Lecture Notes in Computer Science 13354

More information about this series at https://link.springer.com/bookseries/558

Claudio Antares Mezzina ·
Krzysztof Podlaski (Eds.)

Reversible Computation

14th International Conference, RC 2022
Urbino, Italy, July 5–6, 2022
Proceedings

 Springer

Editors
Claudio Antares Mezzina ⓘ
University of Urbino
Urbino, Pesaro-Urbino, Italy

Krzysztof Podlaski ⓘ
University of Łódź
Lodz, Poland

ISSN 0302-9743   ISSN 1611-3349 (electronic)
Lecture Notes in Computer Science
ISBN 978-3-031-09004-2   ISBN 978-3-031-09005-9 (eBook)
https://doi.org/10.1007/978-3-031-09005-9

This Springer imprint is published by the registered company Springer Nature Switzerland AG
The registered company address is: Gewerbestrasse 11, 6330 Cham, Switzerland

Preface

This volume contains the papers presented at the 14th Conference on Reversible Computation (RC 2022), held during July 5–6, 2022, and hosted by University of Urbino, in Italy. For the past two years, the RC conference has been held online, due to the COVID-19 pandemic situation. This year, we attempted to get back to normality by holding the event in person in Urbino.

The RC conference brings together researchers from computer science, mathematics, engineering, and physics to discuss new developments and directions for future research in the emerging area of Reversible Computation. This includes, for example, reversible formal models, reversible programming languages, reversible circuits, and quantum computing.

This year, the conference received 20 submissions, and we would like to thank everyone who submitted. Each submission was reviewed by at least three reviewers, who provided detailed evaluations as well as constructive comments and recommendations. After careful reviewing and extensive discussions, the Program Committee (PC) accepted 11 full papers and five short papers for presentation at the conference. We would like to thank the PC members and all the additional reviewers for their truly professional work and strong commitment to the success of RC 2022. We are also grateful to the authors for taking into account the comments and suggestions provided by the referees during the preparation of the final versions of their papers.

Reversibility is catering to a lot of interest from industry. To mark this aspect, the conference program included two invited talks from industry. Robert O'Callahan discussed "Reverse Execution In The rr Debugger" and Vincent van Wingerden gave a talk on "An introduction to Azure Quantum and the Microsoft QDK".

Finally, we want to thank the University of Urbino for supporting the conference and the Department of Pure and Applied Sciences (DiSPeA) for providing the facilities and various other support for the success of the conference. Also, we would like to thank Rodolfo Rossini and his company Vaire for having partially supported RC 2022.

May 2022

Claudio Antares Mezzina
Krzysztof Podlaski

Organization

Program Committee Chairs

Claudio Antares Mezzina   University of Urbino, Italy
Krzysztof Podlask   University of Łódź, Poland

Steering Committee

Rolf Drechsler   University of Bremen, Germany
Robert Glück   University of Copenhagen, Denmark
Ivan Lanese   Inria and University of Bologna, Italy
Irek Ulidowski   University of Leicester, UK
Robert Wille   Technical University of Munich, Germany, and
     SCCH GmbH, Austria

Program Committee

Clément Aubert   Augusta University, USA
Kamila Barylska   Nicolaus Copernicus University, Poland
Robert Glück   University of Copenhagen, Denmark
Ivan Lanese   Inria and University of Bologna, Italy
Hernan Melgratti   ICC, Universidad de Buenos Aires and
     CONICET, Argentina
Keisuke Nakano   Tohoku University, Japan
Alexandru Paler   Aalto University, Finland
Iain Phillips   Imperial College London, UK
G. Michele Pinna   University of Cagliari, Italy
Neil Julien Ross   Dalhousie University, Canada
Bruno Schmitt   EPFL, Switzerland
Harun Siljak   Trinity College Dublin, Ireland
Yasuhiro Takahashi   NTT Communication Science Laboratories, Japan
Irek Ulidowski   University of Leicester, UK
Benoît Valiron   LMF, CentraleSupelec, Université Paris-Saclay,
     France
Robert Wille   Technical University of Munich, Germany, and
     SCCH GmbH, Austria
Shigeru Yamashita   Ritsumeikan University, Japan
Shoji Yuen   Nagoya University, Japan

Additional Reviewers

Vikraman Choudhury
Giovanni Fabbretti
Anna Gogolinska
James Hoey
Lukasz Mikulski

Contents

Reversible and Quantum Circuits

Reversible Computation in Integrated Photonics

Alexis De Vos[✉]

Vakgroep Elektronika, Universiteit Gent, Ghent, Belgium
alexis.devos@ugent.be

Abstract. Sold-state microphotonics allows to build circuits which transform w light beams in a unitary way. Such a circuit transforms a w-dimensional complex vector by means of a unitary $w \times w$ matrix. For the synthesis of the optical circuit, we can learn a lot from properties of quantum circuits, subject to adaptation of the interpretation of the matrix decompositions.

Keywords: reversible computation · integrated optics · photonics · phase shift · beam splitter · unitary matrix · ZXZ decomposition · block-ZXZ decomposition

1 Introduction

Linear transformations between optical modes have become a powerful tool in both optical and microwave photonics. Linear optical networks are integrated in silicon and indium phosphide technologies [1,2] as well as in lithium niobate [3]. In these optical systems light is manipulated in a unitary way: the transformation between input and output vectors is described by means of a unitary matrix [4]. The size of this matrix is $w \times w$, where w is the width of the circuit, i.e. the number of input channels as well as the number of output channels.

Linear optical quantum computation can make use of linear optics as a medium for quantum computation [5]. Such linear transformation, however, is less powerful than the full quantum-mechanical transformation, which is described by a $2^w \times 2^w$ unitary matrix [6]. The $w \times w$ transform therefore cannot manipulate quantum entanglement. It passively manipulates w light modes in a lossless way. Nevertheless several applications in computation and communication have been developed [7].

Unitary optical computing is distinct not only from quantum computing, but also from classical boolean reversible computing, described by $2^w \times 2^w$ permutation matrices [8], as it basicly performs an analog computation.

2 Building Blocks

We will consider two different libraries of building blocks:

C. A. Mezzina and K. Podlaski (Eds.): RC 2022, LNCS 13354, pp. 3–19, 2022.
https://doi.org/10.1007/978-3-031-09005-9_1

– the basic library and
– the enlarged library.

In the smaller library, we have just two building blocks:

– the phase shift, acting on a single light beam, having one real parameter θ, and realizing the 1×1 unitary matrix

$$P = (x) ,$$

where x is a complex number on the unit circle of the complex plane: $x = e^{i\theta}$
– the beam splitter, acting on two light beams, having no parameter[1], and realizing the 2×2 unitary matrix [11–13]

$$Q = \frac{1}{\sqrt{2}} \begin{pmatrix} 1 & i \\ i & 1 \end{pmatrix} . \tag{1}$$

The circuit symbols for these two blocks are:

$$P = \boxed{x} \qquad \text{and} \qquad Q = \boxed{Q} ,$$

respectively.

The larger library contains, besides the blocks P and Q, one more (parameterless) building block:

– the cross-over, swapping two light beams, having no parameter, and realizing the 2×2 permutation matrix

$$S = \begin{pmatrix} & 1 \\ 1 & \end{pmatrix} . \tag{2}$$

This additional block is not necessary, as it can be synthesized by means of the P and Q blocks[2]:

$$S = \begin{pmatrix} -i & \\ & -i \end{pmatrix} Q^2 . \tag{3}$$

The symbol and the decomposition for the swap block are:

$$S \quad = \quad \times \quad = \quad \boxed{Q}\ \boxed{Q}\ \boxed{-i} \\ \boxed{-i} .$$

---

[1] Unfortunately, there seems to be no consensus in the literature about the definition of 'beam splitter', some authors [9,10] giving this name to a one-parameter or even two-or-three-parameter building block, consisting of a beam splitter (as defined in the present paper) plus one or two, or three phase shifters.
[2] In some technologies direct fabrication of an S may be cheaper than fabrication of two Qs and two Ps, such that this decomposition is not desirable.

3   Properties

Theorem 1 *Any 2-beam unitary circuit can be synthesized by applying four or less shift gates and two or less beam splitters.*

Proof is based on the representation of an arbitrary U(2) matrix, as written with the help of four real parameters (θ, φ, ψ, and χ):

$$U = \begin{pmatrix} \cos(\varphi)\, e^{i(\theta+\psi)} & \sin(\varphi)\, e^{i(\theta+\chi)} \\ -\sin(\varphi)\, e^{i(\theta-\chi)} & \cos(\varphi)\, e^{i(\theta-\psi)} \end{pmatrix}$$

and its ZXZ decomposition [14]:

$$U = \begin{pmatrix} \alpha & 0 \\ 0 & \beta \end{pmatrix} \frac{1}{2} \begin{pmatrix} 1+\gamma & 1-\gamma \\ 1-\gamma & 1+\gamma \end{pmatrix} \begin{pmatrix} 1 & 0 \\ 0 & \delta \end{pmatrix}$$

or

$$U = \begin{pmatrix} \alpha & \\ & \beta \end{pmatrix} H \begin{pmatrix} 1 & \\ & \gamma \end{pmatrix} H \begin{pmatrix} 1 & \\ & \delta \end{pmatrix},$$

where

$$\alpha = e^{i(\theta+\varphi+\psi)}$$
$$\beta = i\, e^{i(\theta+\varphi-\chi)}$$
$$\gamma = e^{-2i\varphi}$$
$$\delta = -i\, e^{i(-\psi+\chi)} \tag{4}$$

and H denotes the Hadamard matrix, a.k.a. the discrete Fourier matrix F_2:

$$H = F_2 = \frac{1}{\sqrt{2}} \begin{pmatrix} 1 & 1 \\ 1 & -1 \end{pmatrix}. \tag{5}$$

With the identity

$$H = \begin{pmatrix} 1 & \\ & -i \end{pmatrix} Q \begin{pmatrix} 1 & \\ & -i \end{pmatrix}$$

or

this leads to

$$U = \begin{pmatrix} \alpha & \\ & -i\beta \end{pmatrix} Q \begin{pmatrix} 1 & \\ & -\gamma \end{pmatrix} Q \begin{pmatrix} 1 & \\ & -i\delta \end{pmatrix},$$

i.e.

q.e.d.

    The above decomposition (3) of the matrix S constitutes an example.

Theorem 2 *Any unitary circuit can be synthesized by applying exclusively shift gates and beam splitters.*

Proof is based on the ZXZ decomposition of an arbitrary $n \times n$ unitary matrix U [14–16]:

$$U = Z_1 X Z_2 ,$$

where both Z_1 and Z_2 are $n \times n$ diagonal unitary matrices and X is an $n \times n$ unitary matrix with all line sums equal to 1.

On the one hand, both matrices Z_1 and Z_2 can be synthesized by means of n phase shifters. On the other hand, the matrix X can be decomposed as follows:

$$X = F_n \begin{pmatrix} 1 & \\ & V \end{pmatrix} F_n^{-1} ,$$

where F_n is the $n \times n$ discrete Fourier matrix and V is an appropriate $(n-1) \times (n-1)$ unitary matrix. In Appendix 1, we demonstrate that, for $n \geq 3$, both F_n and F_n^{-1} can be decomposed into four $(n-1) \times (n-1)$ unitary matrices. Hence, the matrix X can be decomposed into nine $(n-1) \times (n-1)$ unitary matrices. By recursion on n, we thus can synthesize matrix U with exclusively U(1) and U(2) blocks. As a U(1) block is a phase shift and a U(2) block can, after Theorem 1, be built with phase shifts and beam splitters, the theorem is proved[3].

Theorem 3 *Any circuit built by combining exclusively shift gates is the synthesis of a member of a U(1)^w subgroup of the unitary group U(w).*

This property follows from the fact that the cascade of two shift gates is equivalent to a single phase shift.

Theorem 4 *Any circuit, with width w greater than 2, built by combining exclusively beam splitters is the synthesis of a member of a countably infinite subgroup of U(w).*

Proof is in Appendix 2. In contrast, beam-splitter circuits of width w equal to 2, can only synthesize eight different U(2) matrices, as the matrix group generated by the matrix Q has order eight[4].

4 Synthesis in Case $w = 2^u$

Synthesis methods for unitary linear transformations with arbitrary width w have been presented in the literature [9,17]. In the present paper, we focus on

---

[3] As the proof is constructive, it can be used as a synthesis algorithm. However, the resulting circuit is very costly with respect to gate count. More efficient synthesis methods may be developed.

[4] The group is cyclic and consists of the eight matrices $Q^0 = J$, $Q^1 = Q$, $Q^2 = iS$, $Q^3 = -Q^{-1}$, $Q^4 = -J$, $Q^5 = -Q$, $Q^6 = -iS$, and $Q^7 = Q^{-1}$, where J denotes the 2×2 unit matrix $\begin{pmatrix} 1 & \\ & 1 \end{pmatrix}$.

the particular case where w is a power of 2. If the width w happens to be a power of 2, say $w = 2^u$, then we can apply the block-ZXZ decomposition of the $U(w)$ matrix [14, 18, 19]:

$$U = Z_1 X Z_2 .$$

Here, both Z_1 and Z_2 are $w \times w$ block-diagonal unitary matrices:

$$Z_1 = \begin{pmatrix} A & \\ & B \end{pmatrix} \quad \text{and} \quad Z_2 = \begin{pmatrix} I & \\ & D \end{pmatrix} ,$$

where A, B, and D are appropriate $(w/2) \times (w/2)$ unitary matrices and I is the $(w/2) \times (w/2)$ unit matrix. The matrix X is a $w \times w$ unitary matrix with all four block sums equal to I. The matrix X can be decomposed as follows:

$$X = G_w \begin{pmatrix} I & \\ & C \end{pmatrix} G_w^{-1} ,$$

where $G_w = G_w^{-1}$ is the Kronecker product of $F_2 = H$ and I:

$$G_w = H \otimes I = \frac{1}{\sqrt{2}} \begin{pmatrix} I & I \\ I & -I \end{pmatrix}$$

and C is an appropriate $(w/2) \times (w/2)$ unitary matrix. The four $(w/2) \times (w/2)$ unitary matrices A, B, C, and D are to be computed according to the algorithm of Appendix 3.

For the transformation matrix G_w, we have

$$G_2 = H ,$$

$$G_4 = \frac{1}{\sqrt{2}} \begin{pmatrix} 1 & & 1 & \\ & 1 & & 1 \\ 1 & & -1 & \\ & 1 & & -1 \end{pmatrix} = \begin{pmatrix} 1 & & & \\ & S & & \\ & & & 1 \end{pmatrix} \begin{pmatrix} H & \\ & H \end{pmatrix} \begin{pmatrix} 1 & & & \\ & S & & \\ & & & 1 \end{pmatrix} ,$$

and

$$G_8 = \begin{pmatrix} 1 & & & \\ & 1 & & \\ & & S & \\ & & & 1 \\ & & & & 1 \end{pmatrix} \begin{pmatrix} 1 & & & \\ & 1 & & \\ & S & & \\ & & S & \\ & & & 1 \end{pmatrix} \begin{pmatrix} 1 & & & \\ & 1 & & \\ & & 1 & \\ & & S & \\ & & & 1 \end{pmatrix}$$

$$\begin{pmatrix} G_4 & \\ & G_4 \end{pmatrix} \begin{pmatrix} 1 & & & \\ & 1 & & \\ & & S & \\ & & & 1 \\ & & & & 1 \end{pmatrix} \begin{pmatrix} 1 & & & \\ & 1 & & \\ & S & & \\ & & S & \\ & & & 1 \end{pmatrix} \begin{pmatrix} 1 & & & \\ & 1 & & \\ & & 1 & \\ & & S & \\ & & & 1 \end{pmatrix}$$

or

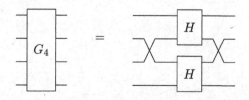

and

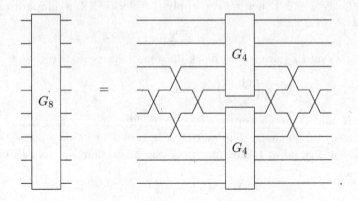

For arbitrary u, we have

$$G_w = H \otimes I = R_w \ (I \otimes H) \ R_w^{-1} \ , \tag{6}$$

where the two rearrangements R_w of the w light beams, in fact, convert the easy-to-implement Kronecker product $I \otimes H$ into the desired Kronecker product $H \otimes I$. This constitutes an example of the fact that the Kronecker products $M_1 \otimes M_2$ and $M_2 \otimes M_1$ of two arbitrary square matrices M_1 and M_2 are permutation equivalent. Decomposition (6) is realized by recursively applying

$$G_w = K_w \begin{pmatrix} G_{w-1} & \\ & G_{w-1} \end{pmatrix} K_w^{-1} \ ,$$

where $K_w = K_w^{-1}$ consists of $(w/4)^2 = 2^{2u-4}$ swaps, e.g.

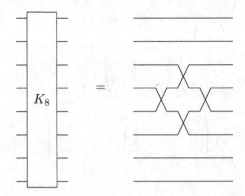

and

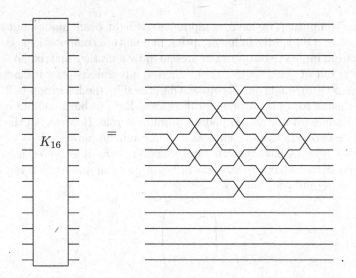

The transformation G_w needs as many as $\frac{1}{4} w(w-2)$ beam swaps, besides $w/2$ Hadamards. As, after

$$U = \begin{pmatrix} A \\ & B \end{pmatrix} G_w \begin{pmatrix} I \\ & C \end{pmatrix} G_w \begin{pmatrix} I \\ & D \end{pmatrix},$$

an arbitrary U(w) circuit consits of two G_w circuits and four U($w/2$) circuits, we conclude that an arbitrary U(w) circuit needs at most $\frac{1}{2} w(w-2)$ beam swaps, w Hadamards and four U($w/2$) circuits. Hence, in total an arbitrary U(w) needs at most

- $w(wu - 2w + 2)/2$ beam swaps,
- $w(w-1)$ Hadamards, and
- w^2 phase shifts,

where u is $\log_2(w)$. This means we need at most

- $w(wu - 2w + 2)/2$ beam swaps,
- $w(w-1)$ beam splitters, and
- $w(3w-2)$ phase shifts

or

- $w(wu - w + 1)$ beam splitters and
- $w^2(u+1)$ phase shifts.

Among the $w^2(u+1)$ phase shifts, as many as $w^2 u$ implement the 1×1 matrix $(-i)$, thus having parameter θ equal to $3\pi/2$, the remaining w^2 shifts having an angle parameter to be computed according to Appendix 3.

5 Comparison with Quantum Computation

In quantum computing, we have, as inputs, not w light-beam modes, but w quantum bits, a.k.a. qubits. Like in linear optics, in quantum computations, the transformation from inputs to outputs is represented by a unitary matrix, however not of size $w \times w$ but of size $2^w \times 2^w$. Thus: whereas integrated optics is described by the Lie group $U(w)$, quantum circuits are described by the Lie group $U(2^w)$. This distinction leads to some surprising differences. E.g., in both computation systems, the Hadamard matrix (5) plays a prominent role. However, in the present paper, it is a two-wire circuit, whereas in quantum computation it is a one-wire circuit. Both systems have a swap gate. However, here, it is represented by the 2×2 permutation matrix (2), whereas in quantum computation it is represented by the 4×4 permutation matrix

$$\begin{pmatrix} 1 & & & \\ & & 1 & \\ & 1 & & \\ & & & 1 \end{pmatrix}.$$

A huge difference between quantum unitary circuits, compared to linear unitary circuits, is the existence of controlled subcircuits. Let us e.g. consider the $2^n \times 2^n$ matrix M:

$$M = \begin{pmatrix} I & \\ & V \end{pmatrix},$$

where I is the $(2^n/2) \times (2^n/2)$ unit matrix and V is some $(2^n/2) \times (2^n/2)$ unitary matrix. In quantum computing, this matrix represents an n-qubit circuit, where the uppermost qubit controls the transformation of the $n-1$ remaining qubits. In classical computing, this matrix represents a 2^n-lightbeam circuit, where the $(2^n/2)$ upper beams are unaffected and the $(2^n/2)$ lower beams are transformed according to matrix V, whatever the values of the upper beams.

In spite of the above difference, in both cases we can apply the block-ZXZ decomposition of Sect. 4. E.g. an 8×8 unitary matrix U represents, in the framework of quantum computing, a 3-qubit circuit. Its block-ZXZ decomposition leads to four controlled 2-qubit circuits:

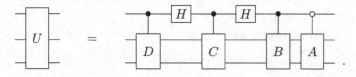

In the framework of classical optics, however, the very same matrix represents an 8-beam circuit and the very same decomposition leads to four uncontrolled

4-beam circuits:

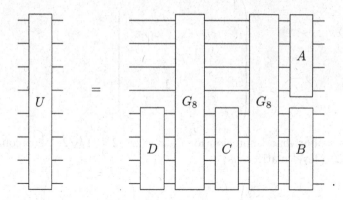

6   A Finite Library

We note that the above synthesis methods, in fact, make use of an infinite library of building blocks, as the block P constitutes a non-countable infinitum of blocks, the angle parameter θ being allowed to vary smoothly from 0 to 2π. It is interesting to investigate what happens if we restrict the angle θ to a single value. We choose here the value $\pi/4$ and thus $x = \omega$, where ω denotes the eighth root of unity, i.e. $e^{i\pi/4} = \frac{1+i}{\sqrt{2}}$. The matrix group generated by matrix P then has order eight[5].

We have the following property:

Theorem 5 *Any circuit, with width w greater than 1, built by combining exclusively beam splitters and (ω) phase shifters, is the synthesis of a member of a countably infinite subgroup of U(w).*

Proof is in Appendix 4. Coversely, we have

Theorem 6 *For w > 1, any U(w) matrix, with all w^2 entries of the form $(a\omega^3 + b\omega^2 + c\omega + d)/2^f$ with a, b, c, d, and f an integer, can be synthesized with exclusively beam splitters and (ω) phase shifters.*

The theorem immediately follows from Lemma 6 of Gilles and Selinger [20]. Advanced synthesis is provided by Niemann et al. [21]. We stress that the so-called one-level and two-level matrices in the Gilles–Selinger decomposition, in the context of linear photonics, do not lead to multiply-controlled gates, as they do in the context of quantum computing. We illustrate this fact by the following

---

[5] The group is cyclic and consists of eight phase shift matrices: $(\omega^0) = (1)$, $(\omega^1) = (\omega)$, $(\omega^2) = (i)$, $(\omega^3) = (i\omega)$, $(\omega^4) = (-1)$, $(\omega^5) = (-\omega)$, $(\omega^6) = (-i)$, and $(\omega^7) = (-i\omega)$.

simple 8×8 example:

$$\begin{pmatrix} 1 & & & & & & & \\ & 1 & & & & & & \\ & & \Omega & & & \Omega & & \\ & & & 1 & & & & \\ & & & & & \omega & & \\ & & & & 1 & & & \\ & & \Omega & & & -\Omega & & \\ & & & & & & & 1 \end{pmatrix},$$

where Ω is a short-hand notation for $(-\omega^3 + \omega)/2 = 1/\sqrt{2}$. Its decomposition into three two-level matrices is

$$\begin{pmatrix} 1 & & & & & & & \\ & 1 & & & & & & \\ & & 1 & & & & & \\ & & & 1 & & & & \\ & & & & 0 & & 1 & \\ & & & & & 1 & & \\ & & & & 1 & & 0 & \\ & & & & & & & 1 \end{pmatrix} \begin{pmatrix} 1 & & & & & & & \\ & 1 & & & & & & \\ & & 1 & & & & & \\ & & & 1 & & & & \\ & & & & \cdot 1 & & & \\ & & & & & 1 & 0 & \\ & & & & & 0 & \omega & \\ & & & & & & & 1 \end{pmatrix} \begin{pmatrix} 1 & & & & & & & \\ & 1 & & & & & & \\ & & \Omega & & & \Omega & & \\ & & & 1 & & & & \\ & & & & 1 & & & \\ & & & & & 1 & & \\ & & \Omega & & & -\Omega & & \\ & & & & & & & 1 \end{pmatrix}.$$

In quantum computation, this leads to a 3-qubit circuit with three doubly-controlled not gates (a.k.a. Toffoli gates), a doubly-controlled T gate, and a doubly-controlled Hadamard gate:

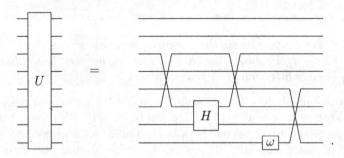

In contrast, in linear optics, the same decomposition leads to an 8-beam circuit with a Hadamard gate, a phase shift, and three swap gates[6], all uncontrolled:

As an example of transformation which can be implemented by the finite library, we mention the 4×4 discrete Fourier transform

---

[6] In most practical technologies, the swaps between non-adjacent wires have to be decomposed into a sequence of swaps between neighbouring wires.

$$F_4 = \frac{1}{2} \begin{pmatrix} 1 & 1 & 1 & 1 \\ 1 & i & -1 & -i \\ 1 & -1 & 1 & -1 \\ 1 & -i & -1 & i \end{pmatrix} ,$$

a transformation exploited in many applications [22]. By applying Sect. 4 and hence five times Appendix 3, we indeed obtain the following synthesis:

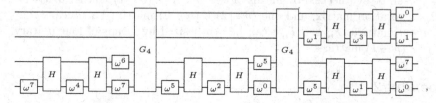

where all $w^2 = 16$ phase gates have an angle parameter θ equal to a multiple of $\pi/4$.

7   Conclusion

Integrated optics allows to implement reversible transformations represented by unitary matrices. We have investigated the synthesis of such passive linear photonic circuits, by means of three different libraries of building blocks:

- the beam splitter Q and a continuum of phase shifters P,
- the beam splitter Q, a continuum of phase shifters P, and the beam swapper S,
- the beam splitter Q and the single phase shifter $P = (\omega)$.

We have revealed some similarities to as well as differences with quantum computation.

Acknowledgement. The author thanks Stijn De Baerdemacker (University of New Brunswick) and Otto Muskens (University of Southampton) for valuable discussions.

Appendix 1

We postulate the following decomposition of the $n \times n$ discrete Fourier matrix (with $n \geq 3$):

$$F_n = \begin{pmatrix} 1 & \\ & F_{n-1} \end{pmatrix} G \begin{pmatrix} 1 & \\ & F_{n-1}^{-1} \end{pmatrix} ,$$

as well as its inverse:

$$F_n^{-1} = \begin{pmatrix} 1 & \\ & F_{n-1} \end{pmatrix} G^{-1} \begin{pmatrix} 1 & \\ & F_{n-1}^{-1} \end{pmatrix} .$$

Straightforward computation of $\begin{pmatrix} 1 & \\ & F_{n-1}^{-1} \end{pmatrix} F_n \begin{pmatrix} 1 & \\ & F_{n-1} \end{pmatrix}$ yields

$$G = \begin{pmatrix} c & s & \\ s & -c & \\ & & L \end{pmatrix} ,$$

where $c = 1/\sqrt{n} = \cos(\varPhi)$ and $s = \sqrt{n-1}/\sqrt{n} = \sin(\varPhi)$, with $\varPhi = \text{Atan}(\sqrt{n-1})$, and L is an $(n-2) \times (n-2)$ unitary matrix. Hence, both F_n and F_n^{-1} can be synthesized by means of two $(n-1) \times (n-1)$ Fourier matrices, one 2×2 rotation matrix, and one $(n-2) \times (n-2)$ matrix. This means that both $n \times n$ matrices F_n and F_n^{-1} can be synthesized by means of four unitary $(n-1) \times (n-1)$ matrices.

Appendix 2

Assume an $n \times n$ matrix M with n distinct eigenvalues z_k. Then, according to the Cayley–Hamilton theorem, we have

$$M^j = \sum_{k=0}^{n-1} c_k z_k^j ,$$

where the n coefficients c_k are appropriate $n \times n$ matrices, to be determined by the n initial conditions

$$\sum_{k=0}^{n-1} z_k^j c_k = M^j ,$$

where j obeys $0 \leq j \leq n - 1$. Hence, with the help of the finite sequence $\{M^0, M^1, ..., M^{n-1}\}$, we can compute any member M^j of the infinite sequence $\{M^n, M^{n+1}, ...\}$, without having to compute any matrix from $\{M^n, M^{n+1}, ..., M^{j-1}\}$.

We consider the following circuit of width $w = 3$:

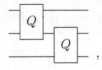

consisting of merely two beam splitters. It is represented by the 3×3 unitary matrix

$$M = \begin{pmatrix} 1 & \\ & Q \end{pmatrix} \begin{pmatrix} Q & \\ & 1 \end{pmatrix} = \frac{1}{2} \begin{pmatrix} \sqrt{2} & i\sqrt{2} & 0 \\ i & 1 & i\sqrt{2} \\ -1 & i & \sqrt{2} \end{pmatrix} .$$

Its eigenvalue equation is

$$(z - 1) \left[2z^2 - (2\sqrt{2} - 1)z + 2 \right] = 0 .$$

Hence, its three eigenvalues are

$$z_0 = 1$$

$$z_1 = \frac{1}{4} \left(2\sqrt{2} - 1 + i \sqrt{7 + 4\sqrt{2}} \right)$$

$$z_2 = \frac{1}{4} \left(2\sqrt{2} - 1 - i \sqrt{7 + 4\sqrt{2}} \right)$$

or $z_0 = 1$, $z_1 = e^{i\theta}$, and $z_2 = e^{-i\theta}$ with $\theta = \arccos((2\sqrt{2} - 1)/4)$.

With the help of the matrices M^0, M^1, and M^2, we are able to compute the matrices c_0, c_1, and c_2 and thus obtain the arbitrary power of M:

$$M^j = z_0^j\, c_0 + z_1^j\, c_1 + z_2^j\, c_2 \ .$$

Suffice it here to note that the matrices c_1 and c_2 are distinct from the zero matrix.

According to Jahnel [23], the only angles which are a rational multiple of π (between 0 and $\pi/2$) with cosine equal to a quadratic irrational are $\pi/6, \pi/5, \pi/4$, and $2\pi/5$ (which have cosines equal to $\sqrt{3}/2, \sqrt{5}/4+1/4, \sqrt{2}/2$, and $\sqrt{5}/4-1/4$, respectively). Hence, the angle θ with $\cos(\theta) = \sqrt{2}/2 - 1/4$ is not a rational portion of 2π. Thus, as a function of k, neither $z_1^k c_1$ nor $z_2^k c_2$ is periodic. We conclude that the infinite sequence $\{M^0, M^1, ...\}$ is not periodic and that M thus generates an infinitum of different matrices. Because the matrices generated by M (and M^{-1}) form a cyclic subgroup of the group generated by beam splitters, we finally conclude that the order of the latter group is infinity.

Each matrix generated by the two generators $\begin{pmatrix} 1 & \\ & Q \end{pmatrix}$ and $\begin{pmatrix} Q & \\ & 1 \end{pmatrix}$ has all of its nine entries of the form $(a + b\sqrt{2} + ci + di\sqrt{2})/(\sqrt{2})^f$ with a, b, c, d, and f an integer. Therefore the number of possible entries is countable. We conclude that the infinite order of the group is countable.

Appendix 3

Let n be an arbitrary even number. We consider the given $n \times n$ unitary matrix U as composed of four $(n/2) \times (n/2)$ blocks:

$$U = \begin{pmatrix} U_{11} & U_{12} \\ U_{21} & U_{22} \end{pmatrix} ,$$

where U_{11}, U_{12}, U_{21}, and U_{22} are $(n/2) \times (n/2)$ matrices, usually not unitary. We perform two polar decompositions:

$$U_{21} = P_{21}V_{21}$$
$$U_{22} = P_{22}V_{22} ,$$

where P_{21} and P_{22} are positive semidefinite matrices and V_{21} and V_{22} are unitary matrices. With V_{21} and V_{22}, we compute the unitary matrix D:

$$D = i V_{21}^\dagger V_{22} \ .$$

With D, we compute the two unitary matrices A and B:

$$A = U_{11} + U_{12}D^{\dagger}$$
$$B = U_{21} + U_{22}D^{\dagger} .$$

With A and B, we compute the unitary matrix C:

$$C = A^{\dagger}U_{11} - B^{\dagger}U_{21} .$$

One easily checks that, for $n = 2$, the above expressions for D, A, B, and C become the values (4) of δ, α, β, and γ.

Appendix 4

We consider the 2×2 matrix M representing the following circuit with four beam splitters Q and four phase shifters $P = (\omega)$:

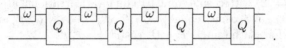

We have

$$M = \left[Q \begin{pmatrix} \omega & \\ & 1 \end{pmatrix} \right]^4 .$$

We rewrite the matrix Q of (1) as follows:

$$Q = \frac{1}{2} \begin{pmatrix} -\omega^3 + \omega & \omega^3 + \omega \\ \omega^3 + \omega & -\omega^3 + \omega \end{pmatrix} .$$

Straightforward computation then yields

$$M = \frac{1}{4} \begin{pmatrix} -3\omega^3 - \omega^2 - \omega - 1 & -\omega^3 + \omega^2 - \omega + 1 \\ \omega^3 - \omega^2 + \omega + 1 & -\omega^3 - \omega^2 - 3\omega + 1 \end{pmatrix} .$$

Applying the short-hand notation $abcd$ for $a\omega^3 + b\omega^2 + c\omega + d$, its residue modulo 2 is

$$\overline{M} = \frac{1}{4} \begin{pmatrix} 1111 & 1111 \\ 1111 & 1111 \end{pmatrix}$$

and its residue modulo 4 is

$$\overline{\overline{M}} = \frac{1}{4} \begin{pmatrix} 1333 & 3131 \\ 1311 & 3311 \end{pmatrix} .$$

We now note the following identity for two matrices modulo 2:

$$\frac{1}{2^a} \begin{pmatrix} 1111 & 1111 \\ 1111 & 1111 \end{pmatrix} \frac{1}{2^b} \begin{pmatrix} 1111 & 1111 \\ 1111 & 1111 \end{pmatrix} = \frac{1}{2^{a+b}} \begin{pmatrix} 0000 & 0000 \\ 0000 & 0000 \end{pmatrix} ,$$

such that this matrix product is reducible. Next, we note the following identity for two matrices modulo 4:

$$\frac{1}{2^a} \begin{pmatrix} 1333 & 3131 \\ 1311 & 3311 \end{pmatrix} \frac{1}{2^b} \begin{pmatrix} 1333 & 3131 \\ 1311 & 3311 \end{pmatrix} = \frac{1}{2^{a+b}} \begin{pmatrix} 2222 & 2222 \\ 2222 & 2222 \end{pmatrix},$$

such that the matrix product is not reducible a second time. Together, the two observations lead to the conclusion that, after simplifying fractions, the product is of modulo-2 type

$$\frac{1}{2^{a+b-1}} \begin{pmatrix} 1111 & 1111 \\ 1111 & 1111 \end{pmatrix}.$$

We apply this result to the case $a = j$ and $b = 2$ and conclude that the matrix M^j (i.e. the product of M^{j-1} and M) is of modulo-2 type

$$\frac{1}{2^{j+1}} \begin{pmatrix} 1111 & 1111 \\ 1111 & 1111 \end{pmatrix}.$$

Indeed, we have

$$M = \frac{1}{4} \begin{pmatrix} -3\omega^3 - \omega^2 - \omega - 1 & -\omega^3 + \omega^2 - \omega + 1 \\ \omega^3 - \omega^2 + \omega + 1 & -\omega^3 - \omega^2 - 3\omega + 1 \end{pmatrix}$$

$$M^2 = \frac{1}{8} \begin{pmatrix} 5\omega^3 - 3\omega^2 - 3\omega - 1 & -3\omega^3 - \omega^2 - \omega - 3 \\ -\omega^3 - \omega^2 - 3\omega + 3 & 3\omega^3 + 3\omega^2 - 5\omega - 1 \end{pmatrix}$$

$$M^3 = \frac{1}{16} \begin{pmatrix} -\omega^3 + 13\omega^2 - 3\omega - 3 & 5\omega^3 + 3\omega^2 - 3\omega - 5 \\ 3\omega^3 - 3\omega^2 - 5\omega - 5 & -3\omega^3 + 13\omega^2 - \omega + 3 \end{pmatrix}$$

$$M^4 = \frac{1}{32} \begin{pmatrix} 3\omega^3 - 5\omega^2 + 19\omega + 1 & -5\omega^3 + 17\omega^2 + 17\omega - 5 \\ 17\omega^3 + 17\omega^2 - 5\omega + 5 & -19\omega^3 + 5\omega^2 - 3\omega + 1 \end{pmatrix}$$

$$M^5 = \frac{1}{64} \begin{pmatrix} -15\omega^3 + 19\omega^2 - 21\omega + 27 & -21\omega^3 - 27\omega^2 + 27\omega + 21 \\ -27\omega^3 + 27\omega^2 + 21\omega + 21 & -21\omega^3 + 19\omega^2 - 15\omega - 27 \end{pmatrix}$$

etc.

Moreover, we see that M^5 is of the same modulo-4 type as M. We conclude that the irreducible denominator of M^j continues to increase like 2^{j+1}, without limit. Hence, within the infinite sequence $\{M, M^2, M^3, ...\}$, all denominators and thus all matrices are different.

Thus this sequence constitutes an infinite set within the matrix group generated by $\left(\begin{smallmatrix} \omega & \\ & 1 \end{smallmatrix} \right)$ and Q. We thus are allowed to say that the group has infinite order. Because all four entries of each matrix have the form $(a\omega^3 + b\omega^2 + c\omega + d)/2^f$ with a, b, c, d, and f an integer, we additionally conclude that the infinite order of the group is countable.

References

1. Politi, A., Cryan, M., Rarity, J., Yu, S., O'Brien, J.: Silica-on-silicon waveguide quantum circuits. Science **320**, 646 (2008)
2. Tang, R., Tanemura, T., Nakano, Y.: Integrated reconfigurable unitary optical mode converter using MMI couplers. IEEE Photonics Technol. Lett. **29**, 971–974 (2017)
3. Baets, R., Kuyken, B.: High speed phase modulators for silicon photonic integrated circuits: a role for lithium niobate? Adv. Photonics **1**, 030502 (2019)
4. Saygin, M., Kondratyev, I., Dyakonov, I., Mironov, S., Straupe, S., Kulik, S.: Robust architecture for programmable universal unitaries. Phys. Rev. Lett. **124**, 010501 (2020)
5. Kok, P., Munro, W., Nemoto, K., Ralph, T., Dowling, J., Milburn, G.: Linear optical quantum computing with photonic qubits. Rev. Modern Phys. **79**, 135–174 (2007)
6. Nielsen, M., Chuang, I.: Quantum Computation and Quantum Information, Cambridge University Press, Cambridge (2000). ISBN 9780521635035
7. Dinsdale, N., et al.: Deep learning enabled design of complex transmission matrices for universal optical components. A.C.S. Photonics **8**, 283–295 (2021)
8. De Vos, A.: Reversible computing, Wiley - VCH, Weinheim (2010). ISBN 9783527409921
9. Reck, M., Zeilinger, A., Bernstein, H., Bertani, P.: Experimental realization of any discrete unitary operator. Phys. Rev. Lett. **73**, 58–61 (1994)
10. Knill, E., Laflamme, R., Milburn, G.: A scheme for efficient quantum computation with linear optics. Nature **409**, 46–52 (2001)
11. Pan, J., Chen, Z., Lu, C., Weinfurter, H., Zeilinger, A., Żukowski, M.: Multiphoton entanglement and interferometry. Rev. Mod. Phys. **84**, 777–790 (2012)
12. Fang, M., Manipatruni, S., Wierzynski, C., Khosrowshahi, A., De Weese, M.: Design of optical neural networks with component imprecisions. Opt. Express **27**, 14009 (2019)
13. Macho-Ortiz, A., Pérez-López, D., Capmany, J.: Optical implementation of 2×2 universal unitary matrix transformations (Supporting information). Laser Photonics Rev. **2021**, 2000473 (2021)
14. De Vos, A., De Baerdemacker, S., Van Rentergem, Y.: Synthesis of quantum circuits versus synthesis of classical reversible circuits, Synthesis Lectures on Digital Circuits and Systems, vol. 54, Morgan & Claypool, La Porte (2018). ISBN 9781681733814
15. De Vos, A., De Baerdemacker, S.: Scaling a unitary matrix. Open Syst. Inf. Dyn. **21**, 1450013 (2014)
16. Idel, M., Wolf, M.: Sinkhorn normal form for unitary matrices. Linear Algebra Appl. **471**, 76–84 (2015)
17. Clements, W., Humphreys, P., Metcalf, B., Kolthammer, W., Walmsley, I.: Optimal design for universal multiport interferometers. Optica **3**, 1460–1465 (2016)
18. Führ, H., Rzeszotnik, Z.: On biunimodular vectors for unitary matrices. Linear Algebra Appl. **484**, 86–129 (2015)
19. De Vos, A., De Baerdemacker, S.: Block-ZXZ synthesis of an arbitrary quantum circuit. Phys. Rev. A **94**, 052317 (2016)
20. Gilles, B., Selinger, P.: Exact synthesis of multiqubit Clifford+T circuits. Phys. Rev. A **87**, 032332 (2013)

21. Niemann, P., Wille, R., Drechsler, R.: Advanced exact synthesis of Clifford+T circuits. Quantum Inf. Process. **19**(9), 1–23 (2020). https://doi.org/10.1007/s11128-020-02816-0
22. Barak, R., Ben-Aryeh, Y.: Quantum fast Fourier transform and quantum computation by linear optics. J. Opt. Soc. Am. **24**, 231–240 (2007)
23. Jahnel, J.: When is the (co)sine of a rational angle equal to a rational number? http://www.uni-math.gwdg.de/jahnel/linkstopapers.html

Optimization of Quantum Boolean Circuits by Relative-Phase Toffoli Gates

Shohei Kuroda[✉] and Shigeru Yamashita[ID]

Ritsumeikan University, Kusatsu, Japan
sousai@ngc.is.ritsumei.ac.jp

Abstract. To realize quantum Boolean circuits, Toffoli gates are often used as logic primitives. Then Toffoli gates are decomposed to physically realizable gates, i.e., CNOT, H and T gates when we consider fault-tolerant implementation. The realization cost of a T gate is huge compared to the other gates, and thus we often consider the number of T gates. We need seven T gates to decompose a Toffoli gate. However, if we allow to add some relative phases to some output quantum states, we can implement a Toffoli gate by only four T gates. Such an approximate Toffoli gate is called a relative-phase Toffoli gate (RTOF). This paper proposes an optimization method of quantum circuit by using RTOFs. When we optimize a circuit by replacing a Toffoli gate with a RTOF, some relative phase errors are added. Our method tries to correct such relative phases by using S gates.

Keywords: Relative Phase Toffoli Gate · T Gate · Optimization

1 Introduction

To perform a quantum algorithm to solve a logical problem, we usually need to design a so-called *quantum Boolean circuit* to calculate some Boolean functions related to the target problem [2]. To realize such quantum Boolean circuits, a Toffoli gate is often used as a logic primitive. After designing a circuit by Toffoli gates, we decompose each Toffoli gate into physically realizable gates. When we consider fault-tolerant quantum computation, we consider T, H and CNOT gates as physically realizable gates, among which the cost of a T gate is considered to be very expensive. Thus, we often focus on the number of T gates which is called *T-count*.

A variant of Toffoli gate called a *Relative-Phase Toffoli gate (RTOF, hereafter)* [1] has been proposed recently. The T-count of an RTOF is only 4 whereas T-count of a Toffoli gate is 7. An RTOF can calculate the same logic function as a Toffoli gate, but the phases of some quantum basis states become different after performing an RTOF; we say that an RTOF adds *relative phase* errors. Because of the relative phase errors, we cannot simply replace a Toffoli gate with an RTOF in general, but RTOFs can be utilized when we decompose a generalized Toffoli gate because the relative phase errors can be canceled between two

C. A. Mezzina and K. Podlaski (Eds.): RC 2022, LNCS 13354, pp. 20–27, 2022.
https://doi.org/10.1007/978-3-031-09005-9_2

RTOFs in the decomposition. Therefore, we can replace Toffoli gates which do not change the state of the function of the circuit with RTOFs without adding *relative phase* errors.

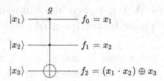

Fig. 1. Functional representations for the output of a Toffoli gate.

This paper seeks the way to replace Toffoli gates which change the state of the function of the circuit with RTOFs. More concretely, we propose a method to erase relative phase errors due to RTOFs. Then, by using our method, we may be able to decrease T-count of a circuit consisting of Toffoli gates as follows: first we replace each Toffoli gate with an RTOF gate, and then we erase the relative phase errors added by RTOFs by using our method. In the following, we present our idea how to erase relative phase errors efficiently; our method does not use T gates, but uses S gates whose implementation cost is much less than T gates.

2   Preliminary

2.1   Quantum Boolean Circuits

In this paper, we consider quantum Boolean circuits consisting of Toffoli gates, T gates, S gates and relative-phase Toffoli gates (RTOFs) [1]. Then, as we will explain later, it is enough to consider the functionality of such quantum circuits by using classical Boolean function with phase information independently.

First let us explain our notations how to represent functions in quantum Boolean circuits. We denote the primary inputs of a circuit by $x_1, x_2, \cdots, x_n$ when we have n primary inputs. Each qubit state in a circuit consisting Toffoli and RTOF gates can be represented by a Boolean function with respect to $x_1, x_2, \cdots, x_n$.

For example, Fig. 1 shows a circuit consisting of a Toffoli gate. The primary inputs are x_1, x_2 and x_3, and the functions to represent the qubit states after the gate are $f_1 = x_1, f_2 = x_2, f_3 = (x_1 \cdot x_2) \oplus x_3$ as shown in Fig. 1.

A quantum Boolean circuit calculates a Boolean function on a target qubit, and usually the other qubits should be restored to the input states if the circuit is used in a quantum algorithm. We can do so very easily by just attaching the reversed circuit of G without the gates which change the state of the target qubit on which G calculates the function. In addition, we do not have to consider the phase information of the gates of G because the relative phase errors are canceled between G and reversed circuit of G.

2.2   T Gates and S Gates

After designing a quantum Boolean circuits consisting of Toffoli gates, we need to decompose each Toffoli gate into physically realizable primitive gates. For fault-tolerant quantum computation, such primitive gates are often considered to be CNOT, T and H gates. A T gate is a quantum-specific gate which acts on one qubit, and it adds $+\frac{\pi}{4}$ phase to the quantum state if the qubit is in $|1\rangle$. A $T^\dagger$ gate adds $-\frac{\pi}{4}$ phase.

In this paper, we also use S and $S^\dagger$ gates which add $+\frac{\pi}{2}$ and $-\frac{\pi}{2}$ phases, respectively similar to T gates. In other words, an S gate corresponds to two T gates. However, note that the realization cost of an S gate is much smaller than a T gate. Thus, in this paper, we utilize S or $S^\dagger$ gates when we need to add $+\frac{\pi}{2}$ and $-\frac{\pi}{2}$ phases.

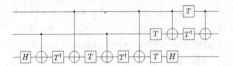

Fig. 2. A Toffoli gate by primitive gates.

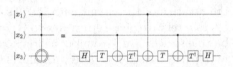

Fig. 3. An RTOF gate by primitive gates.

Table 1. Added phases by an RTOF.

input	$F_{\pi/2}$	F_π	$F_{3\pi/2}$
000	0	0	0
001	0	0	0
010	0	0	0
011	0	0	0
100	0	0	0
101	0	1	0
110	1	0	0
111	0	0	1

Table 2. An example of phase functions.

input	$F_{\pi/2}$	F_π	$F_{3\pi/2}$
000	0	0	0
001	0	0	0
010	0	0	0
011	0	0	0
100	0	0	0
101	0	1	0
110	1	0	0
111	0	0	1

2.3   Relative-Phase Toffoli Gates (RTOFs)

An RTOF (Relative-Phase Toffoli) gate [1] has two control bits and one target bit. It inverts the state of the target bit (i.e., $|1\rangle$ to $|0\rangle$ and $|0\rangle$ to $|1\rangle$) when the states of the both control bits are $|11\rangle$. A Toffoli gate consists of 7 T gates as shown in Fig. 2 whereas an RTOF consists of 4 T gates as shown in Fig. 3.

As Fig. 3, an RTOF has three inputs; the input quantum basis states are $|000\rangle$ to $|111\rangle$. Similar to Toffoli gates, an RTOF swaps $|110\rangle$ and $|111\rangle$. In addition to this logic operation, an RTOF adds some phases to some quantum states unlike Toffoli gates. The added phase are as shown in Table 1. For example, when the input state is $|110\rangle$, a phase $+\pi/2$ is added.

3   Optimization By Using RTOFs

To explain our method, first we need to introduce some terminologies to analyze the added phases by T ($\text{T}^\dagger$) and S ($\text{S}^\dagger$) gates in the following.

3.1   Phase Functions

Definition 1. *For an n-input quantum circuit consisting of RTOF and Toffoli gates, an* **added phase function** *is defined as a mapping from one specific pattern of n inputs, X, to the added phase to the input state corresponding to X by the circuit. In the following, we use the following notation $P(X)$ to denote an added phase function: $P(X) = \theta$ $(0 \le \theta < 2\pi)$.*

For example, we can consider that Table 1 shows the truth table for the added phase function of the circuit as shown in Fig. 3.

We also need the following definition to explain our method.

Definition 2. *For an added phase function $P(X)$ of a quantum circuit, we define a* **phase function** *which is the following Boolean function with respect to the input variables X of the circuit:*

$$F_\theta(X) = 1 \ if \ (P(X) = \theta), \ 0 \ otherwise.$$

For example, for the added phase function as shown in Table 1, three phase functions, $F_{\frac{\pi}{2}}, F_\pi, F_{\frac{3\pi}{2}}$ can be shown in Table. 2. Note that a phase 2π is equivalent to a phase 0. Thus a phase $-\frac{\pi}{2}$ is equivalent to a phase $\frac{3\pi}{2}$.

We also use the following notation.

Definition 3. *$ON(F)$ is defined as the number of input patterns such that F becomes 1.*

3.2   Erasing Relative Phases

Now we are ready to explain our method to optimize a quantum Boolean circuit consisting of Toffoli gates. First we replace each Toffoli gate with an RTOF. Then T-count becomes 4/7 times because T-count of a Toffoli gate is 7 and T-count of an RTOF is 4. However, the circuit should have undesired added relative phases by RTOFs.

Thus our main problem considered in this paper is to erase such relative phases efficiently. For the problem, our first observation is as follows. An RTOF adds only relative phases of $\frac{\pi}{2}, \pi$ or $\frac{3\pi}{2}$. These phases corresponds to 2, 4, 6 times of applications of T gates. Because $T^2 = S$, we can cancel the above relative phases by S and $S^\dagger$ gates. Therefore our idea is to use S and $S^\dagger$ gates, and do not use T or $T^\dagger$ gates whose implementation cost would be much higher than those of S and $S^\dagger$ gates for the future fault-tolerant realization.

The outline of our method is as follows: we apply an $S^\dagger$ gate to all the input states, X, such that $P(X) = \frac{\pi}{2}$. Then we can make $ON(F_{\frac{\pi}{2}})$ to be 0. Our basic strategy to do so is to put the following sub-circuit at the beginning. The added circuit works as follows: (1) it first calculates $P(X)$ at one qubit, then (2) it applies $S^\dagger$ gate on the qubit, and (3) it calculates $P(X)$ again to reverse all the operations to calculate $P(X)$. For the states, X, such that $P(X) = \pi$ or $P(X) = \frac{3\pi}{2}$, we can modify the relative phases in similar ways where the number of S or $S^\dagger$ gates may be different. For example, we need to apply $S^\dagger$ twice to erase phase π.

As explained, our basic strategy is to make sub-circuits to calculate functions which are used to erase the relative phases. If useful functions to erase relative phases already exist, we can utilize them instead of making new sub-circuits. Thus, we try to find a useful function f such that the ON-set of f is included in the ON-set of F_θ for some θ; we apply S or $S^\dagger$ gates appropriate times on a qubit where f is calculated in order to erase the relative phase of θ. By this operation, we can decrease $ON(F_\theta)$ with only adding S or $S^\dagger$ gates. So we try to find such useful functions and apply S or $S^\dagger$ gates as much as possible before we make the above-mentioned additional sub-circuits. The above procedure can be summarized in Algorithm 1.

Algorithm 1. Erasing Relative Phases.

Input: A quantum Boolean circuit consisting of RTOFs.

Output: A modified quantum Boolean circuit without relative phase errors.

Calculate each function after each gate, and the final relative phases for all the quantum states for the given circuit.

while a useful function f exists to decrease $ON(F_\theta)$ for each θ such that $ON(F_\theta) \neq 0$ **do**

    Apply S or $S^\dagger$ gates appropriate times on a qubit where f is calculated.

end while

for $\theta = \frac{\pi}{2}, \pi, \frac{3\pi}{2}$ **do**

    if $ON(F_\theta) \neq 0$ **then**

        Add a sub-circuit to calculate a Boolean function $F_\theta(X)$ at the beginning.

        Apply S or $S^\dagger$ gates appropriate times on a qubit where $F_\theta(X)$ is calculated.

        Add a sub-circuit to calculate a Boolean function $F_\theta(X)$ again after the above S or $S^\dagger$ gates.

    end if

end for

Let us show an example how our method can erase the relative phases. Suppose we are given a circuit consisting of Toffoli gates as shown in Fig. 4, and we

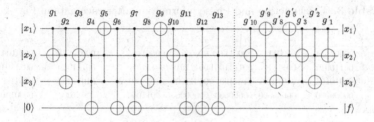

Fig. 4. Input: a circuit consisting of Toffoli gates.

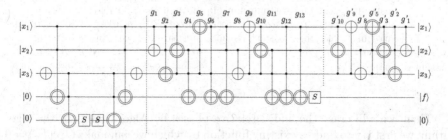

Fig. 5. Output: a circuit after erasing the relative phase errors.

want to optimize the circuit. The circuit has three inputs, and one ancilla qubit where we calculate a function. The function realized after each gate can be represented in Table 3. Because we have three variables, the truth table for each function has eight $0/1$ entries, which can be represented by an 8-bit $0/1$ string. Thus, in the table, each function is represented by an 8-bit $0/1$ string. For example, the second row of column "g_1" (00111100) corresponds to $x_1 \oplus x_2$. The left-most bit of the bit string corresponds to the input pattern: $(x_1, x_2, x_3) = (0, 0, 0)$, and the right-most bit corresponds to the input pattern: $(x_1, x_2, x_3) = (1, 1, 1)$.

First we replace all the Toffoli gates in the circuit with RTOFs. Then T-count becomes 4/7 times, but some undesired relative phases are added. Note that when we design a quantum Boolean circuit we need to restore the input states (i.e., $|x_1\rangle$ to $|x_3\rangle$ in the above example). To do so, we have pairs of identical Toffoli gates whose target bits are on the first three bits in this example. When we replace such a pair of two identical Toffoli gates with two RTOFs, we can cancel the added phases; we make the phases by the two RTOFs opposite. Therefore, we only consider the added phases by RTOFs whose target bits are the forth bit where we calculate the target function f in the following.

In Table 3, we show the added phase by each gate whose target bits are the forth bit in "Added Phase." "Total Phase" in a column "g_i" is the sum of "Added Phase" up to g_i. For example, "Total Phase" of the column "g_6" ($0000\frac{\pi}{2}00\frac{\pi}{2}$) means the total added phases by g_4 and g_6. The added phase function of the circuit can be represented by $P1 = 0\frac{3\pi}{2}\frac{3\pi}{2}0\frac{3\pi}{2}0\pi\frac{3\pi}{2}$. This representation is similar to the above representation for logic functions. For example, the second $\frac{3\pi}{2}$ means that the circuit adds phase $\frac{3\pi}{2}$ to state $|001\rangle$.

Table 3. The Function and Phase information after each gate in Fig. 4.

input		g_1	g_2	g_3	g_4	g_5	g_6
x_1	00001111	00001111	00001111	00001111	00001111	00010111	00010111
x_2	00110011	00111100	00111100	00111010	00111010	00111010	00111010
x_3	01010101	01010101	01011001	01011001	01011001	01011001	01011001
$|0\rangle$	00000000	00000000	00000000	00000000	00011000	00011000	00001001
Added Phase					$000\frac{\pi}{2}\frac{\pi}{2}000$		$000\frac{3\pi}{2}000\frac{\pi}{2}$
Total Phase					$000\frac{\pi}{2}\frac{\pi}{2}000$		$0000\frac{\pi}{2}00\frac{\pi}{2}$

input	g_7	g_8	g_9	g_{10}	g_{11}	g_{12}	g_{13}
x_1	00010111	00010111	01110100	01110100	01110100	01110100	01110100
x_2	00111010	00111010	00111010	01011010	01011010	01011010	01011010
x_3	01011001	01100011	01100011	01100011	01100011	01100011	01100011
$|0\rangle$	00011011	00011011	00011011	00011011	01011001	01011001	01101001
Added Phase	$000\frac{\pi}{2}00\frac{\pi}{2}\frac{2\pi}{2}$				$0\frac{3\pi}{2}0\pi\pi0\frac{\pi}{2}0$	$0\frac{3\pi}{2}\pi\pi0000$	$0\frac{\pi}{2}\pi\frac{3\pi}{2}0000$
Total Phase	$000\frac{\pi}{2}\frac{\pi}{2}0\frac{\pi}{2}\frac{3\pi}{2}$				$0\frac{3\pi}{2}0\frac{3\pi}{2}\frac{3\pi}{2}0\pi\frac{3\pi}{2}$	$0\pi\frac{\pi}{2}\frac{3\pi}{2}\frac{3\pi}{2}0\pi\frac{3\pi}{2}$	$0\frac{3\pi}{2}\frac{3\pi}{2}0\frac{3\pi}{2}0\pi\frac{3\pi}{2}$

Then, we will erase the added relative phases by Algorithm 1. In the algorithm, we first try to find an existing function by which we can make $ON(F_\pi) = 0$ or $ON(F_{\frac{3\pi}{2}}) = 0$. The function on the forth bit after g_{13} is such a function. Thus, we put an S gate on the forth bit after g_{13} by which the added phase function of the circuit is changed to $P2 = 000000\pi0$; $ON(F_\pi)$ becomes 1.

There is no more function to erase more phases from $P2$, thus we go to the next step; we make a function $f = 00000010$ (which is $x_1 \cdot x_2 \cdot \overline{x_3}$) at the beginning of the circuit, and then we put two S gates after that in order to cancel the phase π. The transformed circuit is as shown in Fig. 5.

In this example, we can reduce T-count by $3 \times 6 = 18$ when we replace the Toffoli gates whose target bits are on the forth bit (where we calculate the target function f) with RTOFs at first. Then we need to add four RTOFs gates to erase the relative phase errors; T-count is increased by $4 \times 4 = 16$. Therefore, in total, our method can decrease T-count by 2.

Note that in the above example we do not use Toffoli gates, but we use RTOFs to make an additional function. The reason is as follows. We can always pair two identical RTOFs in the added circuit in our algorithm. For example, in the left-hand sub-circuit before the dotted line in Fig. 5, we have two pairs of identical RTOFs. If there are two identical RTOFs, we can cancel the relative phases by swapping T and T† in one RTOF so that the relative phases added by one RTOF becomes totally opposite to those by the other RTOF.

4   Conclusion

This paper proposed an optimization of quantum circuits consisting of Toffoli gates by utilizing RTOFs. Our key idea is to use S/S† gates to erase undesired relative phases. Obviously our work is not completed; we need to apply our optimization methods to benchmark circuits to analyze how our method can optimize circuits.

References

1. Maslov, D.: Advantages of using relative-phase toffoli gates with an application to multiple control toffoli optimization. Phys. Rev. A **93**(2), 022311 (2016)
2. Yamashita, S., Minato, S.I., Miller, D.M.: Ddmf: an efficient decision diagram structure for design verification of quantum circuits under a practical restriction. IEICE Tran. Fund. Electroni. Commun. Comput. Sci. **E91-A**(12), 3793–3802 (2008). https://doi.org/10.1093/ietfec/e91-a.12.3793, http://hdl.handle.net/2115/47392

Constructing All Qutrit Controlled Clifford+T gates in Clifford+T

Lia Yeh[1]([⊠])([iD]) and John van de Wetering[1,2]([iD])

[1] University of Oxford, Oxford, UK
lia.yeh@cs.ox.ac.uk
[2] Radboud University Nijmegen, Nijmegen, Netherlands

Abstract. For a number of useful quantum circuits, qudit constructions have been found which reduce resource requirements compared to the best known or best possible qubit construction. However, many of the necessary qutrit gates in these constructions have never been explicitly and efficiently constructed in a fault-tolerant manner. We show how to exactly and unitarily construct any qutrit multiple-controlled Clifford+T unitary using just Clifford+T gates and without using ancillae. The T-count to do so is polynomial in the number of controls k, scaling as $O(k^{3.585})$. With our results we can construct ancilla-free Clifford+T implementations of multiple-controlled T gates as well as all versions of the qutrit multiple-controlled Toffoli, while the analogous results for qubits are impossible. As an application of our results, we provide a procedure to implement any ternary classical reversible function on n trits as an ancilla-free qutrit unitary using $O(3^n n^{3.585})$ T gates.

Keywords: Qutrits · Gate Synthesis · Clifford+T

1 Introduction

Classical computing technology works with bits, where the state of the fundamental information unit can be in one of two states. It is then not surprising that quantum computing researchers have mostly studied *qu*bits, where the fundamental unit of information can be in a superposition of two states. However, there are several benefits we can get by working instead with qu*dits*, where we work with higher-dimensional systems. One such benefit is that many proposed physical types of qubits are actually restricted subspaces of higher-dimensional systems, where the natural dimension can be much higher. By working with qudits we can exploit the additional degrees of freedom present in the system. Qudit quantum processors based on ion traps [49] and superconducting devices [4,55,56] have already been demonstrated. By using the otherwise wasted dimensions accessible in a qudit we increases the device's information density, which leads to advantages in for instance runtime efficiency, resource requirements, magic state distillation noise thresholds, and noise resilience in communication [10,12,44,53].

C. A. Mezzina and K. Podlaski (Eds.): RC 2022, LNCS 13354, pp. 28–50, 2022.
https://doi.org/10.1007/978-3-031-09005-9_3

For qudits to make a good foundation for a quantum computer, we need techniques to do fault-tolerant computation with them. A well-studied approach for fault-tolerant computation with qubits is based on the observation that many quantum error correcting codes can natively implement Clifford gates, so that we only need to realise a fault-tolerant implementation of some non-Clifford gate. A popular choice for this gate is the T gate, a single-qubit gate that can be implemented by injecting its magic state into a circuit. As these magic states can be distilled to a desired level of fidelity, we can then implement approximately universal quantum computation fault-tolerantly [9]. Qudit analogues of this Clifford+T gate set have been developed, so that this approach of magic state distillation and injection can be used to do fault-tolerant computation for qudits of any dimension [11].

In this paper we will work with qu*trits*, three-dimensional systems. These are the most well-studied higher-dimensional qudit. Qutrits have been used to reduce the circuit complexity of implementing multi-controlled qubit gates [20, 27,31,36,46]. By replacing some or all of the information carriers to be qutrits instead of qubits, the $|2\rangle$ energy level of the qutrit can be utilised to reduce resource requirements in terms of number of ancillae, entanglement complexity, gate depth and gate count, and non-Clifford gate count. For instance, in Ref. [20] they showed how to implement an n-controlled (qubit) Toffoli gate in $O(\log n)$ depth, using just $O(n)$ two-qutrit gates and no ancillae. More generally, we say a qutrit circuit *emulates* a qubit gate when the action on the $\{|0\rangle, |1\rangle\}$ subspace is equal to the qubit gate. Emulating a qubit logic gate with a qutrit unitary can be more efficient than only using qubits. This is because we can utilise the additional $|2\rangle$ state as an intermediate storage to decrease the cost of implementation. The gates used in these constructions involve what we will call $|2\rangle$-*controlled gates*— controlled unitaries that only fire when the control qutrit is in the $|2\rangle$ state, so that this gate acts as the identity on the target if the control is in the $|0\rangle$ or $|1\rangle$ state. In fact, many qutrit-native algorithms use $|2\cdots2\rangle$-controlled logic gates, including various ternary adders and incrementers [20,24,30].

Because of the ubiquity of qutrit-controlled gates, it is crucial to understand how we can implement these fault-tolerantly if we wish to use them for practical purposes. Unfortunately, while there is a 'naive' decomposition into qutrit Clifford+T gates of for instance the $|2\cdots2\rangle$-controlled X gate which uses $O(n)$ clean ancilla for n ternary controls [30], ancilla-free implementations require either uniformly controlled Givens rotations [28] or qutrit-controlled qubit gates [15], both of which are not fault-tolerant (at least as stated). The construction of Ref. [42] is conceivably fault-tolerant, but it utilises an exponential number of gates. This raises the question of how we can implement these $|2\cdots2\rangle$-controlled gates efficiently using more primitive and fault-tolerant gates.

In this paper we show that when we have any qutrit Clifford+T unitary U, we can construct an ancilla-free exact Clifford+T implementation of the $|2\cdots2\rangle$-controlled U unitary which uses a number of gates polynomial in the number of controls. Specifically, for k controls we require $O(k^{3.585})$ gates (this number comes from $\log_2 6 \approx 3.585$). Our work means in particular that we have fault-tolerant and ancilla-free implementations of all the constructions mentioned above. Note that our result, constructing controlled Clifford+T unitaries for any Clifford+T unitary, is not possible with qubits when we don't allow ancillae. For instance, it is not possible to construct a qubit controlled-T gate [33] or a three-controlled Toffoli [17] using just Clifford+T gates and no ancillae. The constructions in this paper build on our work in a previous paper where we showed how to construct the qutrit single-controlled Hadamard and S gates, which we used to exactly synthesise the qutrit metaplectic gate [18]. A software implementation of some of our constructions can be found on Github[1].

As an application of our construction we give an algorithm for implementing any reversible classical trit function $f: \{0,1,2\}^n \rightarrow \{0,1,2\}^n$ as a unitary n-qutrit Clifford+T circuit using at most $O(3^n n^{3.585})$ Clifford+T gates. We find a lower bound for this problem of $O(3^n \cdot n/\log n)$ so that our result here is within a polynomial factor of optimal.

The paper is structured as follows. In Sect. 2, we recall the basics of the qutrit Clifford+T gate set and the different types of control wires for qutrit unitaries, and we recall several known results for controlled qutrit unitaries. Then in Sect. 3, we present exact ancilla-free Clifford+T constructions of any $|2\rangle^{\otimes n}$-controlled Clifford+T unitary. In Sect. 4 we show how we can use our results to implement any ternary classical reversible function as a Clifford+T ancilla-free unitary. Finally, we end with some concluding remarks in Sect. 5.

2   Preliminaries

A qubit is a two-dimensional Hilbert space. Similarly, a qutrit is a three-dimensional Hilbert space. We will write $|0\rangle$, $|1\rangle$, and $|2\rangle$ for the standard computational basis states of a qutrit. Any normalised qutrit state can then be written as $|\psi\rangle = \alpha |0\rangle + \beta |1\rangle + \gamma |2\rangle$ where $\alpha, \beta, \gamma \in \mathbb{C}$ and $|\alpha|^2 + |\beta|^2 + |\gamma|^2 = 1$.

Several concepts for qubits extend to qutrits, or more generally to qu*dits*, which are d-dimensional quantum systems. In particular, the concept of Pauli's and Cliffords.

Definition 1. *For a d-dimensional qudit, the Pauli X and Z gates are defined as*

$$X |k\rangle = |k+1\rangle \qquad Z |k\rangle = \omega^k |k\rangle \qquad (1)$$

where $\omega := e^{2\pi i/d}$ is such that $\omega^d = 1$, and the addition $|k+1\rangle$ is taken modulo d [23, 26]. We define the Pauli group as the set of unitaries generated by tensor products of the X and Z gate. We write $\mathcal{P}_n^d$ for the Paulis acting on n qudits.

For qubits this X gate is just the NOT gate, while $Z = \text{diag}(1, -1)$. For the duration of this paper we will work solely with qutrits, so we take ω to always be equal to $e^{2\pi i/3}$.

---

[1] https://github.com/lia-approves/qudit-circuits/tree/main/qutrit_control_Clifford_T.

For a qubit there is only one non-trivial permutation of the standard basis states, which is implemented by the X gate. For qutrits there are five non-trivial permutations of the basis states. By analogy we will all call these ternary X gates. These gates are X_{+1}, X_{-1}, X_{01}, X_{12}, and X_{02}. The gate $X_{\pm 1}$ sends $|t\rangle$ to $|(t \pm 1) \bmod 3\rangle$ for $t \in \{0, 1, 2\}$; X_{01} is just the qubit X gate which is the identity when the input is $|2\rangle$; X_{12} sends $|1\rangle$ to $|2\rangle$ and $|2\rangle$ to $|1\rangle$, and likewise for X_{02}. Note that the qutrit Pauli X gate is the X_{+1} gate, while $X^\dagger = X^2 = X_{-1}$.

2.1   The Clifford+T gate set

Another concept that translates to qutrits (or more general qudits) is that of Clifford unitaries.

Definition 2. *Let U be a qudit unitary acting on n qudits. We say it is* Clifford *when every Pauli is mapped to another Pauli under conjugation by U. I.e. if for any $P \in \mathcal{P}_n^d$ we have $UPU^\dagger \in \mathcal{P}_n^d$.*

Note that the set of n-qudit Cliffords forms a group under composition. For qubits, this group is generated by the S, Hadamard and CX gates. The same is true for qutrits, for the right generalisation of these gates.

Throughout the paper we will write ζ for the ninth root of unity $\zeta = e^{2\pi i/9}$. Note that $\zeta^3 = \omega$ and $\zeta^9 = 1$.

Definition 3. *The qutrit S gate is $S := \zeta^8 \operatorname{diag}(1, 1, \omega)$. I.e. it multiplies the $|2\rangle$ state by the phase ω (up to a global phase).*

We adopt the convention of this global phase of ζ^8 from Ref. [19], as it will make some of our results more elegant to state (without it we would often have to say 'up to global phase').

For qubits, the Hadamard gate interchanges the Pauli Z eigenbasis $\{|0\rangle, |1\rangle\}$ and the X eigenbasis, consisting of the states $|\pm\rangle := \frac{1}{\sqrt{2}}(|0\rangle \pm |1\rangle)$. The same holds for the qutrit Hadamard. In this case the X basis consists of the following states:

$$|+\rangle := \frac{-i}{\sqrt{3}}(|0\rangle + |1\rangle + |2\rangle) \tag{2}$$

$$|\omega\rangle := \frac{-i}{\sqrt{3}}(|0\rangle + \omega|1\rangle + \omega^2|2\rangle) \tag{3}$$

$$|\omega^2\rangle := \frac{-i}{\sqrt{3}}(|0\rangle + \omega^2|1\rangle + \omega|2\rangle) \tag{4}$$

Definition 4. *The qutrit Hadamard gate H is the gate that maps $|0\rangle \mapsto |+\rangle$, $|1\rangle \mapsto |\omega\rangle$ and $|2\rangle \mapsto |\omega^2\rangle$. As a matrix:*

$$H := \frac{-i}{\sqrt{3}} \begin{pmatrix} 1 & 1 & 1 \\ 1 & \omega & \omega^2 \\ 1 & \omega^2 & \omega \end{pmatrix} \tag{5}$$

We choose the global phase of the H gate to be $-i$ to be in line with Refs. [18, 19].

Note that, unlike the qubit Hadamard, the qutrit Hadamard is *not* self-inverse. Instead we have $H^2 = -X_{12}$ so that $H^4 = \mathbb{I}$. This means that $H^\dagger = H^3$.

We have $Z = H^\dagger X_{+1} H$, and hence we can call $Z = Z_{+1}$ by analogy. We can then also define the 'Z permutation gates' by analogy. For instance, $Z_{01} := H X_{01} H^\dagger$. It will in fact be helpful to define a larger class of Z phase gates.

Definition 5. *We write $Z(a, b)$ for the phase gate that acts as $Z(a, b)|0\rangle = |0\rangle$, $Z(a, b)|1\rangle = \omega^a |1\rangle$ and $Z(a, b)|2\rangle = \omega^b |2\rangle$ where we take $a, b \in \mathbb{R}$.*

We define $Z(a, b)$ in this way, taking a and b to correspond to phases that are multiples of ω, because $Z(a, b)$ will turn out to be Clifford iff a and b are integers, so that we can easily see from the parameters whether the gate is Clifford or not. Note that the collection of all $Z(a, b)$ operators constitutes the group of diagonal single-qutrit unitaries modded out by a global phase. Composition of these operations is given by $Z(a, b) \cdot Z(c, d) = Z(a + c, b + d)$. Note that up to a global phase we have $S = Z(0, 1)$.

In Definition 5 we defined the Z phase gate. Similarly, we can define the X phase gates, that give a phase to the X basis gates.

Definition 6. *We define the X phase gates to be $X(a, b) := H Z(a, b) H^\dagger$ where $a, b \in \mathbb{R}$.*

We have in fact already seen examples of such X phase gates: $X_{+1} = X(2, 1)$ and $X_{-1} = X(1, 2)$.

Note that any single-qutrit Clifford can be represented (up to global phase) as a composition of Clifford Z and X phase gates. In particular, we can represent the qutrit Hadamard in the following ways [21]:

$$H = Z(2, 2)X(2, 2)Z(2, 2) = X(2, 2)Z(2, 2)X(2, 2) \tag{6}$$
$$H^\dagger = Z(1, 1)X(1, 1)Z(1, 1) = X(1, 1)Z(1, 1)X(1, 1) \tag{7}$$

In analogy to its qubit counterpart, we will call these *Euler decompositions* of the Hadamard.

The final Clifford gate we need is the qutrit CX gate.

Definition 7. *The* qutrit CX gate *is the unitary that acts as $CX|i, j\rangle = |i, i + j\rangle$ where the addition is taken modulo 3.*

Proposition 1. *Let U be a qutrit Clifford unitary. Then up to a global phase U can be written as a composition of the S, H and CX gates.*

Clifford gates are efficiently classically simulable, so we need to add another gate to get a universal gate set for quantum computing [23]. This brings us to the definition of the qutrit T gate.

Definition 8. *The qutrit T gate is the Z phase gate defined as $T := \operatorname{diag}(1, \zeta, \zeta^8)$ [11, 26, 45].*

Note that we could have written $T = Z(1/3, -1/3)$ as well.

Like the qubit T gate, the qutrit T gate belongs to the third level of the Clifford hierarchy, can be injected into a circuit using magic states, and its magic states can be distilled by magic state distillation. This means that we can fault-tolerantly implement this qutrit T gate on many types of quantum error correcting codes. Also as for qubits, the qutrit Clifford+T gate set is approximately universal, meaning that we can approximate any qutrit unitary using just Clifford gates and the T gate [13, Theorem 1].

2.2   Controlled Unitaries

When we have an n-qubit unitary U, we can speak of the controlled gate that implements U. This is the $(n+1)$-qubit gate that acts as the identity when the first qubit is in the $|0\rangle$ state, and implements U on the last n qubits if the first qubit is in the $|1\rangle$ state.

For qutrits there are multiple notions of control.

Definition 9. *Let U be a qutrit unitary. Then the $|2\rangle$-controlled U is the unitary that acts as*

$$|0\rangle \otimes |\psi\rangle \mapsto |0\rangle \otimes |\psi\rangle \qquad |1\rangle \otimes |\psi\rangle \mapsto |1\rangle \otimes |\psi\rangle \qquad |2\rangle \otimes |\psi\rangle \mapsto |2\rangle \otimes U |\psi\rangle$$

I.e. it implements U on the last qutrits if and only if the first qutrit is in the $|2\rangle$ state.

Note that by conjugating the first qutrit with X_{+1} or X_{-1} gates we can make the gate also be controlled on the $|1\rangle$ or $|0\rangle$ state.

A different notion of qutrit control was introduced in Ref. [8]:

Definition 10. *Given a qutrit unitary U we define*

$$\Lambda(U) |c\rangle |t\rangle = |c\rangle \otimes (U^c |t\rangle). \tag{8}$$

I.e. we apply the unitary U a number of times equal to to the value of the control qutrit, so that if the control qutrit is $|2\rangle$ we apply U^2 to the target qutrits.

The Clifford CX gate defined earlier is in this notation equal to $\Lambda(X_{+1})$. Note that we can get this latter notion of control from the former one: just apply a $|1\rangle$-controlled U, followed by a $|2\rangle$-controlled U^2. Adding controls to a Clifford gate generally makes it non-Clifford. In the case of the CX gate, which is $\Lambda(X_{+1})$, it is still Clifford, while the $|2\rangle$-controlled X_{+1} gate is *not* Clifford.

A number of Clifford+T constructions for controlled qutrit unitaries are already known. For instance, all the $|2\rangle$-controlled permutation X gates can be built from the constructions given in Ref. [6], which we present, suitably modified to be consistent with our notation. The $|0\rangle$-controlled Z gate can be constructed by the following 3 T gate circuit [8, Figure 6]:

$$\tag{9}$$

Here the circles with a 0 or Λ inside denote controls of the types defined above. By conjugating the control qutrit by either $X^\dagger$ before and X after, or X before and $X^\dagger$ after, the $|1\rangle$- and $|2\rangle$-controlled versions of Z are respectively obtained. Taking the adjoint of Eq. (9) has the effect of changing the target operation from Z to $Z^\dagger$. Finally, the target can be changed to X or to $X^\dagger$, by conjugating by a H and $H^\dagger$ pair. Using these gates we can build the $|2\rangle$-controlled X_{01} gate, which is a variation of Ref. [6, Figure 17]:

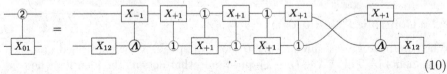

$$\tag{10}$$

Conjugating by the appropriate single-qutrit Clifford gates, these two circuits (9) and (10) suffice to construct any singly-controlled permutation X or Z gate. Note that the blue and red colors of the controls here are just to more clearly show which type of control the gate has and that the colors have no further significance.

The work done in Ref. [6] also describes an approach which could be applied to constructing the $|2\rangle^{\otimes k}$-controlled Z_{+1} gate for any k, and hence also the $|2\rangle^{\otimes k}$-controlled Z_{-1}, X_{+1} and X_{-1} gates for any k, by solving a system of linear equations modulo 3 where the number of equations is exponential in k. They present the explicit circuit for this for $k = 1$, but not for any $k > 1$. Their method does not suffice to construct the k-controlled X_{01} gate due to the X_{01} gate not being diagonal when conjugated by Hadamards.

A complication when trying to construct controlled unitaries, is that usually irrelevant global phases becomes 'local' and hence must be dealt with accordingly [1, Lemma 5.2].

Definition 11. *A controlled global phase gate is a controlled unitary where the unitary is $e^{i\phi}\mathbb{I}$, for an identity matrix I and some phase ϕ.*

The number of qutrits the identity matrix acts on in this definition is irrelevant as the phase factor can be "factored out" from the tensor product of the controlled and target qutrits:

$$\tag{11}$$

Here we wrote the global phase ϕ as $\phi = \gamma \cdot 2\pi/3$ so that we can represent the phase gate as a multiple of ω.

We will see that it can be easier or more cost effective to construct a controlled unitary 'up to a controlled global phase', and that to implement the unitary exactly, additional work must be done. A generalisation of this idea was used to find more efficient decompositions for qubit controlled gates in Ref. [38].

In previous work [18] we also found a construction of the $|2\rangle$-controlled S gate and the $|2\rangle$-controlled Hadamard gate:

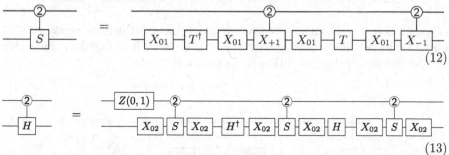

$$(12)$$

$$(13)$$

Note that while in Ref. [18] these constructions were only correct up to a controlled global phase, in this paper we defined S and H to include these global phases, so they don't appear here. While these are thus exact constructions for adding one $|2\rangle$-control to the S and H gates, if we wish to use the gates in these circuits as a base for adding more controls, we will need to also add controls to the $Z(0,1)$ gate in Eq. 13.

3 Adding Controls to Clifford+T Gates

In this section we will implement each the $|2\rangle^{\otimes k}$-controlled versions of every qutrit Clifford+T unitary. As Clifford+T unitaries are built out of Hadamard, CX, S and T gates, it suffices to show how we can construct k-controlled versions of each of these gates.

We will do this in stages, first showing how to construct the X permutation gates with two controls, and then any number of controls, before moving on to the other Clifford+T gates.

3.1 Permutation Gates with Two Controls

Before we can make the step to having an arbitrary number of controls, we first need to construct the permutation gates with two controls and specifically the $|22\rangle$-controlled X_{01} gate. To do this we use the following lemma that allows us to add more controls to a unitary, once we know how to construct it with just one control.

Lemma 1. *For any qutrit unitary V with a construction for $|2\rangle$-controlled V and $|2\rangle$-controlled $V^\dagger$, we can build the circuit consisting of the $|22\rangle$-controlled*

V *multiplied by the* $|21\rangle$*-controlled* V^2 *unitary:*

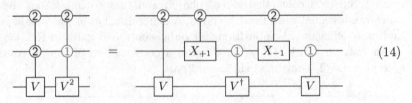

$$(14)$$

Lemma 1 is easily shown to be correct by doing case distinctions on the control wires. While we believe this construction to be new, it is based on the qubit Sleator-Weinfurter decomposition [1, Lemma 6.1]:

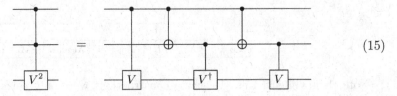

$$(15)$$

We note that Corollary 1 contradicts the statement of Ref. [41] that "a 5-gates Barenco et al. type of realization of a ternary (generalised) Toffoli gate without adding an ancillary line is simply not possible"; their analysis of ternary generalizations of the Sleator-Weinfurter decomposition did not account for decompositions of the form of Eq. (14).

If we pick $V = X_{01}$ in Lemma 1, then we have $V^2 = \mathbb{I}$, so that this construction gives us a way to construct the $|22\rangle$-controlled X_{01} using just $|2\rangle$-controlled X_{01}, X_{+1} and X_{-1} gates, which we already know how to construct in Clifford+T.

Lemma 2. *We can construct the* $|22\rangle$*-controlled* X_{01} *gate in Clifford+T without using any ancilla.*

Note that by conjugating by the appropriate single-qutrit Cliffords on the bottom qutrit, we can also construct the $|22\rangle$-controlled X_{12} and X_{02} gates.

Remark 1. The $|22\rangle$-controlled X_{01} gate was first decomposed by Di and Wei [15] in terms of qubit Clifford+T operations, where the CX gate could be performed pairwise on any two of the three qutrit Z-basis states; as far as we are aware, there does not exist an error correction protocol that can, without code switching, correct qubit Clifford operations on all three pairs of Z-basis states. Moraga [42] found an alternative decomposition of the $|22\rangle$-controlled X_{01} gate, in terms of $|2\rangle$-controlled qutrit X gates—which around the same time was shown by Bocharov et.al. to be constructable in qutrit Clifford+T [6]. Hence, it was in principle already known how to construct the qutrit $|22\rangle$-controlled X_{01} gate in Clifford+T, but this was never pointed out explicitly. Note furthermore that our construction has the benefit of arising in a systematic way from a general qutrit Sleator-Weinfurter construction, which enables us to add controls to a wide variety of unitaries.

We can use the $|22\rangle$-controlled X_{01} gate to build the $|22\rangle$-controlled X_{+1} gate. To do this we will adapt a well-known construction for qubit controlled phases. Recall that if we can implement k-controlled Toffoli gates and the square root of a phase gate, that we can then also implement the k-controlled phase gate [1]:

$$
\vdots \quad \boxed{Z(\alpha)} \quad \cong \quad \vdots \quad \boxed{Z(\alpha/2)} \oplus \boxed{Z(-\alpha/2)} \oplus \tag{16}
$$

This works because when the Toffoli 'fires' the X gate is applied, and we have $XR_Z(\alpha)X \propto Z(-\alpha)$.

Lemma 3. *We can construct the $|22\rangle$-controlled X_{+1} gate in Clifford+T without using any ancillae.*

Proof. Consider the following circuit:

$$
\begin{array}{c}
②\\
②\\
\boxed{X_{+1}}
\end{array}
\quad = \quad
\begin{array}{c}
②\qquad②\\
②\qquad②\\
\boxed{X_{-1}}\ \boxed{X_{12}}\ \boxed{X_{+1}}\ \boxed{X_{12}}
\end{array}
\tag{17}
$$

This works because $X_{12}X_{+1}X_{12} = X_{-1}$ and $X_{-1}^2 = X_{+1}$.

By conjugating by appropriate Clifford gates we then see we have the following corollary.

Corollary 1. *We can construct with ancillae in Clifford+T any $|xy\rangle$-controlled X permutation gate where $x, y \in \{0, 1, 2\}$.*

3.2 Permutation Gates with Any Number of Controls

Now let's see how we can generalise these constructions to have any number of controls. Here instead of building the controlled X_{+1} gate out of the controlled X_{01}, we will go in the opposite direction. In order to efficiently build the $|2\rangle^{\otimes k}$-controlled X_{+1} gate, we will adapt a construction for multiple-controlled Toffolis for qubits that requires one *borrowed ancilla*.

Definition 12. *A borrowed ancilla is an ancilla that can be in any state, and that is returned to the same state after the operation is finished.*

Having a borrowed ancilla just means that in the circuit we are considering there is at least one other qutrit that is not directly involved with our construction.

We base our construction on the following qubit identity for Toffolis [1, Lemma 7.3]:

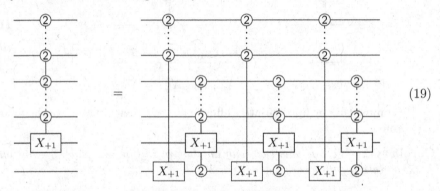

$$(18)$$

Using this construction, a k-controlled Toffoli where $k = 2^m$ can be decomposed into 4 Toffolis with $k/2 = 2^{m-1}$ controls. Iterating this procedure then requires $O(k^2)$ 'standard' Toffolis with 2 controls each.

Lemma 4. *We can construct the $|2\rangle^{\otimes k}$-controlled X_{+1} gate using $O(k^{2.585})$ Clifford+T gates and using one borrowed ancilla.*

Proof. Consider the following identity:

$$(19)$$

To see this is correct first note that it is the identity when any of the top control wires is not in the $|2\rangle$ state (as doing X_{+1} three times is just the identity). As such, let us assume they are all in the $|2\rangle$ state so that we can ignore these control wires. We are cycling the value of the ancilla three times, which means that the controlled X_{+1} gate on the target qutrit fires exactly once, namely when the ancilla is put into the $|2\rangle$ state. As we cycle the value of the ancilla three times, it is put back into the state that it started in.

We can use Eq. (19) to reduce the implementation of a $|2\rangle^{\otimes k}$-controlled X_{+1} gate where $k = 2^m$ to a sequence of 6 $|2\rangle^{\otimes k/2}$-controlled X_{+1} gates. Letting $C(m)$ denote the number of $|22\rangle$-controlled X_{+1} gates needed to write the 2^m-controlled X_{+1} gate, we then get the relation $C(m) = 6C(m-1)$. As $C(1) = 1$ we calculate $C(m) = 6^{m-1} = \frac{1}{6}2^{m\log_2 6}$. Substituting $k = 2^m$ we then see we require $O(k^{\log_2 6})$ of the base gate, which we can round up to $O(k^{2.585})$.

Lemma 5. *We can construct the $|2\rangle^{\otimes k}$-controlled X_{01} gate using $O(k^{3.585})$ Clifford+T gates without using any ancillae.*

Proof. Consider the following generalised version of Eq. (14), for which the qubit analogue is [1, Lemma 7.5]:

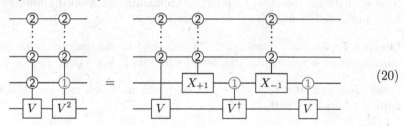

$$(20)$$

Again taking $V = X_{01}$, we see that we can reduce the construction of the $|2\rangle^{\otimes k}$-controlled X_{01} gate to the construction of the $|2\rangle^{\otimes k-1}$-controlled X_{01} gate at the cost of introducing two $|2\rangle^{\otimes k-1}$-controlled X_{+1} gates and two $|2\rangle$-controlled X_{01} gates. Iterating the procedure we see then that the full construction requires $2k$ $|2\rangle$-controlled X_{01} gates and $2k$ $|2\rangle^{\otimes m}$-controlled X_{+1} gates where $m \leq k - 1$. The cost of this is dominated by the controlled X_{+1} gates, which cost $O(k^{2.585})$ gates each. As we have $O(k)$ of these, we require $O(k^{3.585})$ Clifford+T gates to build the $|2\rangle^{\otimes k}$-controlled X_{01} gate. Note that as the controlled X_{+1} gates are not controlled on all the wires that we have access to at least one borrowed ancilla, so that we can in fact use the construction of Lemma 4.

This construction doesn't require any borrowed ancillae. We can now use a generalised version of Eq. (17) to complete the circle and construct a many-controlled version of the X_{+1} gate that does not require any borrowed ancillae (at the cost of worse polynomial scaling).

Lemma 6. *We can construct the $|2\rangle^{\otimes k}$-controlled X_{+1} gate using $O(k^{3.585})$ Clifford+T gates without using any ancillae.*

Proof. Follows from the following circuit that generalises Eq. (17):

$$(21)$$

As this requires two copies of $|2\rangle^{\otimes k}$-controlled X_{01}, the cost is asymptotically the same as in Lemma 5. □

Note that we can change what the unitary is controlled on by conjugating any number of control qutrits by the appropriate qutrit X gate in $\{X_{+1}, X_{-1}, X_{01}, X_{02}, X_{12}\}$. Successive application of tritstring-controlled X gates leads to selective control on all possible combinations of tritstrings. We hence have the following.

Corollary 2. *We can construct any qutrit generalisation of a multiple-controlled Toffoli in Clifford+T unitarily without ancillae.*

3.3   Building Multiple-Controlled Clifford+T gates

Now we have all the tools to build the remaining controlled Clifford+T gates: CX, Hadamard, S and T.

Lemma 7. *The $|2\rangle^{\otimes k}$-controlled CX gate can be constructed unitarily without ancillae using a polynomial number of Clifford+T gates in k.*

Proof. Just consider the following construction, which can be obtained from applying Lemma 1 with $V = X_{-1}$:

$$\tag{22}$$

For the many-controlled T gate we use the 'square-root trick' of Eq. (16). Here to find the square root we can use the fact $(T^5)^2 = T$ as $T^9 = \mathbb{I}$, and hence T^5 acts like a $\sqrt{T}$ gate. Similarly, T^4 is like $\sqrt{T}^{\dagger}$. It is then easily verified that we have the following construction for the controlled T gate.

Lemma 8. *We can build the $|2\rangle^{\otimes k}$-controlled T gate unitarily without ancillae using a polynomial number of Clifford+T gates in k.*

Proof. Consider the following circuit identity:

$$\tag{23}$$

Its correctness follows because $X_{12}T^4X_{12} = T^5$.

That we can implement the $|2\rangle$-controlled T in Clifford+T without ancillae is interesting as this is not possible in the qubit setting. With qubits, to construct the controlled T gate we have to either employ the $\sqrt{T}$ gate, or a clean ancilla [32, 33, 50].

To add controls to the S gate, we extend our construction from Ref. [18]:

Lemma 9. *The $|2\rangle^{\otimes k}$-controlled S gate can be constructed unitarily without ancillae using a polynomial number of Clifford+T gates in k.*

Proof. We straightforwardly generalise Eq. (12):

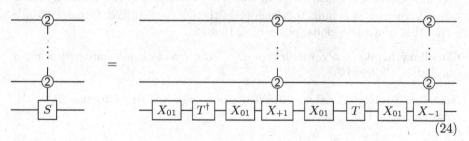

$$(24)$$

We will shortly show how to control the H gate. To do this we will need to handle some controlled global phase for which we need the following results.

Lemma 10. *The $|2\rangle^{\otimes k}$-controlled $Z(2,2) = diag(1,\omega^2,\omega^2)$ gate can be constructed up to a controlled global phase of ζ^2. This Clifford+T construction is unitary and ancilla-free, with T-count polynomial in k.*

Proof. Use the following circuit:

$$(25)$$

Its correctness can be verified by direct computation, or by commuting S and X_{02}.

With one borrowed ancilla, we can construct the $|2\rangle^{\otimes k}$-controlled $\zeta S = Z(0,1)$ gate:

Lemma 11. *The $|2\rangle^{\otimes k}$-controlled $Z(0,1)$ gate can be constructed unitarily with one borrowed ancilla using only Clifford+T gates, with T-count polynomial in k.*

Proof. Use the following circuit:

$$(26)$$

The correctness follows from the fact that $Z_{-1}X_{02}Z_{-1}X_{02} = \omega\mathbb{I}$, and from Eq. (11).

While not really necessarily for the remainder of the paper, let us note that we can compose the construction of this $|2\rangle^{\otimes k}$-controlled ζS with the adjoint of the construction of Lemma 9 (which gives the $|2\rangle^{\otimes k}$-controlled $S^\dagger$ gate) to give a resulting controlled global phase of ζ. Hence:

Corollary 3. *We can construct the $|2\rangle^{\otimes k}$-controlled $\zeta\mathbb{I}$ gate unitarily without ancillae in Clifford+T.*

Note that by Eq. (11) this controlled global phase is equal to the $|2\rangle^{\otimes(k-1)}$-controlled $Z(0, 1/3)$ gate.

Lemma 12. *The $|2\rangle^{\otimes k}$-controlled Hadamard gate can be implemented unitarily without ancillae using a polynomial number of Clifford+T gates in k.*

Proof. Consider the following circuit:

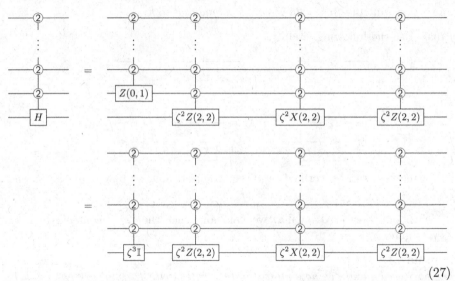

$$(27)$$

Each of these gates can be constructed unitarily in Clifford+T without ancillae and with a polynomial number of gates using Lemmas 10 and 11. To see why it is correct, note that when the gates fire it implements a $\zeta^9 Z(2,2)X(2,2)Z(2,2)$ gate, and as $\zeta^9 = 1$ and $Z(2,2)X(2,2)Z(2,2) = H$ by Eq. (6) the construction is indeed correct.

3.4 The Main Theorem

We have now seen how to exactly and unitarily construct without ancillae the $|2\rangle^{\otimes k}$-controlled CX, S, H, T and permutation gates. Each of our constructions used at most $O(k^{3.585})$ Clifford+T gates.

We hence have the following theorem.

Theorem 1. *Let U be any n-qutrit Clifford+T unitary consisting of N CX, S, H and T gates. Then there is an $n + k$-qutrit Clifford+T circuit implementing the $|2\rangle^{\otimes k}$-controlled U unitary using $O(Nk^{3.585})$ gates.*

As noted in Corollaries 1 and 2, by conjugating the control qutrits by certain Clifford operations, we can make the unitary controlled on every possible tritstring in the Z- or X-basis. Furthermore, by repeated application of the decomposition on different control values, more specific definitions of ternary control, including that of Definition 10 may be realised.

4   Building Trit Permutation Gates in Clifford+T

A *ternary classical reversible* function is a bijective map $f : \{0,1,2\}^n \rightarrow \{0,1,2\}^n$. Ternary classical reversible circuits have been well-studied with a variety of applications. In contrast with irreversible logic, which necessarily dissipates energy in order to perform computation, reversible logic is of interest for energy efficient and sustainable computing. Ternary classical reversible functions are of importance to quantum algorithms involving oracles, which are implementations of classical functions as quantum gates. One reason to expect comparative advantage of qutrits over qubits for this application is that it is impossible to build ancilla-free qubit Clifford+T Toffolis with 3 or more controls [17]. Therefore, ancilla-free implementations of classical reversible functions as qubit Clifford+T unitaries are limited to bitstrings of length $n \leq 3$.

However, the decomposition of ternary classical reversible circuits into a fault-tolerant quantum gate set such as Clifford+T has not been explicitly presented before. Given a ternary classical reversible function f on n trits, our goal will be to find an n-qutrit Clifford+T unitary U that implements that function on its Z basis states: $U|x_1,\ldots,x_n\rangle = |f(x_1,\ldots,x_n)\rangle$. Additionally, we want this construction to require the fewest number of T gates.

Let's first note that if we put some previously appeared papers together, that there is in fact a procedure to build arbitrary ternary reversible functions as ancilla-free Clifford+T circuits, although to our knowledge, this has never been pointed out explicitly before. Namely, Fan *et al.* [16] proved that a gate set consisting of only the single-qutrit gates X_{01}, X_{02}, and X_{12} and the two-qutrit $|1\rangle$-controlled X_{+1} gate can implement without ancillae all the ternary classical reversible circuits. They do this by proving that the $|2\rangle^{\otimes(n-1)}$-controlled X gates needed to build reversible functions can be broken down in terms of single-qutrit X gates and the $|1\rangle$-controlled X_{+1} gate (although this is not done in an explicit manner, and actually extracting the concrete circuits to do so is cumbersome).

Separately, Bocharov, Roetteler, and Svore [8, Figure 6] constructed the $|1\rangle$-controlled X_{+1} gate as a two-qutrit Clifford+T unitary. Combining these results then yields ancilla-free Clifford+T implementations of any ternary classical reversible function.

Various past works have compared optimisation procedures for specific benchmark ternary classical reversible circuits [2,29,34,37,47,48]. Rather than focus on optimising individual circuits, we will instead focus on providing an asymptotic upper bound of the Clifford+T gate count needed to construct an arbitrary ternary classical reversible circuit. This same upper bound then also caps the asymptotic T-count of these previous decompositions. We hope that our algorithm can then serve as a baseline for circuit complexity of ternary classical reversible circuit synthesis, to which empirical gate counts for specific constructions can be compared.

As was observed in Ref. [54], we can view a reversible classical function on n trits as just a permutation of the set $\{0, 1, 2\}^n$. The following classic result shows that any permutation is generated by just the 2-cycles.

Definition 13. *Let S_k be a symmetric group of symbols $\{d_1, d_2, ..., d_k\}$, then $(d_{i_1}, d_{i_2}, ..., d_{i_j})$ is called a j-cycle, where $j \leq k, 1 \leq i_1, i_2, ..., i_j \leq k$.*

Lemma 13. *The 2-cycles generate all permutations.*

Proof. Any permutation can be written as product of some disjoint cycles. So we only need to show that every cycle $(d_1, d_2, ..., d_k)$ can be expressed as a product of some 2-cycles. When we have a k-cycle we can reduce it to a $(k-1)$-cycle:

$$(d_1, d_2, ..., d_k) = (d_1, d_2)(d_1, d_3, ..., d_k) \tag{28}$$

By repeating this equation, each cycle can then be reduced to a 2 cycle.

It hence suffices to show how to implement an arbitrary 2-cycle on the set $\{0, 1, 2\}^n$. Such a 2-cycle is called a *two-level axial reflection* in Ref. [8, Def. 1]. That is, a two-level axial reflection is a qutrit operation which permutes two tritstrings, and acts as the identity on all other tritstrings.

Definition 14. *A two-level axial reflection is a gate*

$$\tau_{|j\rangle, |k\rangle} = \mathbb{I}^{\otimes n} - |j\rangle \langle j| - |k\rangle \langle k| + |j\rangle \langle k| + |k\rangle \langle j| \tag{29}$$

where $|j\rangle, |k\rangle$ are two different standard n-qudit basis vectors.

In Ref. [7, Section 4], later improved by a constant factor in Ref. [5], they presented a method for *approximate* synthesis of any n-qutrit two-level axial reflection in the Clifford+R gate set, where $R = \text{diag}(1, 1, -1)$ is the non-Clifford gate for attaining universality, with asymptotic R-count $5\log_3(1/3\epsilon) + O(\log(\log(1/\epsilon)))$, such that $c |0\rangle^{\otimes n}$ approximates $|u\rangle$ to precision $\epsilon/(2\sqrt{(2)})$.

We show that the same operation, an n-qutrit two-level axial reflection, can be *exactly* synthesised as an ancilla-free Clifford+T unitary with a T-count that scales asymptotically as $O(n^{3.585})$. This is because we show we can construct it using a single instance of a qutrit Toffoli controlled on $n-1$ wires which requires $O(n^{3.585})$ gates.

Proposition 2. *Let $a = (a_1, ..., a_n)$ and $b = (b_1, ..., b_n)$ be any two tritstrings of length n. Then we can exactly implement the two-level axial reflection on a and b as an ancilla-free n-qutrit Clifford+T unitary with T-count $O(n^{3.585})$.*

Proof. We assume $a \neq b$, or the 2-cycle would just be the identity operation on all inputs. As a and b differ, they must differ by at least one character. Without loss of generality suppose that $a_n \neq b_n$. Consider the following circuit:

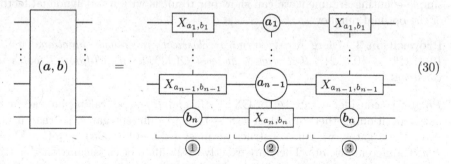

$$(30)$$

Here the circles denote controls on the value of an a_j or b_j, which control whether a X_{a_j,b_j} operation is applied (which we take to be the identity if $a_j = b_j$). Hence, the gate in Step 2 is a many-controlled X_{a_n,b_n} gate, which we know how to build by Lemma 5 using $O(n^{3.585})$ gates. We conjugate this gate, in Steps 1 and 3, by $n - 1$ gates that are each Clifford equivalent to the $|2\rangle$-controlled X_{12} gate. Hence these steps require $O(n)$ gates to implement.

This circuit indeed implements the (a, b) 2-cycle, which we can see by enumerating the possible input cases.

– When the input is a: Only steps 2 and 3 fire (as $b_n \neq a_n$), outputting b.
– When the input is b: Steps 1 and 2 fire, outputting a.

Observe that when Step 2 does not fire, Steps 1 and 3 always combine to the identity gate. Therefore, we only need to consider the remaining cases where Step 2 does fire.

– When both Steps 1 and 2 fired: The input had to have been b.
– When Step 2 fired, but Step 1 didn't fire: Either the input was a, or the last input character was neither a_n nor b_n in which case the overall operation is the identity.

Therefore, the circuit in Eq. (30) maps a to b, b to a, and is identity on all other tritstrings. Lastly, the T-count is asymptotically that of the gate in Step 2, which is $O(n^{3.585})$.

Theorem 2. *For any ternary classical reversible function* $f : \{0, 1, 2\}^n \to \{0, 1, 2\}^n$ *on n trits, we can construct an n-qutrit ancilla-free Clifford+T circuit which exactly implements it, with T-count* $O(3^n n^{3.585})$.

Proof. We view f as a permutation of size 3^n. This permutation consists of cycles, each of which can be decomposed into 2-cycles using Lemma 13. This full decomposition requires at most $3^n - 1$ 2-cycles. Implementing each of these 2-cycles requires $O(n^{3.585})$ T gates. Therefore, the asymptotic T-count of the overall construction is $O(3^n n^{3.585})$.

At first glance the number of gates needed here may seem excessive, but as noted in Ref. [54], the asymptotic scaling we find is still "exponentially lower than the complexity of a breadth-first-search synthesis algorithm". Additionally, with a simple counting argument we can show our result is within a polynomial factor of the optimal number.

Proposition 3. *There exist ternary classical reversible functions* f : $\{0, 1, 2\}^n \rightarrow \{0, 1, 2\}^n$ *that require at least* $O(n3^n/\log n)$ *Clifford+T gates to construct.*

Proof. We consider a gate set of CX, S, T, and H gates. Taking into account qutrit positioning there are then $n(n-1) + 3n$ different gates, so that using N of these gates, we can construct at most $(n(n-1) + 3n)^N \leq (2n^2)^N = 2^N n^{2N}$ different circuits. There are exactly $(3^n)!$ different classical reversible trit functions on n trits (where $k!$ denotes the factorial of k). In order to write down every such permutation we must hence have a number of gates N such that at least $2^N n^{2N} \geq (3^n)!$. Taking the logarithm on both sides and using $\log(k!) \geq \frac{1}{2}k \log k$ we can rewrite this inequality to $N \log 2 + 2N \log n \geq \frac{1}{2}3^n \cdot n \log 3$. Factoring out N gives $N \geq \frac{\log 3}{2} \frac{n3^n}{\log 2 + 2 \log n} \geq \frac{\log 3}{6} \frac{n3^n}{\log n}$ showing that we must have $N = O(n3^n/\log n)$.

We believe it might be possible to improve the implementation of the X_{01} gate with n controls to require just $O(n)$ gates, in which case the construction of Theorem 2 would require $O(n3^n)$ gates, making it optimal to within a logarithmic factor.

Although our construction resembles that for qubits in Ref. [54], their construction uses $O(n2^n)$ multiple-controlled X gates (each with $n-1$ controls). In contrast, our construction requires $O(3^n)$ of this gate's qutrit equivalent. This factor of n improvement in asymptotic circuit complexity can be applied to the qubit setting of Ref. [54] as well, resulting in a more efficient construction. Additionally, our observation that only a single ternary $(n-1)$-controlled Toffoli is needed to implement the two-level axial reflection can be used to improve the algorithm of Fan *et al.* [16] as well. Finally, let us note that our decomposition can be readily generalised to any qudit dimension provided we can construct single-qudit X permutation gates controlled on an arbitrary dit string.

5   Conclusion

We have shown how to construct any many-controlled qutrit Clifford+T unitary, using just Clifford+T gates and without using ancillae. Our construction uses $O(k^{3.585})$ gates in the number of controls k. Using our results we have shown how any classical permutation on n trits can be realised as an n-qutrit ancilla-free Clifford+T unitary circuit with $O(3^n n^{3.585})$ gates.

We suspect that the $O(k^{3.585})$ scaling is not optimal. In future work we would like to find better ways to decompose the many controlled X_{+1} gate into fewer-controlled gates, using the fact that after the first iteration of the decomposition we have many borrowed ancillae available, which would possibly be used to lead to better asymptotic scaling. In particular, we would like to see whether the linear T-count construction of the qubit n-controlled Toffoli construction where $n-2$ borrowed ancilla are available from Ref. [1, Lemma 7.2] can be adapted to qutrits. Improvements in this scaling will directly lead to improvements in the Clifford+T synthesis of reversible trit functions of Theorem 2 and will bring it closer to the theoretical lower bound. It would also directly improve the decompositions using the techniques of for instance Refs. [14, 35, 47, 54]. It would also be interesting to find lower bounds on the T-count of our constructions using techniques extended from the qubit setting [3, 22, 25, 39, 40, 43, 51, 52].

Our results pave the way to a full characterisation of the unitaries that can be constructed over the qutrit Clifford+T gate set. We conjecture that, as in the qubit case [17], any qutrit unitary with entries in the number ring generated by the Clifford+T gate set can be exactly synthesised over Clifford+T.

Finally, we aim to use our results to emulate qubit logic circuits on qutrits. Work in this area has already shown to lead to several benefits [20], so it will be interesting to to identify where more asymptotic improvements for qubit computation in the fault-tolerant regime can be made.

Acknowledgments. The authors wish to thank Andrew Glaudell and Neil J. Ross for discussions regarding the consequences of our results and Andrew Glaudell specifically for pointing out Eq. (23). We additionally wish to thank Shuxiang Cao and Razin Shaikh for assistance in preparing the figures in an early draft of this paper. JvdW is supported by an NWO Rubicon personal fellowship. LY is supported by an Oxford - Basil Reeve Graduate Scholarship at Oriel College with the Clarendon Fund.

References

1. Barenco, A., et al.: Elementary gates for quantum computation. Phys. Rev. A **52**(5), 3457–3467 (1995). https://doi.org/10.1103/physreva.52.3457
2. Basu, S., Mandal, S.B., Chakrabarti, A., Sur-Kolay, S., Choudhury, A.K.: An efficient synthesis method for ternary reversible logic. In: 2016 IEEE International Symposium on Circuits and Systems (ISCAS), pp. 2306–2309 (2016). https://doi.org/10.1109/ISCAS.2016.7539045
3. Beverland, M., Campbell, E., Howard, M., Kliuchnikov, V.: Lower bounds on the non-Clifford resources for quantum computations. Quantum Sci. Technol. **5**(3), 035009 (2020). https://doi.org/10.1088/2058-9565/ab8963
4. Blok, M.S., et al.: Quantum Information Scrambling on a Superconducting Qutrit Processor. Phys. Rev. X **11**, 021010 (2021). https://doi.org/10.1103/PhysRevX.11.021010
5. Bocharov, A.: A note on optimality of quantum circuits over metaplectic basis. Quantum Inf. Comput. **18** (2016). https://doi.org/10.26421/QIC18.1-2-1
6. Bocharov, A., Cui, S., Roetteler, M., Svore, K.: Improved quantum ternary arithmetics. Quantum Inf. Comput. **16**, 862–884 (2016). https://doi.org/10.26421/QIC16.9-10-8
7. Bocharov, A., Cui, X., Kliuchnikov, V., Wang, Z.: Efficient topological compilation for a weakly integral anyonic model. Phys. Rev. A **93**(1) (2016). https://doi.org/10.1103/physreva.93.012313

8. Bocharov, A., Roetteler, M., Svore, K.M.: Factoring with qutrits: Shor's algorithm on ternary and metaplectic quantum architectures. Phys. Rev. A **96**, 012306 (2017). https://doi.org/10.1103/PhysRevA.96.012306

9. Bravyi, S., Kitaev, A.: Universal quantum computation with ideal Clifford gates and noisy ancillas. Phys. Rev. A **71**, 022316 (2005). https://doi.org/10.1103/PhysRevA.71.022316

10. Campbell, E.T.: Enhanced fault-tolerant quantum computing in d-level systems. Phys. Rev. Lett. **113**, 230501 (2014). https://doi.org/10.1103/PhysRevLett.113.230501

11. Campbell, E.T., Anwar, H., Browne, D.E.: Magic-state distillation in all prime dimensions using quantum reed-muller codes. Phys. Rev. X **2**, 041021 (2012). https://doi.org/10.1103/PhysRevX.2.041021

12. Cozzolino, D., Da Lio, B., Bacco, D., Oxenløwe, L.K.: High-dimensional quantum communication: benefits, progress, and future challenges. Adv. Quantum Technol. **2**(12), 1900038 (2019). https://doi.org/10.1002/qute.201900038

13. Cui, S.X., Wang, Z.: Universal quantum computation with metaplectic anyons. J. Math. Phys. **56**(3), 032202 (2015). https://doi.org/10.1063/1.4914941

14. Datta, K., Sengupta, I., Rahaman, H.: Group theory based reversible logic synthesis. In: 2012 5th International Conference on Computers and Devices for Communication (CODEC), pp. 1–4 (2012). https://doi.org/10.1109/CODEC.2012.6509346

15. Di, Y.M., Wei, H.R.: Synthesis of multivalued quantum logic circuits by elementary gates. Phys. Rev. A **87**, 012325 (2013). https://doi.org/10.1103/PhysRevA.87.012325

16. Fan, F., Yang, G., Yang, G., Hung, W.N.N.: A synthesis method of quantum reversible logic circuit based on elementary qutrit quantum logic gates. J. Circ. Syst. Comput. **24**(08), 1550121 (2015). https://doi.org/10.1142/S0218126615501212

17. Giles, B., Selinger, P.: Exact synthesis of multiqubit Clifford+T circuits. Phys. Rev. A **87**(3) (2013). https://doi.org/10.1103/physreva.87.032332

18. Glaudell, A., J. Ross, N., van de Wetering, J., Yeh, L.: Qutrit metaplectic gates are a subset of Clifford+T. In: 17th Conference on the Theory of Quantum Computation, Communication and Cryptography (TQC 2022). Leibniz International Proceedings in Informatics (LIPIcs), Schloss Dagstuhl - Leibniz-Zentrum für Informatik (In press). https://arxiv.org/abs/2202.09235

19. Glaudell, A.N., Ross, N.J., Taylor, J.M.: Canonical forms for single-qutrit Clifford+T operators. Ann. Phys. **406**, 54–70 (2019). https://doi.org/10.1016/j.aop.2019.04.001

20. Gokhale, P., Baker, J.M., Duckering, C., Brown, N.C., Brown, K.R., Chong, F.T.: Asymptotic improvements to quantum circuits via qutrits. In: Proceedings of the 46th International Symposium on Computer Architecture, June 2019. https://doi.org/10.1145/3307650.3322253

21. Gong, X., Wang, Q.: Equivalence of Local Complementation and Euler Decomposition in the Qutrit ZX-calculus, April 2017

22. Gosset, D., Kliuchnikov, V., Mosca, M., Russo, V.: An algorithm for the T-count. Quantum Info. Comput. **14**(15–16), 1261–1276 (2014). https://doi.org/10.5555/2685179.2685180

23. Gottesman, D.: Fault-tolerant quantum computation with higher-dimensional systems. Chaos Solitons Fractals **10**(10), 1749–1758 (1999). https://doi.org/10.1016/s0960-0779(98)00218-5

24. Haghparast, M., Wille, R., Monfared, A.T.: Towards quantum reversible ternary coded decimal adder. Quantum Inf. Process. **16**(11), 1–25 (2017). https://doi.org/10.1007/s11128-017-1735-3

25. Howard, M., Campbell, E.: Application of a resource theory for magic states to fault-tolerant quantum computing. Phys. Rev. Lett. **118**, 090501 (2017). https://doi.org/10.1103/PhysRevLett.118.090501

26. Howard, M., Vala, J.: Qudit versions of the qubit $\pi/8$ gate. Phys. Rev. A **86**, 022316 (2012). https://doi.org/10.1103/PhysRevA.86.022316

27. Ionicioiu, R., Spiller, T., Munro, W.: generalized toffoli gates using qudit catalysis. Phys. Rev. A **80**, 012312 (2009). https://doi.org/10.1103/PhysRevA.80.012312

28. Khan, F.S., Perkowski, M.: Synthesis of multi-qudit hybrid and d-valued quantum logic circuits by decomposition. Theor. Comput. Sci. **367**(3), 336–346 (2006). https://doi.org/10.1016/j.tcs.2006.09.006

29. Khan, M., Perkowski, M.: Genetic algorithm based synthesis of multi-output ternary functions using quantum cascade of generalized ternary gates. In: Proceedings of the 2004 Congress on Evolutionary Computation (IEEE Cat. No.04TH8753), vol. 2, pp. 2194–2201 (2004). https://doi.org/10.1109/CEC.2004.1331169

30. Khan, M.H.A., Perkowski, M.A.: Quantum ternary parallel adder/subtractor with partially-look-ahead carry. J. Syst. Archit. **53**(7), 453–464 (2007). https://doi.org/10.1016/j.sysarc.2007.01.007

31. Kiktenko, E.O., Nikolaeva, A.S., Xu, P., Shlyapnikòv, G.V., Fedorov, A.K.: Scalable quantum computing with qudits on a graph. Phys. Rev. A **101**(2) (2020). https://doi.org/10.1103/physreva.101.022304

32. Kim, T., Choi, B.S.: Efficient decomposition methods for controlled-rń using a single ancillary qubit. Sci. Rep. **8**(1), 5445 (2018). https://doi.org/10.1038/s41598-018-23764-x

33. Kliuchnikov, V., Maslov, D., Mosca, M.: Fast and efficient exact synthesis of single-qubit unitaries generated by Clifford and T gates. Quantum Info. Comput. **13**(7–8), 607–630 (2013)

34. Kole, A., Rani, P.M.N., Datta, K., Sengupta, I., Drechsler, R.: Exact synthesis of ternary reversible functions using ternary toffoli gates. In: 2017 IEEE 47th International Symposium on Multiple-Valued Logic (ISMVL), pp. 179–184 (2017). https://doi.org/10.1109/ISMVL.2017.51

35. Kole, D.K., Rahaman, H., Das, D.K., Bhattacharya, B.B.: Optimal reversible logic circuit synthesis based on a hybrid DFS-BFS technique. In: 2010 International Symposium on Electronic System Design, pp. 208–212 (2010). https://doi.org/10.1109/ISED.2010.47

36. Lanyon, B.P., et al.: Simplifying quantum logic using higher-dimensional Hilbert spaces. Nat. Phys. **5**(2), 134–140 (2009). https://doi.org/10.1038/nphys1150

37. Mandal, S.B., Chakrabarti, A., Sur-Kolay, S.: Quantum ternary circuit synthesis using projection operations (2012). https://doi.org/10.48550/ARXIV.1205.2390, https://arxiv.org/abs/1205.2390

38. Maslov, D.: Advantages of using relative-phase toffoli gates with an application to multiple control toffoli optimization. Phys. Rev. A **93**, 022311 (2016). https://doi.org/10.1103/PhysRevA.93.022311

39. Maslov, D.: Optimal and asymptotically optimal NCT reversible circuits by the gate types. Quantum Inf. Comput. **16**(13 & 14) (2016). https://doi.org/10.26421/qic16.13-14

40. Meuli, G., Soeken, M., Roetteler, M., De Micheli, G.: Enumerating optimal quantum circuits using spectral classification. In: 2020 IEEE International Symposium on Circuits and Systems (ISCAS), pp. 1–5 (2020). https://doi.org/10.1109/ISCAS45731.2020.9180792

41. Moraga, C.: On some basic aspects of ternary reversible and quantum computing. In: Proceedings of the 2014 IEEE 44th International Symposium on Multiple-Valued Logic, pp. 178–183. ISMVL 2014, IEEE Computer Society, USA (2014). https://doi.org/10.1109/ISMVL.2014.39

42. Moraga, C.: Quantum p-valued toffoli and deutsch gates with conjunctive or disjunctive mixed polarity control. In: 2016 IEEE 46th International Symposium on Multiple-Valued Logic (ISMVL), pp. 241–246 (2016). https://doi.org/10.1109/ISMVL.2016.22

43. Mosca, M., Mukhopadhyay, P.: A polynomial time and space heuristic algorithm for T-count. Quantum Sci. Technol. 7(1), 015003 (2021). https://doi.org/10.1088/2058-9565/ac2d3a

44. Prakash, S.: Magic state distillation with the ternary golay code. Proc. R. Soc. A Math. Phys. Eng. Sci. 476(2241), 20200187 (2020). https://doi.org/10.1098/rspa.2020.0187

45. Prakash, S., Jain, A., Kapur, B., Seth, S.: Normal form for single-qutrit Clifford+T operators and synthesis of single-qutrit gates. Phys. Rev. A 98(3) (2018). https://doi.org/10.1103/physreva.98.032304

46. Ralph, T.C., Resch, K.J., Gilchrist, A.: Efficient toffoli gates using qudits. Phys. Rev. A 75(2) (2007). https://doi.org/10.1103/physreva.75.022313

47. Rani, P.M.N., Datta, K.: Improved ternary reversible logic synthesis using group theoretic approach. J. Circuits Syst. Comput. 29(12), 2050192 (2020). https://doi.org/10.1142/S0218126620501923

48. Rani, P.M.N., Kole, A., Datta, K., Chakrabarty, A.: Realization of ternary reversible circuits using improved gate library. Procedia Comput. Sci. 93, 153–160 (2016). https://doi.org/10.1016/j.procs.2016.07.195

49. Ringbauer, M., et al.: A universal qudit quantum processor with trapped ions (2021). https://arxiv.org/abs/2109.06903

50. Selinger, P.: Quantum circuits of t-depth one. Phys. Rev. A 87(4), 042302 (2013). https://doi.org/10.1103/PhysRevA.87.042302

51. Shende, V.V., Markov, I.L.: On the CNOT-Cost of TOFFOLI Gates. Quantum Info. Comput. 9(5), 461–486 (2009)

52. Song, G., Klappenecker, A.: Optimal realizations of simplified toffoli gates. Quantum Info. Comput. 4(5), 361–372 (2004)

53. Wang, Y., Hu, Z., Sanders, B.C., Kais, S.: Qudits and high-dimensional quantum computing. Front. Phys. 8, 479 (2020). https://doi.org/10.3389/fphy.2020.589504

54. Yang, G., Xie, F., Song, X., Hung, W., Perkowski, M.: A constructive algorithm for reversible logic synthesis. In: 2006 IEEE International Conference on Evolutionary Computation, pp. 2416–2421 (2006). https://doi.org/10.1109/CEC.2006.1688608

55. Ye, B., Zheng, Z.F., Zhang, Y., Yang, C.P.: Circuit QED: single-step realization of a multiqubit controlled phase gate with one microwave photonic qubit simultaneously controlling $n - 1$ microwave photonic qubits. Opt. Exp. 26(23), 30689 (2018). https://doi.org/10.1364/oe.26.030689

56. Yurtalan, M.A., Shi, J., Kononenko, M., Lupascu, A., Ashhab, S.: Implementation of a walsh-hadamard gate in a superconducting qutrit. Phys. Rev. Lett. 125, 180504 (2020). https://doi.org/10.1103/PhysRevLett.125.180504

Fast Control for Reversible Processors

Torben Ægidius Mogensen[(✉)]

DIKU, University of Copenhagen,
Universitetsparken 5, 2100 Copenhagen, Denmark
torbenm@di.ku.dk

Abstract. Reversible processors implemented using reversible gates has
a potential for extreme low power dissipation. Very few designs for
reversible processors have been made – we are aware only of the Pendulum and Bob processors. The Pendulum processor has a reversible
instruction set (PISA), and has been implemented using classical, irreversible logic gates in CMOS. Bob has a gate-level design using reversible
gates, but has not been realised in physical hardware.

In this paper, we will focus on the control part of reversible processors,
assuming very little about the available data-processing instructions and
their implementation.

The reversible instruction sets PISA and BobISA (the ISA for
Bob) use identical control-flow mechanisms that ensure instruction-level
reversibility without imposing restrictions on instruction sequences. We
review this mechanism and find it relatively costly. So we propose two
modifications to the mechanism that allow faster implementation in
reversible hardware and which do not significantly complicate code generation. We show a reversible circuit diagram for the complete control
step for 16-bit instruction addresses.

1 Introduction

Reversible programming languages (such as Janus [3,8] or Hermes [4,9]) use high-
level syntactic restrictions to ensure reversibility of control structures, but that
is not possible in low-level reversible machine language: Here, every instruction
must in isolation be reversible.

Reversible microprocessor designs have used different methods to ensure
reversible control flow. Early versions of the PISA instruction set for the Pendulum architecture architecture [6] use a branch stack: Whenever a branch is
made, a "return" address is pushed onto a stack. A comefrom instruction pops
an address from this stack and jumps there. By having a comefrom instruction
immediately before every branch target, control flow can be reversible. This approach suffers from a lack of local reversibility: Programs need special instructions
at branch targets to be reversible – otherwise running a program backwards will
not undo the effect of running it in the forwards direction. Later versions of the
PISA instruction set [1,7] remedies this by making branch instructions locally
reversible without restrictions on branch targets (although programs are rarely

C. A. Mezzina and K. Podlaski (Eds.): RC 2022, LNCS 13354, pp. 51–64, 2022.
https://doi.org/10.1007/978-3-031-09005-9_4

meaningful unless branch targets are also branch instructions). A later architecture, Bob, and its instruction set BobISA [5], use the same mechanism for
control.

Instruction sequences in both PISA and BobISA can be executed both forwards and backwards, controlled by a direction bit. When running backwards,
data-processing instructions are inverted. For example, an instruction that does
addition when running forwards does subtraction when running backwards, and
vice-versa.

That is the easy part, the difficult part is how to handle jumps in a reversible
manner. A traditional jump, where control is passed to a specified address is not
reversible unless the instruction(s) at the target address has sufficient information to know from where the jump came, and will inevitably jump back to this
place if the direction of execution is reversed: It is not enough that the target
of the jump *can* jump back when the direction of execution is reversed, it *must*
do so. Furthermore, if control passes to a potential jump target not through a
jump, but by falling through from the previous instruction, reverse execution
must also fall through instead of jumping. So, the following information must be
available:

– Was a jump performed to get to the current address?
– If so, where did the jump originate?

and, no matter which instruction occupies the current address, reversing the
direction of execution will cause control to flow back to the instruction that was
executed immediately prior to the instruction at the current address, regardless of whether this was a jump or a data-processing instruction at the address
immediately preceding the current address.

We will start by reviewing the control mechanism used in the PISA and
BobISA instruction sets. We then propose modifications to the control mechanism that allow simpler and faster implementation at gate level and show a
complete gate-level design for the proposed control mechanism.

2   The Control Mechanism in PISA and BobISA

PISA and BobISA use the same model of control. Execution of code is an interleaving of data steps and control steps:

    . . .
    control step
    data step
    control step
    data step
    control step
    . . .

The data steps can not directly change control, but can set up the control steps
for doing so. When executing in reverse, the sequence is inverted (but is still
an interleaving of data and control steps), and each step is locally inverted. For

example, an add instruction is inverted to a sub instruction. We will not go into details about the data instructions except where a data instruction affects the following control step. There are three control registers:

PC is the *program counter*, which points to the current instruction.
BR is the *branch register*, which in most cases is 0, but will contain non-zero values before and after jumps.
DR is the *direction register*, a single bit that indicates the direction of execution. Conceptually, it holds the value +1 when executing forwards and -1 when executing backwards.

The data step can not modify PC, but it can modify BR and DR. There is no instruction for the control step – it is implicit in the instruction stream and always the same. The control step operates entirely on the control registers, which it can read and modify. The data registers are not touched. The control step uses the following rules:

– If BR = 0, PC := PC + DR
– If BR ≠ 0, PC := PC + DR·BR

Note that if BR ≠ 0 before the control step, BR ≠ 0 afterwards (and vice versa). As DR is negated when running backwards, the control step is its own inverse.

PISA and BobISA have data-processing instructions that can modify BR and DR. For generating code for control structures, we will use the following instructions:

Instruction	Action
add r, k	$r := r + k$
sub r, k	$r := r - k$
negate r	$r := -r$
br *offset*	BR := BR + DR·*offset*
brz r, *offset*	if $(r = 0)$ BR := BR + DR·*offset*
brnz r, *offset*	if $(r \neq 0)$ BR := BR + DR·*offset*
swapbr r	$(BR, r) := (r, BR)$
rswapbr r	$(BR, r, DR) := (r, BR, -DR)$

where r is a register and k is a constant. A processor will have additional data-processing instructions, but we will not use them here. When running in reverse, instructions are inverted as follows:

Instruction	Inverse
add r, k	sub r, k
sub r, k	add r, k
negate r	negate r
br *offset*	br $(-offset)$
brz r, *offset*	brz r, $(-offset)$
brnz r, *offset*	brnz r, $(-offset)$
swapbr r	swapbr r
rswapbr r	rswapbr r

Using these, an unconditional jump can be made as

```
l0 : br offset to l1
        ⋮
l1 : br offset to l0
```

Note that the offsets are relative to the instructions in which they occur, so $(\textit{offset to } l1) + (\textit{offset to } l0) = 0$.

When running forwards (DR = +1) starting at PC = $l0$ with BR = 0, the instruction at $l0$ adds *offset to l1* to BR, so BR becomes *offset to l1*. Since BR is now non-zero, PC is set to PC + DR·*offset to l1* = $l1$. The instruction at $l1$ adds *offset to l0* to BR, which becomes $(\textit{offset to } l1) + (\textit{offset to } l) = 0$. Since BR is now 0, execution continues after $l1$.

When running backwards (DR = -1) starting at PC = $l1$ with BR = 0, the instruction at $l1$ subtracts *offset to l0* from BR (because the instruction is inverted), so BR becomes -(*offset to l0*). Since BR is now non-zero, PC is set to PC + DR·(-(*offset to l0*)) = PC + ·*offset to l0* = $l0$. The instruction at $l0$ subtracts *offset to l1* from BR, which (because $(\textit{offset to } l1) + (\textit{offset to } l0) = 0$) becomes 0. Since BR is now 0, execution continues backwards from the instruction preceding $l0$.

Conditional branches use conditional branch instructions, but are otherwise done the same way. Given a conditional statement

```
if (x==0)  s₁ else  s₂
```

where the statements s_1 else s_2 do not modify x, we can generate the following code

```
l0 : brnz Rx, offset to l2
        code for s₁
l1 : br offset to l3
l2 : br offset to l0
        code for s₂
l3 : brz Rx, offset to l1
```

where Rx contains the value of x. The codes for s_1 and s_2 do not modify Rx. Again, we assume BR = 0 when entering the code.

If Rx is zero, the conditional branch instruction at $l0$ does nothing, so the code for s_1 is executed and a branch from $l1$ to $l3$ is done. Since Rx is zero, this adds to BR the offset to $l1$, making BR zero, so execution continues with the instructions after $l3$.

If, conversely, Rx is nonzero, the conditional branch instruction at $l0$ adds to BR the offset to $l2$, so a jump is made from $l0$ to $l2$. The branch instruction at $l2$ resets BR to 0, so the code for s_2 is executed, followed by the conditional branch at $l3$. Since Rx is nonzero, this does nothing, so execution continues with the instructions after $l3$.

In the examples above, branch targets are branch instructions that reset BR to 0. While this makes sense from a code generation perspective, it is not required for reversibility. If BR is not reset, the control step after the instruction at the branch target will just jump again. For example, the instruction br 2 will cause every other instruction to be executed until BR is modified again.

2.1   Procedure Calls

Instructions `swapbr` and `rswapbr` are used for procedure calls. A call (without parameters) to a procedure P is done with the following sequence:

```
l0 : add R1, offset to P from l1
l1 : swapbr R1
l2 : add R1, offset to P from l1
```

It is assumed that BR and R1 both contain 0 at the start of the sequence. The first instruction makes R1 equal to the offset to P from the `swapbr` instruction. The `swapbr` instruction sets BR to this offset (while clearing R1), so the control step will jump to P.

As an invariant, the procedure will return to the calling `swapbr` instruction with R1 equal to 0 and BR equal to $-(offset to P from l1)$. The `swapbr` instruction sets BR to 0 and R1 to the negative offset. The final instruction thus clears R1.

When running in reverse, the `add` instructions are inverted to `sub` instructions, so after executing $l2$, R1 holds the negative offset to P. The `swapbr` instruction at $l1$ swaps this with BR, and since the direction register is multiplied to the offset in the control step, this jumps to P. Cleanup is done with the `add` instruction at $l0$ (which is a `sub` instruction when executing backwards).

A reverse call (uncall) to P uses an `rswapbr` instruction, which reverses the direction of execution both when transferring control to P and when returning therefrom. Handling both execution directions requires procedure P to use the following structure:

```
l3 : br offset to l4
P :  swapbr R1
     ⋮
     negate R1
l4 : br offset to l3
```

such that when P is entered with backwards execution direction, a jump is made to the end of the procedure body, which is then executed backwards. Note that R1 is negated so the return branch will use the negated offset.

3   Making the Control Step More Efficient

The control mechanism used in PISA and BobISA works well and it is fairly easy to generate code for this (assuming the source language is reversible). But it is relatively costly, in particular the second case (BR $\neq$ 0) where an offset is either added to or subtracted from PC depending on the value of the direction bit requires a full addition. The first case (BR $=$ 0) requires increment or decrement of PC, so it is a bit faster than the second case, but even an increment takes at least log(wordsize) time in the worst case.

Speculatively doing the common case (fall through) in parallel with the data step can alleviate the cost, but that will require stalling and uncomputation if

BR is made non-zero in the data step, effectively making branches even more costly. We will, instead, try to reduce the cost of both the common case (fall through) and the less common case (jumps). We start with jumps, as these are both more costly and easier to optimise.

3.1   Optimising Jumps

In reversible logic, a conditional swap of two values is faster (and simpler) than a conditional addition or subtraction of an offset. A conditional swap can be done using Fredkin gates, and for swapping n-bit values, the n Fredkin gates can be executed in parallel, making the logic depth equal to 1. See Sect. 4 for a concrete implementation. In contrast, addition (conditional or not) requires carry propagation. An n-bit ripple-carry adder has $O(n)$ logic depth, and an n-bit carry-lookahead adder has $O(\log(n))$ logic depth. So we will replace the addition used for branching by a swap.

We use the same control registers (PC, BR, and DR) as PISA and BobISA, but the second case of control step (when BR $\neq 0$) is altered:

– If BR = 0, PC := PC + DR
– If BR $\neq 0$, (PC, BR) := (BR, PC)

Note that we need PC$\neq$0 for this to be reversible, as the second case would not preserve BR$\neq$0 if PC=0, making the choice for inverse execution ambiguous. If we can know that there are no jumps out of address 0, the ambiguity is resolved, so hard-wiring the instruction at address 0 to a non-branching instruction solves the issue.

The control instructions are modified to fit the new model:

Instruction	Action
br *target*	BR := BR XOR *target*
brz *r, target*	if $(r = 0)$ BR := BR XOR *target*
brnz *r, target*	if $(r \neq 0)$ BR := BR XOR *target*
swapbr *r*	(BR, *r*) := (*r*, BR)
rswapbr *r*	(BR, *r*, DR) := (*r*, BR, -DR)

Note that branch instructions now use absolute target addresses instead of relative offsets, so branch instructions are now their own inverses. All other instructions, including swapbr and rswapbr are unchanged.

An unconditional jump can now be implemented as:

    l0 : br l1
      ⋮
    l1 : br l0

If BR = 0 at the start of this sequence, the instruction at *l0* sets BR = *l1*, which is non-zero, so in the control step BR and PC are swapped, making PC = *l1* and BR = *l0*. At *l1*, BR is set to 0 by XORing with *l0*, so execution continues after *l1*. The backwards execution is equivalent.

For the conditional statement
 if (x==0) s_1 else s_2
where the statements s_1 else s_2 do not modify x, we can generate the following code

```
l0: brnz Rx, l2
      code for s₁
l1: br l3
l2: br l0
      code for s₂
l3: brz Rx, l1
```

Again, apart from using absolute addresses instead of offsets, the code is the same as before.

Procedure calls are similarly changed to use absolute addresses:

```
l0: add R1, P
l1: swapbr R1
l2: sub R1, P
```

We, as before, assume that R1 contains 0 when entering this sequence. Note that the call should now (by a new invariant) preserve R1 (instead of negating it), so we need to subtract P after the call. The procedure structure is now

```
l0: br l1
P:  swapbr R1
       ⋮
l1: br l0
```

Note that we no longer negate R1 in the procedure body, so we save an instruction. Apart from using absolute branch addresses instead of offsets, the code generation is very similar to the scheme using the control structure of the PISA and BobISA instruction sets.

For code generation, the main difference is whether absolute addresses or offsets are used. Neither of these are significantly more difficult than the other.

The cost of branching is now so low that fall through dominates the cost of the control step, as this still needs a binary increment or decrement.

3.2   Making Fall Through More Efficient

The time used in the control step is, as mentioned, now dominated by the increment or decrement of PC when BR = 0. An increment is marginally simpler and faster than a full addition, but it is far from constant time. With a simple ripple-carry mechanism increment requires $O(n)$ logic depth for an n-bit PC, and with a carry-lookahead mechanism it requires $O(\log(n))$ logic depth. We would, ideally, want to reduce the logic depth the control step to constant time. The idea for getting close to this is to change the control step rules to

– If BR = 0 and DR = +1, PC := $f(PC)$
– If BR = 0 and DR = -1, PC := $f^{-1}(PC)$

– If $BR \neq 0$, $(PC, BR) := (BR, PC)$

where f is a bijective function that has the following properties:

1. The sequence $x_1 = f(1)$, $x_2 = f(x_1)$, $x_3 = f(x_2)$, ..., $x_1 = f(x_j)$ should have a cycle j that is one less than the size of the program memory, and $x_i \neq 0$ for all i.
2. $f(PC)$ is faster to compute (has lower logic depth) than incrementing the PC.

The requirement that $x_i \neq 0$ ensures that $PC = 0$ can neither happen by jumps (as $BR = 0$ implies no jump) nor by falling through from a preceding or following instruction (in either direction of computation) – we know that this can never happen if the processor initialises PC to 1 (or some other nonzero value). The requirement that the cycle should be one less than the size of program memory is to ensure that a program can use all the program memory (except address 0).

We have found the following family of functions (Galois linear-feedback shift registers [2]) to work:

$$f(x) = 2x \qquad\qquad\qquad \text{when } x < 2^{n-1}$$
$$f(x) = (2x - 2^n + 1)\ \text{XOR}\ k \quad \text{when } x \geq 2^{n-1}$$

where n is the word size and $0 < k < 2^{n-1}$ is an even integer constant. Any such k makes the function bijective in the interval $[0, 2^n - 1]$, mapping 0 to 0 and non-zero values to non-zero values, but the cycle starting at 1 is not always maximal.

$f(x)$ can be implemented by a left rotate followed by an XOR with k if the least significant bit is 1. This can be implemented in constant time using reversible logic. The inverse is an XOR with k when the least significant bit is 1 followed by a right rotate.

Most values of k give much shorter periods than $2^n - 1$ when starting with $x = 1$. In addition to giving the maximal period, we also want k to have the fewest number of 1-bits (called "taps" in the theory of linear-feedback registers [2]), as we need a gate for each such bit to do the XOR with k. We have found that for no number of address bits between 8 and 34 are one or two taps sufficient for achieving the maximal cycle, but for all of these we have found many values of k with three 1-bits.

Theory [2] tells that it is always possible to find k that gives the maximal period, but the author does not know of any general results about the minimal number of taps for Galois LFSRs[1]. We conjecture that three taps are sufficient for all word sizes. Table 1 shows for word sizes between 8 and 34 bits the five smallest values of k (in hexadecimal) with three taps that achieve the maximal cycle (so $f(x)$ will cycle through all values from 1 to $2^n - 1$).

It can seem weird that instructions that are executed sequentially are not adjacent in memory, but a compiler can easily lay out code using this addressing scheme. It does, however, mean that the full address space for code must be

---

[1] This may easily be due to the author's insufficient search skills.

Table 1. Maximal-cycle values of k with three taps for different address sizes

Address bits	Five smallest Maximal-cycle values of k with three taps				
8	0x1c	0x2a	0x2c	0x4c	0x64
9	0x1a	0x2c	0x32	0x58	0x68
10	0x1a	0x26	0x2c	0x64	0x8a
11	0x16	0x2a	0x2c	0x46	0x62
12	0x52	0x68	0x98	0xd0	0x106
13	0x1a	0x26	0x34	0x52	0x64
14	0x2a	0x38	0x52	0xa8	0x10c
15	0x16	0x2c	0x34	0x86	0x92
16	0x2c	0x38	0x52	0x1a0	0x214
17	0xe	0x2c	0x32	0x54	0x68
18	0x26	0x4c	0x106	0x190	0x20a
19	0x26	0x46	0x52	0x58	0x62
20	0x52	0x64	0x68	0x222	0x228
21	0x26	0x64	0x92	0x106	0x148
22	0x38	0xc2	0x128	0x160	0x222
23	0x2a	0x2c	0x32	0x4c	0x64
24	0x1a	0x86	0xb0	0x124	0x224
25	0xe	0x2c	0x92	0xc4	0x10c
26	0x46	0x4c	0xb0	0xe0	0x118
27	0x26	0xd0	0x128	0x130	0x182
28	0x52	0xe0	0x222	0x320	0x40a
29	0x16	0x1c	0x8c	0xc2	0x118
30	0x52	0x112	0x148	0x290	0x2c0
31	0xe	0x2c	0x34	0x46	0x54
32	0xc4	0x124	0x20c	0x228	0x824
33	0x52	0x68	0x86	0x98	0xa2
34	0x118	0x222	0x250	0x428	0x460

physically present. For 16-bit addresses, this is not an issue, as 64K instruction words is a rather small code area. For 32-bit addresses, it is large but not unrealistic, as 2^{32} instructions of 32 bits each is 16 GB. But a full 64-bit address space is out of the question.

So we suggest that instruction addresses need not use a number of bits that is a power of 2, even if data words do. For example, a processor can use 32 bits for data words and data addresses and 24 bits for instruction addresses, or 64 bits for data words and data addresses and 32 bits for instruction addresses. The low addresses (except 0) can then be used for code, while the main part of memory is used for data. It is convenient to allow code to read and write code memory (as that can allow, for example, loading new programs). To ease this, instructions that implement f and f^{-1} can be supported.

For branch instructions, it is simple to limit the number of bits for the target address (and omit 0), but swapbr instructions can, for example, swap a 32-bit data register with a 24-bit BR. A solution could be to swap only as many bits from the data register as the size of BR and leave the rest if the bits in the data register unchanged.

4   Gate-Level Realisation

In Fig. 1, we show a gate-level realisation of control for a processor with 16-bit instruction addresses. Inputs are the PC ($p_0 \ldots p_{15}$), BR ($b_0 \ldots b_{15}$), and 16 ancillae that are initially 0 and will be returned to 0 at the end. The circuit is for forwards execution (DR = +1). For backwards execution (DR = −1), the circuit can be run right to left. We will later present a circuit that takes DR as input runs left-to-right regardless of its value.

Between the first two vertical grey lines (marked A), the circuit computes a Boolean that is 1 if BR=0 and 0 otherwise. The next section (marked B) uncomputes the intermediate values of this comparison while copying the result to all 16 ancillae. Gates that horizontally are drawn very close can be done in parallel. Section C swaps BR and PC when the ancillae are 0 (meaning BR≠0). Section D rotates PC one bit left (up) if BR=0. This is done by first conditionally swapping even and odd bits, which places the even bits in their (now odd) correct positions. Then, half of the ancillae are conditionally (using the other half of the ancillae) swapped with the incorrectly placed bits, which are then conditionally swapped into their right positions. We can do this because all ancillae have the same value. Again, horizontally close gates can be done in parallel, so the logic depth of this section is only 3. Section E XORs PC with $0x2c = 101100_2$ (for $k = 0x2c = 44$) when BR=0 and p_0=1. Lastly, we do B^{-1} and A^{-1} to clear the ancillae.

The total logic depth is 4+4+1+3+3+4+4 = 23. Note that sections A, B and their inverses only involve BR, so they can be done in parallel with calculations that do not involve BR. Since the first thing that happens after the control step is that the instruction at PC is fetched, this can naturally start right after section E and in parallel with sections B^{-1} and A^{-1}. Dually, an "unfetch" step that happens before the control step can be done in parallel with sections A and B. If so, the actual cost of the control step is only 7 gate delays.

The logic depth of sections C and D is independent of the number of bits in PC and BR. Section E uses a number of sequential Toffoli gates equal to the number of bits in k, which can be 3 for all address spaces between 8 and 34 bits (and conjectured to be 3 also for larger address spaces). So we conjecture that the logic depth of sections C, D and E is a total of 7 gates regardless of the word size. The logic depth of sections A, B, B^{-1}, and A^{-1} are each equal to the (base 2) logarithm of the size of instruction addresses (rounded up), so the total logic depth for n-bit addresses is $4 * \lceil \log_2(n) \rceil + 7$.

The gate count for section A (and A^{-1}) is $2n-1$ Toffoli gates. Section B and B^{-1} each use $2n-1$ Toffoli gates and $n-1$ controlled NOT gates. Section C uses n Fredkin (controlled swap) gates, section D uses $\frac{3n}{2}$ Fredkin gates, and section E uses 3 Toffoli gates. So the total gate count is $8n-1$ Toffoli gates, $2n-2$ controlled NOT gates, and $\frac{5n}{2}$ Fredkin gates.

4.1   Making DR Explicit

It may not always be practical to change the direction in which (sub)circuits are executed, so we present an alternative that takes the direction bit as input and always runs left-to-right.

We note that most of the circuit in Fig. 1 is self-inverse. In fact, to get the effect of reverse-direction control, we just need to remove/inactivate section D and add/activate a D^{-1} section after section E. So we can add an input representing DR and let this control which of the two sections are executed. A block diagram of this is shown in Fig. 2. The d input represents DR by $d = 1$ when DR $= 1$ and $d = 0$ when DR $= -1$. We can control the choice between activating section D or section D^{-1} by adding an extra control on all the gates in these sections, turning singly-controlled swap (Fredkin) gates into doubly-controlled gates. Since there are eight gates in parallel in these sections, we want eight copies of the d bit as input.

The logic depth of this circuit is 3 higher than that of the circuit in Fig. 1.

5   Summary and Discussion

We have reviewed the control mechanism used in the two reversible instruction sets BobISA and PISA.

We have made two suggestions for changing the control step with the aim of making it implementable using fewer reversible gates and with lower logic depth. We have shown a diagram for a circuit for the control step for 16-bit instruction addresses to support this claim.

The changes do not make code generation significantly different, and the instruction count is basically the same (and one instruction shorter for procedures). The main change is that absolute addresses rather than relative offsets

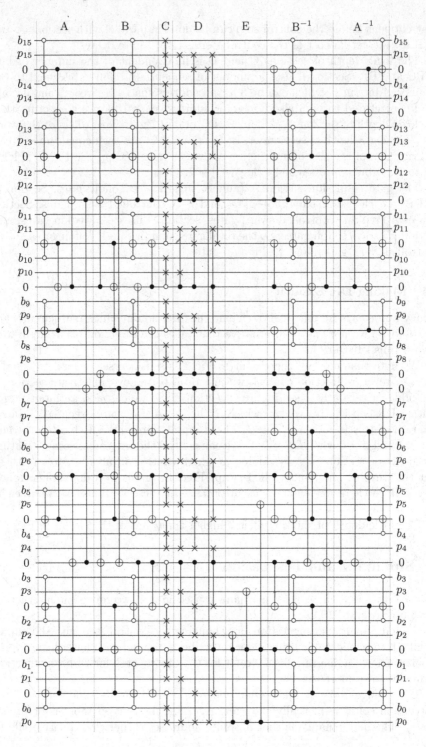

Fig. 1. Circuit for the proposed control mechanism (16 bits)

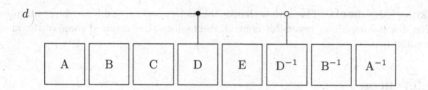

Fig. 2. Adding direction as input

are used for jumps and that instruction adjacency does not follow address adjacency. Code generation can be made in two steps: First, a symbolic assembly language using labels as branch targets (as in the examples shown in this paper) is used as target language, and then an assembler lays this out in memory while translating labels to absolute addresses. That instruction addresses are non-sequential does not complicate this. The main issue is that relocating code is more complicated.

Using linear-feedback shift-register for calculating the address of the next instruction implies that instructions in a sequence are spread out in memory, so spatial locality is reduced. This means that an instruction cache (if any such is used) should not use cache lines longer than one instruction word, as adjacent words in memory are unlikely to contain instructions that will be used in near future. Temporal locality is, however, unaffected: An instruction that has been recently fetched is likely to be fetched again in the near future.

5.1   Future Work

In this paper, we have looked only at the control step of executing a reversible instruction sequence, but it wold be interesting to look at optimising the data processing step as well.

There is also potential for further optimisation of the control step. A significant part of the circuit shown in Fig. 1 is taken by testing if BR = 0 (sections A and B and their inverses). If we align all instructions to even addresses, we could use BR = 1 for indicating fall through and set BR to an even address for indicating a jump. This way, we need only test one bit of BR, so we can eliminate section A and its inverse from the circuit. But we still need to propagate this bit to all the ancillae (half of section B and its inverse), so we still have $O(\log(n))$ gate delay, albeit with a smaller constant factor. If sections A and B and their inverses can be done in parallel with fetching and unfetching instructions, this change is probably not worth it.

There is also potential for investigating alternative reversible functions for stepping through the instruction address space. While the chosen family of functions has constant logic depth (six gate delays), it is possible that functions with even smaller logic depth can be found.

Acknowledgements. The author thanks Niklas Deworetzki and Uwe Meyer for interesting discussions about reversible control, discussions that inspired some of the ideas presented here.

References

1. Frank, M.P.: Modifications to PISA architecture to support guaranteed reversibility and other features. MIT Reversible Computing Project Memo #M7 (1997)
2. Goresky, M., Klapper, A.: Fibonacci and galois representations of feedback-with-carry shift registers. Inf. Theor. IEEE Trans. **48**, 2826–2836 (2002)
3. Lutz, C.: Janus: a time-reversible language. A Lett. Landauer. (1986)
4. Mogensen, T.Æ.: Hermes: a language for light-weight encryption. In: Lanese, I., Rawski, M. (eds.) RC 2020. LNCS, vol. 12227, pp. 93–110. Springer, Cham (2020). https://doi.org/10.1007/978-3-030-52482-1_5
5. Thomsen, M.K., Axelsen, H.B., Glück, R.: A reversible processor architecture and its reversible logic design. In: De Vos, A., Wille, R. (eds.) RC 2011. LNCS, vol. 7165, pp. 30–42. Springer, Heidelberg (2012). https://doi.org/10.1007/978-3-642-29517-1_3
6. Vieri, C.: A reversible computer architecture. Master's thesis, MIT Artificial Intelligence Laboratory (1995)
7. Vieri, C.: Reversible computer engineering and architecture. Doctoral thesis, MIT (1999)
8. Yokoyama, T., Glück, R.: A reversible programming language and its invertible self-interpreter. In: PEPM 2007: Proceedings of the 2007 ACM SIGPLAN Symposium on Partial Evaluation and Semantics-Based Program Manipulation, New York, pp. 144–153. ACM (2007)
9. Ægidius Mogensen, T.: Hermes: a reversible language for lightweight encryption. Sci. Comput. Program. **215**, 102746 (2022)

Designing a Reversible Stack Machine

Niklas Deworetzki[(✉)] and Uwe Meyer

Technische Hochschule Mittelhessen,
Wiesenstr. 14, 35390 Giessen, Germany
{niklas.deworetzki,uwe.meyer}@mni.thm.de

Abstract. Reversible computing is a continuously advancing area of active research and an increasing number of available reversible programming languages, compilers, and interpreters are primarily based on register-based execution environments, such as PISA. In this paper, we report on our progress in developing a novel reversible stack machine, which combines the inherent reversibility of stacks with a clean instruction set to create a highly performant reversible machine. The instruction set, as well as strategies for implementing reversible arithmetic and control flow, will be explained.

Keywords: reversible computation · reversible algorithms · stack machines · computer architecture

1 Introduction

Reversible computing as an area of active research seemingly provides a continuous stream of insights into information theory, programming languages, algorithms, and even advanced computational concepts. Yet, there is still a considerable gap when comparing the diversity of software, programming languages, and abstract machines in classical and reversible computing. Current reversible machines can be roughly divided into two categories: Abstract machines used as an execution environment for existing programming languages, such as a machine for the Oz language by Lienhardt, Lanese, Mezzina, and Stefani [7], and instruction set architectures, which primarily explore RISC-like register machines. Examples of the latter include designs by Vieri [10], Frank [3], Hall [4], or the recent work by Axelsen, Glück, and Yokoyama [1]. This paper tries to contribute to this category of machines by exploring the design of a reversible stack-based machine and its instruction set architecture.

The proposed machine uses an argument stack to perform computations. Instructions manipulate values on the stack, eliminating the need for general-purpose registers. After presenting an overview of the machine design (Sect. 2), we will look at how arithmetic (Sect. 3) and control flow (Sect. 4) might be implemented reversibly, followed by a short discussion on the representation and execution of instructions (Sect. 5). The current state of development and other features of the machine are outlined in the final chapter (Sect. 6).

© The Author(s), under exclusive license to Springer Nature Switzerland AG 2022
C. A. Mezzina and K. Podlaski (Eds.): RC 2022, LNCS 13354, pp. 65–72, 2022.
https://doi.org/10.1007/978-3-031-09005-9_5

2   Stack-based Architecture Design

During our recent work on translation and optimization of reversible intermediate languages [2,6], we had two insights that largely influenced the design of this machine model: The extended version of Janus proposed by Yokoyama, Axelsen and Glück [11] introduces stacks as a native data structure to the language. Stacks seem to work very well in a reversible setting as their two basic operations *push* and *pop* are the exact inverse of each other. Additionally, we discovered that it is challenging to translate Reversible Static-Single Assignment (RSSA) as proposed by Mogensen [9] into efficient and compact program code for register machines. The reason for this lies in the complexity of individual RSSA instructions: Instructions used for control flow potentially accept an infinite number of operands passed from and to labels in the intermediate code. This makes RSSA a fantastic tool for program analysis and optimizations, as it is explicit about the flow of information and data within a program. However, encoding and especially decoding complex instructions carries additional runtime costs. Our basic idea is to combine those concepts, defining the design goals for our abstract machine: Provide a simple instruction set, allowing a high execution rate for instructions, and use a stack to manage operands. By reducing the work required to decode complex instructions or manage operands with a limited number of registers, it seems possible to provide a fast execution environment for reversible programs.

The machine is modeled after the Harvard architecture [5, Chapter L.2], having distinct memory areas for instructions, data, and the argument stack. This allows for a simple execution cycle. Special precautions must be taken when instructions and data do not reside in distinct memory regions, as this would allow self-modifying code which could interfere with reversibility [10]. In addition to these memory regions, we use three registers to implement control flow operations as suggested by Axelsen, Glück, and Yokoyama [1]: A program counter (pc) refers to the currently executed instruction in memory. A direction register (dir) encodes the current execution direction, holding the value 1 during forward execution and -1 during backward execution. The additional branching register (br) is used to perform jumps, as its value determines the change of pc during each execution cycle (see Fig. 1).

$$\frac{br = 0}{(pc, br, dir) \rightarrow (pc + dir, br, dir)} \qquad \frac{br \neq 0}{(pc, br, dir) \rightarrow (pc + br \cdot dir, br, dir)}$$

Fig. 1. Control logic of the reversible execution cycle as defined in [1].

Extending this model, our machine requires a stack pointer (sp) as an additional register. It points to the next free memory cell on top of the stack and is modified when pushing or popping operands on the stack. A frame pointer (fp) is also included as a second additional register to aid the creation of stack frames and to support local variables. Including these registers, our machine uses a total of only five registers, as shown in Fig. 2.

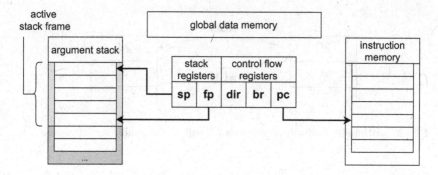

Fig. 2. Overview of the machine model.

3   Reversible Arithmetic

In our machine, instructions come in pairs, where each instruction is the inverse of the other. Consider an instruction `pushc` (push constant) that uses the exclusive-or operation to write a value to the cleared stack cell pointed to by sp and increments this register by one. The inverse instruction `popc` decrements the sp register and then uses the exclusive-or operation to clear the value of the stack cell. If both instructions are executed with the same operands, their effects cancel each other out, and the original machine state is thus restored.

During reverse execution, those pairs swap their meaning: A `pushc` instruction executed in reverse pops a value from the stack, while a reverse `popc` instruction now pushes a value onto the stack. This way, it is possible to invert programs and use their inverse semantics during regular execution. Similar to the concepts presented in Janus [8], reversibility is not seen as a restriction but provided as a tool for the programmer.

However, this concept of reversible instruction pairs comes with restrictions for each individual instruction. In order for a reverse instruction to exist, every instruction needs to be reversible in the first place. Simple operations such as placing values onto the stack, removing them, or shuffling stack items' positions, are trivially reversible. But, especially with arithmetic operations, it becomes quite challenging to ensure reversibility. For a few selected operations, it is possible to update the top element on the stack with the lower elements unchanged as parameters for this update. These operations are the same that Janus and RSSA allow as part of their assignments. Namely, they are addition, subtraction, and the exclusive-or, where addition and subtraction are mutually inverse and the exclusive-or is self-inverse. Figure 3 shows how the stack is modified under this scheme, using addition and subtraction as example operations.

This scheme cannot be used to implement all arithmetic operations; only those that are injective on the updated parameter. Other operations, such as multiplication or division, cannot be implemented this way, as they do not guarantee the reversibility of the performed update. As an example, consider the multiplication with 0, which would irreversibly update the top stack element to

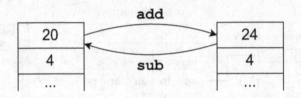

Fig. 3. Arithmetic performed on the stack using a reversible update operation.

0. Instead, we extend the notion of a reversible update as presented in [1]. As a result, we allow an arbitrary deterministic operation $\odot_n$ that accepts $n \in \mathbb{N}_0$ parameters to be computed in conjunction with push and pop operations. The stack is hereby referred to as a function $S : \mathbb{Z}_{32} \to \mathbb{Z}_{32}$, mapping 32-bit addresses to 32-bit words on the stack, with sp pointing to the next free element of the stack. We use the notation $S[a \mapsto v]$ to indicate that the stack at address a should be updated to hold value v.

Pushing Values. To push the result of a complex operation, we first have to compute it. Since arguments are placed on the stack, we can use them directly by referencing $S[sp-1]$, $S[sp-2]$ and so on. Just focussing on the stack pointer and the stack, we can write the push operation as:

$$\frac{}{(sp, S) \to_{\text{push}\odot_n} (sp+1, S[sp \mapsto \odot_n(S(sp-1), S(sp-2), \ldots, S(sp-n))])}$$

Popping Values. In order to reversibly remove a value obtained by performing a complex operation from the stack, we compute it again. Since the operands from pushing the value are unchanged on the stack, we can compute the same result of the operation. If the value stored on top of the stack equals this value, it is possible to zero clear the stack cell and decrement the stack pointer afterward.

$$\frac{S(sp-1) = \odot_n(S(sp-2), S(sp-3), \ldots, S(sp-(n+1)))}{(sp, S) \to_{\text{pop}\odot_n} (sp-1, S[sp-1 \mapsto 0])}$$

Using this technique, we can define instruction pairs for arbitrary complex operations. In a fully reversible implementation, it is possible to let $\odot_n$ generate garbage that is immediately uncomputed within a single execution step. Figure 4 shows how such a reversible push operation may be implemented. The different components of the stack on the left-hand side represent the operands used by $\odot_n$. The result of this operation is copied into the empty stack cell on top of the stack using an exclusive-or operation (written $\oplus$). The result and produced garbage are then immediately consumed by running $\odot_n$ in reverse. Meanwhile, the stack pointer is incremented.

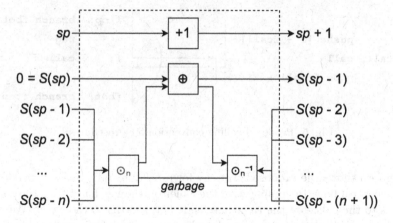

Fig. 4. Schematic illustration of a reversible push operation, showing how stack cells are used and generation of garbage can be avoided.

4   Reversible Control Flow

One of the most challenging aspects of a reversible execution environment is the implementation of reversible control flow. As we adapted the control flow design from [1], we can use a **branch** instruction similar to the **BRA** instruction in PISA for our needs. This instruction adds the offset to a label onto the br register, which sets the pc to the given label for the next instruction cycle. A paired **branch** instruction at the target label, adding the inverse offset to the register, resets the value of br to 0 and therefore continues normal execution. Similar instructions **brt** and **brf** (<u>br</u>anch on <u>t</u>rue, <u>br</u>anch on <u>f</u>alse) modify the br register in the same way if a corresponding truth value lies on top of the stack.

The standard pattern used for procedure calls in PISA is not applicable to our stack machine without adaption. It uses a **SWAPBR** instruction that swaps the contents of the br register and a general-purpose register. As we do not have general-purpose registers, we have to use other means to provide an offset for a call. Naturally, we use the stack for this task.

The process of calling a procedure can be implemented as follows:

1. The caller pushes an offset to a target onto the stack.
2. A **call** instruction is executed, swapping the contents of the br register and the top stack element.
3. The callee accepts the call with another **call** instruction, which again swaps the contents of the br register and the top stack element, effectively restoring the value of br and placing the originating offset on the stack.
4. After the execution of the procedure finishes, the offset on the stack is negated using a **negate** instruction, yielding the offset required to return to the caller.
5. The **call** instruction is executed again, loading the return offset into the br register.
6. The caller accepts the return and can pop the offset from the stack.

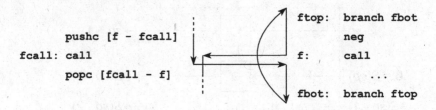

Fig. 5. Proposed calling convention for procedures.

Figure 5 shows the proposed strategy for procedure calls with arrows depicting the control flow. Beginning with the caller on the left-hand side, the control changes to the callee on the right-hand side and returns to the caller. We allow simple expressions between [ ] bracket characters to perform static address and offset calculations.

5   Encoding and Executing Instructions

Instructions, like all other values, are represented as 32-bit words. For the purpose of this machine, 32-bit words representing instructions consist of two components: A 16-bit opcode and a 16-bit immediate value, the latter being used to parameterize instructions like pushc or branch. One bit of the opcode is reserved as the *direction bit*. Inverse instructions have an identical representation, differing only in the direction bit, as Fig. 6 shows.

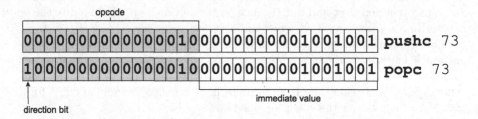

Fig. 6. Encoding of instructions as 32-bit word, showing the purpose of each bit.

This allows fast inversion of instructions. As seen in Fig. 7, only the direction bit has to be inverted when the machine is running in reverse (the *dir* register holds a value of −1). The execution mechanism shown fetches the executed instruction, extracts the opcode from it and then selects a corresponding action based on the opcode.

```
int32_t instruction = program[pc];
int32_t opcode = EXTRACT_OPCODE(instruction);
if (dir == -1) opcode = opcode ^ DIRECTION_BIT;
switch (opcode) {
  case OPCODE_PUSHC:
      ...
  case OPCODE_POPC:
      ...
```

Fig. 7. Execution mechanism of the stack machine implemented in C++.

6 Current Progress and Future Work

Currently, we identified an instruction set consisting of 36 reversible instruction pairs. These instructions support basic stack operations, stack shuffling, arithmetic, control flow, procedure calls, stack frames, and memory manipulation. All operations defined in RSSA can be expressed as a combination of these instructions. A virtual machine implementation written in C++ that parses assembler code-like source files and executes them is publicly available.[1] A formal description of all supported machine operations and an translation scheme from RSSA is under development.

Experiments with the virtual machine show that an efficient implementation of machine instructions and the execution mechanism is possible. On modern consumer hardware, the machine executes more than 100 million virtual instructions per second. Comparisons with existing backends of the RC3 compiler [6] show that this machine is a viable alternative for the execution of reversible programs. In the current state, stack machines represent a promising and low-level runtime environment for reversible programs with a potential for efficient execution and good performance.

Acknowledgements. We would like to thank Torben Æ. Mogensen for his work on RSSA, which we use as the main back-end of our compiler, and for the fruitful discussions during an earlier stage of the project. Also, we would like to thank the reviewers who had provided valuable feedback and suggestions for improvement.

References

1. Axelsen, H., Glück, R., Yokoyama, T.: Reversible machine code and its abstract processor architecture. In: Proceedings of the Second International Conference on Computer Science: Theory and Applications, pp. 56–69. Ekaterinburg, Russia (2007)

---

[1] The implementation together with example programs and documentation is available at https://git.thm.de/ndwr15/stackmachine.

2. Deworetzki, N., Meyer, U.: Program analysis for reversible languages. In: Proceedings of the 10th ACM SIGPLAN International Workshop on the State Of the Art in Program Analysis, pp. 13–18. Virtual, Canada (2021)
3. Frank, M.: Reversibility for efficient computing. PhD thesis, CISE Department, University of Florida (1999)
4. Hall, J.: A reversible instruction set architecture and algorithms. In: Proceedings Workshop on Physics and Computation. Dallas, USA (1994)
5. Hennessy, J., Patterson, D.A.: Computer Architecture - A Quantitative Approach, 5th edn. Morgan Kaufmann, Waltham (2012)
6. Kutrib, M., Meyer, U., Deworetzki, N., Schuster, M.: Compiling Janus to RSSA. In: Yamashita, S., Yokoyama, T. (eds.) RC 2021. LNCS, vol. 12805, pp. 64–78. Springer, Cham (2021). https://doi.org/10.1007/978-3-030-79837-6_4
7. Lienhardt, M., Lanese, I., Mezzina, C.A., Stefani, J.B.: A reversible abstract machine and its space overhead. In: Formal Techniques for Distributed Systems, pp. 1–17. Stockholm, Sweden (2012)
8. Lutz, C.: Janus - a time-reversible language, Letter to R. Landauer (1986)
9. Mogensen, T.Æ.: RSSA: a reversible SSA form. In: Perspectives of System Informatics, pp. 203–217. Kazan and Innopolis, Russia (2016)
10. Vieri, C.: Reversible computer engineering and architecture. Phd thesis, Department of Electrical Engineering and Computer Science, Massachusetts Institute of Technology (1999)
11. Yokoyama, T., Axelsen, H., Glück, R.: Principles of a reversible programming language. In: 5th Conference on Computing Frontiers, pp. 43–54. Ischia, Italy (2008)

Applications of Quantum Computing

Directed Graph Encoding in Quantum Computing Supporting Edge-Failures

D. Della Giustina, C. Piazza, B. Riccardi, and R. Romanello[✉]

Department of Mathematics, Computer Science and Physics, University of Udine,
Udine, Italy
{dellagiustina.davide,riccardi.brian,romanello.riccardo}@spes.uniud.it,
carla.piazza@uniud.it

Abstract. Graphs are one of the most common data structures in classical computer science and graph theory has been widely used in complexity and computability. Recently, the use of graphs in application domains such as routing, network analysis and resource allocation has become crucial. In these areas, graphs are often evolving in time: for example, connection links may fail due to temporary technical issues, meaning that edges of the graph cannot be traversed for some time interval and alternative paths have to be followed. In classical computation, where graphs are represented as adjacency matrices or lists, these problems are well studied and ad-hoc visit procedures have been developed. For specific problems quantum computation, through superpositions and entanglement has provided faster algorithms than their classical counterpart. However, in this model, only reversible operations are allowed and this poses the quest of augmenting a graph in order to be able to reverse edge traversals. In this paper we present a novel graph representation in quantum computation supporting dynamic connectivity typical of real-world network applications. Our proposal has the advantage of being closer than others in literature to the adjacency matrix of the graph. This makes easy dynamic edge-failure modeling. We introduce optimal algorithms for computing our graph encoding and we show the effectiveness of our proposal with some examples.

Keywords: Quantum walks · Graphs · Edge-failure

1 Introduction

Graphs are ubiquitous in computer science and mathematics. They are formal and flexible frameworks used to model a wide class of problems from different fields, ranging from Complexity Theory [25], Flow Theory [2] and Software Verification [20], to more application-oriented domains such as Routing [29], Machine

This work is partially supported by PRIN MUR project Noninterference and Reversibility Analysis in Private Blockchains (NiRvAna) - 20202FCJM and by GNCS INdAM project LESLIE.

C. A. Mezzina and K. Podlaski (Eds.): RC 2022, LNCS 13354, pp. 75–92, 2022.
https://doi.org/10.1007/978-3-031-09005-9_6

Learning [16] and Social Networks [11]. Randomization plays a central role in collecting informations from ever growing and dynamically evolving networks, and with the advent of quantum computing as a more and more useful tool, it is mandatory to define efficient encodings for graphs in quantum circuits.

Quantum computation is constitutionally reversible being based upon unitary transformations that are always reversible. Only measurements/observables collapse quantum states into classical ones with a loss of information that is not reversible. As a matter of fact, classical circuit (i.e., classical boolean functions) can be simulated by quantum ones, but it is necessary to pay the encoding in terms of space dimension. In the case of boolean functions the standard technique for doing this consists in representing a function $f : \{0,1\}^n \to \{0,1\}^m$ as the reversible function $f' : \{0,1\}^{n+m} \to \{0,1\}^{n+m}$ with $f'(x,y) = (x, y \oplus f(x))$.

So, on the one hand, quantum computation allows to exactly solve in polynomial time problems that are in the time complexity class EXP for classical computation, thus proving that $QP \neq P$ (see, e.g., [10,27]). Moreover, it allows to solve with bounded probability of error in polynomial time the factorization problem for which at present there are no classical polynomial algorithms with bounded probability of error. The impact of superposition and entanglement in such speed-up has been evaluated in the literature from different perspectives (e.g., [5,6,17]).

On the other hand, the possibility of using only reversible operators causes an increase of space requirements as shown in the simple case of boolean functions and imposes to redefine each step of classical algorithms in terms of linear unitary (reversible) transformations.

The theory of quantum walks, the quantum counterpart of random walks, has been first introduced in [1]. As for the classical case [8,23], there is a distinction between continuous and discrete time models [30]. The former is introduced in [13] and further investigated in [7,21]: in this case, the main tool is the exponentiation of a suitable hermitian matrix derived from the adjacency matrix of the graph. The latter is described in [1] as a *coined* walk, where a suitable matrix – the coin – is introduced to implement the random choice while maintaining unitarity of the encoding matrix. Algorithmic applications of the discrete time model have been presented in [4,19], while in [14] it has been shown that quantum random walks can obtain better hitting and mixing time with respect to their classical counterpart. For further details and applications description we refer the reader to [18,26,31].

The aim of our work is to encode graphs in the quantum formalism, so that algorithms, such as random walks, can be efficiently developed also in dynamic settings where edges/nodes can be temporary unavailable. We extend the work done in [28] by providing a procedure to optimally compute a unitary matrix from the line of an eulerian graph. In this way, the obtained graph representation has its focus on the edges rather than on the nodes, as it was in [1,21]. In the general case of non-eulerian graphs, we describe an embedding which can be implemented in the quantum framework through projectors. The projectors allow us to *hide* the edges added from the embedding. Moreover, they can be fruitfully exploited for managing edge failures, without recomputing the encoding matrices. As stated in [18], problems related to vertex reachability *"have been efficiently solved using a quantum walk, but studying the impact of . . . and dynamically changing graph topology . . . can be seen as a critical area for research"*. Our work goes into such direction.

The paper is structured as follows. In Sect. 2 we briefly recall some basic definitions from Quantum Computation, Graph Theory and Quantum Random Walks. An optimal procedure to obtain a unitary matrix from any eulerian multigraph is presented in Sect. 3. The following section has the goal to show how to embed any multigraph into an eulerian one. In Sect. 5 we describe the quantum circuit obtained using the results from the previous sections. The efficient management of edge failures in explained in Sect. 6. Finally, Sect. 7 illustrates some comparisons with related literature with examples.

2 Preliminaries

2.1 Quantum Computing

The most used model of Quantum Computation relies on the formalism of state vectors, unitary operators and projectors. At high level we can say that state vectors evolve during the computation through unitary operators, then projectors are used to remove part of the uncertainty on the internal state of the system.

The state of the system is represented by a unitary vector over $\mathbb{C}^n$ with $n = 2^m$ for some $m \in \mathbb{N}$. The concept of a bit of classical computation is replaced by that of a qubit. While a bit can have value 0 or 1 a qubit is a unitary vector of $\mathbb{C}^2$. When the two components of the qubit are the complex numbers $\alpha = x + iy$ and $\beta = z + iw$, the squared norms $|\alpha|^2 = x^2 + y^2$ and $|\beta|^2 = z^2 + w^2$ represent the probability of measuring the qubit thus reading 0 and 1, respectively. In the more general case of m qubits the unitary vectors range in $\mathbb{C}^n$ with $n = 2^m$. Adopting the standard Dirac notation we denote a column vector $v \in \mathbb{C}^n$ by $|v\rangle$, and its conjugate transpose $v^\dagger$ by $\langle v|$. A *quantum state* is a unitary vector

$$|\psi\rangle = \sum_h c_h |v_h\rangle$$

for some basis $\{|v_h\rangle\}$. When not specified, we refer to the *canonical basis*. Further details can be found in [24].

Unitary operators and projectors are linear operators, so before introducing their definitions, we fix the notation on matrices. We rely on the same notation also for graphs represented through adiacency matrices in classical computation.

Let M be a matrix, $M_{i,j}$ is the element in the i-th row and j-th column of M. Moreover, we denote by M_i the entire i-th row. Whenever we refer to the product of two rows of a matrix, we refer to the *dot product* (scalar product) between the former and the conjugate transpose of the latter, i.e., $M_i M_j = \sum_k M_{i,k} M_{j,k}^*$, where $M_{j,k}^*$ is the complex conjugate of $M_{j,k}$.

Unitary operators are a particular class of reversible linear operators. They preserve both the angles between vectors and their lengths. In other terms, unitary operators are transformation from one orthonormal basis to another. Hence, they are represented by unitary matrices. Let U be a square matrix over $\mathbb{C}$. U is said to be *unitary* iff $UU^\dagger = U^\dagger U = I$. We describe the application of a unitary matrix U to a state $|\psi\rangle$ by writing

$$|\psi'\rangle = U\,|\psi\rangle$$

meaning that the state $|\psi\rangle$ becomes $|\psi'\rangle$ after applying the operator U.

In order to extract informations from a quantum state $|\phi\rangle$ a *measurement* must be performed. The most common measurements are projectors. Let $|u\rangle$ be a quantum state. The *projector* operator P_u along the direction of $|u\rangle$ is the linear operator defined as:

$$P_u = \frac{|u\rangle\langle u|}{\langle u\rangle}$$

where $|u\rangle\langle u|$, being the product between a column vector and a row one both of size n, returns a matrix of size $n \times n$. Since throughout the paper we only use unitary vectors, the term $\langle u\rangle$ is always 1 and can be ignored.

2.2   Graph Theory

Graphs are a standard data structure in computer science for the representation of binary relations. They are used in Computability Theory for representing the flow of computations [25], in Network Theory to describe the network topology [2], in Routing [29], etc. We report below some standard definitions on graphs, while we refer the reader to [15] for further details. A directed *graph* G is a pair (V, E) where V is a non empty set of *nodes* and $E \subseteq V \times V$ is a set of *edges*. We say that an edge (u, v) is *directed* from u to v and that u is *adjacent* to v. We also say that u is the *source* and v is the *target* of (u, v). Two edges of the form (u, v) and (v, w) are said to be *consecutive*. We say that a graph is *undirected* iff E is symmetric. The *underlying undirected graph* of G is a new graph whose edge set is the symmetric closure of E.

In classical computation, graphs are usually stored as either adjacency matrices or adjacency lists. In this paper we mainly refer to the adjacency matrix representation. Given a set of nodes V, we assume a fixed order over the elements of V, i.e., each node of V can be identified as an integer between 1 and $|V|$. For a graph $G = (V, E)$ with $|V| = n$, the *adjacency matrix* of G is a (0–1)-matrix M of size $n \times n$ such that $M_{u,v} = 1$ iff $(u, v) \in E$.

A *multigraph* $G = (V, E)$ is a graph in which many edges can connect the same pair of nodes. So, if there are two edges from u to v these are two distinct primitive objects. In other terms, E is a set (of edges) and two functions $s, t :$ $E \to V$ assign to each edge both a source node and a target one. For the sake of readability, we will use the notation (u, v) also on multigraphs to refer to a generic edge having source u and target v. The aim of this paper is providing a quantum representation for graphs. However, it is useful to refer to multigraphs which allow us to overcome some technical issues.

Definition 1 (Incoming and Outgoing edges). *Let* $G = (V, E)$ *be a multigraph,* $v \in V$. *We define the set of its* incoming *edges as:*

$$\delta^-(v) = \{i : i \in E \text{ and } i \text{ has target } v\}$$

and the set of its outgoing *edges as:*

$$\delta^+(v) = \{k : k \in E \text{ and } k \text{ has source } v\}$$

Moreover, the indegree *of* v *is defined as* $d^-(v) = |\delta^-(v)|$ *and analogously its* outdegree *is defined as* $d^+(v) = |\delta^+(v)|$.

The *balance* of a node v is $b(v) = d^+(v) - d^-(v)$. A multigraph $G = (V, E)$ is *balanced* iff for each node $v \in V$, $b(v) = 0$. This property is crucial for directly encoding multigraphs in terms of Quantum Computation since it ensures the possibility of reversing walks over the graph [1]. The following is a well known result from Graph Theory which basically states that the global balance of a multigraph is always null.

Theorem 1. *Let* $G = (V, E)$ *be a multigraph. Let* $B^+ = \{v \in V \ : \ b(v) > 0\}$ *and* $B^- = \{v \in V \ : \ b(v) < 0\}$. *Then,*

$$\sum_{v \in B^+} b(v) + \sum_{v \in B^-} b(v) = 0$$

As for graphs, also on multigraphs a *path* is a sequence of distinct adjacent nodes. A *cycle* is a path where the last node coincides with the first one. A multigraph that does not contain cycles is said to be acyclic. While in the case of graphs, paths can be equivalently defined as sequences of consecutive edges, in the case of multigraphs the definition based on consecutive edges is more informative. In order to avoid confusion, we refer to such definition using the term *tour*. *Eulerian tours* traverse each edge of the multigraph exactly once. A multigraph is *eulerian* iff it admits an eulerian tour which is also a cycle.

The notions of balanced multigraphs and eulerian multigraphs coincide when we consider only connected graphs. We introduce here some more notions about connectivity that will be useful in our technique for encoding multigraphs in quantum data structures. Two nodes of a graph are *mutually reachable* iff there exists a path from the first to the second and viceversa.

A multigraph G is said to be *strongly connected* if each pair of nodes $u, v \in V$ are mutually reachable. It is said to be weakly connected, or just *connected*, if its underlying undirected graph is strongly connected. The following result formalizes the equivalence between balanced and eulerian multigraphs [9].

Theorem 2. *A connected multigraph* G *is balanced iff it is eulerian.*

In [28] it has been proved that there exists a relationship between eulerian graphs and unitary matrices. Such relationship involves the notion of line graph.

Definition 2 (Line Graph). *Let $G = (V, E)$ be a multigraph. The* line graph *of G is the graph $\overrightarrow{G} = (\overrightarrow{V}, \overrightarrow{E})$, where:*

$$\overrightarrow{V} = E \qquad \overrightarrow{E} = \big\{ (i, k) : i, k \in E \text{ and } i \text{ and } k \text{ are consecutive} \big\}$$

The elements of a unitary matrix are not necessarily 0 and 1. To associate a graph to a matrix, we first introduce the notion of *support* of a matrix. Given a matrix M its support is the (0–1)-matrix M^S where $M_{i,j}^S = 1$ iff $M_{i,j} \neq 0$.

Definition 3 (Graph of a Matrix). *The* graph *of a matrix M is the graph whose adjacency matrix is M^S.*

In [28] it has been proved that the line graph of an eulerian multigraph has an adjacency matrix that is the support of a unitary one.

Theorem 3. *Let G be a multigraph and $\overrightarrow{G}$ be its line graph. Then $\overrightarrow{G}$ is the graph of a unitary matrix iff G is eulerian or the disjoint union of eulerian components.*

Since the aim of this paper is to implement quantum random walks on graphs, it is useless to consider disconnected multigraphs. Therefore, in what follows we will consider only connected multigraphs.

2.3   Quantum Random Walks

In classical computation, when we visit a graph choosing randomly the next edge to cross, we say that we are making a *random walk* on the graph. In quantum computing, the counterpart of this concept is the *quantum random walk (QRW)*. Since the only way to change a quantum state is through unitary matrices, the most reasonable way to implement a QRW is based on the ability of encoding the adjacency properties of any graph inside a unitary matrix.

The visit, in both classical and quantum computation, can be made at either continuous or discrete time. In the case of continuous time QRWs, the Hamiltonian of the system is provided and using matrix exponentiation the system evolves through time [21]. On the other hand, in discrete time QRWs, the most common method is through *coined* walks [1]. Such method is based on a pair of Hilbert spaces: the first one is for the graph nodes, while the second one is for the coin. Encoding the graph with this technique generates an unitary matrix which makes the computation reversible.

3   Unitary Matrix of an Eulerian Multigraph

In this section we introduce a procedure which allows us to transform any eulerian multigraph G into a unitary matrix, encoding the adjacency properties of G. The procedure passes through the construction of the line graph of G, then

Theorem 3 from [28] lies at the heart of the transformation. However, the focus in [28] is on the proof of the result, more than on the algorithmic construction of a unitary matrix. Instead, in this section we are going to actually build a unitary matrix starting from a line graph adjacency matrix. Such unitary matrix is not unique and our construction is parametric with respect to a family of unitary matrices which are required as input. As for the computational complexity of the technique, we anticipate that it is linear in the size of the resulting matrix. Notice that it is common usage to build unitary matrices by columns. In our approach, since we edit the adjacency matrix, the resulting unitary will be by rows. In this way we keep a closer relationship to the initial graph. Therefore, the reader should be aware that in the circuit and in the examples we will use the conjugate transpose of the matrix.

3.1 From a Graph to Its Line

Let $G = (V, E)$ be an eulerian multigraph. The function LINEARIZE in Algorithm 1 returns the adiacency matrix $\widetilde{M}$ of the line graph $\overrightarrow{G}$. It can be easily checked that its time complexity is $\Theta(|E|^2)$.

Algorithm 1. Construct the line graph of a given multigraph.

1: **function** LINEARIZE(V, E)
2:    $\widetilde{M} \leftarrow$ SQUAREMATRIX$(|E|)$ ▷ Creating an all zero square matrix
3:    **for all** $i \in E$ **do**
4:       $v \leftarrow$ TARGET(i) ▷ i is of the form (u, v)
5:       **for all** $k \in \delta^+(v)$ **do**   ▷ k is of the form (v, w)
6:          $\widetilde{M}_{i,k} \leftarrow 1$
7:    **return** $\widetilde{M}$
8: **end function**

We now point out some structural properties of $\widetilde{M}$ that follow from the fact that G is eulerian.

Lemma 1. *Let $i = (u, v)$ and $j = (u', v')$ be two edges. It holds that:*

$$\widetilde{M}_i = \widetilde{M}_j \quad iff \quad v = v'$$

Proof. Let i, j be two edges of G. Consider some edge $k \in E$. By definition of $\overrightarrow{G}$, $\widetilde{M}_{i,k} = 1$ iff i and k are consecutive edges. The same is true for j. So, if $v = v'$ it is immediate to conclude that $\widetilde{M}_i = \widetilde{M}_j$. Otherwise, if $\widetilde{M}_i = \widetilde{M}_j$, then since G is eulerian it cannot be the case that $\widetilde{M}_i$ and $\widetilde{M}_j$ have only 0 elements. This means that $\exists k$ such that $\widetilde{M}_{i,k} \neq 0$. Hence, by hypothesis also $\widetilde{M}_{j,k} \neq 0$. Let $k = (v'', w)$, since $\widetilde{M}_{i,k} \neq 0$ it has to be $v = v''$. Moreover, from $\widetilde{M}_{j,k} \neq 0$ we get $v' = v''$. So, $v = v'$.   □

As a consequence of the above lemma we immediately get that each node v induces as many equal rows in $\widetilde{M}$ as its indegree.

Lemma 2. *For every edge* $i = (u, v)$*, there are exactly* $d^+(v)$ *edges* j *such that* $\widetilde{M}_{i,j} \neq 0$*. Moreover, there are exactly* $d^-(v)$ *rows equal to* $\widetilde{M}_i$*.*

In Lemmata 1 and 2 we introduce a relationship between rows describing edges that have a common target. We can generalize the result formalizing it in the case of any pair of rows.

Lemma 3. *Let* $i, j \in E$*. Let* $A = \{k : \widetilde{M}_{i,k} \neq 0\}$ *and* $B = \{l : \widetilde{M}_{j,l} \neq 0\}$*. Then, either* $A = B$ *or* $A \cap B = \varnothing$*.*

Proof. If $A = B$ there is nothing to prove. Suppose $A \neq B$ and assume, for the sake of contradiction, that $k = (v, w) \in A \cap B$. By definition of A and B, it has to be $\widetilde{M}_{i,k} = 1 = \widetilde{M}_{j,k}$. Hence i and j share v as common target. By Lemma 1, $\widetilde{M}_i = \widetilde{M}_j$ and $A = B$. This is a contradiction. ☐

In what follows we say that two rows are *disjoint* if $A \cap B = \varnothing$, where A, B are defined as in the above lemma. In other terms, two rows are disjoint if and only if they correspond to edges having different targets.

3.2   Construction of the Unitary Matrix

We now describe the procedure UNITARIZE which transforms $\widetilde{M}$ into a unitary matrix $\widehat{M}$ whose support is $\widetilde{M}$. The input of the function are the adjacency matrix $\widetilde{M}$ and a family of unitary matrices U. The family has to satisfy:

$$\forall v \in V \; \exists U \in \text{U} \; \text{ of size } d^-(v) \times d^-(v)$$

The goal of UNITARIZE in Algorithm 2 is to edit $\widetilde{M}$ in order to obtain a unitary matrix which encodes the adjacency properties of G. At each iteration of the while loop, a node v is extracted from Q and, for each edge i directed to v, row $\widetilde{M}_i$ is edited through the procedure SPARSESUB exploiting a unitary matrix of suitable dimension. In particular, SPARSESUB(r, r') replaces the h-th non-zero element of r by r'_h.

Let r be a vector and A be a set of indexes of r, we use the notation $r(A)$ to denote the subvector of r obtained by considering only the indexes in A.

Lemma 4. *After applying* SPARSESUB *at line 9, the subvector* $\widehat{M}_i(\delta^+(v))$ *is equal to* U_c*.*

Algorithm 2. Compute a unitary matrix from the line graph.

```
 1: function UNITARIZE(M̃, U)
 2:     M̂ ← M̃
 3:     Q ← V
 4:     while Q ≠ ∅ do
 5:         v ← POP(Q)
 6:         U ← U(d⁻(v))                    ▷ Choose some d⁻(v) × d⁻(v) matrix from U
 7:         c ← 1
 8:         for all i ∈ δ⁻(v) do
 9:             SPARSESUB(M̂ᵢ, Uᶜ)
10:             c ← c + 1
11:     return M̂
12: end function
13:
14: procedure SPARSESUB(r, r′)
15:     h ← 1
16:     for all k ∈ E do
17:         if rₖ ≠ 0 then
18:             rₖ ← r′ₕ
19:             h ← h + 1
20: end procedure
```

Proof. By definition of $\widetilde{M}$, $r_k \neq 0$ holds iff $k \in \delta^+(v)$. By construction, U_c has size $n = d^-(v) = d^+(v) = |\delta^+(v)|$. The result follows immediately. □

Theorem 4. $\widehat{M}$ *is a unitary matrix.*

Proof. It is sufficient to show that the rows of $\widehat{M}$ form an orthonormal basis. By Lemma 4, each row of $\widehat{M}$ is a row of some unitary matrix interleaved by zeros. Hence, the product of each row with itself is 1. Let $i, j \in E$ be distinct edges. If $\widetilde{M}_i$ and $\widetilde{M}_j$ are disjoint, also $\widehat{M}_i$ and $\widehat{M}_j$ are. Therefore $\widehat{M}_i \widehat{M}_j = 0$. Otherwise, by construction of UNITARIZE, $\widehat{M}_i$ and $\widehat{M}_j$ refer to the same unitary matrix. Since their product depends only on their non-zero elements, and since they correspond to unitary rows, $\widehat{M}_i \widehat{M}_j = 0$. □

Since each line of $\widehat{M}$ is edited once and U can be stored efficiently, we get that UNITARIZE has time complexity $\Theta(|E|^2)$.

Example 1. We now provide an example to clarify the structure of $\widehat{M}$ after the procedure UNITARIZE. For sake of readability, we omitted the scalar multipliers from the matrices in U inside $\widehat{M}$.

$$\mathcal{U} = \left\{ \frac{1}{\sqrt{3}} \begin{pmatrix} 1 & 1 & 1 \\ 1 & \omega & \omega^2 \\ 1 & \omega^2 & \omega^4 \end{pmatrix}, \ \frac{1}{\sqrt{2}} \begin{pmatrix} 1 & 1 \\ 1 & -1 \end{pmatrix}, \ \begin{pmatrix} 0 & 1 \\ 1 & 0 \end{pmatrix} \right\} \qquad \omega = \exp\left\{ \frac{2\pi i}{3} \right\}$$

$$\widetilde{M} = \begin{pmatrix} 1 & 1 & & & & \\ & 1 & 1 & 1 & & \\ & 1 & 1 & 1 & & \\ & & & & 1 & 1 \\ & 1 & 1 & 1 & & \\ & & & & 1 & 1 \\ 1 & 1 & & & & \end{pmatrix} \qquad\qquad \widehat{M} = \begin{pmatrix} 1 & 1 & & & \\ & 1 & 1 & 1 & \\ & 1 & \omega & \omega^2 & \\ & & & & 0 & 1 \\ & 1 & \omega^2 & \omega^4 & \\ & & & & 1 & 0 \\ 1 & -1 & & & \end{pmatrix}$$

4   Embedding Multigraphs into Eulerian Ones

In the previous section we showed how to produce a unitary matrix from an eulerian multigraph. The aim of this section is to introduce a procedure called EULERIFY, based on Theorem 2, that takes as input the nodes set V of a connected multigraph $G = (V, E)$ and the array b of the balances of the nodes. It gives as output a set of additional edges $E_\perp$ such that the multigraph $G' = (V, E \cup E_\perp)$ is eulerian. We recall that, since we are interested in quantum random walks, we are interested only in connected graphs.

Algorithm 3. Edit the graph to make every node balanced.

1: **function** EULERIFY(V, b)
2:     $E_\perp \leftarrow \varnothing$
3:     $B^+ \leftarrow \{v \in V : b_v > 0\}$
4:     $B^- \leftarrow \{v \in V : b_v < 0\}$
5:     **while** $B^- \neq \varnothing$ **do**
6:         $u \leftarrow$ POP(B^-)
7:         **while** $b_u < 0$ **do**
8:             $v \leftarrow$ CHOOSE(B^+)   ▷ Choose without extracting
9:             $E_\perp \leftarrow E_\perp \cup \{(u, v)\}$
10:            $(b_u, b_v) \leftarrow (b_u + 1, b_v - 1)$
11:            **if** $b_v = 0$ **then**
12:                $B^+ \leftarrow B^+ \setminus \{v\}$
13:     **return** $E_\perp$
14: **end function**

The procedure takes as input the set of nodes V together with the vector b of size $|V|$ initialized with the balance of the nodes, i.e., the v-th element of b is $b_v = b(v)$. The idea is to iteratively fix each node in deficiency of balance adding edges to nodes in surplus of balance. The choice of the deficient node u is done at line 6. The loop at lines 7–12 is responsible for adding edges from u to surplus nodes v until u is balanced. Theorem 1 both ensures that for each u there are always surplus nodes to choose at line 8 and that when we exit the loop 5–12 the sets B^+ and B^- are empty.

It is clear that the time computational complexity of EULERIFY is proportional to $\Theta(|V| + |E_\perp|) \subseteq O(|V| + |E|)$, since we never add more edges than the existing ones. This is the technical point were the use of multigraphs helps us. We can both add new edges and new copies of existing ones.

The adjacency properties of G could be different from those of G'. In particular, such differences are witnessed by the set $E_\perp$. Our aim is to visit the graph G through a quantum random walk. However, since G' is eulerian, the walk will be performed exploiting the unitary matrix constructed on the line graph of G'. So, we must ensure that such walk only uses edges of E. Therefore, all the edges inside $E_\perp$ are used in the UNITARIZE procedure, but will be forbidden during the walk. In order to do this we will use a projector defined as follows:

$$P_G = I - \sum_{e \in E_\perp} |e\rangle \langle e|$$

Notice that even if in $E_\perp$ we add an edge between two adjacent nodes of G, the projector removes the new edge, while it does not affect the one existing in G.

Example 2. The following toy example show the construction of P_G.

$$E = \{00, 01, 10, 11\} \qquad P_G = \begin{pmatrix} 1 & 0 & 0 & 0 \\ 0 & 0 & 0 & 0 \\ 0 & 0 & 1 & 0 \\ 0 & 0 & 0 & 0 \end{pmatrix}$$
$$E_\perp = \{01, 11\}$$

5   The Quantum Circuit: With and Without Projections

In the previous sections we introduced two procedures, namely UNITARIZE and EULERIFY. While the first is in charge of constructing a unitary matrix from an eulerian multigraph, the second one embeds a connected multigraph into an eulerian one. In this section we put the two procedures together and describe the resulting quantum circuit running the quantum walk. Finally, we propose a way to reduce the size of such circuit avoiding the use of projectors in the case of strongly connected graphs.

Given any connected multigraph $G = (V, E)$, we first check whether it is balanced. If not, we apply the procedure EULERIFY obtaining some G' – which is now eulerian. We also compute a projector P_G which "eliminates" the effect of the edges of $E_\perp$ along the walk. After that, we use the procedure UNITARIZE on G' to obtain a unitary matrix $\widehat{M}$ that would allow us to make one discrete step in the visit of G'. So, a walk on G can be implemented by using each time P_G after $\widehat{M}$ as shown in Fig. 1.

In particular, in the circuit in Fig. 1 a number of qubits proportional to the logarithm of the edges of G' have to be initialized to $|0\rangle$. Then, an equiprobable

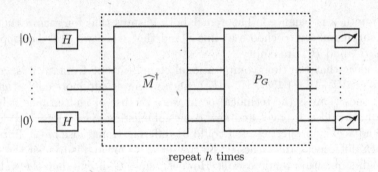

repeat h times

Fig. 1. Quantum circuit for the walk.

superposition of edges is generated using Hadamard operator H. At this point, by applying $\widehat{M}$ and P_G to the state for h times, h steps of the walk on G are performed. Finally, the measurement returns one edge of G whose target node can be interpreted as the last node of the quantum walk.

In terms of circuit complexity, the repeated application of P_G is time consuming. For this reason, we briefly introduce an alternative solution to the problem of embedding a multigraph into an eulerian one. Such alternative solution avoids the use of projections. The idea is that of balancing the multigraph by adding copies of edges that are already present. In this way, the adjacencies of G will not be altered and the projector P_G will not be needed anymore.

First, please notice that if G is not strongly connected, there is no way to embed it into a eulerian multigraph without adding authentic new edges. So, let us assume that G is strongly connected. We are interested in introducing the minimum number of copies of edges to make the graph eulerian: this is in fact an instance of the Directed Chinese Postman Problem. There is extensive literature on the problem, see e.g. [12], but for our purpose it is sufficient to know that for strongly connected graphs it always admits a solution computable in polynomial time. In terms of physical circuit implementation, if we adopt such solution the matrix P_G would disappear from the circuit in Fig. 1.

6   Edges/Nodes Failures

The overall procedure described in the previous sections has a time computational complexity proportional to $\Theta(|E|^2)$ and generates matrices of such size. As we will see in Sect. 7 other methods in literature have the advantage of relying on matrices of size $\Theta(|V|^2)$ (e.g., [21]). However, as a trade off, we show how in our method editing in the original graph G in terms of deletion of either edges or nodes does not result in the matrix $\widehat{M}$ to be recomputed. The only involved cost comes from the update of the projector P_G introduced in Sect. 4. Editing P_G for a single edge requires time $\Theta(1)$, while it requires time $\Theta(d^+(v) + d^-(v))$ for removing a node. In fact, the application of P_G after every step of the walk (see Fig. 1) has the effect of *hiding* some edges.

We know that each step of the visit is a composition of the unitary matrix $\widehat{M}$ followed by an application of the projector P_G. If we suppose that an edge i is temporarily removed from the graph, e.g., a failure in the network occurs, we do not need to edit the matrix $\widehat{M}$. We just need to update a single element of P_G. In terms of matrix operations, we know that i is an element of the basis of the edges. Therefore, we just need to edit P_G setting the i-th element of its diagonal to 0. Notice that P_G only has 1s on some elements of the diagonal and 0 elsewhere. In terms of computational complexity, this operation takes time $\Theta(1)$. At later stages, if the same edge is re-added, e.g., the failure is fixed, it takes again time $\Theta(1)$ to undo the previous edit on P_G. Therefore, our encoding efficiently supports both deleting edges and re-adding them.

In case of edge addition, the matrix $\widehat{M}$ should be entirely recomputed. However, the proposed method can be adapted to be efficient also in the case of edge additions at the cost of a more space-consuming matrix $\widehat{M}$. In particular, consider the case in which we have a set N of edges that could potentially be added to G. This could be the case for a network infrastructure that we know will be strengthened in a near future adding connections that have already been recognized as strategic. At present the graph representing the network is $G = (V, E)$, but in a near future it will become $GN = (V, E \cup N)$. In this case we construct the matrix $\widehat{M}$ for GN and we project away the edges of N. As soon as the new edges are available, we re-introduce them by modifying the projector.

At a high cost in term of space, one could decide to work by assuming that each edge could be added. This is equivalent to consider N as $V \times V$. The reader should be aware that in the worst case the size of GN could be quadratic with respect to the size of G. This occurs when G is sparse.

Finally, if we consider a node failure as a failure of all its incoming and outgoing edges, then also node failure can be easily handled. In fact, if node v fails, the cost of removing all of its edges is exactly $\Theta(d^+(v) + d^-(v))$.

7   Comparisons and Examples

In this section we compare the proposed method with two alternatives from literature. Both techniques tackle the problem of QRWs and therefore they need a way to encode a graph by means of a unitary matrix. The first one [21] regards *continuous time* QRWs. Therefore, the authors use matrix exponentiation to obtain a unitary matrix, typical of continuous time quantum processes. Meanwhile, the second technique [1] deals with *discrete time* QRWs. It labels the edges of the graph in such a way that each node has exactly one incoming and one outgoing edge per label. It then equips each node of degree d with a $d \times d$ unitary matrix – the *coin* – which encodes the possible choices of the next edge to cross.

Besides these encodings, other approaches can be found in literature. For example, in [22], the concept of *reversible* graph was introduced and used to restrict the class of directed graph over which a discrete quantum random walk is modeled. A complete and recent review of the existing proposals can be found in [18].

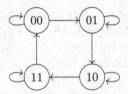

Fig. 2. Four nodes cyclic graph.

7.1   Continuous Time Walk from [21]

Let G be the cyclic graph depicted in Fig. 2 and M be its adjacency matrix. Let $\pi = \begin{pmatrix} 1 & 1 & 1 & 1 \end{pmatrix}$ be the unique non-negative eigenvector of M, $\Pi = \mathrm{DIAG}(\pi)$ and $L = \Pi - \frac{1}{2}(\Pi\, M + M^\dagger\, \Pi)$

$$L = \frac{1}{2}\begin{pmatrix} 0 & 1 & 0 & 1 \\ 1 & 0 & 1 & 0 \\ 0 & 1 & 0 & 1 \\ 1 & 0 & 1 & 0 \end{pmatrix}$$

The unitary matrix used for the walk at time $t \in \mathbb{R}$ is $U^t = e^{-itL}$.

The matrix is not directly related to the graph topology. Moreover, if an edge-failure occurs, the matrix M changes, and both Π and L need to be recomputed. However, in [21] the focus was not on developing visit algorithms but on defining a measure of similarity between graphs.

7.2   Discrete Time Walk from [1]

We consider again the graph of Fig. 2. In the case of this example the *coin* matrix C and the *shift* matrix S are as follows

$$C = \frac{1}{\sqrt{2}}\begin{pmatrix} 1 & 1 \\ 1 & -1 \end{pmatrix} \qquad S = \begin{pmatrix} 0 & 0 & 0 & 1 & 0 & 0 & 0 & 0 \\ 1 & 0 & 0 & 0 & 0 & 0 & 0 & 0 \\ 0 & 1 & 0 & 0 & 0 & 0 & 0 & 0 \\ 0 & 0 & 1 & 0 & 0 & 0 & 0 & 0 \\ 0 & 0 & 0 & 0 & 1 & 0 & 0 & 0 \\ 0 & 0 & 0 & 0 & 0 & 1 & 0 & 0 \\ 0 & 0 & 0 & 0 & 0 & 0 & 1 & 0 \\ 0 & 0 & 0 & 0 & 0 & 0 & 0 & 1 \end{pmatrix}$$

The self loops were labelled – colored – with the same color.

The resulting unitary matrix is

$$U = S \cdot (C \otimes I) = \frac{1}{\sqrt{2}} \begin{pmatrix} 0 & 0 & 0 & 1 & 0 & 0 & 0 & 1 \\ 1 & 0 & 0 & 0 & 1 & 0 & 0 & 0 \\ 0 & 1 & 0 & 0 & 0 & 1 & 0 & 0 \\ 0 & 0 & 1 & 0 & 0 & 0 & 1 & 0 \\ 1 & 0 & 0 & 0 & -1 & 0 & 0 & 0 \\ 0 & 1 & 0 & 0 & 0 & -1 & 0 & 0 \\ 0 & 0 & 1 & 0 & 0 & 0 & -1 & 0 \\ 0 & 0 & 0 & 1 & 0 & 0 & 0 & -1 \end{pmatrix}$$

In this case the matrix seems to be more descriptive in terms of the initial graph topology. However, in the case of an edge-failure, the procedure must start by recomputing again the edge labelling.

7.3 Our Method

We now want to obtain a unitary matrix for G in Fig. 2 with our new method. Since G is eulerian, the set $E_\perp$ is empty. The adjacency matrix of $\overrightarrow{G}$ is

$$\widetilde{M} = \begin{pmatrix} 1 & 1 & 0 & 0 & 0 & 0 & 0 & 0 \\ 0 & 0 & 1 & 1 & 0 & 0 & 0 & 0 \\ 0 & 0 & 1 & 1 & 0 & 0 & 0 & 0 \\ 0 & 0 & 0 & 0 & 1 & 1 & 0 & 0 \\ 0 & 0 & 0 & 0 & 1 & 1 & 0 & 0 \\ 0 & 0 & 0 & 0 & 0 & 0 & 1 & 1 \\ 0 & 0 & 0 & 0 & 0 & 0 & 1 & 1 \\ 1 & 1 & 0 & 0 & 0 & 0 & 0 & 0 \end{pmatrix}$$

We now apply UNITARIZE($\widetilde{M}, U$) to obtain $\widehat{M}$

$$U = \left\{ \frac{1}{\sqrt{2}} \begin{pmatrix} 1 & 1 \\ 1 & -1 \end{pmatrix} \right\} \qquad \widehat{M} = \frac{1}{\sqrt{2}} \begin{pmatrix} 1 & 1 & 0 & 0 & 0 & 0 & 0 & 0 \\ 0 & 0 & 1 & 1 & 0 & 0 & 0 & 0 \\ 0 & 0 & 1 & -1 & 0 & 0 & 0 & 0 \\ 0 & 0 & 0 & 0 & 1 & 1 & 0 & 0 \\ 0 & 0 & 0 & 0 & 1 & -1 & 0 & 0 \\ 0 & 0 & 0 & 0. & 0 & 0 & 1 & 1 \\ 0 & 0 & 0 & 0 & 0 & 0 & 1 & -1 \\ 1 & -1 & 0 & 0 & 0 & 0 & 0 & 0 \end{pmatrix}$$

The above matrix was computed fixing the following encoding of the edges of G

$|000\rangle = (00, 00)$	$|001\rangle = (00, 01)$	$|010\rangle = (01, 01)$	$|011\rangle = (01, 10)$
$|100\rangle = (10, 10)$	$|101\rangle = (10, 11)$	$|110\rangle = (11, 11)$	$|111\rangle = (11, 00)$

Suppose we start in state $|\psi_0\rangle = |000\rangle$. After one step, we are in state

$$|\psi_1\rangle = \widehat{M}^\dagger |000\rangle = \frac{1}{\sqrt{2}}(|000\rangle + |001\rangle)$$

and after another step we reach

$$|\psi_2\rangle = \frac{1}{2}\big(\,|000\rangle + |001\rangle + |010\rangle + |011\rangle\,\big)$$

Notice that since $E_\perp = \varnothing$, the associated projector P_G is the identity matrix.

Suppose that after the second step the edge $|001\rangle$ fails. Using our method we can react to this event by adding the edge $(00, 01)$ to $E_\perp$. The matrix P_G is updated as introduced in the previous section, and it becomes $I - |001\rangle\langle001|$.

Hence, by applying P_G to $|\psi_2\rangle$ we would delete $|001\rangle$ from the state.

7.4   Random Thoughts on Random Walks

Last but not least, for those who are familiar with Markov Chains, we add a brief note about QRWs distributions. In particular, we give an intuitive argument about the non-existence of a stationary distribution as for the classical case. Let $U \in \mathbb{C}^{n \times n}$ be a unitary matrix. The *graph of the states of U* is $G_U = (V_U, E_U)$:

$$V_U = \big\{\, |\psi\rangle \;:\; \langle\psi\rangle = 1, |\psi\rangle \in \mathbb{C}^n \big\} \qquad E_U = \big\{(|\psi\rangle, U|\psi\rangle) \;:\; |\psi\rangle \in V_U \big\}$$

It is straightforward to see that, since U is unitary – hence invertible – each $|\psi\rangle \in V_U$ has exactly one incoming and one outgoing edge. Therefore, G_U is disjoint union of cycles and infinite lines. In particular, if there exists a $t \in \mathbb{N}^+$ such that $U^t|\psi\rangle = |\psi\rangle$, then $U^i|\psi\rangle$, $i \in \mathbb{Z}$ forms a cycle. If such t does not exists, then $|\psi\rangle$ will be a part of an infinite line of states.

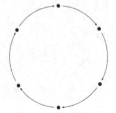

(a) A cyclic state evolution.   (b) An infinite line state evolution.

8   Conclusions

Quantum computing is becoming more and more important in computer science. The laws of Quantum Mechanics, that rule quantum algorithms, require every operation to belong to a restricted class of linear operators. Therefore, also common data structures like graphs must be encoded in such class of matrices in order to be visited using quantum algorithms. In our proposal we introduced a method to encode any graph into a unitary matrix using the notion of *eulerian* graph, and eventually a projector. This new technique produces a matrix that has a closer relationship to the initial graph topology than other methods in literature (i.e., [1,21]). Moreover, the presence of a projector is useful to support edge-failures. We showed that by just changing one single element in the projector we can react to the failure of an edge. We also described how to use our technique in order to obtain edge addition.

As future work we are interested in investigating the limiting distributions of our QRWs. For a restricted class of graphs we are already able to obtain the same results of [1]. However, simulations suggest that the class can be extended.

Moreover, as briefly said in Sect. 5, the Direct Chinese Postman Problem (DCPP) can be exploited in order to avoid projectors at each step. We intend to further study in this direction with particular reference to the problem of keeping the probabilities unchanged after the application of DCPP.

Finally, we are interested in developing graph reduction techniques, such as lumpabilities [3], in order to reduce the quantum circuits size.

References

1. Aharonov, D., Ambainis, A., Kempe, J., Vazirani, U.: Quantum walks on graphs. In: Proceedings of the Thirty-Third Annual ACM Symposium on Theory of Computing, pp. 50–59 (2001)
2. Ahuja, R.K., Magnanti, T.L., Orlin, J.B.: Network Flows - Theory, Algorithms and Applications. Pearson, London (1993)
3. Alzetta, G., Marin, A., Piazza, C., Rossi, S.: Lumping-based equivalences in markovian automata: algorithms and applications to product-form analyses. Inf. Comput. **260**, 99–125 (2018)
4. Ambainis, A.: Quantum walks and their algorithmic applications. Int. J. Quantum Inf. **1**(04), 507–518 (2003)
5. Ambainis, A., Schulman, L.J., Vazirani, U.V.: Computing with highly mixed states. In: Proceedings of the Thirty-Second Annual ACM Symposium on Theory of Computing, pp. 697–704 (2000)
6. Biham, E., Brassard, G., Kenigsberg, D., Mor, T.: Quantum computing without entanglement. Theor. Comput. Sci. **320**(1), 15–33 (2004)
7. Chung, F.: Laplacians and the cheeger inequality for directed graphs. Ann. Comb. **9**(1), 1–19 (2005)
8. Çinlar, E.: Probability and Stochastics, vol. 261. Springer, New York (2011). https://doi.org/10.1007/978-0-387-87859-1
9. Cygan, M., Marx, D., Pilipczuk, M., Pilipczuk, M., Schlotter, I.: Parameterized complexity of eulerian deletion problems. Algorithmica **68**(1), 41–61 (2014)
10. Deutsch, D., Jozsa, R.: Rapid solution of problems by quantum computation. Proc. R. Soc. London. Ser. A Math. Phys. Sci. **439**(1907), 553–558 (1992)
11. Easley, D., Kleinberg, J.: Networks, Crowds, and Markets: Reasoning about a Highly Connected World. Cambridge University Press, Cambridge (2010)
12. Edmonds, J., Johnson, E.L.: Matching, euler tours and the Chinese postman. Math. Program. **5**(1), 88–124 (1973)
13. Farhi, E., Gutmann, S.: Quantum computation and decision trees. Phys. Rev. A **58**(2), 915–928 (1998)
14. Godsil, C., Zhan, H.: Discrete-time quantum walks and graph structures. J. Comb. Theor. Ser. A **167**, 181–212 (2019)
15. Harary, F.: Graph Theory. Addison Wesley Series in Mathematics. Addison-Wesley, Boston (1971)

16. Haykin, S.: Neural Networks and Learning Machines, 3/E. Pearson Education India, Chennai (2010)

17. Jozsa, R., Linden, N.: On the role of entanglement in quantum-computational speed-up. Proc. R. Soc. London. Ser. A. Math. Phys. Eng. Sci. **459**(2036), 2011–2032 (2003)

18. Kadian, K., Garhwal, S., Kumar, A.: Quantum walk and its application domains: a systematic review. Comput. Sci. Rev. **41**, 100419 (2021)

19. Magniez, F., Nayak, A., Roland, J., Santha, M.: Search via quantum walk. SIAM J. Comput. **40**(1), 142–164 (2011)

20. Manna, Z., Pnueli, A.: Temporal Verification of Reactive Systems: Safety. Springer, New York (2012)

21. Minello, G., Rossi, L., Torsello, A.: Can a quantum walk tell which is which? a study of quantum walk-based graph similarity. Entropy **21**(3), 328 (2019)

22. Montanaro, A.: Quantum walks on directed graphs. Quantum Inf. Comput. **7**(1), 93–102 (2007)

23. Motwani, R., Raghavan, P.: Randomized Algorithms. Cambridge University Press, Cambridge (1995)

24. Nielsen, M.A., Chuang, I.: Quantum Computation and Quantum Information (2002)

25. Christos, H.: Papadimitriou. Computational complexity, Pearson, New York (1993)

26. Paparo, G.D., Martin-Delgado, M.A.: Google in a quantum network. Sci. Rep. **2**(1), 1–12 (2012)

27. Qiu, D., Zheng, S.: Revisiting deutsch-jozsa algorithm. Inf. Comput. **275**, 104605 (2020)

28. Severini, S.: On the digraph of a unitary matrix. SIAM J. Matrix Anal. Appl. **25**(1), 295–300 (2003)

29. Tanenbaum, A.S., Wetherall, D.: Computer networks, 5th Edition. Pearson, New York (2011)

30. Salvador Elias Venegas-Andraca: Quantum walks: a comprehensive review. Quantum Inf. Process. **11**(5), 1015–1106 (2012)

31. Xia, F., Liu, J., Nie, H., Yonghao, F., Wan, L., Kong, X.: Random walks: a review of algorithms and applications. IEEE Trans. Emerg. Top. Comput. Intell. **4**(2), 95–107 (2020)

Reordering Decision Diagrams for Quantum Computing Is Harder Than You Might Think

Stefan Hillmich[1]([✉])(iD), Lukas Burgholzer[1]([✉])(iD), Florian Stögmüller[1], and Robert Wille[2,3]([✉])(iD)

[1] Institute for Integrated Circuits, Johannes Kepler University Linz, Linz, Austria
[2] Chair for Design Automation, Technical University of Munich, Munich, Germany
[3] Software Competence Center Hagenberg GmbH (SCCH), Hagenberg, Austria
{stefan.hillmich,lukas.burgholzer}@jku.at, robert.wille@tum.de
https://www.cda.cit.tum.de

Abstract. Decision diagrams have proven to be a useful data structure in both, conventional and quantum computing, to compactly represent exponentially large data in many cases. Several approaches exist to further reduce the size of decision diagrams, i.e., their number of nodes. *Reordering* is one such approach to shrink decision diagrams by changing the order of variables in the representation. In the conventional world, this approach is established and its availability taken for granted. For quantum computing however, first approaches exist, but could not fully exploit a similar potential yet. In this paper, we investigate the differences between reordering decision diagrams in the conventional and the quantum world and, afterwards, unveil challenges that explain why reordering is much harder in the latter. A case study shows that, also for quantum computing, reordering may lead to improvements of several orders of magnitude in the size of the decision diagrams, but also requires substantially more runtime.

1 Introduction

Quantum computers are promising to solve important problems significantly faster than conventional computers ever could. Shor's algorithm [1] and Grover's search [2] are two famous examples, albeit especially Shor's algorithm cannot be handled in a scalable fashion by current quantum computers. Still, there are areas where current quantum hardware can provide an advantage today, such as machine learning [3] and chemistry [4]. This computational power mainly stems from the exploitation of *superposition*, i.e., that quantum states can assume a state in which all basis states are represented at the same time, and *entanglement*, which allows operation on one qubit to also influence other qubits as well. The potential of quantum computers is witnessed by the vast efforts undertaken by companies such as IBM, Google, and Rigetti to build the physical hardware and to develop corresponding design automation tools.

© The Author(s), under exclusive license to Springer Nature Switzerland AG 2022
C. A. Mezzina and K. Podlaski (Eds.): RC 2022, LNCS 13354, pp. 93–107, 2022.
https://doi.org/10.1007/978-3-031-09005-9_7

These methods and tools for design automation need to work on conventional hardware but, at the same time, have to deal with the complexity of the quantum world. To this end, representing a quantum state requires an exponential amount of memory with respect to the number of qubits, often represented as a 2^n-dimensional vector. Rooted in the underlying mathematical principles, the worst-case complexity will always be of this exponential kind [5]. However, utilizing more sophisticated and adaptive data structures such as *decision diagrams* (DDs) [6–14] can lead to much more compact representations in many cases.

In the design automation for conventional circuits and systems, decision diagrams have been established since the 90's (see, e.g., [15,16]). There, it has been shown that the size of decision diagrams significantly depends on the order in which the variables (in case of decision diagrams for quantum computing, the qubits) are encoded. Even though determining an optimal *variable order* is a coNP-hard problem [17], the potential reductions in size motivated a plethora of reordering schemes aimed at determining suitable or even the best possible variable orders for a given decision diagram [17–23].

The success of reordering in the conventional design automation raises the question, whether similar approaches are suitable for the quantum world as well. A few attempts of employing reordering schemes for decision diagrams for quantum computing have been made [11,24–26]. However, those attempts have remained rather rare and considered only a prototypical level with small examples yet. Moreover, implementations of decision diagrams such as provided in [11] frequently abort when reordering is applied to larger examples due to inaccuracies in the floating-point numbers storing the edge weights. This necessitates an investigation on the challenges that have prevented a fully-fledged application of reordering in decision diagrams for quantum computing thus far.

In this work, we investigate the challenges of reordering which emerge during the implementation of this feature for decision diagrams with complex edge weights. As the challenges arise due to inaccuracies in the floating-point representation of real numbers, all types with complex edge weights, such as QMDDs [7] and LIMDDs [13], are susceptible. To this end, it becomes apparent that implementing reordering decision diagrams for quantum computing is much harder than originally thought considering the simplicity of the concept itself. Using this knowledge, we present a solution that handles those challenges and evaluate how this eventually affects the performance of reordering. Our case study shows that reordering may allow for substantial improvements (in some cases yielding decision diagrams which are several orders of magnitudes smaller in their size), but also will require substantially more runtime—showing that designers should decide whether reordering pays off in their use case. For the first time, this explains the reluctance of using reordering in decision diagrams for quantum computing, but also shows the potential still available in this optimization scheme.

The remainder of this paper is organized as follows: Sect. 2 briefly reviews the basics of quantum computing and decision diagrams. Section 3 explains the

concepts of reordering in decision diagrams, whereas Sect. 4 discusses challenges
that arise when implementing reordering in decision diagrams for quantum computing together with a corresponding solution. In Sect. 5, we present the results
of our case study. Finally, we conclude the paper in Sect. 6.

2 Background

In order to keep the work self-contained, we briefly review the basics on quantum
computing and decision diagrams in this section.

2.1 Quantum Computing

In quantum computing, the basic unit of information is the *quantum bit* or
qubit [5,27]. As a conventional bit, it can assume the corresponding computa-
tional basis states $|0\rangle$ and $|1\rangle$ (in Dirac notation). However, qubits can addition-
ally assume linear combinations of the basis states. They are, justifiably, in both
states at the same time. A more precise notion is $|\psi\rangle = \alpha_0 \cdot |0\rangle + \alpha_1 \cdot |1\rangle$ where
$\alpha_0, \alpha_1 \in \mathbb{C}$ are referred to as *amplitudes*. If both α_0 and α_1 are non-zero, the
quantum state is said to be in *superposition*. Additionally, in systems with more
than one qubit, the quantum state can be *entangled*, meaning that an operation
on one qubit may affect other qubits as well.

The amplitudes are fundamentally opaque in a physical quantum computer.
The only way to retrieve information on a quantum state is *measurement*. Measurement is probabilistic and results in a single basis state while, at the same
time, superposition and entanglement are destroyed. The probability to measure
any basis state is determined by its amplitude: Given α_i, the squared magnitude
$|\alpha_i|^2$ is the probability to measure the basis state $|i\rangle$. Therefore, the amplitudes of
the quantum state are constrained such that the sum of the squared magnitudes
must equal one—referred to as *normalization constraint*. For a one-qubit system
$|\alpha_0|^2 + |\alpha_1|^2 = 1$ must hold. Quantum states with n qubits have 2^n basis states,
each with a corresponding amplitude. Multi-qubit states are also subject to the
normalization constraint $\sum_{i \in \{0,1\}^n} |\alpha_i|^2 = 1$. Commonly, quantum states are
represented as 2^n-dimensional vectors containing the amplitudes, implemented
as arrays of floating-point numbers.

Example 1. Consider the pure two-qubit quantum state $|\psi\rangle$, which is set to

$$|\psi\rangle = 1/\sqrt{2} \cdot |00\rangle + 0 \cdot |01\rangle + 0 \cdot |10\rangle + 1/\sqrt{2} \cdot |11\rangle.$$

This state is valid, since $|1/\sqrt{2}|^2 + |0|^2 + |0|^2 + |1/\sqrt{2}|^2 = 1$ satisfies the normal-
ization constraint. As a vector, the state is written as $|\psi\rangle = [\,1/\sqrt{2}\ 0\ 0\ 1/\sqrt{2}\,]^T$. Due
to the superposition, measuring this state yields either of the two basis states
$|00\rangle$ or $|11\rangle$ with a probability of $|1/\sqrt{2}|^2 = 1/2$ each. After the measurement, the
superposition is destroyed and the quantum state is fixed to the measured state,
i.e., subsequent measurements yield the same result.

2.2   Decision Diagrams

Quantum states require 2^n-dimensional vectors to represent n qubits if this straightforward representation is chosen. In many cases *decision diagrams* (DDs) can drastically reduce this exponential complexity by exploiting redundancies [6,8–12], although the worst-case complexity remains exponential.

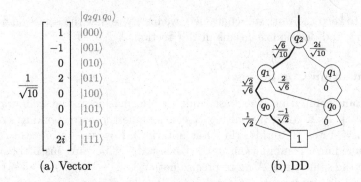

(a) Vector   (b) DD

Fig. 1. Two quantum states with vector and DD representation, respectively

The structural redundancies in vectors can be exploited by shared structures in decision diagrams. More precisely, the vector is split into equally sized upper and lower sub-vectors. There are n levels of splitting for an n-qubit state until the individual elements are reached. If identical sub-vectors occur in this procedure, they are detected and represented by shared nodes. The consistent application of a *normalization scheme* guarantees a canonical representation of quantum states and thus maximally compact decision diagrams (given a fixed variable ordering). In the resulting decision diagram, the amplitudes are encoded in the edge weights. To get the amplitude of a basis state the edge weights along the corresponding path have to be multiplied.

Example 2. Consider the state vector in Fig. 1a. The annotations on the right denote the basis state each amplitude corresponds to. In Fig. 1b, a decision diagram representing the same state is depicted with the normalization introduced in [28]. To access the amplitude of basis state $|001\rangle$, the bolded path in the decision diagram has to be traversed and the edge weights along this path have to be multiplied, e.g., ($q_2 = 0$, $q_1 = 0$, $q_0 = 1$) yielding $1 \cdot \sqrt{6}/\sqrt{10} \cdot \sqrt{2}/\sqrt{6} \cdot -1/\sqrt{2} = -1/\sqrt{10}$.

3   Reordering Decision Diagrams

This section reviews the effect of the variable order in decision diagrams and the conceptual approach to reordering. To this end, we take the findings from reordering decision diagrams in the conventional world (e.g., from [17,19–23])

and adapt them to the corresponding representation of quantum states. Afterwards, we use this as basis to show that certain corner cases frequently occur in reordering of decision diagrams for quantum computing—providing an explanation why reordering has been investigated only in a theoretic or prototypical fashion in the quantum world (e.g., in [10,11,24–26]).

The compaction decision diagrams can achieve significantly depends on the order in which the variables (or qubits) are represented. In fact, the *variable order* has a great influence on the size of the decision diagram [17] and, in particular cases, can be the difference between a compact and an exponential representation with respect to the number of variables/qubits. The variable order is denoted as $q_{i_0} < q_{i_1} < \ldots < q_{i_{n-1}}$ for a system with n variables/qubits and orders the variables/qubits in the decision diagram from the root node at the top to the qubit that appears in the last level before the terminal node.

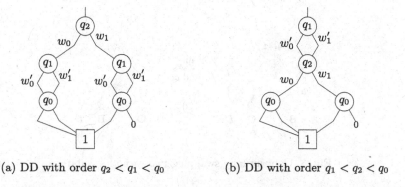

(a) DD with order $q_2 < q_1 < q_0$ (b) DD with order $q_1 < q_2 < q_0$

Fig. 2. Variable swap between q_2 and q_1 decreases the number of nodes

Example 3. Consider the decision diagrams in Fig. 2, both of which represent the same quantum state. In (a), the application of variable order $q_2 < q_1 < q_0$ yields a decision diagram with five non-terminal nodes whereas, in (b), the variable order $q_1 < q_2 < q_0$ yields a decision diagram with only four non-terminal nodes—a 20% reduction of non-terminal nodes.

Changing the variable order is termed *reordering* [19–23]. The simplest change in the variable order is exchanging variables/qubits that are adjacent in the current variable order. For two adjacent variables/qubits $q_{i+1} < q_i$, this requires swapping the "inner edges" representing $|q_{i+1}q_i\rangle = |01\rangle$ and $|q_{i+1}q_i\rangle = |10\rangle$. Keeping in mind that the decision diagrams for quantum states represent vectors, this swap corresponds to the following transformation:

$$
\begin{bmatrix} A \\ B \\ C \\ D \end{bmatrix} \begin{matrix} |00\rangle \\ |01\rangle \\ |10\rangle \\ |11\rangle \end{matrix} \xrightarrow[q_{i+1}\text{ and } q_i]{\text{swap}} \begin{bmatrix} A \\ B \\ C \\ D \end{bmatrix} \begin{matrix} |00\rangle \\ |10\rangle \\ |01\rangle \\ |11\rangle \end{matrix} \xrightarrow[\text{indices}]{\text{sort}} \begin{bmatrix} A \\ C \\ B \\ D \end{bmatrix} \begin{matrix} |00\rangle \\ |01\rangle \\ |10\rangle \\ |11\rangle \end{matrix}.
$$

In this description, A, B, C, and D can be complex numbers (if q_{i+1} and q_i are the only qubits) or sub-vectors themselves (if the system has more qubits). Of course, there may be multiple nodes labeled q_i. In this case, these the variable swapping has to be applied to each such node.

Example 4. The general simplicity of swapping two adjacent variables/qubits in a decision diagram is illustrated in Fig. 3. Only the inner outgoing edges on the lower level need to be swapped and the node labels have to be exchanged.

Changing the variable order from one to another is realized by iteratively exchanging adjacent variables/qubits in the current variable order until the desired variable order is attained. Doing so is also commonly required by heuristics trying to a find good variable order. Finding the minimal solution is an coNP-hard problem [17] and often done via exhaustive search.

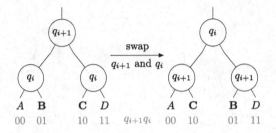

Fig. 3. Conceptually swapping two variables/qubits

In the conventional world, reordering is a standard approach to reduce the size of decision diagrams such as BDDs [17,19]. A well-known reordering heuristic is *sifting*, which has a quadratic complexity in the number of variables/qubits [23]. This approach repeatedly selects a qubit and moves it up and down in the decision diagram to find the minimal position for said variable/qubit. Hence, for a decision diagram with n variables/qubits, there are $n - 1$ positions to consider for each variables/qubit—yielding an efficient heuristic which often yields good enough results. Besides that, a plethora of further works exist which aim to determine good orders or even try to obtain the best possible order as efficiently as possible (see, e.g., [18,20–23]).

4   Challenges in Reordering Decision Diagrams for Quantum Computing

In the quantum world, decision diagrams recently were established as a data structure to efficiently handle quantum states and quantum function descriptions for simulation, synthesis, and verification. However, while reordering is a tried and tested procedure for conventional decision diagrams, it has been rarely used in decision diagrams for quantum computing yet. In fact, reordering for the quantum world has been considered only on a rather conceptual level with small examples [11,25,26]. In this section, we discuss why this might be the case and particularly show the challenges of reordering which emerge in quantum computing when more complex decision diagrams are considered.

Conceptually, reordering decision diagrams of quantum states is conducted similarly to reordering in conventional decision diagrams and consists of one or more variable swaps as illustrated in Fig. 3: Each variable swap involves two adjacent levels swapping their inner out-going edges on the lower level and accordingly relabeling the nodes. However, while this is a conceptually simple procedure and easy to realize for conventional decision diagrams, a corresponding realization for the quantum world has to consider the increased complexity. Indeed, decision diagrams for quantum computing additionally need to represent complex numbers, which are commonly encoded in the edge weights (see Sect. 2.2). This may lead to severe challenges that have not been considered thus far and are investigated in the following.

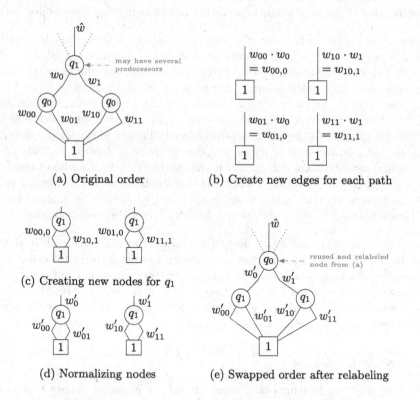

Fig. 4. Step-by-step variable swap for a single node q_1

4.1 Floating-Point Accuracy

Quantum computing uses complex numbers to describe states and functions, so decision diagrams for quantum have to incorporate complex numbers as well ($1/\sqrt{2}$ is an example of a common irrational factor in quantum computing occurring in the real or imaginary parts of a complex number). For design automation tasks on conventional computers, we are left with two choices: Do calculations symbolically to retain absolute accuracy or use some form of approximation, such as floating-point numbers. Exact representations, such as the algebraic representation proposed in [29], are too computationally expensive for all but small benchmarks. In the case of [29], which uses tuples of integers for representation, the integers quickly become larger than natively representable with 64 bits and the implementation therefore introduces an overhead by using arbitrary large integers. Hence, most implementations use floating-point numbers. However, the edge weights encoding the amplitudes of the quantum state are affected by most operations, such as multiplying edge weights of decision diagrams in simulation and reordering. Thus, due to the limited accuracy of floating-point numbers, each modification of the edge weights carries the risk of losing tiny bits of information.

Example 5. Figure 4 illustrates the required computations on the edge weights, when swapping two adjacent qubits in a decision diagram. As illustrated in Fig. 4a (showing the original order) and in Fig. 4e (showing the resulting order), the procedure follows the original idea from the conventional world (see Fig. 3) and just adjusts the inner outgoing edges and the node labels. In addition to that, however, the edge weights also need to be adjusted when decision diagrams for quantum computing are considered. This is particularity shown in Fig. 4b and Fig. 4d—and provides a challenge to be addressed. In fact, multiplying numbers that are not exactly representable with floating-point numbers, such as $1/\sqrt{2}$ or $1/3$, will result in a product that might be slightly off its real value. This difference in actual number and exact number interferes with the detection of identical sub-structures and, hence, leads to larger decision diagrams.

Most state-of-the-art implementations tackle the challenge of lost sharing due to floating-point inaccuracies by employing some form of tolerance when comparing floating-point numbers Commonly, two complex numbers a and b are regarded as equal if $|\operatorname{Re}(a) - \operatorname{Re}(b)| < T$ and $|\operatorname{Im}(a) - \operatorname{Im}(b)| < T$ for some tolerance T. However, using such a tolerance to mitigate floating-point inaccuracies causes another challenge when trying to do reordering.

4.2 Node Collisions

The inaccuracy of floating-point numbers and the common usage of tolerances for comparisons eventually creates a more severe problem for reordering nodes. In theory, doing a variable swap between q_{i+1} and q_i does not change the number of nodes on the level of q_{i+1}. However, in practice, a loss of precision may cause two hitherto different nodes to become identical.

Example 6. Consider the decision diagram shown in Fig. 5 and assume that a tolerance of $T = 0.01$ is applied. Now, the qubits q_1 and q_0 should be swapped. Note that both nodes labeled q_1 are very similar before the variable swap, but the edge weights differ by at least the tolerance. During the swapping procedure, weights of outgoing edges from the left-hand side of q_1's successors are multiplied as shown in Fig. 4b. Because the two q_1-nodes were similar to begin with, the products from the left-hand side q_1-node will be similar to the products from the right-hand side q_1-node as well. During the next steps (see Fig. 4c this may lead to a situation where, due to the applied tolerance, nodes will be considered identical during lookup of existing nodes to exploit redundancies—a *collision* occurs. More precisely, consider the left successors in the decision diagram shown in Fig. 5 as an example (bolded in the figure). Here, we get the products $0.45 \cdot 0.5 = 0.225$ and $0.46 \cdot 0.49 = 0.2254$. Due to the tolerance, both weights will be treated as identical since $|0.225 - 0.2254| < 0.01$—the same holds for the remaining products. As a result, the resulting nodes will be considered equal during lookup of existing nodes.

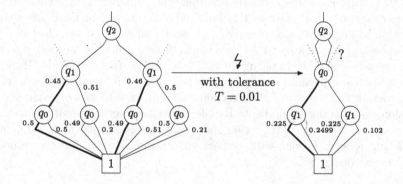

Fig. 5. Decision diagram where exchanging q_1 and q_0 leads to a collision

At a first glance, *collisions* (a term borrowed from unwanted collisions in hash tables) may seem desirable since the number of nodes is reduced. In fact, the number of nodes in a fully populated reduced decision diagram is invariant to the variable ordering (assuming sufficient accuracy in represented numbers), whereas collisions possibly reduce the number of nodes. However, since the nodes on the upper level of the variable swap are re-used to avoid reconstructing the whole decision diagram, this invalidates all edges pointing to the colliding node. Worse yet, keeping nodes regardless of a collision creates a conflict with the commonly used *unique table*. The unique table holds pointers to all inserted nodes and is essential to efficiently identifying identical sub-structures for sharing. As the name suggests, it is supposed to hold unique entries—forcibly inserting duplicates creates unreachable nodes.

Example 6 (Continued). Consider again Fig. 5. Edges pointing to the left-hand side q_1-node in the original decision diagram would work as expected in the reordered version. However, edges pointing to the right-hand side q_1-node in the original decision diagram are invalid in the reordered version. The resulting decision diagram would not correctly represent the state anymore if the collision were ignored.

Previous works (such as [11, 24–26]) did not consider collisions and, hence, failed when node collisions occurred. This may be due to collisions only occurring with increasingly complex decision diagrams and previous works considered rather small examples in their evaluations. In cases where an implementation is available (e.g., [11]), the execution is aborted with an error message if a node collision happens. However, our case study in Sect. 5 confirms that collisions are a common problem in more complex quantum states and, hence, need to be considered.

We propose to mitigate the problem of colliding nodes by readjusting edges pointing to the collided node. To this end, the corresponding parts of the unique table are scanned to find the address of the collided node and substitute the address of the original node. Further, the decision diagram may contain nodes that are yet to be inserted into the unique table and, thus, the current decision diagram is scanned as well. Note that neither scan approach is sufficient: Multiple decision diagrams can exist in the same unique table to increase the sharing potential, so nodes outside the current decision diagram may be affected.

Depending on the structure above the collision, it may be necessary to perform cascading substitutions up to one level below the root node. Handling node collisions, especially when they cascade, drastically increase the overhead of reordering since parts of the decision diagram have to be reconstructed. In addition, the merging of nodes to handle collisions is an irreversible operation. The evaluations in the next section show how this eventually makes the entire reordering process harder with respect to runtime. Before, however, another challenge is considered.

4.3   Normalization

Finally, the canonicity of decision diagrams with the same variable order should be preserved. While canonicity might not be a must-have requirement for an efficient data structure (e.g., in tasks such as simulation or synthesis), it is essential in design tasks such as equivalence checking. However, even if it is not required in tasks such as simulation, canonicity increases the likelihood of detecting identical sub-structures—resulting in a more compact decision diagram.

In conventional BDDs, canonicity is achieved by fixing the variable order and ensuring there are no two different nodes representing the same sub-structure—the decision diagrams have to be *ordered* and *reduced* [17]. For decision diagrams in the quantum world, edge weights have to be considered additionally. Here, edge weights are *normalized* to guarantee canonicity. Unfortunately, normalization schemes may cascade upwards through the decision diagram and thus limit efficiency of this desirable, if not required, operation during reordering. The introduction of *normalization factors* in the nodes as explained in [11] mitigates the premature normalization through the whole decision diagram during the reordering procedure. Nonetheless, after the reordering is performed, the normalization factors have to be applied to the out-going edges with subsequent normalization through the whole decision diagram. This may significantly increase the runtime required to conduct reordering.

5   Case Study

The investigations from above showed that, although core principles can be reused from the conventional world, reordering of decision diagrams is significantly harder in the quantum world. This raises the question of whether this optimization technique, which is well known and established for conventional decision diagrams, is still applicable on a larger scale for decision diagrams for quantum computing as well. To evaluate the applicability, we conducted a case study in which we considered quantum benchmarks such as the Quantum Fourier Transform [30], Grover's search [2], and Google's quantum-supremacy benchmarks [31] (using conditional phase-gates) and studied the effect of reordering corresponding decision diagrams representing the resulting quantum states from them with a tolerance $T = 10^{-13}$. Additionally, the reordering was only conducted on decision diagrams with at least 1000 nodes and less than 90% of a complete decision diagram (i.e., $0.9 \cdot 2^{n-1}$ nodes with n denoting the number of qubits). The evaluations were performed on a server running GNU/Linux using an AMD Ryzen 9 3950X and 128 GiB main memory with GNU parallel [32] to orchestrate the execution. The implementation is based on [11,12,33] and extended by the schemes proposed in Sect. 4 to address the investigated challenges and available at https://github.com/cda-tum/ddsim/tree/reordering under the MIT license.

The results are listed in Table 1 and discussed in the following. The table's first columns list the benchmarks as well as the number of qubits using the following notation:

– "qft_A" denotes the Quantum Fourier Transform with A qubits,
– "grover_A" denotes Grover's algorithm with A being the size of the oracle, and
– "inst_AxB_C_D" denotes a quantum-supremacy circuit on an $A \times B$ grid with C cycles and D being a running number from https://github.com/sboixo/GRCS/ to unambiguously identify individual benchmarks.

The following column lists the runtime needed to simulate the corresponding benchmark and, by this, obtain the desired state as a decision diagram. Afterwards, we applied a reordering scheme (namely sifting as reviewed in the end of Sect. 3) to optimize the resulting decision diagrams. The respectively needed runtime for that as well as the minimal number and maximal number of obtained nodes are listed in Columns 4–6 of Table 1. The remaining columns provide the corresponding absolute and relative difference in the number of nodes as well as the number of collisions that occurred during this process (see Sect. 4.2).

Table 1. Effect of Reordering for Quantum States

Benchmark	Qubits	Simulation	Simulation + Reordering (Sifting) of Resulting Quantum State					
		Time [s]	Time [s]	Min. Nodes	Max. Nodes	Abs. Diff.	Rel. Size	Collisions
qft_21	21	1.2	1.7	22	22	0	1.000	0
qft_23	23	1.5	1.8	24	24	0	1.000	0
qft_24	24	1.5	2.6	25	25	0	1.000	0
qft_25	25	1.1	1.5	26	26	0	1.000	0
grover_11	12	0.4	0.5	23	812	789	0.028	153
grover_14	15	0.5	0.8	29	2 700	2 671	0.011	508
grover_17	18	3.1	41.5	35	41 659	41 624	0.001	7 559
grover_20	21	518.5	1 808.2	41	156 414	156 373	<0.001	34 527
grover_22	23	4 584.3	Timeout	–	–	–	–	–
grover_23	24	11 313.1	Timeout	–	–	–	–	–
inst_4x4_10_0	16	3.0	164.0	54 174	64 445	10 271	0.841	3 440
inst_4x4_10_1	16	1.7	60.7	24 849	61 846	36 997	0.402	3 364
inst_4x4_11_0	16	6.7	148.6	49 925	65 462	15 537	0.763	2 269
inst_4x4_11_1	16	2.0	23.9	24 617	36 909	12 292	0.667	120
inst_4x4_12_0	16	9.7	242.9	65 536	65 536	0	1.000	0
inst_4x4_12_1	16	1.3	48.9	32 769	49 152	16 383	0.667	0
inst_4x4_13_0	16	12.2	210.6	65 536	65 536	0	1.000	0
inst_4x4_13_1	16	1.9	177.2	65 536	65 536	0	1.000	0
inst_4x4_14_0	16	15.8	262.7	65 536	65 536	0	1.000	0
inst_4x4_14_1	16	3.2	158.3	36 697	65 536	28 839	0.560	5 480
inst_4x4_15_0	16	23.1	282.0	65 536	65 536	0	1.000	0
inst_4x4_16_0	16	29.3	282.3	65 536	65 536	0	1.000	0
inst_4x4_16_1	16	9.0	93.3	32 871	65 536	32 665	0.502	2 007
inst_4x5_10_0	20	1 302.5	Timeout	–	–	–	–	–
inst_4x5_10_1	20	1 007.1	Timeout	–	–	–	–	–

Timeout of simulation and sifting combined was set to 24 h.

Firstly, the results clearly show that the effect of reordering really depends on the considered benchmark. For example, the number of nodes needed to represent the QFT-state is always linear with respect to the number of qubits for all considered orders (including the minimal and maximal cases). This is in-line with observations from the conventional world (where, e.g., functions like AND, OR, etc. are also oblivious to the variable order). On the other hand, there are benchmarks where the applied order is essential for a compact representation; most notably shown by the benchmark "grover_20" which, according to the applied order, either may require close to 160 000 nodes (maximal case) or can be represented by just 41 nodes (minimal case)—a difference of several orders of magnitude. Also for the quantum-supremacy benchmarks substantial optimizations can be achieved in some cases, despite the fact that these benchmarks are designed to contain little to no redundancy and, therefore, are considered worst-case scenarios for decision diagrams. These benchmarks also showcase a consequence of collisions: A fully populated decision diagram in theory will remain fully populated regardless of the reordering. In practice however, given the limited accuracy of floating point numbers, collisions may decrease the number of nodes as can be seen for the benchmark "inst_4x4_16_1".

Secondly, the results confirm that reordering of decision diagrams is very much a time-consuming task in the quantum world. Just applying the heuristic sifting scheme on the considered state representations already required substantial computation times (see Column 4 in Table 1) which frequently exceed the runtime needed to generate the state by simulation in the first place (see Column 3 in Table 1). That is, in contrast to conventional decision diagrams, designers really should consider the trade-off between the runtime of reordering and the size of the decision diagram. In most cases of quantum circuit simulation based on decision diagrams fixing the variable order in the beginning is the preferable approach. A rough guideline favors positioning the control qubits on a lower index compared to the position of the target qubits and minimizing the distance between control index and target index.

Finally, the results provide evidence that, indeed, reordering in decision diagrams for quantum computing is harder than originally thought: Challenges such as the node collisions discussed in Sect. 4.2 (whose handling causes a significant portion of the increased computation time) are not rare corner cases, but frequently occur (see Column 9 in Table 1). While previous work such as [11, 24–26] did not consider collisions (leading to decision diagrams where reordering only works for small examples and/or whose execution is aborted with an error message), the solution presented and evaluated in this work shed light on this.

6   Conclusions

The size of decision diagrams significantly depends on the order in which the corresponding variables/qubits are encoded. Changing the variable order, i.e., reordering, is a tried and tested technique to compact decision diagrams in the conventional world. In the quantum world, however, a similar potential has not been exploited yet. In this paper, we investigated why this might be the case and unveiled the challenges that arise in reordering for quantum decision diagrams. Our findings show that reordering in the quantum world indeed is harder compared to conventional decision diagrams—explaining why previous implementations could not handle reordering of larger decision diagrams. A case study eventually confirms that reordering may lead to improvements of several orders of magnitude although it requires substantially more runtime.

Acknowledgments. This work received funding from the European Research Council (ERC) under the European Union's Horizon 2020 research and innovation programme (grant agreement No. 101001318), was part of the Munich Quantum Valley, which is supported by the Bavarian state government with funds from the Hightech Agenda Bayern Plus, and has been supported by the BMK, BMDW, and the State of Upper Austria in the frame of the COMET program (managed by the FFG).

References

1. Shor, P.W.: Polynomial-time algorithms for prime factorization and discrete logarithms on a quantum computer. SIAM J. Comp. **26**(5), 1484–1509 (1997)
2. Grover, L.K., et al.: A fast quantum mechanical algorithm for database search. In: Symposium on Theory of Computing, pp. 212–219 (1996)
3. Riste, D., et al.: Demonstration of quantum advantage in machine learning. Npj Quantum Inf. **3**(1), 1–5 (2017)
4. Cao, Y., Romero, J., Olson, J.P., et al.: Quantum chemistry in the age of quantum computing. Chem. Rev. **119**(19), 10856–10915 (2019)

5. Nielsen, M.A., Chuang, I.L.: Quantum Computation and Quantum Information (10th Anniversary edition). Cambridge University, Press (2016)
6. Bahar, R.I., et al.: Algebraic decision diagrams and their applications. In: International Conference on CAD, pp. 188–191 (1993)
7. Miller, D.M., Thornton, M.A.: QMDD: a decision diagram structure for reversible and quantum circuits. In: International Symposium on Multi-Valued Logic, IEEE Computer Society, p. 30 (2006)
8. Abdollahi, A., Pedram, M.: Analysis and synthesis of quantum circuits by using quantum decision diagrams. In: Design, Automation and Test in Europe, pp. 317–322 (2006)
9. Wang, S., Lu, C., Tsai, I., Kuo, S.: An XQDD-based verification method for quantum circuits. IEICE Trans. Fund. **91-A**(2), 584–594 (2008)
10. Viamontes, G.F., Markov, I.L., Hayes, J.P.: Quantum Circuit Simulation. Springer, Dordrecht (2009). https://doi.org/10.1007/978-90-481-3065-8
11. Niemann, P., Wille, R., Miller, D.M., Thornton, M.A., Drechsler, R.: QMDDs: efficient quantum function representation and manipulation. IEEE Trans. CAD Integr. Circuits Syst. **35**(1), 86–99 (2016)
12. Zulehner, A., Wille, R.: Advanced simulation of quantum computations. IEEE Trans. CAD Integr. Circuits Syst. **38**(5), 848–859 (2019)
13. Vinkhuijzen, L., Coopmans, T., Elkouss, D., Dunjko, V., Laarman, A.: LIMDD a decision diagram for simulation of quantum computing including stabilizer states, CoRR, vol. abs/2108.00931 (2021)
14. Hong, X., Zhou, X., Li, S., Feng, Y., Ying, M.: A tensor network based decision diagram for representation of quantum circuits (2021). arXiv: 2009.02618 [quant-ph]
15. Bryant, R.E.: Symbolic Boolean manipulation with ordered binary-decision diagrams. ACM Comput. Surv. **24**(3), 293–318 (1992)
16. Bahar, R.I., et al.: Algebric decision diagrams and their applications. Formal Methods Syst. Des. **10**(2–3), 171–206 (1997)
17. Bryant, R.E.: Graph-based algorithms for boolean function manipulation. IEEE Trans. Comput. **C-35**(8), 677–691 (1986)
18. Friedman, S.J., Supowit, K.J.: Finding the optimal variable ordering for binary decision diagrams. In: Design Automation Conference (1987)
19. Rudell, R.: Dynamic variable ordering for ordered binary decision diagrams. In: International Conference on CAD, pp. 42–47 (1993)
20. Ishiura, N., Sawada, H., Yajima, S.: Minimization of binary decision diagrams based on exchanges of variables. In: International conference on CAD, pp. 472–473 (1991)
21. Meinel, C., Slobodova, A.: Speeding up variable reordering of OBDDs. In: International Conference on Computer Design VLSI in Computers and Processors, pp. 338–343 (1997)
22. Somenzi, F.: Efficient manipulation of decision diagrams. Int. J. Softw. Tools Technol. Transfer 3(2), 171–181 (2001). https://doi.org/10.1007/s100090100042
23. Meinel, C., Somenzi, F., Theobald, T.: Linear sifting of decision diagrams and its application in synthesis. IEEE Trans. CAD Integr. Circuits Syst. **19**(5), 521–533 (2000)
24. Schaick, S.V., Kent, K.B.: Analysis of variable reordering on the QMDD representation of quantum circuits. In: Euromicro Conf. on Digital System Design, pp. 347–352 (2007)

25. Miller, D.M., Feinstein, D.Y., Thornton, M.A.: QMDD minimization using sifting for variable reordering. Multiple-Valued Logic Soft Comput. **13**(4–6), 537–552 (2007)
26. Miller, D.M., Feinstein, D.Y., Thornton, M.A.: Variable reordering and sifting for QMDD. In: International Symposium on Multi-Valued Logic (2007)
27. Watrous, J.: The Theory of Quantum Information. Cambridge University Press, Cambridge (2018)
28. Hillmich, S., Markov, I.L., Wille, R.: Just like the real thing: fast weak simulation of quantum computation. In: Design Automation Conference (2020)
29. Zulehner, A., Niemann, P., Drechsler, R., Wille, R.: Accuracy and compactness in decision diagrams for quantum computation. In: Design, Automation and Test in Europe, pp. 280–283 (2019)
30. Jozsa, R.: Quantum algorithms and the fourier transform. R. Soc. London. Ser. A **454**(1969), 323–337 (1998)
31. Boixo, S., et al.: Characterizing quantum supremacy in near-term devices. Nat. Phys. **14**(6), 595–600 (2018)
32. Tange, O.: GNU parallel: the command-line power tool. Login Usenix Mag. **36**(1), 42–47 (2011)
33. Zulehner, A., Hillmich, S., Wille, R.: How to efficiently handle complex values? Implementing decision diagrams for quantum computing. In: International Conference on CAD (2019)

Foundations and Applications

Certifying Algorithms and Relevant Properties of Reversible Primitive Permutations with **Lean**

Giacomo Maletto[1] and Luca Roversi[2]([⊠])([iD])

[1] Dipartimento di Matematica, Università Degli Studi di Torino, Turin, Italy
giacomo.maletto@edu.unito.it
[2] Dipartimento di Informatica, Università Degli Studi di Torino, Turin, Italy
luca.roversi@unito.it

Abstract. Reversible Primitive Permutations (RPP) are recursively defined functions designed to model Reversible Computation. We illustrate a proof, fully developed with the proof-assistant **Lean**, certifying that: "RPP can encode every Primitive Recursive Function". Our reworking of the original proof of that statement is conceptually simpler, fixes some bugs, suggests a new more primitive reversible iteration scheme for RPP, and, in order to keep formalization and semi-automatic proofs simple, led us to identify a single pattern that can generate some useful reversible algorithms in RPP: Cantor Pairing, Quotient/Reminder of integer division, truncated Square Root. Our **Lean** source code is available for experiments on Reversible Computation whose properties can be certified.

1 Introduction

Studies focused on questions posed by Maxwell, regarding the solidity of the principles which Thermodynamics is based on, recognized the fundamental role that Reversible Computation can play to that purpose.

Once identified, it has been apparent that Reversible Computation constitutes the context in which to frame relevant aspects in areas of Computer Science; they can span from reversible hardware design which can offer a greener foot-print, as compared to classical hardware, to unconventional computational models—we think of quantum or bio-inspired ones, for example —, passing through parallel computation and the synchronization issues that it rises, or debuggers that help tracing back to the origin of a bug, or the consistent transactions roll-back in data-base management systems, just to name some. The book [18] is a comprehensive introduction to the subject; the book [6], focused on the low-level aspects of Reversible Computation, concerning the realization of reversible hardware, and [13], focused on how models of Reversible Computation like Reversible Turing Machines (RTM), and Reversible Cellular Automata (RCA) can be considered universal and how to prove that they enjoy such a property, are complementary to, and integrate [18].

C. A. Mezzina and K. Podlaski (Eds.): RC 2022, LNCS 13354, pp. 111–127, 2022.
https://doi.org/10.1007/978-3-031-09005-9_8

This work focuses on the *functional model* RPP [17] of Reversible Computation. RPP stands for (the class of) Reversible Primitive Permutations, which can be seen as a possible reversible counterpart of PRF, the class of Primitive Recursive functions [19]. We recall that RPP, in analogy with PRF, is defined as the smallest class built on some given basic reversible function, closed under suitable composition schemes. The very functional nature of the elements in RPP is at the base of reasonably accessible proofs of the following properties:

- RPP is PRF-complete [17]: for every function $F \in$ PRF with arity $n \in \mathbb{N}$, both $m \in \mathbb{N}$ and f in RPP exist such that f encodes F, i.e. $f(z, \overline{x}, \overline{y}) = (z + F(\overline{x}), \overline{x}, \overline{y})$, for every $\overline{x} \in \mathbb{N}^n$, whenever all the m variables in $\overline{y}$ are set to the value 0. Both z and the tuple $\overline{y}$ are *ancille*. They can be thought of as temporary storage for intermediate computations of the encoding.
- RPP can be extended to become Turing-complete [16] by means of a minimization scheme analogous to the one that extends PRF to the Turing-complete class of *Partial* Recursive Functions.
- According to [12], RPP and the reversible programming language SRL [11] are equivalent, so the fix-point problem is undecidable for RPP as well [10].

This work is further evidence that expressing Reversible Computation by means of recursively defined computational models like RPP, *naturally* offers the possibility to certify with *reasonable effort* the correctness, or other interesting properties, of algorithms in RPP, by means of some proof-assistant, also discovering new algorithms. We recall that a proof-assistant is an integrated environment to formalize data-types, to implement algorithms on them, to formalize specifications and prove that they hold, increasing algorithms dependability.

Contributions. We show how to express RPP and its evaluation mechanism inside the proof-assistant Lean [5]. We can certify the correctness of every reversible function of RPP with respect to a given specification which also means certifying that RPP is PRF-complete, the main result in [17]. In more detail:

- we give a strong guarantee that RPP is PRF-complete in three macro steps. We exploit that in Lean mathlib library, PRF is proved equivalent to a class of recursive *unary* functions called primrec. We define a data-type rpp in Lean to represent RPP. Then, we certify that, for any function f:primrec, i.e. any unary f with type primrec in Lean, a function exists with type rpp that encodes f:primrec. Apart from fixing some bugs, our proof is fully detailed as compared to [17]. Moreover it's conceptually and technically simpler;
- concerning simplification, it follows from how the elements in primrec work, and, additionally, it is characterized by the following aspects:
  - we define a *new* finite reversible iteration scheme subsuming the reversible iteration schemes in RPP, and SRL, but which is more primitive;
  - we identify an algorithmic pattern which uniquely associates elements of $\mathbb{N}^2$, and $\mathbb{N}$ by counting steps in specific paths. The pattern becomes a reversible element in rpp once fixed the parameter it depends on. Slightly

different parameter instances generate reversible algorithms whose behavior we can certify in Lean. They are truncated Square Root, Quotient/Reminder of integer division, and Cantor Pairing [2,20]. The original proof in [17] that RPP is PRF-complete relies on Cantor Pairing, used as a stack to keep the representation of a PRF function as element of RPP reversible. Our proof in Lean replaces Cantor Pairing with a reversible representation of functions mkpair/unpair that mathlib supplies as isomorphism $\mathbb{N} \times \mathbb{N} \simeq \mathbb{N}$. The truncated Square Root is the basic ingredient to obtain reversible mkpair/unpair.

Related Work. Concerning the formalization in a proof-assistant of the semantics, and its properties, of a formalism for Reversible Computation, we are aware of [15]. By means of the proof-assistant Matita [1], it certifies that a denotational semantics for the imperative reversible programming language Janus [18, Section 8.3.3] is fully abstract with respect to the operational semantics.

Concerning *functional models* of Reversible Computation, we are aware of [7] which introduces the class of reversible functions RI, which is as expressive as the *Partial* Recursive Functions. So, RI is stronger than RPP, however we see RI as less abstract than RPP for two reasons: (i) the primitive functions of RI depend on a given specific binary representation of natural numbers; (ii) unlike RPP, which we can see as PRF in a reversible setting, it is not evident to us that RI can be considered the natural extension of a total class analogous to RPP.

Contents. This work illustrates the relevant parts of the BSc Thesis [8] which comes with [9], a Lean project that certifies properties, and algorithms of RPP. Section 2 recalls the class RPP by commenting on the main design aspects that characterize its definition inside Lean. Section 3 defines and proves correct new reversible algorithms central to the proof. Section 4 recalls the main aspects of primrec, and illustrates the key steps to port the original PRF-completeness proof of RPP to Lean. Section 5 is about possible developments.

2   Reversible Primitive Permutations (RPP)

We use the data-type rpp in Fig. 1, as defined in Lean, to recall from [17] that the class RPP is the smallest class of functions that contains five base functions, named as in the definition, and all the functions that we can generate by the composition schemes whose name is next to the corresponding clause in Fig. 1. For ease of use and readability the last two lines in Fig. 1 introduce infix notations for series and parallel compositions.

Example 1 (A term of type rpp*).* In rpp we can write (Id 1‖Sw);;(It Su)‖ (Id 1);;(Id 1‖If Su (Id 1) Pr) which we also represent as a diagram. Its inputs are the names to the left of the blocks. The outputs are to their right:

$$w = \begin{cases} y+1 & \text{if } z+x > 0 \\ y & \text{if } z+x = 0 \\ y-1 & \text{if } z+x < 0 \end{cases}.$$

```
inductive rpp : Type
−− Base functions
| Id (n : ℕ) : rpp −− Identity
| Ne : rpp          −− Sign−change
| Su : rpp          −− Successor
| Pr : rpp          −− Predecessor
| Sw : rpp          −− Transposition or Swap
−− Inductively defined functions
| Co (f g : rpp) : rpp   −− Series composition
| Pa (f g : rpp) : rpp   −− Parallel composition
| It (f : rpp) : rpp     −− Finite iteration
| If (f g h : rpp) : rpp −− Selection
infix '‖' : 55 := Pa −− Notation for the Parallel composition
infix ';;' : 50 := Co −− Notation for the Series composition
```

Fig. 1. The class RPP as a data-type rpp in Lean.

We have just built a series composition of three parallel compositions. The first one composes a unary identity Id 1, which leaves its unique input untouched, and Sw, which swaps its two arguments. Then, the x-times iteration of the successor Su, i.e. It Su, is in parallel with Id 1: that is why, one of the outputs of It Su is $z + x$. Finally, If Su (Id 1) Pr selects which among Su, Id 1, and Pr to apply to the argument y, depending on the value of $z + x$; in particular, Pr is the function that computes the predecessor of the argument. Figure 5 will give the operational semantics which defines rpp formally as a class of functions on $\mathbb{Z}$, not on $\mathbb{N}$. ∎

Remark 1 ("Weak weakening" of algorithms in rpp). We typically drop Id m if it is the last function of a parallel composition. For example, term and diagram in *Example* 1 become (Id 1‖Sw);;(It Su);;(Id 1‖If Su (Id 1) Pr) and:

$$
\begin{array}{llll}
x \ \boxed{\text{Id } 1} \ x & x \quad \boxed{\text{Id } 1} \quad x & \\
y \ \boxed{\text{Sw}} \ z & \boxed{\text{It Su}} \ z+x & z+x \quad \boxed{\text{If Su (Id 1) Pr}} \quad z+x & w = \begin{cases} y+1 & \text{if } z+x > 0 \\ y & \text{if } z+x = 0 \\ y-1 & \text{if } z+x < 0 \end{cases} \\
z \ y & y & w
\end{array}
$$

Remark 2 explains why. ∎

The function in Fig. 2 computes the arity of any f:rpp from the structure of f, once fixed the arities of the base functions; f.arity is Lean dialect for the more typical notation "arity(f)".

Figure 3 remarks that rpp considers n-ary identities Id n as primitive; in RPP the function Id n is obtained by parallel composition of n unary identities.

For any given f:rpp, the function inv in Fig. 4 builds an element with type rpp. The definition of inv lets the successor Su be inverse of the predecessor Pr and lets every other base function be self-dual. Moreover, the function inv

```
def arity : rpp → ℕ
  | (Id n)    := n
  | Ne        := 1
  | Su        := 1
  | Pr        := 1
  | Sw        := 2
  | (f ‖ g)   := f.arity + g.arity
  | (f ;; g)  := max f.arity g.arity
  | (It f)    := 1 + f.arity  -- It f has an extra argument compared to f
  | (If f g h) := 1 + max (max f.arity g.arity) h.arity
```

Fig. 2. Arity of every f: rpp.

$$x_0 \quad \textbf{Id 1} \quad x_0$$
$$\vdots$$
$$x_{n-1} \quad \textbf{Id 1} \quad x_{n-1}$$

$$x_0 \qquad\qquad x_0$$
$$\vdots \quad \textbf{Id n} \quad \vdots$$
$$x_{n-1} \qquad\quad x_{n-1}$$

(a) n unary identities of RPP in parallel.   (b) Single n-ary identity rpp.

Fig. 3. n-ary identities are base functions of rpp.

```
def inv : rpp → rpp
  | (Id n)     := Id n -- self-dual
  | Ne         := Ne   -- self-dual
  | Su         := Pr
  | Pr         := Su
  | Sw         := Sw   -- self-dual
  | (f ‖ g)    := inv f ‖ inv g
  | (f ;; g)   := inv g ;; inv f
  | (It f)     := It (inv f)
  | (If f g h) := If (inv f) (inv g) (inv h)
notation f '⁻¹' := inv f
```

Fig. 4. Inverse inv f of every f:rpp.

distributes over finite iteration It, selection If, and parallel composition ‖, while it requires to exchange the order of the arguments before distributing over the series composition ;;. The last line with **notation** suggests that f^{-1} is the inverse of f; we shall prove this fact once given the operational semantics of rpp. *Operational Semantics of* rpp. The function ev in Fig. 5 interprets an element of rpp as a function from a list of integers to a list of integers. Originally, in [17], RPP is a class of functions with type $\mathbb{Z}^n \to \mathbb{Z}^n$. We use list $\mathbb{Z}$ in place of tuples of $\mathbb{Z}$ to exploit Lean library mathlib and save a large amount of formalization.

```
def ev : rpp → list ℤ → list ℤ
| (Id n)    X                   := X
| Ne        (x :: X)            := −x :: X
| Su        (x :: X)            := (x + 1) :: X
| Pr        (x :: X)            := (x − 1) :: X
| Sw        (x :: y :: X)       := y :: x :: X
| (f ;; g)  X                   := ev g (ev f X)
| (f ∥ g)   X                   := ev f (take f.arity X) ++ ev g (drop f.arity X)
| (It f)    (x :: X)            := x :: ((ev f)^[↓x] X)
| (If f g h) (0 :: X)           := 0 :: ev g X
| (If f g h) (((n : ℕ) + 1) :: X) := (n + 1) :: ev f X
| (If f g h) (−[1 + n] :: X)    := −[1 + n] :: ev h X
| _         X                   := X
notation '‹' f '›' := ev f
```

Fig. 5. Operational semantics of elements in rpp.

Let us give a look at the clauses in Fig. 5. Id n leaves the input list X untouched. Ne "negates", i.e. takes the opposite sign of, the head of the list, Su increments, and Pr decrements it. Sw is the transposition, or swap, that exchanges the first two elements of its argument. The series composition f;;g first applies f and then g. The parallel composition f∥g splits X into two parts. The "topmost" one (take f.arity X) has as many elements as the arity of f; the "lowermost" one (drop f.arity X) contains the part of X that can supply the arguments to g. Finally, it concatenates the two resulting lists by the append ++. Our *new finite iteration* It f iterates f as many times as the value of the head x of the argument, if x contains a non negative value; otherwise it is the identity on the whole x::X. This behavior is the meaning of (ev f)^[↓x]. The selection If f g h chooses one among f, g, and h, depending on the argument head x: it is g with x = 0, it is f with x > 0, and h with x < 0. The last line of Fig. 5 sets a handy notation for ev.

Remark 2 (We keep the definition of ev simple). Based on our definition, we can apply any f:rpp to any X:list ℤ. This is based on two observations: first, in Lean it holds:

```
theorem ev_split (f: rpp) (X: list ℤ):
<f> X = (<f> (take f.arity X)) ++ drop f.arity X
```

so that if X.length >= f.arity, i.e. X supplies enough arguments, then f operates on the first elements of X according to its arity. This justifies *Remark 1*. Second, if instead X.length < f.arity holds, i.e. X has not enough elements, f X has an unspecified behavior; this might sound odd, but it simplifies the certified proofs of must-have properties of rpp. ∎

2.1 The Functions `inv f` and `f` are each other inverse

Once defined `inv` in Fig. 4 and `ev` in Fig. 5 we can prove:

```
theorem inv_co_l (f : rpp) (X : list ℤ) : <f ;; f⁻¹> X = X
theorem inv_co_r (f : rpp) (X : list ℤ) : <f⁻¹ ;; f> X = X
```

certifying that f and f^{-1} are each other inverse. We start by focusing on the main details to prove theorem `inv_co_l` in Lean. The proof proceeds by (structural) induction on `f`, which generates 9 cases, one for each clause that defines `rpp`. One can go through the majority of them smoothly. Some comments about two of the more challenging cases follow.

Parallel Composition. Let `f` be some parallel composition, whose main constructor is `Pa`. The step-wise proof of `inv_co_l` is:

```
<f‖g;;(f‖g)⁻¹> X
  = <f‖g;;f⁻¹‖g⁻¹> X        -- by definition
(!) = <(f;;f⁻¹)‖(g;;g⁻¹)> X   -- lemma pa_co_pa, arity_inv below
  = <f;;f⁻¹>(take f.arity X) ++ <g;;g⁻¹>(drop f.arity X)
                              -- by definition
  = take f.arity X ++ drop f.arity X -- by ind. hyp.
  = X                         -- property of ++ (append),
```

where the equivalence (!) holds because we can prove both:

```
lemma pa_co_pa (f f' g g' : rpp) (X : list ℕ) :
  f.arity = f'.arity → <f‖g ;; f'‖g'> X = <(f;;f') ‖ (g;;g')> X ,
lemma arity_inv (f : rpp) : f⁻¹.arity = f.arity .
```

Proving lemma `arity_inv`, i.e. that the arity of a function does not change if we invert it, assures that we can prove lemma `pa_co_pa`, i.e. that series and parallel compositions smoothly distribute reciprocally.   □

Iteration. Let `f` be a finite iterator whose main constructor is `It`. In this case, the most complex goal to prove is `<It f;;It f⁻¹> x::X = x::X` which reduces to `<f⁻¹>^[↓x] (<f>^[↓x] X') = X'`, where, we recall, the notation `<f>^[↓x]` means "`<f>` applied x times, if x is positive". Luckily this last statement is both formalized as `function.left_inverse (g^[n]) (f^[n])`, and proven in the library mathlib of Lean, where `function.left_inverse` is the proposition $\forall$ (g : $\beta \to \alpha$) (f: $\alpha \to \beta$) (x: α), g(f x) = x : Prop, with α, and β generic types.   □

To conclude, let us see how the proof of `inv_co_r` works. It does not copy-cat the one of `inv_co_l`. It relies on proving:

```
lemma inv_involute (f : rpp) : (f⁻¹)⁻¹ = f ,
```

which says that applying `inv` twice is the identity, and on using `inv_co_l`:

```
<f⁻¹ ;; f> X = X -- which, by inv_involute, is equivalent to
<f⁻¹ ;; (f⁻¹)⁻¹> X = X -- which holds because it is an
instance of (inv_co_l f⁻¹) .
```

Remark 3 (On our simplifying choices on ev*).* A less general, but semantically more appropriate version of inv_co_l and inv_co_r could be:

```
theorem inv_co_l (f : rpp) (X : list ℤ) :
           f.arity ≤ X.length → <f ;; f⁻¹> X = X
theorem inv_co_r (f : rpp) (X : list ℤ) :
           f.arity ≤ X.length → <f⁻¹> ;; f> X = X
```

because, recalling *Remark 2*, f X makes sense when f.arity ≤ X.length. Fortunately, the way we defined rpp allows us to state inv_co_l or inv_co_r in full generality with no reference to f.arity ≤ X.length.   ∎

2.2   How rpp differs from original RPP

The definition of rpp in Lean is really very close to the original RPP, but not identical. The goal is to simplify the overall task of formalization and certification. The brief list of changes follows.

- As already outlined, It and If use the head of the input list to iterate or choose: taking the head of a list with pattern matching is obvious. In [17], the last element in the input tuple drives iteration and selection of RPP.
- Id n, for any n:ℕ, is primitive in rpp and derived in RPP.
- Using list ℤ → list ℤ as the domain of the function that interprets any given element f:rpp avoids to let the type of f:rpp depend on the arity of f. To know the arity of f it is enough to invoke arity f. Finally, we observe that getting rid of a dependent type like, say, rpp n, allows us to escape situations in which we would need to compare equal but not definitionally equal types like rpp (n+1) and rpp (1+n).
- The new finite iterator It f (x::t): list ℤ *subsumes* the finite iterators ItR in RPP, and for in SRL, i.e. It is more primitive, equally expressive and simpler for Lean to prove that its definition is terminating.
  We recall that ItR f $(x_0,x_1,\ldots,x_{n-2},x)$ evaluates to $f(f(\ldots f(x_0,x_1,\ldots,x_{n-2})\ldots))$ with $|x|$ occurrences of f. Instead, for(f) x evaluates to $f(f(\ldots f(x_0,x_1\check{C}\ldots,x_{n-2})\ldots))$, with x occurrences of f, if x > 0; it evaluates to $f^{-1}(f^{-1}(\ldots f^{-}1(x_0,x_1,\ldots,x_{n-2})\ldots))$, with -x occurrences of f^{-1}, if x < 0; it behaves like the identity if x = 0.
  We can define both ItR and for in terms of It:

$$\text{ItR f} = (\text{It f}) ;; \text{Ne} ;; (\text{It f}) ;; \text{Ne} \qquad (1)$$

$$\text{for(f)} = (\text{It f}) ;; \text{Ne} ;; (\text{It } f^{-1}) ;; \text{Ne} . \qquad (2)$$

Example 2 (How does (1) *work?).* Whenever x > 0, the leftmost It f in (1) iterates f, while the rightmost one does nothing because Ne in the middle negates x. On the contrary, if x < 0, the leftmost It f does nothing and the iteration is performed by the rightmost iteration, because Ne in the middle negates x. In both cases, the last Ne restores x to its initial sign. But this is the behavior of ItR, as we wanted.   ∎

3 RPP Algorithms Central to Our Proofs

Figure 6 recalls definition, and behavior of some rpp functions in [17]. It is worth commenting on how rewiring $\lceil i_0 \ldots i_n \rceil$ works. Let $\{i_0, \ldots, i_n\} \subseteq \{0, \ldots, m\}$. Let $\{j_1, \ldots, j_{m-n}\}$ be the set of remaining indices $\{0, \ldots, m\} \setminus \{i_0, \ldots, i_n\}$ ordered such that $j_k < j_{k+1}$. By definition, $\lceil i_0, \ldots, i_n \rceil (x_0, \ldots, x_m) = (x_{i_0}, \ldots, x_{i_n}, x_{j_1}, \ldots, x_{j_{m-n}})$, i.e. rewiring brings every input with index in $\{i_0, \ldots, i_n\}$ before all the remaining inputs, preserving the order.

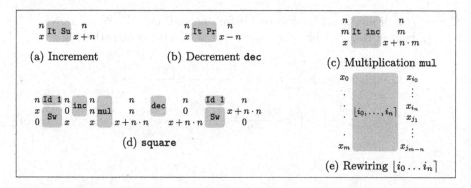

(a) Increment   (b) Decrement dec   (c) Multiplication mul

(d) square

(e) Rewiring $\lceil i_0 \ldots i_n \rceil$

Fig. 6. Some useful functions of rpp (Note that using our definition, the variable n must be non-negative in order to have the shown behavior, otherwise the function acts as the identity. This is why it's called *increment* and not *addition*.)

Figure 7 identifies the new algorithm scheme step[_]. Depending on how we fill the hole [_], we get step functions that, once iterated, draw paths in $\mathbb{N}^2$.

On top of the functions in Figs. 6, and 7 we build Cantor Pairing/Un-pairing, Quotient/Reminder of integer division, and truncated Square Root. It is enough to make the correct instance of step[_] in order to visit $\mathbb{N}^2$ as in Figs. 8a, 8b, and 8c, respectively. The alternative pairing mkpair has a more complex definition, and is a necessary ingredient for the main proof.

Id 1				Id 1
If(Su)(Id 1)(Id 1)	$\lfloor 2,0,1 \rceil$	If(Su|Pr)[_](Id 2)	Sw If(Pr)(Id 1)(Id 1)	Sw

Fig. 7. Algorithm scheme step[_]. The algorithm we can obtain from it depends on how we fill the hole [_].

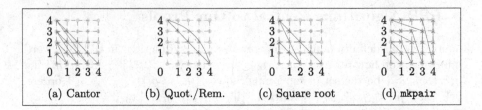

(a) Cantor　　(b) Quot./Rem.　　(c) Square root　　(d) mkpair

Fig. 8. Paths in $\mathbb{N}^2$ that generate algorithms in rpp.

Cantor (Un-)Pairing . The standard definition of Cantor Pairing $\mathsf{cp} : \mathbb{N}^2 \to \mathbb{N}$ and Un-pairing $\mathsf{cu} : \mathbb{N} \to \mathbb{N}^2$, two bijections one inverse of the other, is:

$$\mathsf{cp}(x,y) = \sum_{i=1}^{x+y} i + x = \frac{(x+y)(x+y+1)}{2} + x \qquad (3)$$

$$\mathsf{cu}(n) = \left(n - \frac{i(1+i)}{2}, \frac{i(3+i)}{2} - n \right) , \qquad (4)$$

where $i = \left\lfloor \frac{\sqrt{8n+1}-1}{2} \right\rfloor$.

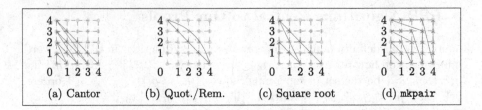

(a) Function cp_in

(b) Function step[Su;;Sw]: detailed behavior with $y > 0$.

(c) Function step[Su;;Sw]: detailed behavior with $y = 0$.

(d) Function cu_in

(e) The function cp　　(f) The function cu

Fig. 9. Cantor Pairing and Un-pairing.

Figure 9 has all we need to define Cantor Pairing `cp:rpp`, and Un-pairing `cu:rpp`. In Fig. 9a, `cp_in` is the natural algorithm in `rpp` to implement (3). As expected, the input pair (x, y) is part of `cp_in` output. The suffix "in" in the name "recalls" exactly this aspect. In order to drop (x, y) from the output of `cp_in`, and obtain `cp` as in Fig. 9e, applying *Bennet's trick*, we need `cu_in`$^{-1}$, i.e. the inverse of `cu_in` which is new, as compared to [17]. The intuition behind `cu_in` is as follows. Let us fix any point $(x, y) \in \mathbb{N}^2$. We can realize that, starting from the origin, if we follow as many steps as the value $cp(x, y)$ in Fig. 8a, we stop exactly at (x, y). The function, expressed in standard functional notation, that, given the current point (x, y), identifies the next one to move to in the path of Fig. 8a is:

$$\text{step}(x, y) = \begin{cases} (x+1, y-1) & y > 0 \\ (0, x+1) & y = 0 \end{cases}.$$

We implement $\text{step}(x, y)$ in `rpp` as `step[Su;;Sw]`. Figures 9b, and 9c represent two runs of `step[Su;;Sw]` to give visual evidence that `step[Su;;Sw]` implements $\text{step}(x, y)$. Colored occurrences of y show the relevant part of the computational flow. Note that we cannot implement $\text{step}(x, y)$ by using the conditional It directly on y, because in the computation we also want to modify the value of y. Finally, as soon as we get `cu_in` by iterating `step[Su;;Sw]` as in Fig. 9d, we can define `cp` (Fig. 9e), and `cu` (Fig. 9f). □

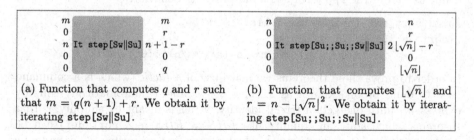

(a) Function that computes q and r such that $m = q(n+1) + r$. We obtain it by iterating `step[Sw‖Su]`.

(b) Function that computes $\lfloor\sqrt{n}\rfloor$ and $r = n - \lfloor\sqrt{n}\rfloor^2$. We obtain it by iterating `step[Su;;Su;;Sw‖Su]`.

Fig. 10. Quotient/Reminder and Square root.

Quotient and Reminder. Let us focus on the path in Fig. 8b. It starts at $(0, n)$ (with $n = 4$), and, at every step, the next point is in *direction* $(+1, -1)$. When it reaches $(n, 0)$ (with $n = 4$), instead of jumping to $(0, n+1)$, as in Fig. 8a, it lands again on $(0, n)$. The idea is to keep looping on the same diagonal. This behavior can be achieved by iterating `step[Sw‖Su]`. Figure 10a shows that we are doing modular arithmetic. Globally, it takes $n + 1$ steps from $(0, n)$ to itself by means of `step[Sw‖Su]`. Specifically, if we assume we have performed m steps along the diagonal, and we are at point (x, y), we have that $x \equiv m \pmod{n+1}$ and $0 \leq x \leq n$. So, if we increase a counter by one each time we get back to $(0, n)$ we can calculate quotient and reminder. □

Truncated Square Root. Let us focus on the path in Fig. 8c. It starts at $(0,0)$. Whenever it reaches $(x,0)$ it jumps to $(0, x+2)$. The behavior can be achieved by iterating `step[Su;;Su;;Sw‖Su]` as in Fig. 10b. In order to compute $\lfloor\sqrt{n}\rfloor$, besides implementing the above path, the function `step[Su;;Su;;Sw‖Su]` counts in k the number of jumps occurred so far along the path. In particular, starting from $(0,0)$, the first jump occurs after 1 step; the next one after 3 steps, then after 5 steps, after 7 etc. Since we know that $1 + 3 + \cdots + (2k-1) = k^2$, for any k, if $n = k^2$, the iteration will stop exactly after k jumps. I.e. $k = \sqrt{k^2} = \sqrt{n}$. Otherwise, if $(k-1)^2 \leq n < k^2$, the iteration will stop after a count of $k-1$ jumps, which approximates $\sqrt{n}$ from below; i.e. $k - 1 = \lfloor\sqrt{n}\rfloor$.   □

Remark 4. The value $2\lfloor\sqrt{n}\rfloor - r$ can be canceled out by adding r, and subtracting $\lfloor\sqrt{n}\rfloor$ twice. What we *cannot* eliminate is the "remainder" $r = n - \lfloor\sqrt{n}\rfloor^2$ because the *function* Square root cannot be inverted in $\mathbb{Z}$, and the algorithm cannot forget it.   ∎

The `mkpair` *function.* Figure 8d shows the behavior of the function `mkpair`. It is very similar to the one of `cp`, but it uses an alternative algorithm described in [4]. Here we do not describe it in detail because it's just a composition of sums, products and square roots, which have already been discussed.

A Note on the Mechanization of Proofs We recall once more that everything defined here above has been proved correct in Lean. For example, in [9], one can define as we did the `rpp` term `sqrt` and prove its behavior:

```
lemma sqrt_def (n : ℕ) (X : list ℤ) :
  <sqrt>(n::0::0::0::0::X) =
          n::(n-√n*√n)::(√n+√n-(n-√*√n))::0::√n::X
```

In order to prove these theorems we make use of a *tactic* (which is a command used to build proofs) known as `simp`, which is able to automatically simplify expressions until one gets a trivial identity. What is meant by simplify, is that theorems which state an equality like $LHS = RHS$ (e.g. `sqrt_def`) can be marked with the attribute `@[simp]`, which means that everytime the `simp` tactic is invoked in another proof, if the equality to be proved has the expression LHS then it will be substituted with RHS, often making it simpler.

This technique is really powerful, because it makes it possible to essentially automate many proofs of theorems which in turn can be marked with `@[simp]` and be used to prove yet more theorems.

4 Proving in Lean that RPP is PRF-complete

We formally show in Lean that the class of functions we can express as (algorithms) in `rpp` contains at least PRF; so, we say "rpp is PRF-complete". The definition of PRF that we take as reference is one of the two available in mathlib library of Lean. Once recalled and commented it briefly, we shall proceed with the main aspects of the PRF-completeness of `rpp`.

```
inductive primrec:(N → N) → Prop
| zero: primrec (λ (n:N), 0)
| succ: primrec succ
| left: primrec (λ (n:N), (unpair n).fst)
| right: primrec (λ (n:N), (unpair n).snd)
| pair {F G}: primrec F → primrec G → primrec (λ (n:N), mkpair (F n) (G n))
| comp {F G}: primrec F → primrec G → primrec (λ (n:N), F (G n))
| prec {F G}: primrec F → primrec G → primrec
(unpaired (λ (z n:N), nat.rec (F z) (λ (y IH:N), G (mkpair z (mkpair y IH))) n))
```

Fig. 11. primrec defines PRF in mathlib of Lean.

4.1 Primitive Recursive Functions primrec of **mathlib**

Figure 11 recalls the definition of PRF from [3] available in mathlib that we take as reference. It is an inductively defined Proposition primrec that requires a *unary* function with type $N \to N$ as argument. Specifically, primrec is the least collection of functions $N \to N$ with a given set of base elements, closed under some composition schemes.

Base Functions. The *constant* function zero yields 0 on every of its inputs. The succ*essor* gives the natural number next to the one taken as input. The two *projections* left, and right take an argument n, and extract a left, or a right, component from it as n was the result of pairing two values x,y:N. The functions that primrec relies on to encode/decode pairs on natural numbers as a single natural one are mkpair:$N \to N \to N$, and unpair:$N \to N \times N$. The first one builds the value mkpair x y, i.e. the number of steps from the origin to reach the point with coordinates (x,y) in the path of Fig. 8d. The function unpair:$N \to N \times N$ takes the number of steps to perform on the same path. Once it stops, the coordinates of that point are the two natural numbers we are looking for. So, mkpair/unpair are an alternative to Cantor Pairing/Un-pairing.

Composition Schemes. Three schemes exist in primrec, each depending on parameters f,g:primrec. The scheme pair builds the function that, taken a value n:N, gives the unique value in N that encodes the pair of values F n, and G n; everything we might pack up by means of pair, we can unpack with left, and right.

The scheme comp composes F,G:primrec.

The *primitive recursion* scheme prec can be "unfolded" to understand how it works; this reading will ease the description of how to encode it in rpp. Let F, G be two elements of primrec. We see prec as encoding the function:

$$H[\mathtt{F},\mathtt{G}](x) = R[\mathtt{G}]\big(\mathtt{F}((x)_1), (x)_2\big) \tag{5}$$

where: (i) $(x)_1$ denotes (unpair x).fst, (ii) $(x)_2$ denotes (unpair x).snd, and (iii) $R[\mathtt{G}]$ behaves as follows:

$$R[\mathtt{G}](z,0) = z$$
$$R[\mathtt{G}](z,n+1) = \mathtt{G}\big(\!\ll z, \ll n, R[\mathtt{G}](z,n)\gg\gg\big) \ ,$$

(6)

defined using the built-in recursive scheme nat.rec on $\mathbb{N}$, and $\ll a, b\gg$ denotes (mkpair a b).

4.2   The Main Point of the Proof

In order to formally state what we mean for rpp to be PRF-complete, in Lean we need to say when, given $\mathtt{F}:\mathbb{N} \to \mathbb{N}$, we can *encode* it by means of some f:rpp:

```
def encode (F:ℤ → ℤ) (f:rpp) :=
    ∀ (z:ℤ) (n:ℕ), <f> (z::n::repeat 0 (f.arity-2))
                       = (z+(F n))::n::repeat 0 (f.arity-2)
```

says that, fixed $\mathtt{F}:\mathbb{N} \to \mathbb{N}$, and f, the statement (encode F f) holds if the evaluation of <f>, applied to any argument (z::n::0::...::0), with as many occurrences of trailing 0s as f.arity-2, gives a list with form ((z+(F n))::n ::0::...::0) such that: (i) the first element is the original value z increased with the result (F n) of the function we want to encode; (ii) the second element is the initial n; (iii) the trailing 0s are again as many as f.arity-2. In Lean we can prove:

```
theorem completeness (F:ℕ → ℕ): primrec F → ∃ f:rpp, encode F f
```

which says that we know how to build f:rpp which encodes F, for every well formed $\mathtt{F}:\mathbb{N} \to \mathbb{N}$, i.e. such that primrec F holds.

The proof proceeds by induction on the proposition primrec, which generates 7 sub-goals. We illustrate the main arguments to conclude the most interesting case which requires to encode the composition scheme prec.

Remark 5. Many aspects we here detail out were simply missing in the original PRF-completeness proof for RPP in [17]. ∎

The inductive hypothesis to show that we can encode prec is that, for any given F,G:$\mathbb{N} \to \mathbb{N}$ such that (primrec F):Prop, and (primrec G):Prop, both f,g:rpp exist such that (encode F f), and (encode G g) hold. This means that f $(z::n::\mathbf{0}) = (z+\mathtt{F}\ n)::n::\mathbf{0}$, and g $z::n::\mathbf{0} = (z+\mathtt{G}\ n)::n::\mathbf{0}$, where $\mathbf{0}$ stands for a sufficiently long list of 0s.

Figure 12a, where we assume $z = 0$, defines prec[f,g]:rpp such that (encode (prec F G) prec[f,g]):Prop holds, and H[f,g] encodes $H[\mathtt{F},\mathtt{G}]$ as in (5). The term It R[g] in H[f,g] encodes (6) by iterating R[g] from the initial value given by f.

Figure 13 splits the definition of R[g] into three logical parts. Figure 13a packs everything up by means of mkpair to build the argument $R[\mathtt{G}](z,n)$ of g; by

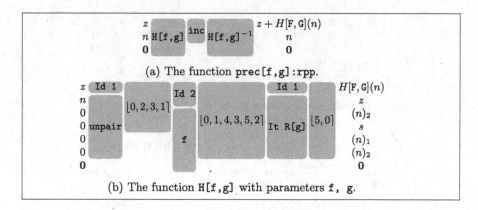

(a) The function prec[f,g]:rpp.

(b) The function H[f,g] with parameters f, g.

Fig. 12. Encoding prec of Fig. 11 in rpp.

induction we get $R[\mathtt{G}](z, n+1)$. In Fig. 13b, unpair unpacks «z, «n, $R[\mathtt{G}](z, n)$»» to expose its component to the last part. Figure 13c both increments n, and packs $R[\mathtt{G}](z, n)$ into s, by means of mkpair, because $R[\mathtt{G}](z, n)$ has become useless once obtained $R[\mathtt{G}](z, n+1)$ from it. Packing $R[\mathtt{G}](z, n)$ into s, so that we can eventually recover it, *is mandatory*. We cannot "replace" $R[\mathtt{G}](z, n)$ with 0 because that would not be a reversible action.

Remark 6. The function cp in Fig. 9e can replace mkpair in Fig. 13c as a bijective map $\mathbb{N}^2$ into $\mathbb{N}$. Indeed, the original PRF-completeness of RPP relies on cp. We favor mkpair to take the most out of mathlib. ∎

5 Conclusion and Developments

We give a concrete example of reversible programming in a proof-assistant. We think it is a valuable operation because programming reversible algorithms is not as much wide-spread as classical iterative/recursive programming, in particular by means of a tool that allows us to certify the result. Other proof assistants have been considered, and in fact the same theorems have also been proved in Coq, but we found that the use of the mathlib library together with the simp tactic made our experience with Lean much smoother. Furthermore, our work can migrate to Lean 4 whose stable release is announced in the near future. Lean 4 exports its source code as efficient C code [14]; our and other reversible algorithms can become efficient extensions of Lean 4, or standalone, and C applications.

The most application-oriented obvious goal to mention is to keep developing a Reversible Computation-centered certified software stack, spanning from a programming formalism more friendly than rpp, down to a certified emulator of Pendulum ISA, passing through compilator, and optimizer whose properties we can certify. For example, we can also think of endowing Pendulum ISA emulators with energy-consumption models linked to the entropy that characterize

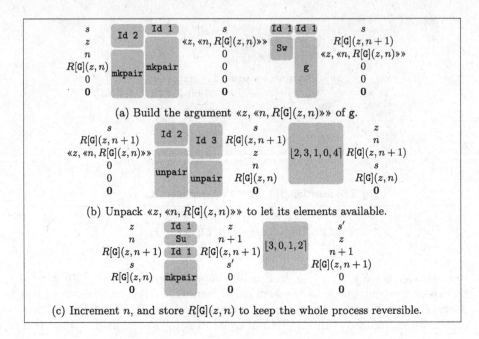

(a) Build the argument $\ll z, \ll n, R[\mathsf{G}](z,n)\gg\gg$ of $\mathbf{g}$.

(b) Unpack $\ll z, \ll n, R[\mathsf{G}](z,n)\gg\gg$ to let its elements available.

(c) Increment n, and store $R[\mathsf{G}](z,n)$ to keep the whole process reversible.

Fig. 13. Encoding $R[\mathsf{G}]$ in (6) as $\mathtt{R[g]:rpp}$.

the reversible algorithms we program, or the Pendulum ISA object code we can generate from them.

A more speculative direction, is to keep exploring the existence of programming schemes in $\mathtt{rpp}$ able to generate functions, other than Cantor Pairing, etc., which we can see as discrete space-filling functions, whose behavior we can describe as steps, which we count, along a path in some space.

References

1. Asperti, A., Coen, C.S., Tassi, E., Zacchiroli, S.: User interaction with the matita proof assistant. J. Autom. Reasoning **39**, 109–139 (2007)
2. Cantor, G.: Ein beitrag zur mannigfaltigkeitslehre. J. für die reine und angewandte Mathematik **1878**(84), 242–258 (1878)
3. Carneiro, M.: Computability.primrec. https://leanprover-community.github.io/mathlib_docs/computability/primrec.html
4. Carneiro, M.: Formalizing computability theory via partial recursive functions. In: 10th International Conference on Interactive Theorem Proving, ITP 2019, 9–12 September 2019, Portland, OR, USA, pp. 12:1–12:17 (2019)
5. de Moura, L., Kong, S., Avigad, J., van Doorn, F., von Raumer, J.: The lean theorem prover (system description). In: Felty, A.P., Middeldorp, A. (eds.) CADE 2015. LNCS (LNAI), vol. 9195, pp. 378–388. Springer, Cham (2015). https://doi.org/10.1007/978-3-319-21401-6_26
6. De Vos, A.: Reversible Computing - Fundamentals, Quantum Computing, and Applications. Wiley, Hoboken (2010)

7. Jacopini, G., Mentrasti, P.: Generation of invertible functions. Theor. Comput. Sci. **66**(3), 289–297 (1989)
8. Maletto, G.: A Formal Verification of Reversible Primitive Permutations. BSc Thesis, Dipartimento di Matematica - Torino, October 2021. https://github.com/GiacomoMaletto/RPP/tree/main/Tesi
9. Maletto, G.: RPP in LEAN. https://github.com/GiacomoMaletto/RPP/tree/main/Lean
10. Matos, A., Paolini, L., Roversi, L.: The fixed point problem of a simple reversible language. TCS **813**, 143–154 (2020)
11. Matos, A.B.: Linear programs in a simple reversible language. Theor. Comput. Sci. **290**(3), 2063–2074 (2003)
12. Matos, A.B., Paolini, L., Roversi, L.: On the expressivity of total reversible programming languages. In: Lanese, I., Rawski, M. (eds.) RC 2020. LNCS, vol. 12227, pp. 128–143. Springer, Cham (2020). https://doi.org/10.1007/978-3-030-52482-1_7
13. K. Morita. Theory of Reversible Computing. Monographs in Theoretical Computer Science. An EATCS Series. Springer, Japan (2017). https://doi.org/10.1007/978-4-431-56606-9
14. Moura, L., Ullrich, S.: The lean 4 theorem prover and programming language. In: Platzer, A., Sutcliffe, G. (eds.) CADE 2021. LNCS (LNAI), vol. 12699, pp. 625–635. Springer, Cham (2021). https://doi.org/10.1007/978-3-030-79876-5_37
15. Paolini, L., Piccolo, M., Roversi, L.: A certified study of a reversible programming language. In: Uustalu, T. (ed.) TYPES 2015 postproceedings, volume 69 of LIPIcs. Schloss Dagstuhl - Leibniz-Zentrum fuer Informatik, Germany (2017)
16. Paolini, L., Piccolo, M., Roversi, L.: On a class of reversible primitive recursive functions and its turing-complete extensions. New Gen. Comput. **36**(3), 233–256 (2018)
17. Paolini, L., Piccolo, M., Roversi, L.: A class of recursive permutations which is primitive recursive complete. Theor. Comput. Sci. **813**, 218–233 (2020)
18. Perumalla, K.S.: Introduction to Reversible Computing. Chapman & Hall/CRC Computational Science. Taylor & Francis, New York (2013)
19. Rogers, H.: Theory of Recursive Functions and Effective Computability. McGraw-Hill Series in Higher Mathematics. McGraw-Hill, New York (1967)
20. Szudzik, M.P.: The Rosenberg-Strong Pairing Function. CoRR, abs/1706.04129, 2017

Algeo: An Algebraic Approach to Reversibility

Fritz Henglein[1], Robin Kaarsgaard[2], and Mikkel Kragh Mathiesen[1(✉)]

[1] Department of Computer Science, University of Copenhagen (DIKU),
Copenhagen, Denmark
mkm@di.ku.dk

[2] School of Informatics, University of Edinburgh, Edinburgh, Scotland

Abstract. We present Algeo, a functional logic programming language based on the theory of infinite dimensional modules. Algeo is reversible in the sense that every function has a generalised inverse, an *adjoint*, which can be thought of as an inverse execution of the forward function. In particular, when the given function is invertible, the adjoint is guaranteed to coincide with the inverse.

Algeo generalises "ordinary" forward-backward deterministic reversible programming by permitting relational and probabilistic features. This allows functions to be defined in a multitude of ways, which we summarise by the motto that "all definitions are extensional characterisations; all extensional characterisations are definitions."

We describe the syntax, type system, and the axiomatic semantics of Algeo, and showcase novel features of the language through examples.

1 Introduction

Reversible programming languages have seen a great deal of research in recent years thanks to their applications in surprisingly diverse areas such as debugging [11,16], robotics [20], discrete event simulation [19] and quantum computing [9,10,18]. For this reason, many different styles of reversible programming have been explored, notably imperative [24], object-oriented [7], functional [13,17,23], and parallel [11,17].

In this paper, we study reversibility in the context of functional logic programming (see, e.g., [1]). As the name suggests, functional logic programming incorporates aspects associated with both functional programming (e.g., pattern matching, strong typing discipline) and logic programming (e.g., nondeterminism, search), making it capable for tasks such as satisfiability modulo theories, querying, and more. The combination of (very liberal) pattern matching with search means that functions can be defined in an indirect way, which makes certain functions expressible in particularly pleasant and succinct ways.

R. Kaarsgaard—Supported by DFF–International Postdoctoral Grant 0131-00025B.
M. K. Mathiesen—Supported by DFF Research Grant 8022-00415B.

C. A. Mezzina and K. Podlaski (Eds.): RC 2022, LNCS 13354, pp. 128–145, 2022.
https://doi.org/10.1007/978-3-031-09005-9_9

path : ⟨**Atom**⟩ → ⟨**Atom** ⊗ **Atom**⟩ → **Atom** → **Atom** → ⟨**Atom**⟩

path v ∗ **p p** ≛ **p** ⋈ **!v**	Start and end agree and are in the vertex set
path v e p q ≛ (	The general case
[**r** : **Atom**] [**s** : **Atom**]	Introduce existential variables
r ≛ **!v**;	Let **r** be a non-deterministically chosen vertex
p ⊗ **r** ≛ **!e**;	Check that there is an edge from **p** to **r**
s ≛ **!path** ⟨**!v** ⋈ **p**⊥⟩ **e r q**;	Find a path recursively that does not contain **p**
(**p** ∥ **s**))	Return either **p** or the vertex found recursively

Fig. 1. Graph search in Algeo. A graph can be represented by a bag of vertices, **v** : ⟨**Atom**⟩, and a bag of edges, **e** : ⟨**Atom** ⊗ **Atom**⟩, and given a start vertex **p** : ⟨**Atom**⟩ and end vertex **q** : ⟨**Atom**⟩, **path v e p q** nondeterministically returns a vertex in a path from **p** to **q**, further weighted by its number of occurences along any path from **p** to **q**.

We present Algeo, a programming language based on the linear algebraic theory of modules. Algeo extends the functional logic paradigm with a notion of reversibility in the form of (Hermitian) *adjoints*, a kind of generalised inverse. These adjoints exist not only for programs which are forward and backward deterministic, but also for arbitary linear maps, which may exhibit nondeterministic behaviours (e.g., relational, probabilistic). Crucially, however, when applied to programs which *are* forward and backward deterministic, the adjoint is guaranteed to coincide with the inverse program.

A unique feature of Algeo is that a value comes equipped with a *multiplicity*. This multiplicity can be taken from any ring, which in turn determines the meaning of this multiplicity. For example, real multiplicities, when restricted to those in the closed unit interval $[0, 1]$, can represent *probabilistic* or *fuzzy* membership. Integral multiplicities, when restricted to nonnegative numbers, can represent *multiset* membership; negative multiplicities provide additive inverse operations, e.g. deleting a row in a database table such that adding it again yields the original table whether or not the row was present to start with. Multiplicities can further be used to give a smooth account of *negation* in logic programming. To properly account for these multiplicities, all functions in Algeo are linear by definition in that they preserve multiplicities. However, since not all useful functions are linear, a form of explicit nonlinearity is also supported, requiring the explicit use of *bags* via bagging ⟨−⟩ and extraction !(−) operations. An example of an Algeo program for searching for paths between given vertices in a graph is shown in Fig. 1.

Paper Outline. Section 2 contains a brief tutorial of the language. We present the syntax and type system of Algeo in Sect. 3, give it an axiomatic semantics in the form of a system of equations, and illustrate its use through examples. In Sect. 4, we detail some applications in the use of fixed points, and give an encoding of *polysets* (i.e., sets with integral and possibly negative multiplicities) in Algeo. We describe related work in Sect. 5, and end with some concluding remarks and directions for future research in Sect. 6.

2   Algeo by Example

We now give an intuition for Algeo by writing some simple programs. In Algeo **Scalar** and $\oplus$ play the role of unit type and sum type respectively. Take **Bool** to be an alias for **Scalar** $\oplus$ **Scalar**, and define:

$$\textbf{true} : \textbf{Bool} \qquad\qquad \textbf{false} : \textbf{Bool}$$
$$\textbf{true} \doteq \text{inl}(*) \qquad\qquad \textbf{false} \doteq \text{inr}(*)$$

Negation of booleans can be written using two clauses.

$$\textbf{not} : \textbf{Bool} \to \textbf{Bool}$$
$$\textbf{not true} \doteq \textbf{false}$$
$$\textbf{not false} \doteq \textbf{true}$$

The *adjoint* of **not** is then given by:

$$\textbf{not}^\dagger : \textbf{Bool} \to \textbf{Bool}$$
$$[\textbf{x} : \textbf{Bool}]\textbf{not}^\dagger \ (\textbf{not x}) \doteq \textbf{x}$$

This definition quantifies over $\textbf{x} : \textbf{Bool}$. Such a quantification represents a nondeterministic choice of a *base value*. In **Bool** the base values are **true** and **false** so the definition is equal to

$$\textbf{not}^\dagger \ (\textbf{not true}) \doteq \textbf{true} \parallel \textbf{not}^\dagger \ (\textbf{not false}) \doteq \textbf{false}$$

where $\parallel$ represents binary nondeterministic choice. By the definition of **not** this reduces to

$$\textbf{not}^\dagger \ \textbf{false} \doteq \textbf{true} \parallel \textbf{not}^\dagger \ \textbf{true} \doteq \textbf{false}$$

which is equivalent to having two clauses:

$$\textbf{not}^\dagger \ \textbf{false} \doteq \textbf{true} \qquad\qquad \textbf{not}^\dagger \ \textbf{true} \doteq \textbf{false}$$

We can thus establish that $\textbf{not}^\dagger = \textbf{not}$, as expected. Note the difference between $=$ and $\doteq$. The former is a relation between expressions and the latter behaves as an operator with type $\tau \to \tau \to \textbf{Scalar}$. A definition of a name x is given by an expression of type **Scalar** which may refer to x. There is no requirement to use $\doteq$. In fact **not** could equivalently have been defined as:

$$\textbf{istrue}, \textbf{isfalse} : \textbf{Bool} \to \textbf{Scalar} \qquad\qquad \textbf{not} : \textbf{Bool} \to \textbf{Bool}$$
$$\textbf{istrue true} \qquad\qquad\qquad\qquad\qquad \textbf{isfalse} \ (\textbf{not true})$$
$$\textbf{isfalse false} \qquad\qquad\qquad\qquad\qquad \textbf{istrue} \ (\textbf{not false})$$

Next, we define conjunction and disjunction:

$$\text{and, or} : \textbf{Bool} \to \textbf{Bool} \to \textbf{Bool}$$
$$[\mathbf{x} : \textbf{Bool}]\text{and true } \mathbf{x} \; \hat{=} \; \mathbf{x}$$
$$\text{and false} * \; \hat{=} \; \textbf{false}$$
$$[\mathbf{x} : \textbf{Bool}][\mathbf{y} : \textbf{Bool}]\text{not (or x y)} \; \hat{=} \; \text{and (not x) (not y)}$$

Let us take the adjoint of **and** with respect to the first argument:

$$\text{and}_1^\dagger : \textbf{Bool} \to \textbf{Bool}$$
$$[\mathbf{x} : \textbf{Bool}]\text{and}_1^\dagger(\text{and } \mathbf{x} *) \; \hat{=} \; \mathbf{x}$$

Applying this function we get $\text{and}_1^\dagger$ **true** = **true** and $\text{and}_1^\dagger$ **false** = **true** ∥ **false** ∥ **false**. When the first argument of **and** and its result are both **false** there are two different possibilities for the value of the second argument, so **false** is listed twice.

A nondeterministic choice between copies of the same value like **false** ∥ **false** can also be written $\overline{2};$ **false**. We say that the *multiplicity* of **false** in this result is 2. In general, multiplicities can also be negative so, e.g., $\overline{-1};$ **false** represents -1 occurences of **false**. This can be used to cancel out positive multiplicities. For instance, we have **false** ∥ $(\overline{-1};$ **false**$) = \emptyset$ (an empty result). Thus, negative multiplicities allow another kind of reversal via cancellation. To see this in action, consider the following alternative definition of conjunction:

and $* * \; \hat{=} \;$ **false**	Conjunction 'usually' returns **false**
and true true $\hat{=} \; (\overline{-1};$ **false**$)$	Not when both arguments are **true**, though
and true true $\hat{=} \;$ **true**	In that case the result should be in fact be **true**

Generally, functions defined in Algeo are linear in the sense that they respect nondeterminism and multiplicities, corresponding to addition and scalar multiplication, respectively. Even before we know the definition of some function **f** we can say that **f** (**true** ∥ **false**) = **f true** ∥ **f false**. Now suppose that the definition is

$$\mathbf{f} \; \mathbf{x} \; \hat{=} \; \text{and } \mathbf{x} \text{ (not x)}.$$

It is clear that **f true** = **f false** = **false** and therefore **f** (**true** ∥ **false**) = $\overline{2};$ **false**. Even though **f** uses its argument twice and the argument is a nondeterministic choice between **true** and **false** the two uses of **x** are 'entangled' and have to make the same nondeterministic choices.

For cases where this behaviour is undesirable Algeo supports bag types, written $\langle \tau \rangle$ and pronounced 'bag of τ'. Bags are formed by writing an expression in angle brackets, e.g., $\langle$**true** ∥ **false**$\rangle$. The bag constructor is explicitly not linear, so $\langle$**true** ∥ **false**$\rangle \neq \langle$**true**$\rangle \parallel \langle$**false**$\rangle$. The contents of a bag can be extracted with the $!(-)$ operator.

$$\tau ::= \mathbf{Atom} \mid \mathbf{Empty} \mid \mathbf{Scalar} \mid \tau_1 \rightarrow \tau_2 \mid \tau_1 \oplus \tau_2 \mid \tau_1 \otimes \tau_2 \mid \langle \tau \rangle$$

$$b ::= x \mid a \mid b_1\, b_2 \mid b_1; b_2 \mid \mathbf{inl}(b) \mid \mathbf{inr}(b) \mid b_1 \otimes b_2 \mid b_1 \mapsto b_2 \mid \langle e \rangle$$

$$d ::= x \mid a \mid d_1\, d_2 \mid d_1; d_2 \mid \mathbf{inl}(d) \mid \mathbf{inr}(d) \mid d_1 \otimes d_2 \mid d_1 \mapsto d_2 \mid \langle e \rangle \mid \emptyset \mid d_1 \bowtie d_2 \mid \diamond e$$

$$e ::= x \mid a \mid e_1\, e_2 \mid e_1; e_2 \mid \mathbf{inr}(e) \mid \mathbf{inr}(e) \mid e_1 \otimes e_2 \mid e_1 \mapsto e_2 \mid \langle e \rangle \mid \emptyset \mid e_1 \bowtie e_2 \mid \diamond e$$

$$\bar{n} \mid e_1 \parallel e_2 \mid [x : \tau] e \mid\, !e$$

Fig. 2. Syntax of types and terms.

Consider a version of $\mathbf{f}$ using bags:

$$\mathbf{g} : \langle \mathbf{Bool} \rangle \rightarrow \mathbf{Bool}$$

$$\mathbf{g}\, \mathbf{x} \stackrel{=}{=} \mathbf{and}\, !\mathbf{x}\, (\mathbf{not}\, !\mathbf{x})$$

We have $\mathbf{g}\, \langle \mathbf{true} \rangle = \mathbf{f}\, \mathbf{true}$ and similarly for **false**. However:

$\mathbf{g}\, \langle \mathbf{true} \parallel \mathbf{false} \rangle$

$= \mathbf{and}\, (\mathbf{true} \parallel \mathbf{false})\, (\mathbf{not}\, (\mathbf{true} \parallel \mathbf{false}))$

$= \mathbf{and}\, \mathbf{true}\, (\mathbf{not}\, \mathbf{true}) \parallel \mathbf{and}\, \mathbf{true}\, (\mathbf{not}\, \mathbf{false}) \parallel \mathbf{and}\, \mathbf{false}\, (\mathbf{not}\, \mathbf{true}) \parallel \mathbf{and}\, \mathbf{false}\, (\mathbf{not}\, \mathbf{false})$

$= \mathbf{false} \parallel \mathbf{true} \parallel \mathbf{false} \parallel \mathbf{false} = \mathbf{true} \parallel \bar{3}; \mathbf{false}$

Essentially, the nondeterminism is postponed until $!(-)$ is applied. For $\mathbf{g}$ this means that the two uses of $!\mathbf{x}$ are not entangled and the result now has the possibility of being **true**. Adjoints also exist when bags are involved, but can be slightly more complicated. For instance, applying the adjoint of $\mathbf{g}$ to **true** we get

$$[\mathbf{a} : \langle \mathbf{Scalar} \rangle][\mathbf{b} : \langle \mathbf{Scalar} \rangle]!\mathbf{a}; !\mathbf{b}; \langle !\mathbf{a}; \mathbf{true} \parallel !\mathbf{b}; \mathbf{false} \rangle$$

which is the totality of all bags containing $\mathbf{a}$ copies of **true** and $\mathbf{b}$ copies of **false** scaled by the product of their multiplicities.

3   Syntax and Semantics

The syntax of types and terms are given in Fig. 2. Alternatives ($\parallel$) have the lowest precedence. Aggregrations ($[x : \tau] \ldots$) extend all the way to right. We employ the following conventions: τ is a type, e is an expression, d is a duplicable expression (see below for further details), b is a base value, a is an atom, n is a number and x, y and z are variables. Any b is also a d, and any d is also an e.

Intuitively base values represent deterministic computations that yield a value exactly once. Duplicable expressions are deterministic computations that either produce a base value or fail. Expressions in general represent nondeterministic computations that might produce any number of results. Variables are thought of as ranging over base values, although we will sometimes carefully substitute nonbase values.

We now describe the constructs of the language. An axiomatic semantics is given in Sect. 3.2. Most operations, exceptions being $\diamond$ and $\langle \cdot \rangle$, are *linear* in the sense that they respect failure ($\emptyset$), alternatives ($\|$) and conjunction (;). For instance, $\bowtie$ is linear in each component so in particular $\emptyset \bowtie e = \emptyset$, $(e_1 \| e_2) \bowtie e_3 = (e_1 \bowtie e_3) \| (e_2 \bowtie e_3)$ and $(e_1; e_2) \bowtie e_3 = e_1; (e_2 \bowtie e_3)$. Hence, understanding these operators reduces to understanding their actions on base values.

- $\emptyset$ is *failure*. It aborts the computation.
- $e_1; e_2$ is *biased conjunction*. The first component is evaluated to a base value, which is discarded. The result of the biased conjunction is then the second component.
- $e_1 \bowtie e_2$ is *join*. It computes the intersection of the two arguments. In particular, the intersection of two base values is their unique value when equal and failure otherwise.
- $e_1 \otimes e_2$ is a *pair*.
- $e_1 \mapsto e_2$ is a *mapping*. It is a function that maps every base value in e_1 to every base value in e_2.
- $\mathbf{inl}(e)$ and $\mathbf{inr}(e)$ are left and right injections for the $\oplus$ type.
- $\langle \tau \rangle$ is the type of bags of τ.
- $\langle e \rangle$ is a *bag*. It collects all the results from e into a single bag. The bag itself is considered a base value.
- $\diamond e$ is an *indicator*. It yields $\overline{0}$ if $e = \emptyset$, otherwise $\overline{1}$. Thus, $\diamond$ is explicitly nonlinear.
- $e_1 \| e_2$ is *alternative*. It represents a nondeterministic choice between e_1 and e_2.
- $[x : \tau]e$ is *aggregation*. It represents a nondeterministic choice of a base value $b : \tau$ which is substituted for x in e.
- $!e$ is *extraction*. It extracts the contents of a bag.
- $\overline{n}$ is a *number*. It represents a computation that succeeds n times. Note that negative values of n are possible. In general, depending on the choice of ring, n can also be rational or even complex.

We will also need the following syntactic sugar:

$e_1 \overset{\cdot}{=} e_2 = e_1 \bowtie e_2; \overline{1}$	Pointwise unification of e_1 and e_2
$e_1 \backslash\backslash e_2 = e_1 \| \overline{-1}; e_2$	Collect the results of e_1 but subtract the results from e_2
$*_\tau = [x : \tau]x$	Wildcard, acts as the unit for $\bowtie$
$e^\perp = * \backslash\backslash e$	Everything except e
$e_1 \oplus e_2 = \mathbf{inl}(e_1) \| \mathbf{inr}(e_2)$	A sum of lefts and rights

Beware: some constructs, e.g. $\overset{\cdot}{=}$, use unfamiliar notation. This is done deliberately to show that these constructs represent new and unfamiliar concepts. A good rule of thumb is that the familiar-looking syntax like $\mathbf{inl}(e)$ means roughly what one would expect, whereas the unfamiliar syntax like $\overset{\cdot}{=}$ has no simple well-known analogue.

In most languages the notion of function embodies both the introduction of variables and the mapping of those variables to some result. In Algeo, by contrast, these are separate concerns. Variable introduction is handled by $[x : \tau]$ whereas mappings are constructed by expressions of the form $e_1 \mapsto e_2$. This separation of concerns is the vital ingredient that makes Algeo so powerful.

$$\mathbf{id} : \tau \to \tau$$
$$\mathbf{id\ x} \doteq \mathbf{x}$$

$$\mathbf{linv} : \langle \tau_1 \to \tau_2 \rangle \to \langle \tau_2 \to \tau_1 \rangle$$
$$\langle !(\mathbf{linv\ f}) \circ !\mathbf{f} \rangle \doteq \langle \mathbf{id} \rangle$$

$$(\circ) : (\tau_1 \to \tau_2) \to (\tau_2 \to \tau_3) \to (\tau_1 \to \tau_3)$$
$$(\mathbf{f} \circ \mathbf{g})\ \mathbf{x} \doteq \mathbf{f}\ (\mathbf{g\ x})$$

$$\mathbf{rinv} : \langle \tau_1 \to \tau_2 \rangle \to \langle \tau_2 \to \tau_1 \rangle$$
$$\langle !\mathbf{f} \circ !(\mathbf{rinv\ f}) \rangle \doteq \langle \mathbf{id} \rangle$$

$$(-^\dagger) : (\tau_1 \to \tau_2) \to \tau_2 \to \tau_1$$
$$\mathbf{f}^\dagger \circ \mathbf{f} \doteq \mathbf{id}$$

$$\mathbf{inv} : \langle \tau_1 \to \tau_2 \rangle \to \langle \tau_2 \to \tau_1 \rangle$$
$$\mathbf{inv\ f} \doteq \mathbf{linv\ f} \bowtie \mathbf{rinv\ f}$$

Fig. 3. Some basic functions in Algeo: identity, composition, adjoints, and (left and right) inverses. Note the use of bags $\langle - \rangle$ to contain nonlinearity.

Finally, we need to explain how (possibly recursive) top-level definitions are encoded as expressions. Suppose we define $x : \tau$ by the clauses $e_1, \ldots, e_n$, each of them typeable as $x : \tau, \widehat{x} : \langle \tau \rangle \vdash e_i : \mathbf{Scalar}$. Intuitively, x refers to (a single component of) the object we are defining and $\widehat{x}$ refers to the completed definition. The completed definition is used for recursive invocations. Note that $\widehat{x}$ is just a name with no a priori relation to x.

Given such a top-level definition and a program e that can refer to x the desugared version is:

$$[\widehat{x} : \langle \tau \rangle]\widehat{x} \doteq \langle [x : \tau](e_1 \parallel \cdots \parallel e_n); x \rangle; e^{x := !\widehat{x}}$$

The notation $e^{x := !\widehat{x}}$ means e with $!\widehat{x}$ substituted for x. This construction works by summing over all basis elements of τ subject to the conditions imposed by $e_1 \parallel \cdots \parallel e_n$. The sum is collected into the bag $\widehat{x}$, which represents the totality of the object we are defining. Each use of x in the program is replaced with $!\widehat{x}$ so each copy is independent. This scheme generalises to mutual recursion. Note that $\doteq$ is not mentioned and has no special status in this regard; it is merely an operator which happens to be useful for imposing suitable constraints when giving definitions.

Figure 3 shows some basic and fundamental functions. While identity and composition are similar to their definition in any functional language, the definition of adjoint $(-^\dagger)$ seems very strange from a functional perspective and further seems to imply that all functions are injective—which isn't so! The trick to understanding this definition is that f quantifies over base values of the form $b_1 \mapsto b_2$ (and *not* entire functions), while $\mathbf{id}$ masquerades over the sum of all base values of the form $b \mapsto b$. In this way, we could just as well define $(\cdot^\dagger)$ as $(x \mapsto y)^\dagger \circ (x \mapsto y) \doteq (x \mapsto x)$ or even the more familiar $(x \mapsto y)^\dagger \doteq (y \mapsto x)$.

The use of search and indirect definition is perhaps more powerfully illustrated by $\mathbf{linv}$ (and, symmetrically, $\mathbf{rinv}$) which says that a left inverse to a function f is anything that behaves like it; in other words, any function that, after composition with $!f$ (needed here since f is used more than once), yields the identity (and symmetrically for $\mathbf{rinv}$). Even further, $\mathbf{inv}$ states that a full inverse to f is anything that behaves *both* as a left inverse *and* as a right inverse, using the join operator to intersect the left inverses with the right inverses.

A function $\mathbf{f}$ is *unitary* if the adjoint is also a two-sided inverse module bagging, i.e. if $\langle \mathbf{f}^\dagger \rangle = \mathbf{inv}\ \langle \mathbf{f} \rangle$. The unitaries include include many interesting

$$\boxed{\Gamma \vdash e : \tau}$$

$$\frac{}{\Gamma \vdash \bar{n} : \textbf{Scalar}} \qquad \frac{}{\Gamma \vdash a : \textbf{Atom}} \qquad \frac{}{\Gamma, x : \tau, \Gamma' \vdash x : \tau} \qquad \frac{}{\Gamma \vdash \emptyset : \tau}$$

$$\frac{\Gamma \vdash e_1 : \tau \quad \Gamma \vdash e_2 : \tau}{\Gamma \vdash e_1 \parallel e_2 : \tau} \qquad \frac{\Gamma \vdash e : \tau_1}{\Gamma \vdash \textbf{inl}(e) : \tau_1 \oplus \tau_2} \qquad \frac{\Gamma \vdash e : \tau_2}{\Gamma \vdash \textbf{inr}(e) : \tau_1 \oplus \tau_2}$$

$$\frac{\Gamma \vdash e_1 : \tau_1 \quad \Gamma \vdash e_2 : \tau_2}{\Gamma \vdash e_1 \otimes e_2 : \tau_1 \otimes \tau_2} \qquad \frac{\Gamma \vdash e_1 : \tau_1 \quad \Gamma \vdash e_2 : \tau_2}{\Gamma \vdash e_1 \mapsto e_2 : \tau_1 \to \tau_2} \qquad \frac{\Gamma \vdash e_1 : \tau' \quad \Gamma \vdash e_2 : \tau}{\Gamma \vdash e_1 ; e_2 : \tau}$$

$$\frac{\Gamma \vdash e_1 : \tau' \to \tau \quad \Gamma \vdash e_2 : \tau'}{\Gamma \vdash e_1\, e_2 : \tau} \qquad \frac{\Gamma, x : \tau' \vdash e : \tau}{\Gamma \vdash [x : \tau'] e : \tau} \qquad \frac{\Gamma \vdash e : \tau}{\Gamma \vdash \diamond e : \textbf{Scalar}}$$

$$\frac{\Gamma \vdash e : \tau}{\Gamma \vdash \langle e \rangle : \langle \tau \rangle} \qquad \frac{\Gamma \vdash e : \langle \tau \rangle}{\Gamma \vdash\, !e : \tau}$$

Fig. 4. The type system of Algeo.

examples, including all classically reversible functions as well as all quantum circuits. In these cases we prefer the adjoint, since it does not require the use of bags and is generally easier to work with.

3.1 Type System

The type system is seen in Fig. 4 and consists of a single judgement $\Gamma \vdash e : \tau$ stating that in type environment Γ the expression e has type τ. These rules should not be surprising, at least for a classical programming language. However, Algeo functions represent linear maps, so why does the type system not track variable use? The reason is that duplication and deletion are relatively harmless operations. Duplicating a value by using a variable multiple times creates 'entangled' copies. They still refer to the same bound variables so any nondeterministic choice is made globally for all copies. Unused variables will still be bound in an aggregration and ultimately the multiplicity of the result will be scaled by the dimension of the type. Thus, such variables are not simply forgotten.

3.2 Axiomatic Semantics

We now present the semantics of Algeo as a set of equations between expressions, see Fig. 5. Equations hold only when well-typed and well-scoped. For instance, $\emptyset = \bar{0}$ implicitly assumes that the $\emptyset$ in question is typed as **Scalar**. The semantics is parametric over the choice of numbers, provided that the numbers form a ring of characteristic 0 (i.e. are the integers or an extension of them) and that for any type τ there is a number $\textbf{dim}(\tau)$ such that:

$$\textbf{dim}(\tau_1 \oplus \tau_2) = \textbf{dim}(\tau_1) + \textbf{dim}(\tau_2) \qquad \textbf{dim}(\textbf{Empty}) = 0$$
$$\textbf{dim}(\tau_1 \otimes \tau_2) = \textbf{dim}(\tau_1) \cdot \textbf{dim}(\tau_2) \qquad \textbf{dim}(\textbf{Scalar}) = 1$$
$$\textbf{dim}(\tau_1 \to \tau_2) = \textbf{dim}(\tau_1) \cdot \textbf{dim}(\tau_2)$$

Biased conjunction

$\bar{1}; e = e$

$x; e = e$

$\langle e_1 \rangle; e_2 = e_2$

$\text{inl}(e_1); e_2 = e_1; e_2$

$\text{inr}(e_1); e_2 = e_1; e_2$

$e_1 \otimes e_2; e_3 = e_1; e_2; e_3$

$e_1 \mapsto e_2; e_3 = e_1; e_2; e_3$

Function application

$(e_1 \mapsto e_2)\, e' = e_1 \bowtie e'; e_2$

Numbers

$\emptyset = \bar{0}$

$\bar{m} \parallel \bar{n} = \overline{m+n}$

$\bar{m}; \bar{n} = \overline{m \cdot n}$

$[x : \tau]\bar{1} = \mathbf{dim}(\tau)$

Aggregation

$[x : \mathbf{Empty}]\, e = \emptyset$

$[x : \mathbf{Scalar}]\, e = e^{x := \bar{1}}$

$[x : \tau_1 \oplus \tau_2]\, e = ([y : \tau_1]\, e^{x := \text{inl}(y)}) \parallel$
$\qquad\qquad\qquad ([y : \tau_2]\, e^{x := \text{inr}(y)})$

$[x : \tau_1 \otimes \tau_2]\, e = [x_1 : \tau_1]\,[x_2 : \tau_2]\, e^{x := x_1 \otimes x_2}$

$[x : \tau_1 \to \tau_2]\, e = [x_1 : \tau_1]\,[x_2 : \tau_2]\, e^{x := x_1 \mapsto x_2}$

$[x : \tau]\, x \bowtie e; x = e$

$[x : \tau]\, e = e^{x := d} \backslash\!\backslash\, e^{x := \emptyset} \parallel [y : \tau]\, e^{x := y \backslash\!\backslash y \bowtie d}$

Extraction

$!\langle e \rangle = e$

$\langle !x \rangle = x$

Join

$d \bowtie d = d$

$\text{inl}(e) \bowtie \text{inl}(e') = \text{inl}(e \bowtie e')$

$\text{inr}(e) \bowtie \text{inr}(e') = \text{inl}(e \bowtie e')$

$\text{inl}(e) \bowtie \text{inr}(e') = \emptyset$

$\text{inr}(e) \bowtie \text{inl}(e') = \emptyset$

$(e_1 \otimes e_2) \bowtie (e_1' \otimes e_2') =$
$\qquad (e_1 \bowtie e_1') \otimes (e_2 \bowtie e_2')$

$(e_1 \mapsto e_2) \bowtie (e_1' \mapsto e_2') =$
$\qquad (e_1 \bowtie e_1') \mapsto (e_2 \bowtie e_2')$

$\langle e_1 \rangle \bowtie \langle e_2 \rangle = (\diamond(e_1 \backslash\!\backslash e_2))^{\perp}; \langle e_1 \rangle$

Possibility

$\diamond \emptyset = \bar{0}$

$\diamond(e_1 \parallel e_2) = \diamond e_1 \parallel \diamond e_2 \backslash\!\backslash \diamond e_1; \diamond e_2$
$\qquad \text{when } e_1 \bowtie e_2 = \emptyset$

$\diamond(e_1; e_2) = \diamond e_1; \diamond e_2$

$\diamond x = \bar{1}$

$\diamond a = \bar{1}$

$\diamond \bar{n} = \bar{1} \quad \text{when } n \neq \emptyset$

$\diamond \langle e \rangle = \bar{1}$

$\diamond \text{inl}(e) = \diamond e$

$\diamond \text{inr}(e) = \diamond e$

$\diamond(e_1 \otimes e_2) = \diamond e_1; \diamond e_2$

$\diamond(e_1 \mapsto e_2) = \diamond e_1; \diamond e_2$

$\diamond(\diamond e) = \diamond e$

Linearity

$([x : \tau]-)$, $(!-)$,

$\text{inl}(-) \text{ and } \text{inr}(-) \text{ are linear}$

$(-;-)$, $(--)$, $(- \bowtie -)$,

$(- \otimes -) \text{ and } (- \mapsto -) \text{ are bilinear}$

Fig. 5. Axiomatic semantics of Algeo.

As the 'standard model' we propose $\mathbb{Z}[\omega]$, i.e. polynomials over the integers in one variable ω. We define $\mathbf{dim}(\mathbf{Atom}) = \mathbf{dim}(\langle \tau \rangle) = \omega$ together with the equations above.

Most operations are defined to be either *linear* or *bilinear* (with the notable exceptions of $\diamond$ and $\langle - \rangle$). For an operation o this entails:

$$o(\emptyset) = \emptyset \qquad\qquad o([x : \tau]e) = [x : \tau]o(e)$$
$$o(e_1; e_2) = e_1; o(e_2) \qquad\qquad o(e_1 \parallel e_2) = o(e_1) \parallel o(e_2)$$

A binary operator $(- \odot -)$ is bilinear if both $(e_1 \odot -)$ and $(- \odot e_2)$ are linear.

3.3   Justification of the Semantics

All axioms are based on intuition from finite-dimensional types, i.e. types whose set of base values is finite. The idea is to extend this to infinite-dimensional types, but with a flavour of 'compactness' keeping the properties of finite-dimensionality. While it is possible to aggregate over infinite types, any given expression will only mention a finite number of distinct base values. We avoid contradiction arising from this approach by *not insisting* that every aggregation be reducible. For example, $[x : \langle \mathbf{Scalar} \rangle]!x$ has type $\mathbf{Scalar}$ but cannot be shown to be equal to any expression of the form $\bar{n}$; indeed, we cannot even establish whether it is zero or nonzero. This reveals a possible connection between Algeo and nonstandard analysis.

Most axioms should be uncontroversial, but some deserve elaboration. Perhaps the most unusual one is $[x : \tau]e = e^{x:=d} \setminus\!\!\setminus e^{x:=\emptyset} \parallel [y : \tau]e^{x:=y\setminus\!\!\setminus y \bowtie d}$. Usually we will exploit the equality $y \setminus\!\!\setminus y \bowtie d = y \bowtie d^{\perp}$ to get the rule $[x : \tau]e = e^{x:=d} \setminus\!\!\setminus e^{x:=\emptyset} \parallel [y : \tau]e^{x:=y\bowtie d^{\perp}}$. Firstly, note that d is only used in the substitutions, so some amount of prescience is required to choose a suitable d. The intuition is that we are splitting into cases depending on whether x is equal to d or not. To see how this works in the finite-dimensional case suppose $\tau = \mathbf{Scalar} \oplus \cdots \oplus \mathbf{Scalar}$ (n copies). Then τ has n distinct base values which we shall refer to as $b_1, \ldots, b_n$. The following reasoning shows how the statement can be shown directly from the other axioms in the finite case. A d of type τ will either be some b_i or $\emptyset$. Without loss of generality let $d = b_1$ (if $d = \emptyset$ the statement is trivial). We then have:

$$
\begin{aligned}
[x : \tau]e &= e^{x:=b_1} \parallel e^{x:=b_2} \parallel \ldots \parallel e^{x:=b_n} \\
&= e^{x:=b_1} \setminus\!\!\setminus e^{x:=\emptyset} \parallel e^{x:=\emptyset} \parallel e^{x:=b_2} \parallel \ldots \parallel e^{x:=b_n} \\
&= e^{x:=b_1} \setminus\!\!\setminus e^{x:=\emptyset} \parallel e^{x:=b_1 \bowtie b_1^{\perp}} \parallel e^{x:=b_2 \bowtie b_1^{\perp}} \parallel \ldots \parallel e^{x:=b_n \bowtie b_1^{\perp}} \\
&= e^{x:=b_1} \setminus\!\!\setminus e^{x:=\emptyset} \parallel [y : \tau]e^{x:=y \bowtie b_1^{\perp}}
\end{aligned}
$$

The possibility operator $\diamond e$ also deserves elaboration. The intuitive description (evaluate e and return $\bar{1}$ if it is not $\emptyset$) sounds similar to negation by failure (evaluate e and return $\bar{1}$ if it *is* $\emptyset$). However, $\diamond e$ is not defined operationally. It has rules for each data constructor as well as $\emptyset$, $\parallel$ and $(;)$, but it does not by itself make progress on e. For example, a subexpression like $\diamond(x \overset{\cdot}{=} y)$ does not simply succeed with a 'unification' of x and y. Rather, the case-split rule (discussed above) should be applied where either x or y is bound, making a global nondeterministic choice on whether x and y are equal.

The combination $(\diamond e)^{\perp}$ expresses the Algeo version of negation by failure. Compared to the usual notion in logic programming it is pure and not dependent on the evaluation strategy.

Finally, we mention $\langle e_1 \rangle \bowtie \langle e_2 \rangle = (\diamond(e_1 \setminus\!\!\setminus e_2))^{\perp}; \langle e_1 \rangle$ which describes how to resolve joins of bags. When comparing bags $\langle e_1 \rangle$ and $\langle e_2 \rangle$ we have to decide whether e_1 and e_2 are equal as Algeo expressions. That is the case precisely when $e_1 \setminus\!\!\setminus e_2 = \emptyset$. If $e_1 = e_2$ then $(\diamond(e_1 \setminus\!\!\setminus e_2))^{\perp} = \bar{1}$ and the whole right-hand side reduces to $\langle e_1 \rangle$ as expected. If $e_1 \neq e_2$ then the condition fails and the right-hand side reduces to $\emptyset$, again as expected.

This rule is the sole reason why $\diamond$ has to be in the language. The possibility operator could otherwise simply be defined as $\diamond e = (\langle e \rangle \doteq \langle \emptyset \rangle)^\perp$, but then the rule for bag joins would not actually make any progress.

3.4 Derived Equations and Evaluation

The semantic equations in Fig. 5 are not reduction rules, although most of them embody some kind of reduction when read from left to right. They can be used for evaluation as well as deriving new equations.

As an example of a derived equation consider $[x : \tau]x \bowtie b; e = e^{x:=b}$. This property states that if a variable is unconditionally subject to a join constraint with a base value, we may dispense with the variable and simply substitute that value. The main idea is to case-split on whether or not x equals b. The last line exploits that all base values are left identities for $(;)$.

$$[x : \tau]x \bowtie b; e = (x \bowtie b; e)^{x:=b} \setminus\!\setminus (x \bowtie b; e)^{x:=\emptyset} \| [y : \tau](x \bowtie b; e)^{x:=y\bowtie b^\perp}$$
$$= b \bowtie b; e^{x:=b} \setminus\!\setminus \emptyset \bowtie b; e^{x:=b} \| [y : \tau]y \bowtie b^\perp \bowtie b; e^{x:=b}$$
$$= b; e^{x:=b} \setminus\!\setminus \emptyset \| [y : \tau]\emptyset = b; e^{x:=b} = e^{x:=b}$$

A generalisation of this lemma suggests that, in the absence of bags, we can emulate the usual operational interpretation of logic programming where variables are instantiated based on unification constraints.

As an example of evaluation consider the problem of calculating how many pairs of atoms are equal and how many are unequal. Equality of x of y can be reified by putting it in a bag, i.e. $\langle x \doteq y \rangle$. The question can then be answered as follows, assuming the standard model where $\mathbf{dim}(\mathbf{Atom}) = \omega$.

$$[x : \mathbf{Atom}][y : \mathbf{Atom}]\langle x \doteq y \rangle$$
$$= [x : \mathbf{Atom}]\langle x \doteq y \rangle^{y:=x} \setminus\!\setminus \langle x \doteq y \rangle^{y:=\emptyset} \| ([z : \mathbf{Atom}]\langle x \doteq y \rangle^{y:=z\bowtie x^\perp})$$
$$= [x : \mathbf{Atom}]\langle x \doteq x \rangle \setminus\!\setminus \langle x \doteq \emptyset \rangle \| ([z : \mathbf{Atom}]\langle x \doteq z \bowtie x^\perp \rangle)$$
$$= [x : \mathbf{Atom}]\langle \overline{1} \rangle \setminus\!\setminus \langle \overline{0} \rangle \| ([z : \mathbf{Atom}]\langle \overline{0} \rangle)$$
$$= [x : \mathbf{Atom}]\langle \overline{1} \rangle \setminus\!\setminus \langle \overline{0} \rangle \| \overline{\mathbf{dim}(\mathbf{Atom})}; \langle \overline{0} \rangle$$
$$= ([x : \mathbf{Atom}]\langle \overline{1} \rangle) \setminus\!\setminus ([x : \mathbf{Atom}]\langle \overline{0} \rangle) \| ([x : \mathbf{Atom}]\overline{\mathbf{dim}(\mathbf{Atom})}; \langle \overline{0} \rangle)$$
$$= \overline{\mathbf{dim}(\mathbf{Atom})}; \langle \overline{1} \rangle \setminus\!\setminus \mathbf{dim}(\mathbf{Atom}); \langle \overline{0} \rangle \| \overline{\mathbf{dim}(\mathbf{Atom}) \cdot \mathbf{dim}(\mathbf{Atom})}; \langle \overline{0} \rangle$$
$$= \overline{\omega}; \langle \overline{1} \rangle \| \overline{\omega^2 - \omega}; \langle \overline{0} \rangle$$

Thus, we see that there are ω pairs of equal atoms and $\omega^2 - \omega$ unequal pairs. This corresponds well with the size of the diagonal and off-diagonal respectively of a hypothetical $\omega \times \omega$ matrix.

3.5   Relation to Linear Algebra

Many operations in Algeo are closely related to linear algebra, in particular K-algebras where K is the ring of elements of type **Scalar**. The correspondence can be seen in Fig. 6. Recall the common definition of the adjoint of f as the unique function $f^\dagger$ satisfying $\langle f(x) \mid y \rangle = \langle x \mid f^\dagger(y) \rangle$ for all x and y. Translating this to Algeo we might write it as $[\mathbf{x}][\mathbf{y}](\mathbf{f}\ \mathbf{x} \doteq \mathbf{y}) \doteq (\mathbf{x} \doteq \mathbf{f}^\dagger\ \mathbf{y})$, which turns out to be a perfectly good definition that is equivalent to our previous one. This gives a new perspective on what the inner product means in linear algebra.

0	$\emptyset$
$x + y$	$x \parallel y$
$n \cdot x$	$\overline{n}; x$
1	$*$
$x \cdot y$	$x \bowtie y$
$\langle x \mid y \rangle$	$x \doteq y$

Fig. 6. Linear algebra versus Algeo

4   Applications

Pattern Matching. The flexibility of Algeo definitions allows us to define functions in many ways. This clearly includes definition by cases using ordinary pattern matching, but further exploration reveals that many extensions of pattern matching can be encoded as well. Note that in Algeo a 'pattern' is nothing more than an expression written on the left-hand side of $\doteq$. Simple examples include $*$ functioning as a wildcard, and definitions in general functioning as pattern synonyms. We list a number of common pattern matching features below along with their representation in Algeo.

- Functional patterns. These are written just like in Curry. For example, suppose $\mathbf{f}$ is defined by $\mathbf{f}\ (\mathbf{g}\ x) \doteq e$. When $\mathbf{f}$ is applied to some e', effectively $\mathbf{g}$ will be run in reverse on e' and x bound to each result.
- View patterns. There is a Haskell extension providing patterns of the form $(f \Rightarrow p)$, which matches a value v if p matches $f\ v$. This syntax is definable as a function in Algeo:

$$(\Rightarrow) : (\tau \to \tau') \to \tau' \to \tau$$
$$\mathbf{f} \Rightarrow \mathbf{p} \doteq (\mathbf{f}\ \mathbf{v} \doteq \mathbf{p}; \mathbf{v})$$

This is effectively a functional pattern where the function is run in reverse.
- Guard patterns. Some functional languages allow pattern guards like $\mathbf{f}\ p \mid c$ where the interpretation is that p is matched and then the boolean condition c is checked. Algeo, like any other logic language, can of course include conditions (i.e. expressions of type **Scalar**) in the body of a function. However, the flexibility of definitions means that we can write $\mathbf{f}\ (c; p)$ to signify that we consider the condition c to be part of the pattern.
- Alias patterns. Many functional languages support patterns like x **as** p where x is bound to the value matched by the entire pattern p. In Algeo the $\bowtie$ operator furnishes a much more general version of this. A pattern like $e_1 \bowtie e_2$ matches e_1 and e_2 simultaneously. When e_1 is a variable this encodes an alias pattern.

– Alternative patterns. Some languages allow patterns like $(p_1 \mid p_2)$ where p_1 and p_2 are nullary constructors. This is interpreted as equivalent to writing two clauses, one with p_1 and one with p_2. In Algeo any two patterns can be combined using $\|$. By linearity $\mathbf{f}\ (e_1 \parallel e_2) \ \hat{=}\ e$ means exactly the same as $\mathbf{f}\ e_1 \ \hat{=}\ e \parallel \mathbf{f}\ e_2 \ \hat{=}\ e$.

– Negative patterns. Generally pattern matching is positive in the sense that patterns describe the shape of the data that we want to match. Matching everything except for some given pattern is typically done with a final default case; this works in functional languages where patterns are ordered and pattern matching works by finding the first match only. Algeo can describe negative patterns directly. Recall that $e^{\perp} = * \parallel e$ for any expression e. As a pattern this can be interpreted as 'everything except e'. For example, deciding equality between two values can be defined as follows:

$$\mathbf{eq?} : \tau \to \tau \to \mathbf{Scalar} \oplus \mathbf{Scalar}$$
$$\mathbf{eq?}\ \mathbf{x}\ \mathbf{x} \ \hat{=}\ \mathbf{inl}(\bar{1})$$
$$\mathbf{eq?}\ \mathbf{x}\ \mathbf{x}^{\perp} \ \hat{=}\ \mathbf{inr}(\bar{1})$$

Linear Algebra. Given that Algeo is built on linear algebra, it will likely come as no surprise that expressing problems from linear algebra is often straightforward. An example of this is matrix multiplication. Given an $m \times n$ matrix A with entries a_{ij}, and a $n \times p$ matrix B with entries b_{ij}, the entries in the $n \times p$ matrix $C = AB$ are given by $c_{ij} = \sum_{k=1}^{n} a_{ik} b_{kj}$, i.e., summing over all possible ways of going first via A and then via B. In Algeo, a matrix from τ_1 to τ_2 is a value of type $\tau_1 \otimes \tau_2$ (i.e., a weighted sum of pairs of base values of τ_1 and τ_2), and their multiplication is expressed as

$$(\cdot) : \tau_1 \otimes \tau_2 \to \tau_2 \otimes \tau_3 \to \tau_1 \otimes \tau_3$$
$$(x \otimes y) \cdot (y \otimes z) \ \hat{=}\ x \otimes z$$

where the implicit aggregation over y corresponds to the summation over k in the definition of c_{ij} from before. Another example is the trace (or sum of diagonal elements) of a square $n \times n$ matrix, $\mathrm{tr}(A) = \sum_{n=1} a_{nn}$, which can be slightly cryptically defined without a right hand side:

$$\mathbf{tr} : (\tau \otimes \tau) \to \mathbf{Scalar}$$
$$\mathbf{tr}\ (x \otimes x)$$

Again, note how the implicit aggregation over x corresponds to summation in the definition from linear algebra.

A much more involved example is (unnormalised) operator diagonalisation, i.e., the representation of an operator F as a composition $F = U^{-1} \circ D \circ U$, where U is an isomorphism, and D is diagonal. We specify this by describing the constraints: U must be an isomorphism, so $U^{-1} \circ U = \mathrm{id}$ and $U \circ U^{-1} = \mathrm{id}$; D must be diagonal, meaning that joining it with the identity should have no effect; and the composition of $U^{-1} \circ D \circ U$ should be F. In Algeo, this becomes

$$\textbf{diagonalise} : \langle \tau \to \tau \rangle \to \langle \tau \to \tau \rangle \otimes \langle \tau \to \tau \rangle \otimes \langle \tau \to \tau \rangle$$
$$\textbf{diagonalise f} \equiv \textbf{u} \otimes \textbf{d} \otimes \textbf{v};$$
$$\langle !\textbf{u} \circ !\textbf{v} \rangle \equiv \langle \textbf{id} \rangle;$$
$$\langle !\textbf{v} \circ !\textbf{u} \rangle \equiv \langle \textbf{id} \rangle;$$
$$\langle !\textbf{d} \bowtie \textbf{id} \rangle \equiv \textbf{d};$$
$$\langle !\textbf{u} \circ !\textbf{d} \circ !\textbf{v} \rangle \equiv \textbf{f}$$

Notice that this is only slightly different than usual diagonalisation, in that this will find diagonalisations for eigenvectors scaled arbitrarily, rather than (as usual) only of length 1.

Polysets and Polylogic. Polysets [8] are a generalisation of multisets which also permit elements to occur a *negative* number of times. This is useful for representing, e.g., (possibly unsynchronised) database states, with elements with *positive* multiplicity representing (pending) data insertions, and elements with *negative* multiplicity representing (pending) data deletions.

Polysets can be represented in Algeo via *polylogic*, an account of propositional logic relying on multiplicities of *evidence* and *counterexamples* (similar to *decisions* as in [15]). Concretely, a truth value in polylogic consists of an amount of evidence (injected to the left) and an amount of counterexamples (injected to the right). For example, $\perp$ has no evidence and a single counterexample, and dually for $\top$, as in

$$\perp, \top \; : \; \textbf{Scalar} \oplus \textbf{Scalar}$$
$$\perp = \emptyset \oplus *$$
$$\top = * \oplus \emptyset$$

As in [15], negation swaps evidence for counterexamples and vice versa, while the evidence of a conjunction is the join of the evidence of its conjuncts, with everything else counterexamples (disjunction dually):

$$\neg(e \oplus e') = e' \oplus e$$
$$(e_1 \oplus e_1') \wedge (e_2 \oplus e_2') = (e_1 \bowtie e_2) \oplus (e_1 \bowtie e_2' \parallel e_1' \bowtie e_2 \parallel e_1' \bowtie e_2')$$
$$(e_1 \oplus e_1') \vee (e_2 \oplus e_2') = (e_1 \bowtie e_2 \parallel e_1 \bowtie e_2' \parallel e_1' \bowtie e_2) \oplus (e_1' \bowtie e_2')$$

A polyset over τ is represented by the type $\tau \oplus \tau$, with all the above definitions generalising directly. That is, a value of this type is an aggregation of evidence (with multiplicity) either for or against each base value of τ. In this way, we can interpret a finite set $\{d_1, \ldots, d_k\}$ by the expression $(d_1 \oplus d_1^{\perp}) \vee \cdots \vee (d_k \oplus d_k^{\perp})$. Note that in this calculus $\vee$ and $\wedge$ form a lattice-esque structure as opposed to $\parallel$ and $\bowtie$, which form a ring structure.

5   Related Work

Algebraic λ-calculi. A related approach to computing with linear algebra is the idea of extending the λ-calculus with linear combinations of terms [2,22], though such approaches do not provide generalised reversibility in the form of adjoints. Extending the λ-calculus in this way is a delicate ordeal that easily leads to collapse (e.g. $\overline{0} = \overline{1}$) from interactions between sums and fixpoints. Algeo evades these problems by taking a different view of functions, namely that base elements of type $\tau_1 \to \tau_2$ are $b_1 \mapsto b_2$ where b_1 and b_2 are base elements, and function application is linear in *both* arguments (this approach was briefly considered in [2] and discarded due to wanting a strict extension of untyped λ-calculus).

It is possible in Algeo to define an abstraction $\lambda x.e$ as syntactic sugar for $[\widehat{x} : \langle \tau_1 \rangle]\widehat{x} \mapsto e^{x := !\widehat{x}}$ of type $\langle \tau_1 \rangle \to \tau_2$. The input must be a bag type to model the nonlinearity of function application in algebraic λ-calculi. However, the fixpoint-esque operators definable in Algeo have different semantics than in standard λ-calculus and do not allow the kind of infinite unfolding that so easily leads to paradoxes. The simplest such operator is **fix** $: (\tau \to \tau) \to \tau$ defined by **fix** $(\mathbf{x} \mapsto \mathbf{x}) \stackrel{\cdot}{=} \mathbf{x}$, which is just a repackaged version of ⋈. To get something approaching the usual concept of fixpoint we again need bags:

$$\mathbf{fix} : \langle \tau \to \tau \rangle \to \tau \qquad\qquad \mathbf{fix\ f} \stackrel{\cdot}{=} !\mathbf{f}\ (!\widehat{\mathbf{fix}}\ \mathbf{f})$$

Even ignoring the bag operations **fix** is not a fixpoint combinator in the λ-calculus sense since **fix** $e = !e\ (!\widehat{\mathbf{fix}}\ e)$ does not hold in general when e is a not a base value. We can try to create a paradox by considering e.g. $e = \mathbf{fix}\ \langle [\mathbf{x} : \tau]\mathbf{x} \mapsto \overline{-1}; \mathbf{x}\rangle$. It is indeed the case that $e = (\overline{-1}; e)$ and therefore that $e = 0$, but this only emphasises what we already know: that Algeo is powerful enough to express arbitrary constraints and that recognising 0 is uncomputable in general.

Reversible and Functional Logic Programming. The functional logic paradigm of programming was pioneered by languages such as Curry [1,6] and Mercury [21]. Along with reversible functional programming languages such as Rfun [23], Core-Fun [12], and Theseus [14], they have served as inspiration for the design of Algeo. Unlike Algeo, neither of the conventional functional logic programming languages come with an explicit notion of multiplicity and the added benefits in expressing data of a probabilistic, fractional, or an "inverse" nature, nor do they have adjoints. On the other hand, while the reversible functional languages all have a notion of inversion, their execution models and notions of reversibility differ significantly from those found in Algeo.

Modules, Databases, and Query Languages. Free modules can be seen as a form of generalised multisets. When permitting negative multiplicities, this allows the representation of database table schemas as (certain) free modules, tables as vectors of these free module, and linear maps as operations (e.g., insertion, deletion, search, aggregation, joins, and much more) acting on these tables. The structural theory of modules that led to the development of Algeo, and its relation to database representation and querying, is described in [8].

Abstract Stone Duality. Abstract Stone duality (see, e.g., [3]) is a synthetic approach to topology and analysis inspired by Stone's famous duality theorem between categories of certain topological spaces and certain order structures. An interesting feature of abstract Stone duality is that it permits the indirect definition of numbers from a description (i.e., a predicate) via a method known simply as *definition by description*, provided that it can be shown that a description is true for exactly one number. This is not unlike the indirect description of terms in Algeo, though instead of requiring descriptions to be unique, the result of an indirect description in Algeo is instead the *aggregation* over all terms satisfying this description.

6 Conclusion and Future Work

We have presented the reversible functional logic programming language Algeo, described its syntax and type system, and given it semantics in the form of a system of equations. We have illustrated the use of Algeo through applications and examples, and described applications in areas such as database querying and logic programming with an improved notion of negation.

As regards avenues for future research, we consider developing an implementation based on this work to be a logical next step. However, this is not as trivial as it may appear at first glance, as it requires the development of strategies for performing nontrivial rewriting using the equational theory. In particular, we don't believe that there is an obvious optimal evaluation strategy for Algeo, as it would have to optimally solve all expressible problems (e.g., matrix diagonalisation, three-way joins).

An extension to Algeo not considered here is that of *dual types*, reflecting the notion of *dual* modules and vector spaces in linear algebra. To include these would permit Algeo to use multiplicities in the complex numbers, in turn paving the way for using Algeo to express quantum algorithms.

We would also find it interesting to use Algeo to study polylogic (as described in Sect. 4), in particular its use as a reasonable semantics for negation not involving the impure and unsatisfying negation-as-failure known from Prolog. Finally, since Algeo permits aggregating over infinite collections of values, it seems that there is at least some connection to nonstandard analysis and linear algebra (see also [5]) which could be interesting to elaborate. In fact, permitting the use of nonstandard real (or complex) numbers as multiplicities would allow automatic differentiation (see [4] for a recent, combinatory approach to automatic differentiation on Hilbert spaces) to be specified in an exceedingly compact manner, which could lead to further applications in machine learning and optimization.

References

1. Antoy, S., Hanus, M.: Functional logic programming. Commun. ACM **53**(4), 74–85 (2010)
2. Arrighi, P., Dowek, G.: Linear-algebraic λ-calculus: higher-order, encodings, and confluence. In: Voronkov, A. (ed.) RTA 2008. LNCS, vol. 5117, pp. 17–31. Springer, Heidelberg (2008). https://doi.org/10.1007/978-3-540-70590-1_2
3. Bauer, A., Taylor, P.: The Dedekind reals in abstract Stone duality. Math. Struct. Comput. Sci. **19**(4), 757–838 (2009)
4. Elsman, M., Henglein, F., Kaarsgaard, R., Mathiesen, M.K., Schenck, R.: Combinatory adjoints and differentiation. Accepted for Ninth Workshop on Mathematically Structured Functional Programming (MSFP 2022) (2022, to appear)
5. Gogioso, S., Genovese, F.: Infinite-dimensional categorical quantum mechanics. In: Duncan, R., Heunen, C. (eds.) Proceedings 13th International Conference on Quantum Physics and Logic (QPL 2016). Electronic Proceedings in Theoretical Computer Science, vol. 236. OSA (2016)
6. Hanus, M.: Functional logic programming: from theory to curry. In: Voronkov, A., Weidenbach, C. (eds.) Programming Logics. LNCS, vol. 7797, pp. 123–168. Springer, Heidelberg (2013). https://doi.org/10.1007/978-3-642-37651-1_6
7. Hay-Schmidt, L., Glück, R., Cservenka, M.H., Haulund, T.: Towards a unified language architecture for reversible object-oriented programming. In: Yamashita, S., Yokoyama, T. (eds.) RC 2021. LNCS, vol. 12805, pp. 96–106. Springer, Cham (2021). https://doi.org/10.1007/978-3-030-79837-6_6
8. Henglein, F., Kaarsgaard, R., Mathiesen, M.K.: The programming of algebra. Accepted for Ninth Workshop on Mathematically Structured Functional Programming (MSFP 2022) (2022, to appear)
9. Heunen, C., Kaarsgaard, R.: Bennett and Stinespring, together at last. In: Proceedings 18th International Conference on Quantum Physics and Logic (QPL 2021). Electronic Proceedings in Theoretical Computer Science, vol. 343, pp. 102–118. OPA (2021)
10. Heunen, C., Kaarsgaard, R.: Quantum information effects. Proc. ACM Program. Lang. **6**(POPL) (2022)
11. Hoey, J., Ulidowski, I.: Reversible imperative parallel programs and debugging. In: Thomsen, M.K., Soeken, M. (eds.) RC 2019. LNCS, vol. 11497, pp. 108–127. Springer, Cham (2019). https://doi.org/10.1007/978-3-030-21500-2_7
12. Jacobsen, P.A.H., Kaarsgaard, R., Thomsen, M.K.: CoreFun: a typed functional reversible core language. In: Kari, J., Ulidowski, I. (eds.) RC 2018. LNCS, vol. 11106, pp. 304–321. Springer, Cham (2018). https://doi.org/10.1007/978-3-319-99498-7_21
13. James, R.P., Sabry, A.: Information effects. ACM SIGPLAN Not. **47**(1), 73–84 (2012)
14. James, R.P., Sabry, A.: Theseus: a high level language for reversible computing (2014). https://www.cs.indiana.edu/~sabry/papers/theseus.pdf. Work-in-progress report
15. Kaarsgaard, R.: Condition/decision duality and the internal logic of extensive restriction categories. In: Proceedings of the Thirty-Fifth Conference on the Mathematical Foundations of Programming Semantics (MFPS XXXV). Electronic Notes in Theoretical Computer Science, vol. 347, pp. 179–202. Elsevier (2019)

16. Lanese, I., Nishida, N., Palacios, A., Vidal, G.: CauDEr: a causal-consistent reversible debugger for erlang. In: Gallagher, J.P., Sulzmann, M. (eds.) FLOPS 2018. LNCS, vol. 10818, pp. 247–263. Springer, Cham (2018). https://doi.org/10.1007/978-3-319-90686-7_16

17. Nishida, N., Palacios, A., Vidal, G.: A reversible semantics for erlang. In: Hermenegildo, M.V., Lopez-Garcia, P. (eds.) LOPSTR 2016. LNCS, vol. 10184, pp. 259–274. Springer, Cham (2017). https://doi.org/10.1007/978-3-319-63139-4_15

18. Sabry, A., Valiron, B., Vizzotto, J.K.: From symmetric pattern-matching to quantum control. In: Baier, C., Dal Lago, U. (eds.) FoSSaCS 2018. LNCS, vol. 10803, pp. 348–364. Springer, Cham (2018). https://doi.org/10.1007/978-3-319-89366-2_19

19. Schordan, M., Jefferson, D., Barnes, P., Oppelstrup, T., Quinlan, D.: Reverse code generation for parallel discrete event simulation. In: Krivine, J., Stefani, J.-B. (eds.) RC 2015. LNCS, vol. 9138, pp. 95–110. Springer, Cham (2015). https://doi.org/10.1007/978-3-319-20860-2_6

20. Schultz, U.P., Laursen, J.S., Ellekilde, L.-P., Axelsen, H.B.: Towards a domain-specific language for reversible assembly sequences. In: Krivine, J., Stefani, J.-B. (eds.) RC 2015. LNCS, vol. 9138, pp. 111–126. Springer, Cham (2015). https://doi.org/10.1007/978-3-319-20860-2_7

21. Somogyi, Z., Henderson, F., Conway, T.: The execution algorithm of Mercury, an efficient purely declarative logic programming language. J. Log. Program. **29**(1), 17–64 (1996)

22. Vaux, L.: The algebraic lambda calculus. Mathe. Struct. Comp. Sci. **19**(5), 1029–1059 (2009). https://doi.org/10.1017/S0960129509990089

23. Yokoyama, T., Axelsen, H.B., Glück, R.: Towards a reversible functional language. In: De Vos, A., Wille, R. (eds.) RC 2011. LNCS, vol. 7165, pp. 14–29. Springer, Heidelberg (2012). https://doi.org/10.1007/978-3-642-29517-1_2

24. Yokoyama, T., Glück, R.: A reversible programming language and its invertible self-interpreter. In: Partial Evaluation and Program Manipulation. Proceedings, pp. 144–153. ACM (2007)

Concurrencies in Reversible Concurrent Calculi

Clément Aubert[✉][iD]

School of Computer and Cyber Sciences, Augusta University, Augusta, USA
caubert@augusta.edu
https://spots.augusta.edu/caubert/

Abstract. The algebraic specification and representation of networks of agents have been greatly impacted by the study of reversible phenomena: reversible declensions of the calculus of communicating systems (CCSK and RCCS) offer new semantic models, finer congruence relations, original properties, and revisits existing theories and results in a finer light. But much remains to be done: concurrency, a central notion in establishing *causal consistency*–a crucial property for reversible systems–, was never given a syntactical definition in CCSK. We remedy this gap by leveraging a definition of concurrency developed for forward-only calculi using proved transition systems, and prove that CCSK still enjoys causal consistency for this elegant and syntactical notion of reversible concurrency. We also compare it to a definition of concurrency inspired by reversible π-calculus, discuss its relation with structural congruence, and prove that it can be adapted to any CCS-inspired reversible system and is equivalent—or refines—existing definitions of concurrency for those systems.

Keywords: Formal semantics · Process algebras · Concurrency

1 Introduction: Reversibility, Concurrency–Interplays

Concurrency Theory is being reshaped by reversibility: fine distinctions between causality and causation [37] contradicted Milner's expansion laws [30, Example 4.11], and the study of causal models for reversible computation led to novel correction criteria for causal semantics—both reversible and irreversible [17]. "Traditional" equivalence relations have been captured syntactically [6], while original observational equivalences were developed [30]: reversibility triggered a global reconsideration of established theories and tools, with the clear intent of providing actionable methods for reversible systems [26], novel axiomatic foundations [31] and original non-interleaving models [4,17,24].

Two Formalisms extend the Calculus of Communicating Systems (CCS) [34]—the godfather of π-calculus [38], among others—with reversible features. Reversible CCS (RCCS) [18] and CCS with keys (CCSK) [37] are similarly the source of most [1,17,32,33]—if not all—of later formalism developed to

C. A. Mezzina and K. Podlaski (Eds.): RC 2022, LNCS 13354, pp. 146–163, 2022.
https://doi.org/10.1007/978-3-031-09005-9_10

enhance reversible systems with some respect (rollback operator, name-passing abilities, probabilistic features, ...). Even if those two systems share a lot of similarities [28], they diverge in some respects that are not fully understood—typically, it seems that different notions of "contexts with history" led to establish the existence of congruences for CCSK [30, Proposition 4.9] or the impossibility thereof for RCCS [8, Theorem 2]. However, they also share some shortcomings, and we offer to tackle one of them for CCSK, by providing a syntactical definition of concurrency, easy to manipulate, that satisfies the usual sanity checks.

Reversible Concurrency is of course a central notion in the study of RCCS and CCSK, as it enables the definition of causal consistency—a principle that, intuitively, states that backward reductions can undo an action only if its consequences have already been undone—and to obtain models where concurrency and causation are decorrelated [37]. As such, it has been studied from multiple angles, but, in our opinion, never in a fully satisfactory manner. In CCSK, sideways and reverse diamonds properties were proven using conditions on keys and "joinable" transitions [37, Propositions 5.10 and 5.19], but to our knowledge no "definitive" definition of concurrency was proposed. Ad-hoc definitions relying on memory inclusion [25, Definition 3.1.1] or disjointness [18, Definition 7] for RCCS, and semantical notions for both RCCS [4–6] and CCSK [24,36,40] have been proposed, but, to our knowledge, none of those have ever been 1. compared to each other, 2. compared to pre-existing forward-only definitions of concurrency.

Our Contribution introduces the first syntactical definition of concurrency for CCSK (Sect. 3.1), by extending the "universal" concurrency developed for forward-only CCS [19], that leveraged *proved* transition systems [22]. We make crucial use of the loop lemma (Lemma 5) to define concurrency between coinitial traces in terms of concurrency between composable traces—a mechanism that considerably reduces the definition and proof burdens: typically, the square property is derived from the sideways and reverse diamonds. We furthermore establish the correctness of this definition by proving the expected reversible properties—causal consistency (Sect. 3.3), among others—and by discussing how our definition relates to definitions of concurrency in similar systems—obtained by porting our technique to RCCS [18,25] and its "identified" declensions [8], or by restricting a notion of concurrency for π-calculus—and to structural congruence (Sect. 4). With respect to this last point, we prove that our technique gives a notion of concurrency that either match or subsumes existing definitions, that sometimes lack a notion of concurrency for transitions of opposite directions.

Additional details are contained in our preliminary technical report [3], i.e. all proofs [3, Sect. B], and the technical justification of the claims made in Sect. 4 about the "universality" of our approach [3, Sect. C].

2 Finite and Reversible Process Calculi

2.1 Finite, Forward-Only CCS

Finite Core CCS. We briefly recall the (forward-only) "finite fragment" of the core of CCS (simply called CCS) following a standard presentation [14].

Definition 1 ((Co-)names and labels). *Let* $\mathsf{N} = \{a, b, c, \dots\}$ *be a set of names and* $\overline{\mathsf{N}} = \{\overline{a}, \overline{b}, \overline{c}, \dots\}$ *its set of* co-names. *The set of* labels L *is* $\mathsf{N} \cup \overline{\mathsf{N}} \cup \{\tau\}$, *and we use* α, β *(resp.* λ*) to range over* L *(resp.* $\mathsf{L}\backslash\{\tau\}$*). A bijection* $\overline{\cdot} : \mathsf{N} \to \overline{\mathsf{N}}$, *whose inverse is also written* $\overline{\cdot}$, *gives the* complement *of a name.*

Definition 2 (Operators). *We let* P, Q *range over CCS processes, defined as usual, using restriction* $(P\backslash\alpha)$, *sum* $(P + Q)$, *prefix* $(\alpha.P)$ *and parallel composition* $(P \mid Q)$. *The inactive process* 0 *is omitted when preceded by a prefix, and the binding power of the operators [34, p. 68], from highest to lowest, is* $\backslash\alpha$, $\alpha.$, $\mid$ *and* $+$, *so that e.g.* $\alpha.P + Q\backslash\alpha \mid P + a$ *is to be read as* $(\alpha.P) + (((Q\backslash\alpha) \mid P) + (a.0))$. *In a process* $P \mid Q$ *(resp.* $P + Q$*), we call* P *and* Q threads *(resp.* branches*).*

The labeled transition system for CCS, denoted $\xrightarrow{\alpha}$, is reminded in Fig. 1.

Action and Restriction

$$\frac{}{\alpha.P \xrightarrow{\alpha} P} \text{ act.} \qquad\qquad \alpha \notin \{a, \overline{a}\} \quad \frac{P \xrightarrow{\alpha} P'}{P\backslash a \xrightarrow{\alpha} P'\backslash a} \text{ res.}$$

Parallel Group

$$\frac{P \xrightarrow{\alpha} P'}{P \mid Q \xrightarrow{\alpha} P' \mid Q} \mid_{\mathrm{L}} \qquad \frac{P \xrightarrow{\lambda} P' \quad Q \xrightarrow{\overline{\lambda}} Q'}{P \mid Q \xrightarrow{\tau} P' \mid Q'} \text{ syn.} \qquad \frac{Q \xrightarrow{\alpha} Q'}{P \mid Q \xrightarrow{\alpha} P \mid Q'} \mid_{\mathrm{R}}$$

Sum Group

$$\frac{P \xrightarrow{\alpha} P'}{Q + P \xrightarrow{\alpha} P'} +_{\mathrm{L}} \qquad\qquad \frac{Q \xrightarrow{\alpha} Q'}{Q + P \xrightarrow{\alpha} Q'} +_{\mathrm{R}}$$

Fig. 1. Rules of the labeled transition system (LTS) for CCS

2.2 CCSK: A "Keyed" Reversible Concurrent Calculus

CCSK captures uncontrolled reversibility using two symmetric LTS—one for forward computation, one for backward computation—that manipulates *keys* marking executed prefixes, to guarantee that reverting synchronizations cannot be done without both parties agreeing. We use the syntax of the latest paper on the topic [30], that slightly differs [30, Remark 4.2] with the classical definition [37]. However, those changes have no impact since we refrain from using CCSK's newly introduced structural congruence, but discuss it in Sect. 4.

Definition 3 (Keys, prefixes and CCSK processes). *Let* $\mathsf{K} = \{m, n, \dots\}$ *be a set of* keys, *we let* k *range over them. Prefixes are of the form* $\alpha[k]$—*we call them* keyed labels—*or* α. *CCSK processes are CCS processes where the prefix can also be of the form* $\alpha[k]$, *we let* X, Y *range over them.*

The forward LTS for CCSK, that we denote $\xrightarrow{\alpha[k]}$, is given in Fig. 2—with key and std defined below. The reverse LTS $\xrightarrow{\alpha[k]}\!\!\!\!\!\rightsquigarrow$ is the exact symmetric of $\xrightarrow{\alpha[k]}$ [30, Figure 2] (it can also be read from Fig. 3), and we write $X \xrightarrow{\alpha[k]}\!\!\!\!\!\rightsquigarrow Y$ if $X \xrightarrow{\alpha[k]}\!\!\!\!\!\rightsquigarrow Y$ or $X \xrightarrow{\alpha[k]} Y$. For all three types of arrows, we sometimes omit the label and keys when they are not relevant, and mark with * their transitive closures. As usual, we restrict ourselves to reachable processes, defined below.

Definition 4 (Standard and reachable processes). *The set of keys occuring in* X *is written* $\mathrm{key}(X)$, *and* X *is standard*—$\mathrm{std}(X)$—*iff* $\mathrm{key}(X) = \emptyset$. *If there exists a process* O_X *s.t.* $\mathrm{std}(O_X)$ *and* $O_X \longrightarrow^* X$, *then* X *is reachable.*

The reader eager to see this system in action can fast-forward to Example 1, but should be aware that this example uses proved labels, introduced next.

Action, Prefix and Restriction

$$\mathrm{std}(X) \; \frac{}{\alpha.X \xrightarrow{\alpha[k]} \alpha[k].X} \; \text{act.} \qquad\qquad k \neq k' \; \frac{X \xrightarrow{\beta[k]} X'}{\alpha[k'].X \xrightarrow{\beta[k]} \alpha[k'].X'} \; \text{pre.}$$

$$\alpha \notin \{a, \overline{a}\} \; \frac{X \xrightarrow{\alpha[k]} X'}{X\backslash a \xrightarrow{\alpha[k]} X'\backslash a} \; \text{res.}$$

Parallel Group

$$k \notin \mathrm{key}(Y) \; \frac{X \xrightarrow{\alpha[k]} X'}{X \mid Y \xrightarrow{\alpha[k]} X' \mid Y} \; |_{\mathrm{L}} \qquad\qquad k \notin \mathrm{key}(X) \; \frac{Y \xrightarrow{\alpha[k]} Y'}{X \mid Y \xrightarrow{\alpha[k]} X \mid Y'} \; |_{\mathrm{R}}$$

$$\frac{X \xrightarrow{\lambda[k]} X' \quad Y \xrightarrow{\overline{\lambda}[k]} Y'}{X \mid Y \xrightarrow{\tau[k]} X' \mid Y'} \; \text{syn.}$$

Sum Group

$$\mathrm{std}(Y) \; \frac{X \xrightarrow{\alpha[k]} X'}{X + Y \xrightarrow{\alpha[k]} X' + Y} \; +_{\mathrm{L}} \qquad \mathrm{std}(X) \; \frac{Y \xrightarrow{\alpha[k]} Y'}{X + Y \xrightarrow{\alpha[k]} X + Y'} \; +_{\mathrm{R}}$$

Fig. 2. Rules of the forward labeled transition system (LTS) for CCSK

3   A New Causal Semantics for CCSK

The only causal semantics for CCS with replication we are aware of [19][1] remained unnoticed, despite some interesting qualities: 1. it enables the definition of causality for replication while agreeing with pre-existing causal semantics of CCS and CCS with recursion [19, Theorem 1] 2. it leverages the technique of *proved* transition systems that encodes information about the derivation in the labels [22], 3. it was instrumental in one of the first results connecting implicit computational complexity and distributed processes [23], 4. last but not least, as we will see below, it allows to define an elegant notion of causality for CCSK with "built-in" reversibility, as *the exact same definition will be used for forward and backward transitions*, without making explicit mentions of the keys or directions. We believe our choice is additionally compact, elegant and suited for reversible computation: defining concurrency on composable transitions first allows *not* to consider keys in our definition, as the LTS guarantees that the same key will not be re-used. *Then*, the loop lemma allows to "reverse" transitions so that concurrency on coinitial transitions can be defined from concurrency on composable transitions. This allows to carry little information in the labels—the direction is not needed—and to have a definition insensitive to keys and identifiers for the very modest cost of prefixing labels with some annotation tracking the thread(s) or branch(es) performing the transition.

3.1   Proved Labeled Transition System for CCSK

We adapt the proved transition system [15,19,20] to CCSK: this technique enriches the transitions label with prefixes that describe parts of their derivation, to keep track of their dependencies or lack thereof. We adapt an earlier formalism [21]—including information about sums [19, footnote 2]—but extend the concurrency relation to internal (i.e. τ-) transitions, omitted from recent work [19, Definition 3] but present in older articles [15, Definition 2.3].

Definition 5 (Enhanced keyed labels). *Let* v, v_{L} *and* v_{R} *range over strings in* $\{|_{\mathrm{L}}, |_{\mathrm{R}}, +_{\mathrm{L}}, +_{\mathrm{R}}\}^*$, *enhanced keyed labels are defined as*

$$\theta := v\alpha[k] \ \| \ v\langle|_{\mathrm{L}} \ v_{\mathrm{L}}\alpha[k], |_{\mathrm{R}} \ v_{\mathrm{R}}\overline{\alpha}[k]\rangle$$

We write E *the set of enhanced keyed labels, and define* $\ell : \mathsf{E} \to \mathsf{L}$ *and* $\Bbbk : \mathsf{E} \to \mathsf{K}$:

$$\ell(v\alpha[k]) = \alpha \qquad\qquad \ell(v\langle|_{\mathrm{L}} \ v_{\mathrm{L}}\alpha[k], |_{\mathrm{R}} \ v_{\mathrm{R}}\overline{\alpha}[k]\rangle) = \tau$$
$$\Bbbk(v\alpha[k]) = k \qquad\qquad \Bbbk(v\langle|_{\mathrm{L}} \ v_{\mathrm{L}}\alpha[k], |_{\mathrm{R}} \ v_{\mathrm{R}}\overline{\alpha}[k]\rangle) = k$$

We present in Fig. 3 the rules for the *proved* forward and backward LTS for CCSK. The rules $|_{\mathrm{R}}$, $|_{\mathrm{R}}^{\bullet}$, $+_{\mathrm{R}}$ and $+_{\mathrm{R}}^{\bullet}$ are omitted but can easily be inferred. This LTS has its derivation in bijection with CCSK's original LTS:

---

[1] We preferred to refer to this work over older presentations [12,13] to be better equipped to later on accommodate replication for reversible calculi [2].

Lemma 1 (Adequacy of the proved labeled transition system). *The transition* $X \xrightarrow{\alpha[m]} X'$ *can be derived using Fig. 2 iff* $X \xrightarrow{\theta} X'$ *with* $\mathscr{k}(\theta) = m$ *and* $\ell(\theta) = \alpha$ *can be derived using Fig. 3.*

Definition 6 (Dependency relation). *The* dependency relation *on enhanced keyed labels is induced by the axioms of Fig. 4, for* $d \in \{\mathrm{L}, \mathrm{R}\}$.

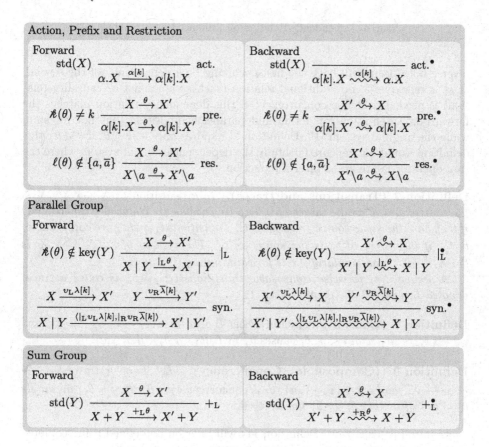

Fig. 3. Rules of the *proved* LTS for CCSK

A dependency $\theta_0 \lessdot \theta_1$ means "whenever there is a trace in which θ_0 occurs before θ_1, then the two associated transitions are causally related". The following definitions will enable more formal examples, but we can stress that 1. the "action" rule enforces that executing or reversing a prefix at top level, e.g. $\alpha.X \xrightarrow{\alpha[k]} \alpha[k].X$ or $\alpha[k].X \overset{\alpha[k]}{\rightsquigarrow} \alpha.X$, makes the prefix $(\alpha[k])$ a dependency of all further transitions; 2. as the forward and backward versions of the same rule share the same enhanced keyed labels, a trace where a transition and its

Action
$\alpha[k] \lessdot \theta$

Palallel Group	
$\vert_d \theta \lessdot \vert_d \theta'$	if $\theta \lessdot \theta'$
$\langle \theta_{\mathrm{L}}, \theta_{\mathrm{R}} \rangle \lessdot \theta$	if $\exists d$ s.t. $\theta_d \lessdot \theta$
$\theta \lessdot \langle \theta_{\mathrm{L}}, \theta_{\mathrm{R}} \rangle$	if $\exists d$ s.t. $\theta \lessdot \theta_d$
$\langle \theta_{\mathrm{L}}, \theta_{\mathrm{R}} \rangle \lessdot \langle \theta'_{\mathrm{L}}, \theta'_{\mathrm{R}} \rangle$	if $\exists d$ s.t. $\theta_d \lessdot \theta'_d$

Sum Group	
$+_d \theta \lessdot +_d \theta'$	if $\theta \lessdot \theta'$
$+_{\mathrm{L}} \theta \lessdot +_{\mathrm{R}} \theta'$	
$+_{\mathrm{R}} \theta \lessdot +_{\mathrm{L}} \theta'$	

Fig. 4. Dependency Relation on Enhanced Keyed Labels

reverse both occur will have the first occurring be a dependency of the second, as $\lessdot$ is reflexive; 3. no additional relation (such as a conflict or causality relation) is needed to define concurrency; 4. this dependency relation matches the forward-only definition for action and parallel composition, but not for sum: while the original system [19, Definition 2] requires only $+_d \theta \lessdot \theta'$ if $\theta \lessdot \theta'$, this definition would not capture faithfully the dependencies in our system where the sum operator is preserved after a reduction.

Definition 7 (Transitions and traces). *In a transition* $t : X \xrightarrow{\theta} X'$, X *is the* source, *and* X' *is the* target *of* t. *Two transitions are* coinitial *(resp.* cofinal*) if they have the same source (resp. target). Transitions* t_1 *and* t_2 *are* composable, $t_1; t_2$, *if the target of* t_1 *is the source of* t_2. *The* reverse *of* $t : X' \xrightarrow{\theta} X$ *is* $t^{\bullet} : X \xrightarrow{\theta} X'$, *and similarly if* t *is forward, letting* $(t^{\bullet})^{\bullet} = t^2$.

A sequence of pairwise composable transitions $t_1; \cdots ; t_n$ *is called a* trace, *denoted* T, *and* ϵ *is the empty trace.*

Definition 8 (Causality relation). *Let* T *be a trace* $X_1 \xrightarrow{\theta_1} \cdots \xrightarrow{\theta_n} X_n$ *and* $i, j \in \{1, \cdots, n\}$ *with* $i < j$, θ_i causes θ_j *in* T $(\theta_i <_T \theta_j)$ *iff* $\theta_i \lessdot \theta_j$.

Definition 9 ((Composable) Concurrency). *Let* T *be a trace* $X_1 \xrightarrow{\theta_1} \cdots \xrightarrow{\theta_n} X_n$ *and* $i, j \in \{1, \cdots, n\}$, θ_i *is* concurrent with θ_j $(\theta_i \smile_T \theta_j$, *or simply* $\theta_i \smile \theta_j)$ *iff neither* $\theta_i <_T \theta_j$ *nor* $\theta_j <_T \theta_i$.

Coinitial concurrency (Definition 11) will later on be defined using composable concurrency and the loop lemma (Lemma 5).

Example 1. Consider the following trace, dependencies, and concurrent transitions, where the subscripts to $\lessdot$ and $\smile$ have been omitted:

---

[2] The existence and uniqueness of the reverse transition is immediate in CCSK. This property, known as the loop lemma (Lemma 5) is sometimes harder to obtain.

And we have, e.g.

$$(a.\bar{b}) \mid (b + c)$$

$$\xrightarrow{\mid_L a[m]} a[m].\bar{b} \mid b + c$$

$$\mid_L a[m] \lessdot \mid_L \bar{b}[n] \qquad\qquad \text{as } a[m] \lessdot \bar{b}[n]$$

$$\mid_L \bar{b}[n] \lessdot \mid_L \bar{b}[n] \qquad\qquad \text{as } \bar{b}[n] \lessdot \bar{b}[n]$$

$$\xrightarrow{\mid_L \bar{b}[n]} a[m].\bar{b}[n] \mid b + c$$

and also

$$\xrightarrow{\mid_R +_R c[n']} a[m].\bar{b}[n] \mid b + c[n']$$

$$\mid_L a[m] \lessdot \langle \mid_L \bar{b}[n], \mid_R +_R b[n] \rangle$$

$$\mid_R +_R c[n'] \lessdot \langle \mid_L \bar{b}[n], \mid_R +_L b[n] \rangle$$

$$\xrightarrow{\mid_L \bar{b}[n]} a[m].\bar{b} \mid b + c[n']$$

but

$$\xrightarrow{\mid_R +_R c[n']} a[m].\bar{b} \mid b + c$$

$$\mid_L \bar{b}[n] \smile \mid_R +_R c[n']$$

$$\xrightarrow{\langle \mid_L \bar{b}[n], \mid_R +_L b[n] \rangle} a[m].\bar{b}[n] \mid b[n] + c$$

since labels prefixed by $\mid_L$ and $\mid_R$ are never causes of each others.

To prove the results in the next section, we need an intuitive and straight-forward lemma (Lemma 2) that decomposes a concurrent trace involving two threads into one trace involving one thread while maintaining concurrency, i.e. proving that a trace e.g. of the form $T : X \mid Y \xrightarrow{\mid_L \theta} X' \mid Y \xrightarrow{\mid_L \theta'} X'' \mid Y$ with $\mid_L \theta \smile_T \mid_L \theta'$ can be decomposed into a trace $T' : X \xrightarrow{\theta} X' \xrightarrow{\theta'} X''$ with $\theta \smile_{T'} \theta'$. A similar lemma is also needed to decompose sums (Lemma 3), and their proofs proceed by simple case analysis and offer no resistance.

Lemma 2 (Decomposing concurrent parallel transitions). *Let $i \in \{1, 2\}$ and $\theta_i \in \{\mid_L \theta_i', \mid_R \theta_i'', \langle \mid_L \theta_i', \mid_R \theta_i'' \rangle\}$, define $\pi_L(X_L \mid X_R) = X_L$, $\pi_L(\mid_L \theta) = \theta$, $\pi_L(\langle \mid_L \theta_L, \mid_R \theta_R \rangle) = \theta_L$, $\pi_L(\mid_R \theta) = undefined$, and define similarly π_R.*
Whenever $T : X_L \mid X_R \xrightarrow{\theta_1} Y_L \mid Y_R \xrightarrow{\theta_2} Z_L \mid Z_R$ with $\theta_1 \smile_T \theta_2$, then for $d \in \{L, R\}$, if $\pi_d(\theta_1)$ and $\pi_d(\theta_2)$ are both defined, then, $\pi_d(\theta_1) \smile_{\pi_d(T)} \pi_d(\theta_2)$ with $\pi_d(T) : \pi_d(X_L \mid X_R) \xrightarrow{\pi_d(\theta_1)} \pi_d(Y_L \mid Y_R) \xrightarrow{\pi_d(\theta_2)} \pi_d(Z_L \mid Z_R)$.

Proof. The trace $\pi_d(T)$ exists by virtue of the rule $\mid_d$, syn. or their reverses. What remains to prove is that $\pi_d(\theta_1) \smile_{\pi_d(T)} \pi_d(\theta_2)$ holds.

The proof is by case on θ_1 and θ_2, but always follows the same pattern. As we know that both $\pi_d(\theta_1)$ and $\pi_d(\theta_2)$ need to be defined, there are 7 cases:

θ_1	$\mid_L \theta_1'$	$\mid_L \theta_1'$	$\mid_R \theta_1'$	$\mid_R \theta_1'$	$\langle \mid_L \theta_1', \mid_R \theta_1'' \rangle$	$\langle \mid_L \theta_1', \mid_R \theta_1'' \rangle$	$\langle \mid_L \theta_1', \mid_R \theta_1'' \rangle$
θ_2	$\mid_L \theta_2'$	$\langle \mid_L \theta_2', \mid_R \theta_2'' \rangle$	$\mid_R \theta_2'$	$\langle \mid_L \theta_2', \mid_R \theta_2'' \rangle$	$\mid_L \theta_2'$	$\mid_R \theta_2'$	$\langle \mid_L \theta_2', \mid_R \theta_2'' \rangle$

By symmetry, we can bring this number down to three:

(case letter)	a)	b)	c)
θ_1	$\mid_L \theta_1'$	$\langle \mid_L \theta_1', \mid_R \theta_1'' \rangle$	$\{\langle \mid_L \theta_1', \mid_R \theta_1'' \rangle\}$
θ_2	$\mid_L \theta_2'$	$\mid_L \theta_2'$	$\{\langle \mid_L \theta_2', \mid_R \theta_2'' \rangle\}$

In each case, assume $\pi_L(\theta_1) = \theta_1' \smile_{\pi_L(T)} \theta_2' = \pi_L(\theta_2)$ does not hold. Then it must be the case that either $\theta_1' \lessdot_{\pi_L(T)} \theta_2'$ or $\theta_2' \lessdot_{\pi_L(T)} \theta_1'$, and since both can be treated the same way thanks to symmetry, we only need to detail the following three cases:

a) If $\theta'_1 <_{\pi_L(T)} \theta'_2$, then $\theta'_1 < \theta'_2$, and it is immediate that $\theta_1 =|_L \theta'_1 <_T |_L \theta'_2 = \theta_2$, contradicting $\theta_1 \smile_T \theta_2$.

b) If $\theta'_1 <_{\pi_L(T)} \theta'_2$, then $\theta'_1 < \theta'_2$, $|_L \theta'_1 < |_L \theta'_2$ and $\langle |_L \theta'_1, |_R \theta''_1\rangle < |_L \theta'_2$, from which we can deduce $\theta_1 <_T \theta_2$, contradicting $\theta_1 \smile_T \theta_2$.

c) If $\theta'_1 <_{\pi_L(T)} \theta'_2$, then $\theta'_1 < \theta'_2$, $|_L \theta'_1 < |_L \theta'_2$ and $\langle |_L \theta'_1, |_R \theta''_1\rangle < \langle |_L \theta'_2, |_R \theta'_2\rangle$, from which we can deduce $\theta_1 <_T \theta_2$, contradicting $\theta_1 \smile_T \theta_2$.

Hence, in all cases, assuming that $\pi_d(\theta_1) \smile_{\pi_d(T)} \pi_d(\theta_2)$ does not hold leads to a contradiction. □

Lemma 3 (Decomposing concurrent sum transitions). *Let $i \in \{1,2\}$ and $\theta_i \in \{+_L\theta'_i, +_R\theta''_i\}$, define $\rho_L(X_L + X_R) = X_L$, $\rho_L(+_L\theta) = \theta$, $\rho_L(+_R\theta) = undefined$, and define similarly ρ_R.*

Whenever $T : X_L + X_R \xrightarrow{\theta_1} Y_L + Y_R \xrightarrow{\theta_2} Z_L + Z_R$ with $\theta_1 \smile_T \theta_2$, then for $d \in \{L,R\}$, if $\rho_d(\theta_1)$ and $\rho_d(\theta_2)$ are both defined, then, $\rho_d(\theta_1) \smile_{\pi_d(T)} \rho_d(\theta_2)$ with $\rho_d(T) : \rho_d(X_L + X_R) \xrightarrow{\rho(\theta_1)} \rho_d(Y_L + Y_R) \xrightarrow{(\theta_2)} \rho_d(Z_L + Z_R)$.

Proof. The trace $\rho_d(T)$ exists by virtue of the rule $+_d$ or its reverse. What remains to prove is that $\rho_d(\theta_1) \smile_{\rho_d(T)} \rho_d(\theta_2)$ holds.

The proof is by case on θ_1 and θ_2, but always follows the same pattern. As we know that both $\rho_d(\theta_1)$ and $\rho_d(\theta_2)$ need to be defined, there are 2 cases:

$$\begin{array}{c||c|c|}\theta_1 & +_L\theta'_1 & +_R\theta'_1\\\hline\theta_2 & +_L\theta'_2 & +_R\theta'_2\end{array}$$

In each case, assume $\rho_L(\theta_1) = \theta'_1 \smile_{\rho_L(T)} \theta'_2 = \rho_L(\theta_2)$ does not hold, then it is immediate to note that $\theta_1 \smile_T \theta_2$ cannot hold either, a contradiction. □

3.2   Diamonds and Squares: Concurrency in Action

Square properties and concurrency diamonds express that concurrent transitions are *actually* independent, in the sense that they can be swapped if they are composable, or "later on" agree if they are co-initial. That our definition of concurrency enables those, *and* to allows inter-prove them, is a good indication that it is resilient and convenient.

Theorem 1 (Sideways diamond). *For all $X \xrightarrow{\theta_1} X_1 \xrightarrow{\theta_2} Y$ with $\theta_1 \smile \theta_2$, there exists X_2 s.t. $X \xrightarrow{\theta_2} X_2 \xrightarrow{\theta_1} Y$.*

The proof, sketched, requires a particular care when X is not standard. Using pre. is transparent from the perspective of enhanced keyed labels, as no "memory" of its usage is stored in the label of the transition. This is essentially because—exactly like for act.—all the dependency information is already present in the term or its enhanced keyed label. To make this more formal, we introduce a function that "removes" a keyed label, and prove that it does not affect derivability.

Definition 10. *Given α and k, we define $\mathrm{rm}_{\alpha[k]}$ by $\mathrm{rm}_{\alpha[k]}(0) = 0$ and*

$$\mathrm{rm}_{\alpha[k]}(\beta.X) = \beta.X \qquad\qquad \mathrm{rm}_{\alpha[k]}(X \mid Y) = \mathrm{rm}_{\alpha[k]}(X) \mid \mathrm{rm}_{\alpha[k]}(Y)$$

$$\mathrm{rm}_{\alpha[k]}(X\backslash a) = (\mathrm{rm}_{\alpha[k]}X)\backslash a \qquad \mathrm{rm}_{\alpha[k]}(X + Y) = \mathrm{rm}_{\alpha[k]}(X) + \mathrm{rm}_{\alpha[k]}(Y)$$

$$\mathrm{rm}_{\alpha[k]}(\beta[m].X) = \begin{cases} X & \text{if } \alpha = \beta \text{ and } k = m \\ \beta[m].\mathrm{rm}_{\alpha[k]}(X) & \text{otherwise} \end{cases}$$

We let $\mathrm{rm}_k^\lambda = \mathrm{rm}_{\lambda[k]} \circ \mathrm{rm}_{\overline{\lambda}[k]}$ if $\lambda \in L\backslash\{\tau\}$, $\mathrm{rm}_k^\tau = \mathrm{rm}_{\tau[k]}$ otherwise.

The function $\mathrm{rm}_{\alpha[k]}$ simply looks for an occurrence of $\alpha[k]$ and removes it: as there is at most one, there is no need for a recursive call when it is found. This function preserves derivability of transitions that do not involve the key removed:

Lemma 4. *For all X, α and k, $X \xrightarrow{\theta} Y$ with $k(\theta) \neq k$ iff $\mathrm{rm}_k^\alpha(X) \xrightarrow{\theta} \mathrm{rm}_k^\alpha(Y)$.*

Proof. Assume $\alpha[k]$ or $\overline{\alpha}[k]$ (if $\alpha \neq \tau$) occur in X (otherwise the result is straightforward), as $k(\theta) \neq k$, the same holds for Y. As keys occur at most twice, attached to complementary names, in reachable processes [30, Lemma 3.4], $k \notin \mathrm{key}(\mathrm{rm}_k^\alpha(X)) \cup \mathrm{key}(\mathrm{rm}_k^\alpha(Y))$. Then the proof follows by induction on the length of the derivation for $X \xrightarrow{\theta} Y$: as neither pre. nor pre.$^\bullet$ change the enhanced keyed label, we can simply "take out" the occurrences of those rules when they concern $\alpha[k]$ or $\overline{\alpha}[k]$ and still obtain a valid derivation, with the same enhanced keyed label, hence yielding $\mathrm{rm}_k^\alpha(X) \xrightarrow{\theta} \mathrm{rm}_k^\alpha(Y)$. For the converse direction, pre. or pre.$^\bullet$ can be reintroduced to the derivation tree and in the appropriate location, as k is fresh in $\mathrm{rm}_k^\alpha(X)$ and $\mathrm{rm}_k^\alpha(Y)$.   □

Proof (of Theorem 1 (sketch)). The proof proceeds by induction on the length of the deduction for the derivation for $X \xrightarrow{\theta_1} X_1$, using Lemmas 2 and 3 to enable the induction hypothesis if θ_1 is not a prefix. The only delicate case is if the last rule is pre.: in this case, there exists α, k, X' and X_1' s.t. $X = \alpha[k].X' \xrightarrow{\theta_1} \alpha[k].X_1' = X_1$ and $k(\theta_1) \neq k$. As $\alpha[k].X_1' \xrightarrow{\theta_2} Y$, $k(\theta_2) \neq k$ [30, Lemma 3.4], and since $\theta_1 \smile \theta_2$, we apply Lemma 4 twice to obtain the trace T:

$$\mathrm{rm}_k^\alpha(\alpha[k].X') = X' \xrightarrow{\theta_1} \mathrm{rm}_k^\alpha(\alpha[k].X_1') = X_1' \xrightarrow{\theta_2} \mathrm{rm}_k^\alpha(Y)$$

with $\theta_1 \smile_T \theta_2$, and we can use the induction hypothesis to obtain X_2 s.t. $X' \xrightarrow{\theta_2} X_2 \xrightarrow{\theta_1} \mathrm{rm}_k^\alpha(Y)$. Since $k(\theta_2) \neq k$, we can append pre. to the derivation of $X' \xrightarrow{\theta_2} X_2$ to obtain $\alpha[k].X' = X \xrightarrow{\theta_2} \alpha[k].X_2$. Using Lemma 4 one last time, we obtain that $\mathrm{rm}_k^\alpha(\alpha[k].X_2) = X_2 \xrightarrow{\theta_1} \mathrm{rm}_k^\alpha(Y)$ implies $\alpha[k].X_2 \xrightarrow{\theta_1} Y$, which concludes this case.   □

Example 2. Re-using Example 1, since $\mid_L \overline{b}[n] \smile \mid_R +_R c[n']$ in

$$a[m].\overline{b} \mid b + c \xrightarrow{\mid_L \overline{b}[n]} a[m].\overline{b}[n] \mid b + c \xrightarrow{\mid_R +_R c[n']} a[m].\overline{b}[n] \mid b + c[n'],$$

Theorem 1 allows to re-arrange this trace as

$$a[m].\bar{b} \mid b + c \xrightarrow{\mid_R +_R c[n']} a[m].\bar{b} \mid b + c[n'] \xrightarrow{\mid_L \bar{b}[n]} a[m].\bar{b}[n] \mid b + c[n'].$$

Theorem 2 (Reverse diamonds).

1. *For all* $X \xrightarrow{\theta_1} X_1 \overset{\theta_2}{\rightsquigarrow} Y$ *with* $\theta_1 \smile \theta_2$, *there exists* X_2 *s.t.* $X \overset{\theta_2}{\rightsquigarrow} X_2 \xrightarrow{\theta_1} Y$.
2. *For all* $X \overset{\theta_1}{\rightsquigarrow} X_1 \xrightarrow{\theta_2} Y$ *with* $\theta_1 \smile \theta_2$, *there exists* X_2 *s.t.* $X \xrightarrow{\theta_2} X_2 \overset{\theta_1}{\rightsquigarrow} Y$.

It should be noted that in the particular case of $t; t^{\bullet} : X \xrightarrow{\theta_1} X_1 \overset{\theta_1}{\rightsquigarrow} X$, or $t^{\bullet}; t$, $\theta_1 \lessdot \theta_1$ by reflexivity of $\lessdot$ and hence the reverse diamonds cannot apply. The name "reverse diamond" was sometimes used for different properties [37, Proposition 5.10], [36, Definition 2.3] that, in the presence of the loop lemma (Lemma 5), are equivalent to ours, once the condition on keys is replaced by our condition on concurrency. It is, however, to our knowledge the first time this property, stated in this particular way, is isolated and studied on its own.

Proof (Sketch). We can re-use the proof of Theorem 1 almost as it is, since Lemmas 4, 2 and 3 hold for both directions.

For 1., the only case that diverges is if the deduction for $X \xrightarrow{\theta_1} X_1$ have for last rule pre. In this case, $\alpha[k].X' \xrightarrow{\theta_1} \alpha[k].X'_1 \overset{\theta_2}{\rightsquigarrow} Y$, but we cannot deduce that $\textit{k}(\theta_2) \neq k$ immediately. However, if $\textit{k}(\theta_2) = k$, then we would have $\alpha[k].X'_1 \overset{\alpha[k]}{\rightsquigarrow} \alpha.Y' = Y$, but this application of act.$^{\bullet}$ is not valid, as $\mathrm{std}(X'_1)$ does not hold, since X'_1 was obtained from X' after it made a *forward* transition. Hence, we obtain that $\mathrm{key}(\theta_2) \neq k$ and we can carry out the rest of the proof as before.

For 2., the main difference lies in leveraging the dependency of sum prefixes between e.g. $+_R \theta_1$ and $+_L \theta_2$ in $X + O_Y \overset{+_R \theta_1}{\rightsquigarrow} O_X + O_Y \xrightarrow{+_L \theta_2} O_X + Y$. □

Example 3. Re-using Example 1, since $\mid_R +_R c[n'] \smile \mid_L \bar{b}[n]$ in

$$a[m].\bar{b}[n] \mid b + c \xrightarrow{\mid_R +_R c[n']} a[m].\bar{b}[n] \mid b + c[n'] \overset{\mid_L \bar{b}[n]}{\rightsquigarrow} a[m].\bar{b} \mid b + c[n'],$$

Theorem 2 allows to re-arrange this trace as

$$a[m].\bar{b}[n] \mid b + c \overset{\mid_L \bar{b}[n]}{\rightsquigarrow} a[m].\bar{b} \mid b + c \xrightarrow{\mid_R +_R c[n']} a[m].\bar{b} \mid b + c[n'].$$

Concurrency on coinitial traces is defined using concurrency on composable traces and the loop lemma, immediate in CCSK.

Lemma 5 (Loop lemma [37, Prop. 5.1]). *For all* $t : X \xrightarrow{\theta} X'$, *there exists a unique* $t^{\bullet} : X' \overset{\theta}{\rightsquigarrow} X$, *and conversely. We let* $(t^{\bullet})^{\bullet} = t$.

Definition 11 (Coinitial concurrency). *Let* $t_1 : X \xrightarrow{\theta_1} Y_1$ *and* $t_2 : X \xrightarrow{\theta_2} Y_2$ *be two coinitial transitions, θ_1 is concurrent with θ_2 ($\theta_1 \smile \theta_2$) iff $\theta_1 \smile \theta_2$ in the trace $t_1^{\bullet}; t_2 : Y_1 \xrightarrow{\theta_1} X \xrightarrow{\theta_2} Y_2$.*

To our knowledge, this is the first time co-initial concurrency is defined from composable concurrency: while the axiomatic approach discussed coinitial concurrency [31, Section 5], it primarily studied independence relations that could be defined in any way, and did not connect these two notions of concurrency.

Theorem 3 (Square property). *For all $t_1 : X \xrightarrow{\theta_1} X_1$ and $t_2 : X \xrightarrow{\theta_2} X_2$ with $\theta_1 \smile \theta_2$, there exist $t_1' : X_1 \xrightarrow{\theta_2} Y$ and $t_2' : X_2 \xrightarrow{\theta_1} Y$.*

Proof (sketch). By Definition 11 we have that $\theta_1 \smile \theta_2$ in $t_1^{\bullet}; t_2 : X_1 \xrightarrow{\theta_1} X \xrightarrow{\theta_2} X_2$. Hence, depending on the direction of the arrows, and possibly using the loop lemma to convert two backward transitions into two forward ones, we obtain by Theorems 1 or 2 $t_1''; t_2'' : X_1 \xrightarrow{\theta_2} Y \xrightarrow{\theta_1} X_2$, and we let $t_1' = t_1''$ and $t_2' = t''_2^{\bullet}$:

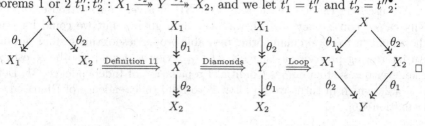

Example 4. Following Example 1, we can get e.g. from $a[m].\bar{b}[n] \mid b+c \xrightarrow{\mid_{R}+_{L}b[n']}$ $a[m].\bar{b}[n] \mid b[n'] + c$ and $a[m].\bar{b}[n] \mid b + c \xrightarrow{\mid_{L}\bar{b}[n]} a[m].\bar{b} \mid b + c$ the transitions converging to $a[m].\bar{b} \mid b[n'] + c$.

3.3 Causal Consistency

Formally, causal consistency (Theorem 4) states that any two coinitial and cofinal traces are causally equivalent:

Definition 12 (Causally equivalent). *Two traces T_1, T_2 are causally equivalent, if they are in the least equivalence relation closed by composition satisfying $t; t^{\bullet} \sim \epsilon$ and $t_1; t_2' \sim t_2; t_1'$ for any $t_1; t_2' : X \xrightarrow{\theta_1} \xrightarrow{\theta_2} Y$, $t_2; t_1' : X \xrightarrow{\theta_2} \xrightarrow{\theta_1} Y$.*

Theorem 4. *All coinitial and cofinal traces are causally equivalent.*

The "axiomatic approach" to reversible computation [31] allows to obtain causal consistency from other properties that are generally easier to prove.

Lemma 6 (Backward transitions are concurrent). *Any two different coinitial backward transitions $t_1 : X \rightsquigarrow X_1$ and $t_2 : X \rightsquigarrow X_2$ are concurrent.*

Proof (Sketch). The proof is by induction on the size of θ_1 and leverages that $k(\theta_1) \neq k(\theta_2)$ for both transitions to be different. $\qquad\square$

Lemma 7 (Well-foundedness). *For all X there exists $n \in \mathbb{N}$, $X_0, \cdots, X_n$ s.t. $X \rightsquigarrow X_n \rightsquigarrow \cdots \rightsquigarrow X_1 \rightsquigarrow X_0$, with $\mathrm{std}(X_0)$.*

This lemma forbids infinite reverse computation, and is obvious in CCSK as any backward transition strictly decreases the number of occurrences of keys.

Proof (of Theorem 4). We can re-use the results of the axiomatic approach [31] since our forward LTS is the symmetric of our backward LTS, and as our concurrency relation (that the authors call the independence relation, following a common usage [39, Definition 3.7]) is indeed an irreflexive symmetric relation: symmetry is immediate by definition, irreflexivity follows from the fact that $\prec$ is reflexive. Then, by Theorem 3 and Lemma 6, the parabolic lemma holds [31, Proposition 3.4], and since the parabolic lemma and well-foundedness hold (Lemma 7), causal consistency holds as well [31, Proposition 3.5].   □

We use here the axiomatic approach [31] in a very narrow sense, to obtain only causal consistency—which was our main goal—, but we could have used those lemmas to obtain many other desirable properties for this system "for free". An interesting problem, as suggested by a reviewer, would also be to establish whenever our system enjoys Coinitial Propagation of Independence [31, Definition 4.2], which in turns would allow it to fulfil Independence of Diamonds [31, Definition 4.6].

Example 5. Re-using the full trace presented in Example 1, we can re-organize the transitions using the diamonds so that every undone transition is undone immediately, and we obtain up to causal equivalence the trace

$$a.\overline{b} \mid b + c \xrightarrow{\mid_L a[m]} a[m].\overline{b} \mid b + c \xrightarrow{\langle \mid_L \overline{b}[n], \mid_R + _L b[n] \rangle} a[m].\overline{b}[n] \mid b[n] + c$$

4   Structural Congruence, Universality and Other Criteria

Causality for a semantics of concurrent computation should satisfy a variety of criteria, the squares and diamonds being the starting point, and causal consistency being arguably the most important. This section aims at briefly presenting additional criteria and at defending the "universality" of our approach. Since this last point requires to introduce two other reversible systems and four other definitions of concurrency, the technical content is only in our research report [3, Sect. C], but we would like to stress that the results stated below are fairly routine to prove—introducing all the material to enable the comparisons is the only lengthy part.

Concurrency-Preserving Structural Congruences. "Denotationality" [17, Section 6] is a criteria stating that structural congruence should be preserved by the causal semantics. Unfortunately, our system only vacuously meets this criteria— since it does not possess a structural congruence. The "usual" structural congruence is missing from all the proved transition systems [15,20,22,23], or missing the associativity and commutativity of the parallel composition [21, p. 242]. While adding such a congruence would benefits the expressiveness, making it interact nicely with the derived proof system *and* the reversible features [30, Section 4], [7] is a challenge we prefer to postpone.

Comparing with Concurrency Inspired by Reversible π-Calculus. It is possible to restrict the definition of concurrency for a reversible π-calculus extending CCSK [32], back to a sum-free version of CCSK. The structural causality [32, Definition 22]—for transitions of the same direction—and conflict relation [32, Definition 25]—for transitions of opposite directions—can then both be proven to match our dependency relation in a rather straightforward way, hence proving the adequacy of notions. However, this inherited concurrency relation cannot be straightforwardly extended to the sum operator, and requires two relations to be defined: for those reasons, we argue that our solution is more convenient to use. It should also be noted that this concurrency does not meet the denotationality criteria either, when the congruence includes renaming of bound keys [30].

A similar work could have been done by restricting concurrency for e.g. reversible higher-order π-calculus [29, Definition 9], reversible π-calculus [16, Definition 4.1] or croll-π [27, Definition 1], but we reserve it for future work, and would prefer to extend our definition to a reversible π-calculus rather than proceeding the other way around.

Comparing with RCCS-Inspired Systems. In RCCS, the definition of concurrency fluctuated between a condition on memory inclusion for composable transitions [25, Definition 3.1.1] and a condition on disjointness of memories on coinitial transitions [18, Definition 7], both requiring the entire memory of the thread to label the transitions, and neither been defined on transitions of opposite directions. It is possible to adapt our proved system to RCCS, and to prove that the resulting concurrency relation is equivalent to those two definitions, when restricted to transitions of equal direction. A similar adaptation is possible for reversible and identified CCS [8], that came with *yet* another definition of concurrency leveraging its built-in mechanism to generate identifiers.

Optimality, Parabolic Lemma, and RPI. The optimality criteria is the adequacy of the concurrency definitions for the LTS and for the reduction semantics [16, Theorem 5.6]. While this criteria requires a reduction semantics and a notion of reduction context to be formally proven, we believe it is easy to convince oneself that the gist of this property—the fact that non-τ-transitions are concurrent iff there exists a "closing" context in which the resulting τ-transitions are still concurrent—holds in our system: as concurrency on τ-transitions is defined in terms of concurrency of its elements (e.g., $\langle \theta_R^1, \theta_L^1 \rangle \smile \langle \theta_R^2, \theta_L^2 \rangle$ iff $\theta_d^1 \smile \theta_d^2$ for at least one $d \in \{L, R\}$), this criteria is obtained "for free".

Properties such as the parabolic lemma [18, Lemma 10]—"any trace is equivalent to a backward trace followed by a forward trace"—or "RPI" [31, Definition 3.3]—"reversing preserves independence", i.e. $t \smile t'$ iff $t^\bullet \smile t'$—follow immediately, by our definition of concurrencies for this latter. We furthermore believe that "baking in" the RPI principle in definitions of reversible concurrencies should become the norm, as it facilitates proofs and forces to have $t_1 \smile t_2$ iff $t_1^\bullet \smile t_2^\bullet$, which seems a very sound principle.

5   Conclusion and Perspectives

We believe our proposal to be not only elegant, but also extremely resilient and easy to work with. It should be stressed that it *does not* require to observe the directions, but also ignore keys or identifiers, that should in our opinion only be technical annotations disallowing processes that have been synchronized to backtrack independently. We had previously defended that identifier should be considered only up to isomorphisms [6, p. 13], or explicitly generated by a built-in mechanism [8, p. 152], and re-inforce this point of view here. From there, much can be done. A first interesting line of work would be to compare our syntactical definition with the semantical definition of concurrency in models of RCCS [4–6] and CCSK [24,36,40]. Of course, as we already mentioned, extending this definition to reversible π-calculi, taking inspiration from e.g. the latest development in forward-only π [23], would allow to re-inforce the interest and solidity of this technique.

Another interesting track would be to consider infinite extensions of CCSK, since infinite behaviors in the presence of reversibility is not well-understood nor studied: an attempt to extend algebras of communicating processes [11], including recursion, seems to have been unsuccessful [41]. A possible approach would be to define recursion and iteration in CCSK, to extend our definition of concurrency to those infinite behaviors, and to attempt to reconstruct the separation results from the forward-only paradigm [35]. Whether finer, "reversible", equivalences can preserve this distinction despite the greater flexibility provided by backward transitions is an open problem. Another interesting point is the study of infinite behaviors that duplicate past events, including their keys or memories: whether this formalism could preserve causal consistency, or what benefits there would be in tinkering this property, is also an open question.

Last but not least, these last investigations would require to define and understand relevant properties, or metrics, for reversible systems. In the forward-only world, termination or convergence were used to compare infinite behaviors [35], and additional criteria were introduced to study causal semantics [17]. Those properties may or may not be suited for reversible systems, but it is difficult to decide as they sometimes even lack a definition. This could help in solving the more general question of deciding *what* it is that we want to observe and assess when evaluating reversible, concurrent systems [9,10].

Acknowledgments. I would like to thank Doriana Medić for suggesting that I adapt the definition of concurrency for a reversible π-calculus extending CCSK [32] and compare it to the concurrency developed in this paper, as done in [3, Sect. C]. I am also extremely thankful to the reviewers for their careful reading of this technical paper, and for their enlightening suggestions.

References

1. Arpit, Kumar, D.: Calculus of concurrent probabilistic reversible processes. In: ICCCT-2017: Proceedings of the 7th International Conference on Computer and Communication Technology, pp. 34–40. ICCCT-2017. ACM, New York (2017). https://doi.org/10.1145/3154979.3155004
2. Aubert, C.: Causal consistent replication in reversible concurrent calculi, October 2021. https://hal.archives-ouvertes.fr/hal-03384482. Under revision
3. Aubert, C.: Concurrencies in reversible concurrent calculi. Technical report, March 2022. https://hal.archives-ouvertes.fr/hal-03605003
4. Aubert, C., Cristescu, I.: Reversible barbed congruence on configuration structures. In: Knight, S., Lluch Lafuente, A., Lanese, I., Vieira, H.T. (eds.) ICE 2015. EPTCS, vol. 189, pp. 68–95 (2015). https://doi.org/10.4204/EPTCS.189.7
5. Aubert, C., Cristescu, I.: Contextual equivalences in configuration structures and reversibility. J. Log. Algebr. Methods Program. **86**(1), 77–106 (2017). https://doi.org/10.1016/j.jlamp.2016.08.004
6. Aubert, C., Cristescu, I.: How reversibility can solve traditional questions: the example of hereditary history-preserving bisimulation. In: Konnov, I., Kovács, L. (eds.) 31st International Conference on Concurrency Theory, CONCUR 2020, 1–4 September 2020, Vienna, Austria. LIPIcs, vol. 2017, pp. 13:1–13:24. Schloss Dagstuhl (2020). https://doi.org/10.4230/LIPIcs.CONCUR.2020.13
7. Aubert, C., Cristescu, I.: Structural equivalences for reversible calculi of communicating systems (oral communication). Research report, Augusta University (2020). https://hal.archives-ouvertes.fr/hal-02571597. Communication at ICE 2020
8. Aubert, C., Medić, D.: Explicit identifiers and contexts in reversible concurrent calculus. In: Yamashita, S., Yokoyama, T. (eds.) RC 2021. LNCS, vol. 12805, pp. 144–162. Springer, Cham (2021). https://doi.org/10.1007/978-3-030-79837-6_9
9. Aubert, C., Varacca, D.: Processes, systems & tests: defining contextual equivalences. In: Lange, J., Mavridou, A., Safina, L., Scalas, A. (eds.) Proceedings 14th Interaction and Concurrency Experience, Online, 18th June 2021. EPTCS, vol. 347, pp. 1–21. Open Publishing Association (2021). https://doi.org/10.4204/EPTCS.347.1
10. Aubert, C., Varacca, D.: Processes against tests: Defining contextual equivalences. Invited submission to the Journal of Logical and Algebraic Methods in Programming (2022). https://hal.archives-ouvertes.fr/hal-03535565
11. Baeten, J.C.M.: A brief history of process algebra. Theor. Comput. Sci. **335**(2–3), 131–146 (2005). https://doi.org/10.1016/j.tcs.2004.07.036
12. Boudol, G., Castellani, I.: A non-interleaving semantics for CCS based on proved transitions. Fund. Inform. **11**, 433–452 (1988)
13. Boudol, G., Castellani, I.: Three equivalent semantics for CCS. In: Guessarian, I. (ed.) LITP 1990. LNCS, vol. 469, pp. 96–141. Springer, Heidelberg (1990). https://doi.org/10.1007/3-540-53479-2_5
14. Busi, N., Gabbrielli, M., Zavattaro, G.: On the expressive power of recursion, replication and iteration in process calculi. MSCS **19**(6), 1191–1222 (2009). https://doi.org/10.1017/S096012950999017X

15. Carabetta, G., Degano, P., Gadducci, F.: CCS semantics via proved transition systems and rewriting logic. In: Kirchner, C., Kirchner, H. (eds.) 1998 International Workshop on Rewriting Logic and its Applications, WRLA 1998, Abbaye des Prémontrés at Pont-à-Mousson, France, September 1998. Electron. Notes Theor. Comput. Sci. **15**, 369–387 (1998). https://doi.org/10.1016/S1571-0661(05)80023-4. https://www.sciencedirect.com/journal/electronic-notes-in-theoretical-computer-science/vol/15/suppl/C

16. Cristescu, I., Krivine, J., Varacca, D.: A compositional semantics for the reversible p-calculus. In: LICS, pp. 388–397. IEEE Computer Society (2013). https://doi.org/10.1109/LICS.2013.45

17. Cristescu, I.D., Krivine, J., Varacca, D.: Rigid families for CCS and the π-calculus. In: Leucker, M., Rueda, C., Valencia, F.D. (eds.) ICTAC 2015. LNCS, vol. 9399, pp. 223–240. Springer, Cham (2015). https://doi.org/10.1007/978-3-319-25150-9_14

18. Danos, V., Krivine, J.: Reversible communicating systems. In: Gardner, P., Yoshida, N. (eds.) CONCUR 2004. LNCS, vol. 3170, pp. 292–307. Springer, Heidelberg (2004). https://doi.org/10.1007/978-3-540-28644-8_19

19. Degano, P., Gadducci, F., Priami, C.: Causality and replication in concurrent processes. In: Broy, M., Zamulin, A.V. (eds.) PSI 2003. LNCS, vol. 2890, pp. 307–318. Springer, Heidelberg (2004). https://doi.org/10.1007/978-3-540-39866-0_30

20. Degano, P., Priami, C.: Proved trees. In: Kuich, W. (ed.) ICALP 1992. LNCS, vol. 623, pp. 629–640. Springer, Heidelberg (1992). https://doi.org/10.1007/3-540-55719-9_110

21. Degano, P., Priami, C.: Non-interleaving semantics for mobile processes. Theor. Comput. Sci. **216**(1–2), 237–270 (1999). https://doi.org/10.1016/S0304-3975(99)80003-6

22. Degano, P., Priami, C.: Enhanced operational semantics. ACM Comput. Surv. **33**(2), 135–176 (2001). https://doi.org/10.1145/384192.384194

23. Demangeon, R., Yoshida, N.: Causal computational complexity of distributed processes. In: Dawar, A., Grädel, E. (eds.) LICS, pp. 344–353. ACM (2018). https://doi.org/10.1145/3209108.3209122

24. Graversen, E., Phillips, I.C.C., Yoshida, N.: Event structure semantics of (controlled) reversible CCS. J. Log. Algebr. Methods Program. **121**, 100686 (2021). https://doi.org/10.1016/j.jlamp.2021.100686

25. Krivine, J.: Algèbres de Processus Réversible - Programmation Concurrente Déclarative. Ph.D. thesis, Université Paris 6 & INRIA Rocquencourt (2006). https://tel.archives-ouvertes.fr/tel-00519528

26. Lanese, I.: From reversible semantics to reversible debugging. In: Kari, J., Ulidowski, I. (eds.) RC 2018. LNCS, vol. 11106, pp. 34–46. Springer, Cham (2018). https://doi.org/10.1007/978-3-319-99498-7_2

27. Lanese, I., Lienhardt, M., Mezzina, C.A., Schmitt, A., Stefani, J.-B.: Concurrent flexible reversibility. In: Felleisen, M., Gardner, P. (eds.) ESOP 2013. LNCS, vol. 7792, pp. 370–390. Springer, Heidelberg (2013). https://doi.org/10.1007/978-3-642-37036-6_21

28. Lanese, I., Medić, D., Mezzina, C.A.: Static versus dynamic reversibility in CCS. Acta Inform. (2019). https://doi.org/10.1007/s00236-019-00346-6

29. Lanese, I., Mezzina, C.A., Stefani, J.: Reversibility in the higher-order π-calculus. Theor. Comput. Sci. **625**, 25–84 (2016). https://doi.org/10.1016/j.tcs.2016.02.019

30. Lanese, I., Phillips, I.: Forward-reverse observational equivalences in CCSK. In: Yamashita, S., Yokoyama, T. (eds.) RC 2021. LNCS, vol. 12805, pp. 126–143. Springer, Cham (2021). https://doi.org/10.1007/978-3-030-79837-6_8

31. Lanese, I., Phillips, I., Ulidowski, I.: An axiomatic approach to reversible computation. In: FoSSaCS 2020. LNCS, vol. 12077, pp. 442–461. Springer, Cham (2020). https://doi.org/10.1007/978-3-030-45231-5_23

32. Medić, D., Mezzina, C.A., Phillips, I., Yoshida, N.: A parametric framework for reversible π-calculi. Inf. Comput. **275**, 104644 (2020). https://doi.org/10.1016/j.ic.2020.104644

33. Mezzina, C.A., Koutavas, V.: A safety and liveness theory for total reversibility. In: Mallet, F., Zhang, M., Madelaine, E. (eds.) 11th International Symposium on Theoretical Aspects of Software Engineering, TASE 2017, Sophia Antipolis, France, 13–15 September, pp. 1–8. IEEE (2017). https://doi.org/10.1109/TASE.2017.8285635. https://ieeexplore.ieee.org/xpl/conhome/8277122/proceeding

34. Milner, R. (ed.): A Calculus of Communicating Systems. LNCS, vol. 92. Springer, Heidelberg (1980). https://doi.org/10.1007/3-540-10235-3

35. Palamidessi, C., Valencia, F.D.: Recursion vs replication in process calculi: expressiveness. Bull. EATCS **87**, 105–125 (2005). http://eatcs.org/images/bulletin/beatcs87.pdf

36. Phillips, I., Ulidowski, I.: Reversibility and models for concurrency. Electron. Notes Theor. Comput. Sci. **192**(1), 93–108 (2007). https://doi.org/10.1016/j.entcs.2007.08.018

37. Phillips, I., Ulidowski, I.: Reversing algebraic process calculi. J. Log. Algebr. Program. **73**(1–2), 70–96 (2007). https://doi.org/10.1016/j.jlap.2006.11.002

38. Sangiorgi, D., Walker, D.: The Pi-calculus. CUP (2001)

39. Sassone, V., Nielsen, M., Winskel, G.: Models for concurrency: towards a classification. Theor. Comput. Sci. **170**(1–2), 297–348 (1996). https://doi.org/10.1016/S0304-3975(96)80710-9

40. Ulidowski, I., Phillips, I., Yuen, S.: Concurrency and reversibility. In: Yamashita, S., Minato, S. (eds.) RC 2014. LNCS, vol. 8507, pp. 1–14. Springer, Cham (2014). https://doi.org/10.1007/978-3-319-08494-7_1

41. Wang, Y.: RETRACTED ARTICLE: an algebra of reversible computation. SpringerPlus **5**(1), 1–35 (2016). https://doi.org/10.1186/s40064-016-3229-7

The ℵ-Calculus

A Declarative Model of Reversible Programming

Hannah Earley[✉] [ID]

Department of Applied Mathematics, University of Cambridge, Cambridge, UK
h.earley@damtp.cam.ac.uk

Abstract. A novel model of reversible computing, the ℵ-calculus, is introduced. It is declarative, reversible-Turing complete, and has a local term-rewriting semantics. Unlike previously demonstrated reversible term-rewriting systems, it does not require the accumulation of history data. Terms in the ℵ-calculus, in combination with the program definitions, encapsulate all program state. An interpreter was also written.

Keywords: Reversible Computing · Term-Rewriting · Declarative Paradigm

1 Introduction

Reversible computing is a response to Szilard's and Landauer's observations [5,7] that the 'erasure' of information, as is common in conventional computing, leads to a fundamental thermodynamic cost in the form of an entropy increase. To avoid this, one should ensure that the computational state transitions are *injective*, i.e. every valid[1] computational state has at most one valid predecessor. This logical reversibility thus circumvents the Landauer-Szilard limit by avoiding the need to erase information via logical reversibility of its operation.

We introduce a novel model of reversible computing, the ℵ-calculus[2]. It is declarative, in that programs describe the logic of the computation whilst the control flow is left implicit. Irreversible declarative languages include `Prolog`, but we believe the ℵ-calculus is the first declarative model of reversible computing. Its semantics are that of a Term-Rewriting System (TRS): A given computation is represented by a term, and this is reversibly transformed by a transition rule to complete the computation. Reversible TRSs have been studied before. For example, Abramsky [1] introduces a general approach to modeling reversible TRSs, although he then applies it to reversibly simulating the irreversible λ-calculus. To reversibly simulate an irreversible system, some computational history must be recorded. This is implicit in Abramsky's treatment, but explicit in the approaches of Di Pierro et al. [3] and Nishida et al. [6]. We believe ours is the first reversible-Turing complete TRS that doesn't require such recording.

---

[1] No such constraint need be applied to invalid computational states [4].

[2] The name of the calculus is inspired by the Greek meaning 'not forgotten', ἀλήθεια.

C. A. Mezzina and K. Podlaski (Eds.): RC 2022, LNCS 13354, pp. 164–171, 2022.
https://doi.org/10.1007/978-3-031-09005-9_11

In Sect. 2 we introduce the ℵ-calculus by example. In Sects. 3 and 4 we formalize the model's definition and its semantics. We conclude with Sect. 5 and briefly discuss some language extensions. In the interest of space, proofs of theorems such as non-ambiguity and reversible-Turing completeness are deferred to an accompanying longer report.

2 Examples

Recursion: Addition and Subtraction. The inductive definition of Peano addition, $a + Z = a$ and $a + Sb = S(a + b)$ where a natural number is either $Z \equiv 0$ or the successor (S) of another natural number, can be readily reversibilized. Reversible addition must return both the sum, and additional information to determine what both addends were. Here, we will keep the second addend: $a + Z = (a, Z)$ and $a + b = (c, b) \implies a + Sb = (Sc, Sb)$. In the ℵ-calculus, this is:

$$! + a\ b\ ();\quad !\ ()\ c\ b\ +;$$
$$+ a\ Z\ () = ()\ a\ Z\ +; \qquad \text{(ADD–BASE)}$$
$$+ a\ (Sb)\ () = ()\ (Sc)\ (Sb)\ +: \qquad \text{(ADD–STEP)}$$
$$+ a\ b\ () = ()\ c\ b\ +. \qquad \text{(ADD–STEP–SUB)}$$

The first line says that terms of the form $+ a\ b\ ()$ and $()\ c\ b\ +$ are halting states (either initial or final), where a, b, c are variable terms. This is stated via the syntax !. Note the () term, pronounced 'unit'; this is an empty set of parentheses that is used by convention for disambiguation between definitions. The second line, definition (ADD–BASE), implements the base rule that $a + Z = (a, Z)$. As this is a Term-Rewriting System (TRS), we have a term on both sides and so the expression is more symmetric. As the term encapsulates all information about program state, we need a *witness* to the fact that an addition (rather than a multiplication or something else) was performed; here this is given by reusing the + symbol (identifier) on the right hand side. The next definition, (ADD–STEP), implements the inductive step and has as a *sub-rule* (ADD–STEP–SUB), which performs the recursion. The above can perhaps best be understood through the below evaluation trace of $3 + 2 = (5, 2)$:

Squiggly arrows represent matching against the patterns in the definitions, and solid arrows refer to instantiation/consumption of 'sub-terms'.

Iteration: Squaring and Square-Rooting. A more involved example is given by reversible squaring and square-rooting. Reversible squaring may be implemented using addition as a sub-routine via the fact $m^2 = \sum_{k=0}^{m-1}(k + k + 1)$. By doing the sum in reverse (i.e. starting with $k = m - 1$ and decrementing it towards 0), m is consumed whilst $n = m^2$ is generated. This also shows how iteration/looping can be implemented in the $\aleph$-calculus. The definition of squaring (SQ) is given below:

$$! \text{ SQ } m \; (); \quad ! \; () \; n \; \text{SQ};$$
$$\text{SQ } m \; () = \text{SQ } Z \; m \; \text{SQ}; \qquad\qquad (\text{SQ–BEGIN})$$
$$\text{SQ } s \; (Sk) \; \text{SQ} = \text{SQ } (Ss'') \; k \; \text{SQ}: \qquad (\text{SQ–STEP})$$
$$+ \; s \; k \; () = () \; s' \; k \; +. \qquad\qquad -- \; s' \leftarrow s + k$$
$$+ \; s' \; k \; () = () \; s'' \; k \; +. \qquad\qquad -- \; s'' \leftarrow s' + k$$
$$\text{SQ } n \; Z \; \text{SQ} = () \; n \; \text{SQ}; \qquad\qquad (\text{SQ–END})$$

In a reversible loop, you have a reverse conditional branch for entering/continuing the loop and a forward conditional branch for continuing/exiting the loop. These are implemented by rules (SQ–BEGIN,–END). Meanwhile rule (SQ–STEP) performs the actual additions of the sum. The reader may notice that SQ appears twice in (SQ–STEP); this is merely for symmetric aesthetics, and to distinguish it from halting terms which are typically marked with (). An example evaluation trace of $3^2 = 9$ (resp. $\sqrt{9} = 3$) is given by:

$$! \quad \text{SQ } 3 \; () = \text{SQ } Z \; 3 \; \text{SQ} = \text{SQ } 5 \; 2 \; \text{SQ} = \text{SQ } 8 \; 1 \; \text{SQ} = \text{SQ } 9 \; Z \; \text{SQ} = () \; 9 \; \text{SQ} \quad !$$

There is no precondition in the forward direction (except that m should be a well-formed natural number), but the reverse direction requires $n = m^2$ be a square number. If we try to take $\sqrt{10}$,

$$! \quad () \; 10 \; \text{SQ} = \text{SQ } 10 \; Z \; \text{SQ} = \text{SQ } 9 \; 1 \; \text{SQ} = \text{SQ } 6 \; 2 \; \text{SQ} = \text{SQ } 1 \; 3 \; \text{SQ} \quad \perp$$

the computation stalls with $\{s'' \mapsto 0, k \mapsto 3\}$ because 3 cannot be subtracted from 0. Specifically, there is no matching rule for the sub-term $()$ Z 3 $+$.

3   Definition

A computation in the $\aleph$-calculus consists of a *term* and a *program* governing the reversible evolution of the term. A term is a tree whose leaves are *symbols*, which are drawn from some infinite set of identifiers (e.g. $+$, SQ, S, Z, MAP); terms are conventionally written with nested parentheses, e.g. SQ $(S(S(SZ)))$ $()$. Equivalently, a term is either a symbol or a string of terms; we call a string of terms a *multiterm*. A program is a series of *definitions*. A definition is either (1) *halting*, e.g. ! SQ n $()$, indicating that multiterms matching the given pattern are in a halting state (annotated with !); or (2) *computational*, e.g. SQ n $() = $ SQ Z n SQ, indicating that multiterms matching the left-pattern may be mapped to a multiterm matching the right-pattern, or vice-versa. Computational definitions may have sub-rules, e.g. $+ \; s \; k \; () = () \; s' \; k \; +$, which need to be invoked to complete the mapping. These are summarized in BNF notation below:

$$\pi ::= \text{SYM} \mid \text{VAR} \mid (\pi^*) \qquad \text{(PATTERN TERM)}$$
$$\rho ::= \pi^* = \pi^* \qquad \text{(RULE)}$$
$$\delta ::= \rho : \rho^* \mid \; ! \; \pi^*; \qquad \text{(DEFINITION)}$$

Determinism Constraints. Like other models of reversible computation, such as Bennett's reversible Turing Machine [2], constraints must be placed on which programs are accepted to ensure unambiguously deterministic reversibility. That is, whilst all the computational definitions are locally reversible—in the sense that their specific action can be uniquely reversed up to sub-rule determinism— there may be a choice of computational rules. Whilst the semantics (Sect. 4) preclude ambiguity, it is useful to reject ambiguous programs before execution. Ensuring determinism is essentially the same as Bennett's approach: the domains and codomains of transitions must be unambiguous. This is slightly complicated in the ℵ-calculus because computational definitions are bidirectional: each definition specifies two rules, one corresponding to the 'forward' direction of the rule and one to its inverse. This means that domains and codomains of definitions are conflated and a multiterm may generally match up to two rules: the 'intended' rule, and the inverse of the rule which produced it. This would lead to ambiguity, except that the ℵ-calculus has a notion of *computational inertia* (Definition 2). The consequence of computational inertia is that, although a multiterm may match up to two rules, there is always a unique choice of which rule to apply at each step for a *given* direction of computation. A necessary and sufficient condition for avoiding ambiguity is given by Theorem 3, and an accompanying algorithm for static analysis of ℵ programs that verifies this condition is provided in the forthcoming extended version of this paper.

Definition 1 (Term Reduction). *In the ℵ-calculus, an input halting multiterm t_0 is 'reduced' to an output halting multiterm t_n, where $n \in \mathbb{N} \cup \{\infty\}$, by a series of n rules $r_{i \to i+1}$. Each rule r has a unique inverse r^{-1}, which gives a trivial inverse reduction from $t'_0 = t_n$ to $t'_n = t_0$ with $r'_{i \to i+1} = r^{-1}_{n-i-1 \to n-i}$.*

Definition 2 (Computational Inertia). *Computational Inertia in the ℵ-calculus is the property that if, in a given reduction (Definition 1), $r_{i \to i+1} = r$, then $r_{i+1 \to i+2}$ cannot be r^{-1}. This would allow for a 'futile cycle' in which no computational progress is made.*

Theorem 3 (Non-Ambiguity). *A program is unambiguously/deterministically reversible if each variable appears exactly twice[3] in a computational*

---

[3] In the examples in Sect. 2 the reader may notice this is violated. This is for programmer convenience, and must be resolved manually or by the compiler.

definition, and if and only if there exists no multiterm matching either (1) three-or-more computational rule patterns, or (2) two-or-more computational rule patterns and one-or-more halting patterns.

4 Semantics

As stated earlier, a computation consists of a multiterm t that evolves reversibly in the context of a program environment, $\mathcal{P}$. $\mathcal{P}$ is a set containing all the definitions making up the program, computational and halting. The $\aleph$-calculus can be formulated without computational inertia (Definition 2), but in the interest of brevity we give the inertial semantics here. In the inertial semantics, each computational definition is assigned a pair of unique identifiers: r, corresponding to the left-to-right rule, and r^{-1}, corresponding to the right-to-left rule. Each halting definition is assigned the identifier !, where for convenience $!^{-1} \equiv !$. $\mathcal{P}$ is then a set of elements $r : \delta$ where δ is a definition and r is the corresponding left-to-right rule identifier; for simplicity, $\mathcal{P}$ is extended with $r^{-1} : \delta^{-1}$ for each computational definition δ where δ^{-1} swaps the left and right sides of the head-rule. Each multiterm $t = t_1 \cdots t_n$ is then tagged as either halting, $[t_1 \cdots t_n | \top]$ for initial multiterms and $[t_1 \cdots t_n | \bot]$ for final multiterms, or 'active', $(t_1 \cdots t_n | r)$ where r is the previously applied rule. As well as tagging active multiterms with the previous rule application, it is important we identify halting tags because sub-multiterms must only be produced/consumed in a halting state or else non-determinism arises[4].

At each computational step, we pick a non-final halting multiterm t (either the 'root' multiterm or a nested multiterm, (SUB–EVAL)) and match it against all the rules in $\mathcal{P}$. The set $\mathcal{M}(t)$ is said set of matching rules, and is generated by rules (UNIT, MATCH). The rules for 'matching' relate to 'unification' and will be described later. If the multiterm is initial-halting, and we find a match of the form $! : \delta \in \mathcal{P}$ then we can map $[t | \top] \to (t | !)$; if there aren't any halting definitions, then the computation enters an invalid state. If the multiterm is active, then there are four valid cases: (1) The tagged multiterm is $(t | !)$ and t matches *only* one-or-more halting definitions $! : \delta$; we map $(t | !) \to [t | \bot]$. (2) The tagged multiterm is $(t | !)$ and t matches one-or-more halting definitions and precisely *one* computational definition $r : \delta$; if r maps $t \xrightarrow{r} t'$, then we map $(t | !) \to (t' | r)$. (3) The tagged multiterm is $(t | r)$ and t matches two computational definitions, $r^{-1} : \delta$ and $s : \varepsilon$, where s may be r but not r^{-1}; then, if s maps $t \xrightarrow{s} t'$, we map $(t | r) \to (t' | s)$. (4) The tagged multiterm is $(t | r)$ and t matches precisely *one* computational definition, $r^{-1} : \delta$, and one-or-more halting definitions; we map $(t | r) \to [t | \bot]$. These five cases above are given by rules (STEP–HALT, STEP–COMP). Any other cases cause computation to enter an invalid state, either because there is no rule specified to continue the multiterm's evolution, or because there is an ambiguity in $\mathcal{P}$. Note that each of the above tagged maps are reversible because

---

[4] The requirement of halting, combined with computational inertia, ensures each sub-multiterm takes on a unique state at production and before consumption.

$$\frac{\bigwedge_i s_i \to t_i}{s_1 \cdots s_n \to t_1 \cdots t_n} \text{ (SUB-EVAL)} \qquad \frac{\sigma \in \text{SYM}}{\sigma \overset{\sigma}{\sim} \varnothing} \qquad \frac{v \in \text{VAR}}{t \overset{v}{\sim} \{v \mapsto t\}} \qquad \frac{\bigwedge_i t_i \overset{T_i}{\sim} T_i \quad \bigcap_i T_i = \varnothing}{[t_1 \cdots t_n | \bot] \overset{T_1 \cdots T_n}{\leadsto} \biguplus_i T_i} \text{ (UNIF)}$$

$$\frac{}{! : !; \in \mathcal{P}} \text{ (UNIT)} \qquad \frac{! : !\pi; \in \mathcal{P} \quad t \overset{\pi}{\sim} V}{! \in \mathcal{M}(t)} \qquad \frac{r : (\lambda = \rho : \Sigma) \in \mathcal{P} \quad t \overset{\lambda}{\sim} V}{r \in \mathcal{M}(t)} \text{ (MATCH)}$$

$$\frac{! \in \mathcal{M}(t)}{[t|\top] \to (t|!)} \quad \frac{\mathcal{M}(t) = \{!\}}{(t|!) \to [t|\bot]} \quad \frac{\mathcal{M}(t) = \{r^{-1}, !\}}{(t|r) \to [t|\bot]} \text{ (STEP-HALT)}$$

$$\frac{\mathcal{M}(t) = \{!, r\} \quad t \overset{r}{\to} t'}{(t|!) \to (t'|r)} \quad \frac{\mathcal{M}(t) = \{r^{-1}, s\} \quad t \overset{s}{\to} t'}{(t|r) \to (t'|s)} \text{ (STEP-COMP)}$$

$$\frac{r : (\lambda = \rho : \Sigma) \in \mathcal{P} \quad \bigwedge_i t_i \overset{\lambda_i}{\sim} T_i \quad \bigcap_i T_i = \varnothing}{t_1 \cdots t_n \overset{r}{\to}_{init} \langle r, \Sigma, \varnothing, \biguplus_i T_i \rangle} \text{ (COMP-INIT)}$$

$$\frac{r : (\lambda = \rho : \Sigma) \in \mathcal{P} \quad \bigwedge_i t_i \overset{\rho_i}{\sim} T_i \quad \bigcap_i T_i = \varnothing}{\langle r, \varnothing, \Sigma, \biguplus_i T_i \rangle \overset{r}{\to}_{fin} t_1 \cdots t_n} \text{ (COMP-FIN)}$$

$$\frac{[s|\top] \to [t|\bot] \quad [s] \overset{\sigma}{\sim} S \quad [t] \overset{\tau}{\sim} T}{\langle r, \{\sigma = \tau.\} \cup \Sigma, \Sigma', R \uplus S \rangle \overset{r}{\to}_{sub} \langle r, \Sigma, \{\sigma = \tau.\} \cup \Sigma', R \uplus T \rangle} \text{ (COMP-SUB}_\ell\text{)}$$

$$\frac{[s|\top] \to [t|\bot] \quad [s] \overset{\sigma}{\sim} S \quad [t] \overset{\tau}{\sim} T}{\langle r, \{\tau = \sigma.\} \cup \Sigma, \Sigma', R \uplus S \rangle \overset{r}{\to}_{sub} \langle r, \Sigma, \{\tau = \sigma.\} \cup \Sigma', R \uplus T \rangle} \text{ (COMP-SUB}_r\text{)}$$

$$\frac{s_1 \cdots s_m \overset{r}{\to}_{init} \overset{r}{\to}^*_{sub} \overset{r}{\to}_{fin} t_1 \cdots t_n}{s_1 \cdots s_m \overset{r}{\to} t_1 \cdots t_n} \text{ (COMP)} \qquad \frac{s \in \text{TERM}^* \quad s \to t \quad t \to u}{s \to s \qquad s \to u} \text{ (CLOSURE)}$$

Listing 1. The semantics of the (inertial) ℵ-calculus. Note that $\langle r, \Sigma \, \Sigma', S \rangle$ represents an intermediate computational state, where r is the rule identifier, Σ is a set sub-rules yet to be applied, Σ' is a set of sub-rules that have been applied, and S is a set of variable bindings.

whenever we consume r it is by identifying exactly two possible rule identifiers, $\{r^{-1}, s\}$, and using this information to consume the old tag r and replace it with s.

In the above, we relied on the notion of a rule $r : (\lambda = \rho : \Sigma)$ inducing the mapping $t \overset{r}{\to} t'$. The semantics, given by rules (COMP,–INIT,–SUB$_\ell$,–SUB$_r$,–FIN), are as follows: The pattern λ is unified against t: here, unification means that t is reversibly consumed by comparison with the pattern λ, in the process producing a variable mapping. Then we pick (without replacement) a sub-rule from Σ where one side consists only of variables in our current mapping. We apply this sub-rule: the variables are substituted into the pattern, the resulting multiterm t is instantiated as $[s|\top]$ and evolved to $[s'|\bot]$, and s' is then matched against and consumed by the other pattern of the sub-rule. This can fail, leading to an invalid state, if the new multiterm doesn't evolve to $[s'|\bot]$ or if s' doesn't unify with the final pattern. This process is repeated until our current variable mapping can be substituted into ρ to yield t', completing the mapping of $t \to t'$.

Unification, rules (UNIF), is simply recursive pattern-matching. If a term t unifies against a pattern π with variable bindings V, we write $t \overset{\pi}{\sim} V$. The pattern $\sigma \in$ SYM only unifies with the term σ. The pattern $v \in$ VAR unifies with any term t with bindings $\{v \mapsto t\}$. The pattern $(\pi_1 \pi_2 \cdots \pi_n)$ unifies with a multiterm $[t_1 t_2 \cdots t_n | \bot]$ if and only if each π_i unifies with t_i with bindings V_i, and the V_i are disjoint (i.e. the π_i don't share any variables); notice that it only unifies with a final-halting state.

These semantics are summarized in Listing 1. Complete computation is achieved via the rules (CLOSURE). An immediate concern is that the application of sub-rules and the evolution of sub-multiterms is non-deterministic/asynchronous. In fact this is a feature, and allows for automatic parallelisation of independent subcomputations in the ℵ-calculus. A necessary condition is confluence, which is satisfied by the ℵ-calculus (Theorem 4). Finally it is important for the usefulness of the ℵ-calculus that it is reversible-Turing complete (Theorem 5).

Theorem 4. *The semantics of the ℵ-calculus are confluent, in the sense that the final result is independent of evaluation order (and possible parallel evaluation).*

Theorem 5. *The ℵ-calculus is reversible-Turing complete, in the sense that it can reversibly simulate (without additional garbage) the reversible Turing Machine defined by Bennett [2] and vice-versa.*

5   Discussion and Future Work

We have introduced a novel model of reversible computing, the ℵ-calculus, that is declarative and has a TRS semantics. We proved (see extended paper) that the calculus is non-ambiguous, reversible-Turing complete, and that its semantics are confluent. An interpreter has also been written and is available online[5]. It may also be extended to support concurrency, with interesting consequences for determinism and causal-consistency. The concurrent and non-inertial variant of the calculus, introduced in the extended paper, gives an alternate positioning of the model in the context of molecular programming: another form of unconventional computing, in which the interactions of specially prepared molecules simulate computation (see Zhang and Seelig [8] for a review of one such approach).

Acknowledgements. The author would like to acknowledge the invaluable help and support of her PhD supervisor, Gos Micklem. This work was supported by the Engineering and Physical Sciences Research Council, project reference 1781682.

---

[5] https://github.com/hannah-earley/alethe-repl

References

1. Abramsky, S.: A structural approach to reversible computation. Theoret. Comput. Sci. **347**(3), 441–464 (2005)
2. Bennett, C.H.: Logical reversibility of computation. IBM J. Res. Dev. **17**(6), 525–532 (1973)
3. Di Pierro, A., Hankin, C., Wiklicky, H.: Reversible combinatory logic. Math. Struct. Comput. Sci. **16**(4), 621–637 (2006)
4. Frank, M.P.: Foundations of generalized reversible computing. In: Phillips, I., Rahaman, H. (eds.) RC 2017. LNCS, vol. 10301, pp. 19–34. Springer, Cham (2017). https://doi.org/10.1007/978-3-319-59936-6_2
5. Landauer, R.: Irreversibility and heat generation in the computing process. IBM J. Res. Dev. **5**(3), 183–191 (1961)
6. Nishida, N., Palacios, A., Vidal, G.: Reversible term rewriting. In: 1st International Conference on Formal Structures for Computation and Deduction (2016)
7. Szilard, L.: Über die Entropieverminderung in einem thermodynamischen System bei Eingriffen intelligenter Wesen. Z. Phys. **53**(11–12), 840–856 (1929)
8. Zhang, D.Y., Seelig, G.: Dynamic DNA nanotechnology using strand-displacement reactions. Nat. Chem. **3**(2), 103–113 (2011)

Formal Translation from Reversing Petri Nets to Coloured Petri Nets

Kamila Barylska[1], Anna Gogolińska[1(✉)], Łukasz Mikulski[1,2], Anna Philippou[3],
Marcin Piatkowski[1], and Kyriaki Psara[3]

[1] Faculty of Mathematics and Computer Science, Nicolaus Copernicus University,
Toruń, Poland
{kamila.barylska,anna.gogolinska,lukasz.mikulski,
marcin.piatkowski}@mat.umk.pl
[2] Institute of Computer Science, Polish Academy of Sciences, Warsaw, Poland
[3] Department of Computer Science, University of Cyprus, Nicosia, Cyprus
{annap,kpsara01}@cs.ucy.ac.cy

Abstract. Reversing Petri nets (RPNs) have recently proposed as a
Petri-net inspired formalism that supports the modelling of causal and
out-of-causal order reversibility. In previous works we proposed a structural way of translating a specific subclass of RPNs into bounded
coloured Petri nets (CPNs). In this paper we extend these results by
removing the restriction of token uniqueness. The proposed transformation from RPNs to CPNs has been implemented in a tool, which allows
building an RPN and converting it to an equivalent CPN.

1 Introduction

Reversible computation is an unconventional form of computing, which allows
operations to reverse at any point during computation. It has been attracting
increasing attention in many applications, e.g. low-power computing, quantum
computation, robotics, and distributed systems. Exploring reversibility through
formal models formulates the theoretical foundations of what reversibility is and
what purpose it serves. As such, reversibility has been an active topic of research
in theoretical models of computation including Petri nets (PNs) [5,6,8–11,13,14].

In this paper, we focus on reversing Petri nets (RPNs) [13] - a Petri net type
that allows transitions to be carried out in both the forward and the reverse
directions in or out of causal order. A challenge that arises is to explore the
relationship between RPNs and classical PNs where no global control is allowed
during transition execution. In our previous work [3] we addressed this challenge
by proposing a translation from a subclass of RPNs into coloured Petri nets
(CPNs) [7]. In comparison to [3], our main contributions of this paper are: *(1)*
lifting the restriction of token uniqueness by allowing multiple instances of the
same type/base, *(2)* a refined approach for transforming RPNs to CPNs that
treats all three semantics of backtracking, causal-order, and out-of-causal-order
reversibility, in unified way, and *(3)* the implementation of the transformation
in a tool.

C. A. Mezzina and K. Podlaski (Eds.): RC 2022, LNCS 13354, pp. 172–186, 2022.
https://doi.org/10.1007/978-3-031-09005-9_12

2   Definition of Reversing Petri Nets

In this section we very briefly introduce Reversing Petri nets (RPNs) and we refer the reader to [8, 15] for more information. RPNs support three reversing semantics: *backtracking*, whereby only the last executed transition can be reversed, *causal reversing*, allowing a transition to rollback if all its effects, if any, have been already undone, and *out-of-causal-order reversing*, where any executed action can be reversed. Undoing a transition during the execution of an RPN requires close monitoring of token manipulation. To enable this, in RPNs tokens are associated with names. In addition, during a transition firing, tokens may become bonded with each other. In this paper we allow occurrences of many tokens of the same type. To distinguish between them we use token instances.

Definition 1. A *reversing Petri net* (RPN) is a tuple (P, T, F, A, B):

1. P is a finite set of *places*,   2. T is a finite set of *transitions*,
3. $F : (P \times T \cup T \times P) \to \mathbb{N}^{A \cup B \cup \overline{A} \cup \overline{B}}$ is a set of directed *arcs*,
4. A is a finite set of *base* or *token types* ranged over by $a, b, \ldots$ Instances of tokens of type a are denoted by a_i where i is unique and the set of all instances of token types in A is denoted by $\mathcal{A}$. Furthermore, we write $\overline{A} = \{\overline{a} \mid a \in A\}$ for the set containing a "negative" form for each token type[1],
5. $B \subseteq A \times A$ is a set of undirected *bond types*. We assume that the relation B is symmetric. The two elements $(a, b), (b, a) \in B$ are represented by $\langle a, b \rangle$ also denoted as $a-b$. Similarly, instances of bonds are elements of $\mathcal{A} \times \mathcal{A}$ and denoted by $\langle a_i, b_j \rangle$ or $a_i - b_j$ for $a_i, b_j \in \mathcal{A}$. The set of all instances of bond types in B is denoted by $\mathcal{B}$. $\overline{B} = \{\overline{\beta} \mid \beta \in B\}$ contains the "negative" form for each bond type.

As in standard Petri nets the association of tokens to places is called a *marking* $M : P \to 2^{A \cup B}$. In addition, we employ the notion of a *history*, which assigns a memory to each transition $H : T \to 2^{\mathbb{N} \times 2^{P \times A}}$ to allow recording of transitions executions. A pair of a marking and a history, $\langle M, H \rangle$, describes a *state* of an RPN with the initial state $\langle M_0, H_0 \rangle$, where $H_0(t) = \emptyset$ for all $t \in T$.

We restrict our attention to acyclic RPNs with transitions of one of three types: (a) transitions T^{TRN} that receive a token instance from their unique input place and transfer it to their unique output place, (b) transitions T^{BC1} that receive two token instances from their unique input place and create a bond between them which is placed to their unique output place, and (c) transitions T^{BC2} which receive two token instances – one from each of their two input places and create a bond between them, which is placed in their unique output place. We refer to a subclass of RPNs that satisfy the above restrictions as *low-level* RPNs.

To better understand the concept of RPNs consider the example presented in Fig. 1. This RPN has five places, three transitions, token types $\{a, b, c\}$, and

---

[1] Elements of A denote the presence of a base, whereas elements of $\overline{A}$ their absence.

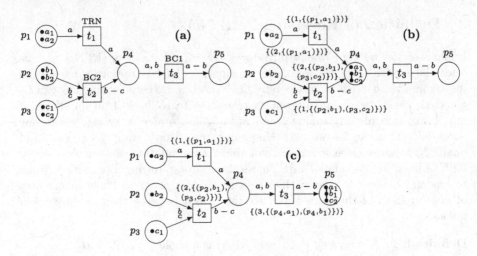

Fig. 1. Exemplary reversing Petri net.

token instances a_1, a_2 of type a, instances b_1, b_2 of type b, and c_1, c_2 of type c. The labels on the arcs between places and transitions specify the tokens or bonds required for the transition to fire (for incoming arcs), and the tokens or bonds produced as the effect of a transition (for outgoing arcs). Here, transition t_1 transfers a token of type a, t_2 requires tokens of types b and c and creates a bond between them, and t_3 takes tokens of types a, b and bonds them. Note that if a token instance is connected to further instances then, if it is employed to fire a transition, the whole connected component has to be used. In Fig. 1(a) an initial marking is presented. Figure 1(b) depicts the marking obtained after execution of transitions t_1 and t_2, which is the same regardless of the order in which the transitions are executed. Let us discuss what happened. Transition t_1 needed a token of type a and there were two possible instances a_1, a_2, of which a_1 was chosen. Similarly, t_2 used b_1 and c_2 and created the bond $\langle b_1, c_2 \rangle$. Note, that any of the combinations $\langle b_1, c_1 \rangle$, $\langle b_2, c_1 \rangle$, $\langle b_2, c_2 \rangle$ would have been possible. The history function is presented above the transitions (for sequence $t_1 t_2$) or below the transitions (for sequence $t_2 t_1$). In both cases the first component of the history values is a number denoting the order in which the transition was executed. The second component contains the names of the transferred token instances and the places from which they were taken.

Assuming the execution sequence $t_1 t_2$, if one decides to reverse a transition in the state presented in Fig. 1(b) using the backtracking semantics, only transition t_2 can be rolled back. It would result in breaking the bond $\langle b_1, c_2 \rangle$ and b_1 would go back to p_2, while c_2 to p_3. Information about the reversed execution would be removed from the history of t_2, hence its history would become empty. However, if the causal semantics were chosen both t_1 and t_2 could be reversed because they are causally independent. Reversing t_2 would proceed the same as in the backtracking case. If t_1 is reversed instead, token a_1 would be transferred back to

p_1 and the history of t_1 would become empty. To keep history values consistent, histories of other transitions with higher number in the sequence of executions have to be decreased by one. This would result in changing the history value of t_2 to $\{(1, \{(p_2, b_1), (p_3, c_2)\})\}$.

After execution of $t_1 t_2 t_3$ – Fig. 1(c) – for backtracking and causal reversing, t_3 is the only transition that can be reversed, because it is the last executed transition (backtracking) and it used effects of both the t_1 and t_2 firings (causal reversing). Undoing t_3 would lead to the state in Fig. 1(b). However, in the out-of-causal-order semantics all three transitions can be reversed. For example, reversing t_2 would result in breaking the bond $\langle b_1, c_2 \rangle$. Instance b_1 would stay in p_5 due to its bond to a_1. In contrast, c_2 has not been used by any non-reversed transition and it would not be connected to any other instance, hence it would return to its initial place p_3. The history of t_2 would be empty, and the value of the history function of t_3 would be updated similarly to the causal example.

3   Transformation and Software

Let us recall that for a given low-level RPN $N_R = (P_R, T_R, A_R, B_R, F_R)$, we have the following decomposition: $T_R = T_R^{BC1} \cup T_R^{BC2} \cup T_R^{TRN}$. To describe the transformation from RPNs to CPNs (see [7] for definition) first we have to define relations and sets, which are used in the transformation.

For an RPN we define relation $\rightarrow$ on $P_R \cup T_R$ as follows: $x \rightarrow y$ if $F(x, y)$ is not empty and we call it a *direct order*. Relation $\prec$ on $P_R \cup T_R$ is the transitive (but irreflexive) closure of $\rightarrow$. We assume that the enumeration of transitions is consistent with $\prec$ (i.e. if $t_i \prec t_j$ then $i < j$).

For any element $x \in P_R \cup T_R$ or transition $t \in T_R$, we consider the following five sets: (1) the *neighborhood* set of x, denoted as $nei(x)$; (2) the set of *dependency counters* of t, denoted as $dpc(t)$; (3) the set of *dependency histories* of t denoted as $dph(t)$; (4) the set of *reversing input places* of t denoted as $rin(t)$; (5) the set of *reversing output places* of t denoted as $rout(t)$. The introduced sets differ depending on the assumed operational semantics of reversing. Apart from these sets, the transformation is identical for all three semantics. In Table 1 we present how these sets are defined depending on the relative semantics.

During the transformation from RPNs to CPNs the state of an RPN $\langle M, H \rangle$ has to be morphed into a marking of a CPN. The main structure of the CPN is the same as the RPN – a CPN contains the same places and transitions (and some additional elements described below). Transferring the marking M is quite straightforward: Token types and token instances are represented by equivalent colours in the CPN. The colour assigned to places in the CPN corresponding to places from the RPN is called a *molecule* and it consists of a pair of two sets: token instances and instances of bonds. The selection of instances required by transitions to be executed is made by transitions guards. Expressions of incoming and outgoing transitions arcs describe transferring of tokens instances and (eventual) creating of bonds. To allow reversing, for every transition $t \in T_R$ a new reversing transition tr is added. Execution of this transition is equivalent

Table 1. Sets *nei*, *dpc*, *dph*, *rin* and *rout* for three operational semantics of reversing.

backtracking
$nei_{BT}(x) = \{y \in P_R \cup T_R \mid (x \to y \vee y \to x) \vee (\exists_{z \in P_R \cup T_R}\, x \to z \to y \vee y \to z \to x)\}$

$dpc_{BT}(t) = T_R \setminus \{t\}$	$dph_{BT}(t) = nei_{BT}(t) \cap T_R$
$rin_{BT}(t) = nei_{BT}(t) \cap P_R$	$rout_{BT}(t) = nei_{BT}(t) \cap P_R$

causal-order reversing
$nei_C(x) = \{y \in P_R \cup T_R \mid (x \to y \vee y \to x) \vee (\exists_{z \in P_R \cup T_R}\, x \to z \to y \vee y \to z \to x)\}$

$dpc_C(t) = nei_C(t) \cap T_R$	$dph_C(t) = nei_C(t) \cap T_R$
$rin_C(t) = nei_C(t) \cap P_R$	$rout_C(t) = nei_C(t) \cap P_R$

out-of-causal-order reversing
$nei_{OOC}(x) = \{y \in P_R \cup T_R \mid x \prec y \vee y \prec x\}$

$dpc_{OOC}(t) = nei_{OOC}(t) \cap T_R$	$dph_{OOC}(t) = nei_{OOC}(t) \cap T_R$
$rin_{OOC}(t) = nei_{OOC}(t) \cap P_R$	$rout_{OOC}(t) = nei_{OOC}(t) \cap P_R$

to the reversing of a selected execution of transition t. More precisely, if t is a transferring transition, tr transfers back the used token instance; if t creates a bond, tr breaks the bond. Transition tr is connected (in both directions) with places from: *(1)* $rin(t)$ to be able to collect the molecule that is affected by the execution to be reversed and *(2)* $rout(t)$ to be able to transfer back the molecule or molecules (possible in case of breaking a bond) obtained after reversing the effect of t. Selection of the correct molecule affected by reversed execution is made by the guard of reversing transition tr. Transferring of the molecule and undoing the effect of the execution of t is achieved by arcs expressions between tr and places from the sets $rin(t)$ and $rout(t)$.

The history function H, which introduces a global control to RPNs, is distributed in CPNs into two types of new places: *transition history places* and *connection history places*. A transition history place (*thp*) is created for every transition and it contains information about the history of executions of that transition. The content of transition history places is important during reversing and to reverse a transition t sometimes it is necessary to check and modify the content of transition history places of other transitions – the set of these transitions is denoted by $dph(t)$. A connection history place is created for a pair of transitions and it contains a number (counter), which describes how many times transitions from the pair were executed. Such places are not created for every pair of transitions, but for a given transition t they are added only for transition t and transitions from $dpc(t)$. Transitions t and tr are connected by arcs in both directions with their own history place, history places of transitions from $dph(t)$, and connection history places created for t and transitions from $dpc(t)$. Expressions of these arcs allow to update the histories.

The CPN obtained for the RPN in Fig. 1(c) is shown in Fig. 2 for out-of-causal-order semantics. In the figure instances are pairs of a token type and the instance index, for example $(a, 1)$ represents a_1 (similarly for bonds). The marking of place p_5 is equivalent to the one presented in Fig. 1(c), p_5 contains seven idle tokens (added for technical reasons) and a molecule consisting of instances: a_1, b_1, c_2 and bonds $\langle a_1, b_1 \rangle$, $\langle b_1, c_1 \rangle$ represented as both pairs. Let us consider the marking of place h_3. It contains a set (implemented as a list) of 4-tuples. One 4-tuple is added to the place for each execution of t_3 and each transition from $dpc(t_3)$, i.e. t_1, t_2 and t_0 (which is added to the net for technical reasons). The first component of a 4-tuple is a number of the considered execution of t_3 in the sequence of executions of t_3 and other transition from $dpc(t_3)$, the second component is an index of transition from $dpc(t_3)$, the third is an index of t_3, the fourth is a list of instances indicating the considered execution. For example $(2, 1, 3, [(a, 1), (b, 1)])$ captures that t_3 was executed in the sequence of executions of transitions of t_1 and t_3 as the second one and it used instances a_1, b_1. For out-of-causal-order semantics all transitions from Fig. 2 can be reversed, hence tr_1, tr_2 and tr_3 are enabled.

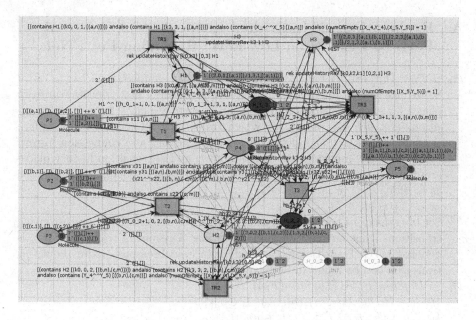

Fig. 2. CPN generated for RPN presented in Fig. 1.

The transformation of RPNs to CPNs described in this paper has been implemented in a java application **RPNEditor**, which may be downloaded at the webpage [2]. The application provides a graphical user interface for displaying and edition of low-level RPNs. A net prepared in the application (alternatively loaded from an XML file) may be transformed into a CPN and stored in the format required by CPN-Tools software [1]. Moreover, at [2] a few examples, as a proof of concept, and the formal description of the presented RPN to CPN transformation are available.

4   Conclusions

In this paper we present work in progress towards examining the relationship between RPNs and *bounded* CPNs. The boundedness assures that the state space is finite and all inhibitors can be dropped by a standard complementary net construction [4,12].

A structural transformation from RPNs to CPNs is provided by encoding the structure of the net along with the execution. In this paper we extend the RPN framework from [3] by lifting the restriction on tokens singularity. To handle token multiplicity in RPNs, and corresponding to them CPNs, semantics of the models have been changed.

Additionally, an algorithmic translation has been implemented in an automated manner using the transformation discussed in this paper. A software solution based on CPN-Tools [7] was employed to illustrate that the translations conform to the semantics of reversible computation.

A   Explanations of Individual Elements of a Coloured Perti Net Based on Low-Level Reversing Petri Net

$P_C = P_R \cup \{h_i \mid t_i \in T_R\} \cup \{h_{ij} \mid t_i, t_j \in T_R; i < j; t_j \in dpc(t_i)\}$

Set of places contains places from the original RPN net, transition history places for each transition and connection history places for pairs of transitions (set dpc determines for which transitions connection history place is added). Notice, that indexes of transition history and connection history places are very important. For transitions t_i and t_j transition history places are denoted as h_i and h_j (respectively), connection history place is denoted as t_{ij} (for $i < j$) or t_{ji} (for $i > j$).

$T_C = T_R \cup \{tr_i \mid t_i \in T_R\} \cup \{t_0\}$

Set of transitions contains transitions from the original RPN and reversing transitions - one for each original transition. A reversing transition for t_i is denoted as tr_i. Transition t_0 is added for technical reasons - more about this transition can be found in Software section.

$D_C = Domain(F_R) \cup (Domain(F_R))^{-1} \cup$
$\{(t_i, h_i), (h_i, t_i), (tr_i, h_i), (h_i, tr_i) \mid t_i \in T_R\} \cup$
$\{(tr_i, h_j), (h_j, tr_i) \mid t_i \in T_R; t_j \in dph(t_i)\} \cup$
$\{(t_i, h_{jk}), (h_{jk}, t_i), (tr_i, h_{jk}), (h_{jk}, tr_i) \mid t_i \in T_R; \{i, l\} = \{j, k\};$
$$t_l \in dpc(t_i)\}$$

This set contains arcs: arcs from RPN N_R, arcs opposite to those from N_R, arcs between every transition t_i and its history places (in both directions), arcs between every reversing transition tr_i and the history place of t_i (in both directions), arcs between every reversing transition tr_i and history places of transitions from $dph(t_i)$ (in both directions), arcs between every transition t_i and all its connection history places (in both directions), arcs between every reversing transition tr_i and all connection history places of t_i (in both directions).

$$\Sigma_C = \mathbb{N}_b \cup A_R \cup B_R \cup \overline{A_R} \cup \overline{B_R} \cup \mathcal{A} \cup \mathcal{B} \cup (2^{\mathcal{A}} \times 2^{\mathcal{B}}) \cup 2^{(\mathbb{N}_b \times T_R \times T_R \times 2^{\mathcal{A}})}$$

We define the following colours: a bounded set of natural numbers, base types, bond types, negative base types, negative bond types, instances of bases, instances of bonds, Cartesian product of subsets of token instances and subsets of bond instances – **molecules**, subsets of 4-tuples (one 4-tuple contains the following information: the second transition in the tuple, in the context of the first one in the tuple, was n-th in the sequence of executions and has used the given base instances).

$$V_C = \{(\mathcal{X}_i, \mathcal{Y}_i) \in (2^{\mathcal{A}} \times 2^{\mathcal{B}}) \mid i \in \mathbb{N}_b\} \cup (\mathcal{X}, \mathcal{Y}) \in (2^{\mathcal{A}} \times 2^{\mathcal{B}}) \cup$$
$$\{(\alpha_i \in \mathcal{A} \mid i \in \mathbb{N}_b\} \cup \{cnt_i \in \mathbb{N}_b \mid i \in \{1, ..., |T_R|\}\} \cup$$
$$\{H_i \in 2^{(\mathbb{N}_b \times T_R \times T_R \times 2^{\mathcal{A}})} \mid i \in \{1, ..., |T_R|\}\}$$

$$C_C = \{p \mapsto (2^{\mathcal{A}} \times 2^{\mathcal{B}}) \mid p \in P_R\} \cup$$
$$\{h_i \mapsto 2^{(\mathbb{N}_b \times T_R \times T_R \times 2^{\mathcal{A}})} \mid t_i \in T_R\} \cup$$
$$\{h_{ij} \mapsto \mathbb{N}_b \mid t_i, t_j \in T_R; i < j; t_j \in dpc(t_i)\}$$

This set describes which colours are assigned to which places (respectively): colour *molecule* to places from RPN, set of 4-tuples to history places, and set of bounded natural numbers to connection history places.

$$G_C = G_C^{TRN} \cup G_C^{BC1} \cup G_C^{BC2} \cup G_C^{t_0} \cup G_C^{\overline{t_0}} \cup G_C^{\overline{TRN}} \cup G_C^{\overline{BC1 \cup BC2}}$$

where

$$G_C^{BC1} = \{t_i \mapsto (\alpha_1 \in \mathcal{X}_1 \wedge \alpha_2 \in \mathcal{X}_2) \vee (\alpha_1, \alpha_2 \in \mathcal{X}_1 \wedge \langle \alpha_1, \alpha_2 \rangle \notin \mathcal{Y}_1$$
$$\wedge (\mathcal{X}_2, \mathcal{Y}_2) = (\emptyset, \emptyset)) \mid$$
$$t_i \in T_R^{BC1}; \{\ell(\alpha_1), \ell(\alpha_2)\} \subset F_R(\bullet t_i, t_i);$$
$$\alpha_1 \neq \alpha_2; \{(\mathcal{X}_1, \mathcal{Y}_1), (\mathcal{X}_2, \mathcal{Y}_2)\} \subseteq Var[E_C(\bullet t_i, t_i)];$$
$$F_R(\bullet t_i, t_i) \cap (\overline{A} \cup \overline{B}) \cap \ell(\mathcal{X}_1 \cup \mathcal{X}_2 \cup \mathcal{Y}_1 \cup \mathcal{Y}_2) = \emptyset\}$$

– Guard of BC1 transition evaluates whether a set of base instances $\mathcal{X}_1$ of a molecule $(\mathcal{X}_1, \mathcal{Y}_1)$ contains an instance α_1 and a set of instances $\mathcal{X}_2$ of a molecule $(\mathcal{X}_2, \mathcal{Y}_2)$ contains an instance α_2, both sets are obtained for the only input place. The types of those instances form a label of an arc between the input place and the transition in the original RPN, α_1 and α_2 differs, and the molecules do not contain negative base nor bond types. It might also happen that a new bond is created within the already existing molecule - in that case both instances α_1, α_2 are unbonded and contained in molecule $(\mathcal{X}_1, \mathcal{Y}_1)$, and the second molecule $(\mathcal{X}_2, \mathcal{Y}_2)$ is empty (an idle token).

$$G_C^{BC2} = \{t_i \mapsto (\alpha_1 \in \mathcal{X}_1 \wedge \alpha_2 \in \mathcal{X}_2) \mid$$
$$t_i \in T_R^{BC2}; \{\ell(\alpha_1), \ell(\alpha_2)\} \subset \bigcup_{X \in F_R(\bullet t_i, t_i)} X;$$
$$\alpha_1 \neq \alpha_2; p_1 \neq p_2 \in \bullet t_i;$$
$$(\mathcal{X}_1, \mathcal{Y}_1) \in Var[E_C(p_1, t_i)]; (\mathcal{X}_2, \mathcal{Y}_2) \in Var[E_C(p_2, t_i)];$$
$$\bigcup_{X \in F_R(\bullet t_i, t_i)} X \cap (\overline{A} \cup \overline{B}) \cap \ell(\mathcal{X}_1 \cup \mathcal{X}_2 \cup \mathcal{Y}_1 \cup \mathcal{Y}_2) = \emptyset\}$$

– Guard of BC2 transition evaluates whether a set of base instances $\mathcal{X}_1$ of a molecule $(\mathcal{X}_1, \mathcal{Y}_1)$ obtained from the first input place contains an instance α_1, set of base instances $\mathcal{X}_2$ of a molecule $(\mathcal{X}_2, \mathcal{Y}_2)$ obtained from the second input place contains an instance α_2, types of those instances form labels of arcs between the input places and the transition in the original RPN, α_1 and α_2 differs, there are two different input places, and the molecules obtained from input places do not contain negative base nor bond types.

$G_C^{TRN} = \{t_i \mapsto (\alpha \in \mathcal{X}) \mid$
$t_i \in T_R^{TRN}; \ell(\alpha) \in F_R(\bullet t_i, t_i); E_C(\bullet t_i, t_i) = \{(\mathcal{X}, \mathcal{Y})\};$
$F_R(\bullet t_i, t_i) \cap (\overline{A} \cup \overline{B}) \cap \ell(\mathcal{X} \cup \mathcal{Y}) = \emptyset\}$

– Guard of TRN transition evaluates whenever a set of base instances $\mathcal{X}$ of a molecule $(\mathcal{X}, \mathcal{Y})$ obtained from the input place contains an instance α, type of α form a label of an arc between the input place and the transition, and the molecule does not contain negative base nor bond types.

$G_C^{t_0} = \{t_0 \mapsto false\}$

– Guard of the initial transition t_0 - always returns $false$, hence the transition cannot be executed.

$G_C^{\overline{t_0}} = \{tr_0 \mapsto false\}$

– Guard of reversing transition for the initial transition t_0 - always returns $false$, hence the transition cannot be executed.

The last two guards are a little bit more complex, that is why we include functions in their descriptions. Those functions are: $isElement$ and $numOfnonEmpty$[2]. The function $isElement$ returns $true$ if its first argument is an element of the set given as the second argument. In the opposite case the function returns $false$. The function $numOfnonEmpty$ counts how many of its arguments are equal to $(\emptyset, \emptyset)$ and returns that number.

Both following guards have the same construction. The first element of a guard is a logical conjunction of $\#dpc(t_i)$ conditions, each of them ensures that the token describing the history of t_i and obtained from the place h_i (which is represented as $E_C(h_i, tr_i)$ in the guards) contains 4-tuple related to the execution which is reversed. In the forward execution of the transition (to be reversed) the base α was transported (for transporting transition) or a bond between instances α_1 and α_2 was created (for BC1 or BC2 transition), which from now on is denoted as $\langle \alpha_1, \alpha_2 \rangle$. This part of the guards is very important because exactly here the choice: *which execution would be reversed?* (which is equivalent to the choice: *execution related to which instances would be reversed?*) is made. In CPN examples, prepared using CPN-Tools, this choice can be made by the user or randomly. The next part of the guards checks whether the set consisting of instances of bases (for TRN transition) or bonds (for BC1 and BC2 transition) obtained from all input places of the transition (to be reversed), contains instances related to its forward execution. The last part of the guards assures that from all tokens obtained from input places only one describes a molecule, the remaining ones should be idle tokens.

$G_C^{\overline{TRN}} = \{tr_i \mapsto (\bigwedge_{t_j \in dpc(t_i)} isElement((k_j, t_j, t_i, \{\alpha\}), E_C(h_i, tr_i));$
$isElement(\alpha, \bigcup_{p_g \in rin(t_i)} \mathcal{X}_g);$
$numOfnonEmpty(\{(\mathcal{X}_g, \mathcal{Y}_g) \mid p_g \in rin(t_i)\})) = 1$
where

---

[2] Exemplary implementations of those functions are included in coloured Petri nets generated by our application. Their formal definitions are included in descriptions of guards.

$$t_i \in T_R^{TRN} \; ; \; \ell(\alpha) \in F_R(t_i, t_i \bullet); \; \forall_{p_g \in rin(t_i)} (\mathcal{X}_g, \mathcal{Y}_g) = b(E_C(p_g, tr_i))$$

isElement$(q, Q) = true$ if and only if $q \in Q$;

numOfnonEmpty$(Q) = \#\{(q_1, q_2) \in Q \mid (q_1, q_2) \neq (\emptyset, \emptyset)\}$ }

$G_C^{\overline{BC1 \cup BC2}} =$

$\{tr_i \mapsto (\bigwedge_{t_j \in dpc(t_i)} \text{isElement}((k_j, t_j, t_i, \{\langle \alpha_1, \alpha_2 \rangle\}), E_C(h_i, tr_i));$

isElement$(\langle \alpha_1, \alpha_2 \rangle, \bigcup_{p_g \in rin(t_i)} \mathcal{Y}_g);$

numOfnonEmpty$(\{(\mathcal{X}_g, \mathcal{Y}_g) \mid p_g \in rin(t_i)\})) = 1$

where

$t_i \in (T_R^{BC1} \cup T_R^{BC2}); \{\ell(\alpha_1), \ell(\alpha_2)\} \in F_R(t_i, t_i \bullet)$;

$\forall_{p_g \in rin(t_i)} (\mathcal{X}_g, \mathcal{Y}_g) = b(E_C(p_g, tr_i));$

isElement$(q, Q) = true$ if and only if $q \in Q$;

numOfnonEmpty$(Q) = \#\{(q_1, q_2) \in Q \mid (q_1, q_2) \neq (\emptyset, \emptyset)\}$ }

$E_C = \{(p, t) \mapsto (\mathcal{X}, \mathcal{Y}) \mid (p, t) \in Domain(F_R); t \in T_R^{TRN} \cup T_R^{BC2}\}$

Description of input arcs from the original RPN for TRN and $BC2$ transitions - the transfer of one molecule $(\mathcal{X}, \mathcal{Y})$ obtained from the place p.

∪

$\{(p, t) \mapsto (1'(\mathcal{X}_1, \mathcal{Y}_1) + +1'(\mathcal{X}_2, \mathcal{Y}_2)) \mid (p, t) \in Domain(F_R); t \in T_R^{BC1}\}$

Description of input arcs from the original RPN for $BC1$ transition - the transfer of two molecules from place p (in the guard it is assumed that one of those molecules may be empty).

∪

$\{(t, p) \mapsto (\emptyset, \emptyset) \mid (p, t) \in Domain(F_R)\}$

Description of arcs opposite to input arcs from the original RPN. An idle token is transferred.

∪

$\{(t, p) \mapsto (\mathcal{X}, \mathcal{Y}) \mid$
$\qquad E_C(\bullet t, t) = \{(\mathcal{X}, \mathcal{Y})\}; t \in T_R^{TRN}; (t, p) \in Domain(F_R)\}$

Description of output arcs for TRN transitions, similar to the ones from RPN. They contain transfer of the molecule obtained from the input place.

∪

$\{(t, p) \mapsto (\mathcal{X}_1 \cup \mathcal{X}_2, \mathcal{Y}_1 \cup \mathcal{Y}_2 \cup \{\langle \alpha_1, \alpha_2 \rangle\}) \mid E_C(\bullet t) = \{(\mathcal{X}_1, \mathcal{Y}_1), (\mathcal{X}_2, \mathcal{Y}_2)\};$
$\{\ell(\alpha_1), \ell(\alpha_2)\} \in F_R(t, p); t \in T_R^{BC1} \cup T_R^{BC2}; (t, p) \in Domain(F_R)\}$

Description of output arcs for BC1 and BC2 transitions. They describe the transfer of the molecules containing the instances of bases and bonds, obtained from the input places (BC2) or place (BC1) and the new bond. Types of the instances in the new bond should be consistent with the label of the arc in RPN.

∪

$\{(p, t) \mapsto (\emptyset, \emptyset) \mid (t, p) \in Domain(F_R); t \in T_R\}$

Description of arcs opposite to input arcs from the original RPN. An idle token is transferred.

∪

$\{(h_{jk}, t_i) \mapsto cnt_l \mid t_i \in T_R; \{i, l\} = \{j, k\}; t_l \in dpc(t_i)\}$

Description of arc from connection history place to a transition. The value obtained from that place is represented by variable cnt_l.

$\cup$

$\{(t_i, h_{jk}) \mapsto E_C(h_{jk}, t_i) + 1 \mid t_i \in T_R; \{i, l\} = \{j, k\}; t_l \in dpc(t_i)\}$

Description of the arc from a transition to its connection history place. It describes the transfer of the value obtained from that place (by the opposite arc) increased by 1.

$\cup$

$\{(h_i, t_i) \mapsto H_l \mid H_l \in 2^{(\mathbb{N}_b \times T_R \times T_R \times 2^A)}\}$

Description of the arc from transition history place to the transition. The value obtained from that place is represented by variable H_l and it contains the whole history of transition t_i (a set of 4-tuples).

$\cup$

$\{(t_i, h_i) \mapsto E_C(h_i, t_i) \cup \bigcup_{t_l \in dpc(t_i)} \{(E_C(h_{jk}, t_i) + 1, t_l, t_i, \{\langle \alpha_1, \alpha_2 \rangle\})\}\}$

where

$t_i \notin T_R^{TRN}; \{i, l\} = \{j, k\}; \langle \ell(\alpha_1), \ell(\alpha_2) \rangle \in F_R(t_i, t_i \bullet)\}$

Description of the arc from BC1 or BC2 transition to its transition history place. The value obtained from the transition history place is transferred back (its described by $E_C(h_i, t_i)$) and a new 4-tuple is added for every transition from $dpc(t_i)$. Each tuple consists of 4 components: the first is a number of current execution of t_i in the sequence of executions of t_i and t_l - this value is obtained from h_{il} or h_{li}, the next two components are identifiers of transitions and the last one is the description of the bond created during the considered execution.

$\cup$

$\{(t_i, h_i) \mapsto E_C(h_i, t_i) \cup \bigcup_{t_l \in dpc(t_i)} \{E_C(h_{jk}, t_i) + 1, t_l, t_i, \{\alpha\})\}$

where

$t_i \in T_R^{TRN}; \{i, l\} = \{j, k\}; \ell(\alpha) \in F_R(t_i, t_i \bullet)\}$

Description of the arc from TRN transition to its transition history place. It is very similar to the previous one, except for the last component of the 4-tuples - in this case it is the description of the base instances which were transferred during the considered execution.

$\cup$

$\{(h_{jk}, tr_i) \mapsto cnt_l \mid t_i \in T_R; \{i, l\} = \{j, k\}; t_l \in dpc(t_i)\}$

Description of the arc from transition history counter place of t_i to its reversing transition tr_i. The value obtained from the place is represented by cnt_l and it is a number of executions of transitions t_i and t_l.

$\cup$

$\{(tr_i, h_{jk}) \mapsto E_C(h_{jk}, tr_i) - 1 \mid t_i \in T_R; \{i, l\} = \{j, k\}; t_l \in dpc(t_i)\}$

Description of the arc from reversing transition tr_i to connection history place of t_i. It describes the transfer of the value obtained from the connection history place by the transition tr_i decreased by one.

$\cup$

$\{(h_j, tr_i) \mapsto H_j \mid (H_j \in 2^{(\mathbb{N}_b \times T_R \times T_R \times 2^A)}; (t_j \in dph(t_i) \vee j = i))\}$

Description of the arc from transition history place of t_i to its reversing transition. The value obtained from that place is represented by variable H_j and it contains the whole history of transition t_i (a set of 4-tuples).

$\cup$

$\{(\boldsymbol{p}, \boldsymbol{tr_i}) \mapsto 2`(\emptyset, \emptyset) \mid (p \in rin(t_i); \forall_{t_j \in T_R} p \notin t_j \bullet)\}$

Description of the arc between a place to a reversing transition. The place has to be in a set $rin(t_i)$ and it cannot be an input place to any transition. Then two idle tokens are transferred from the place.

$\cup$

$\{(\boldsymbol{p}, \boldsymbol{tr_i}) \mapsto (1`(\mathcal{X}, \mathcal{Y}) + +1`(\emptyset, \emptyset)) \mid (p \in rin(t_i); \exists_{t_j \in T_R} p \in t_j \bullet)\}$

Description of the arc between a place to a reversing transition. The place has to be in a set $rin(t_i)$ and it has to be an input place to some transition from the net. Then a molecule and an idle token are transferred from the place (during execution the molecule also can be an idle token).

$\cup$

$\{(\boldsymbol{tr_i}, \boldsymbol{h_j}) \mapsto updateExtHist(k_j \in Var[G_C(tr_i)], E_C(h_j, tr_i))$
where
$t_i \in T_R; t_j \in dph(t_i); (b(k_j), t_j, t_i, Y) \in b(E_C(h_i, tr_i));$
$updateExtHist(k_j, E_C(h_j, tr_i)) =$
$\bigcup_{(k,t_{g \neq i}, t_j, X) \in b(E_C(h_j, tr_i))}(k, t_g, t_j, X) \cup$
$\bigcup_{(k < k_j, t_i, t_j, X) \in b(E_C(h_j, tr_i))}(k, t_i, t_j, X) \cup$
$\bigcup_{(k > k_j, t_i, t_j, X) \in b(E_C(h_j, tr_i))}(k - 1, t_i, t_j, X)\}$

Description of the arc between the reversing transition of t_i and history places of other transitions. It contains calling of $updateExtHist()$ function. The first argument of the function is number k_j which is the first component of 4-tuple from history of transition t_j which have been binded during evaluation of the tr_i guard. The second argument of $updateExtHist()$ consists of elements of t_j's history and the function modifies them: elements not related to the pair t_i and t_j are not changed, elements related to t_i and t_j with the first component k smaller than k_j also are not changed, elements related to t_i and t_j with the firs component k greater than k_j are adjusted by decreasing k by 1.

$\cup$

$\{(\boldsymbol{tr_i}, \boldsymbol{h_i}) \mapsto$
$updateIntHist(K = \{k_j \in Var[G_C(tr_i)] \mid t_j \in dpc(t_i)\}, E_C(h_i, tr_i))$
where
$t_i \in T_R; \forall_{k_j \in K}(b(k_j), t_j, t_i, Y) \in b(E_C(h_i, tr_i));$
$updateIntHist(K, E_C(h_i, tr_i)) =$
$\bigcup_{(k < k_j, t_j, t_i, X) \in b(E_C(h_i, tr_i))}(k, t_j, t_i, X) \cup$
$\bigcup_{(k > k_j, t_j, t_i, X) \in b(E_C(h_i, tr_i))}(k - 1, t_j, t_i, X)\}$
$\cup$

Description of the arc between the reversing transition of t_i and history places of transition t_i. It contains calling of $updateIntHist()$ function. The first argument of the function is the set of numbers k_j which are the first components of 4-tuple from t_i's history related to each pair t_i, t_j, such that $t_j \in dpc(t_i)$ which have been binded during evaluation of the tr_i guard. The second argument of $updateIntHist()$ consist of elements of t_i history and the function modifies them: elements related to t_i and t_j with the first component k smaller than k_j are not changed, elements related to t_i and t_j with k greater than k_j are adjusted by decreasing k by 1.

$\{(\boldsymbol{tr_i}, \boldsymbol{p}) \mapsto (1^{\langle}(\mathcal{X}_1, \mathcal{Y}_1) + +1^{\langle}(\emptyset, \emptyset))$

where

$t_i \in T_R^{TRN}; p \in rout(t_i); \{p\} = t\bullet;$

having $(\mathcal{X}_g, \mathcal{Y}_g) = E_C(p_g, tr_i)$ and $\alpha \in Var[G_C(tr_i)]$:

$(\mathcal{X}_1, \mathcal{Y}_1) = (\emptyset, \emptyset)$ if

$\quad t \neq max((\bigcup_{t_j \in (dph(t_i) \cup t_i)} b(E_C(h_j, tr_i))|_{con(\alpha, \bigcup_{p_g \in rin(t_i)}(\mathcal{X}_g \cup \mathcal{Y}_g))}));$

$\mathcal{X}_1 \cup \mathcal{Y}_1 = con(\alpha, \bigcup_{p_g \in rin(t_i)}(\mathcal{X}_g \cup \mathcal{Y}_g))$ if

$\quad t = max((\bigcup_{t_j \in (dph(t_i) \cup t_i)} b(E_C(h_j, tr_i))|_{con(\alpha, \bigcup_{p_g \in rin(t_i)}(\mathcal{X}_g \cup \mathcal{Y}_g))}))\}$

Description of the arc between reversing transition of transporting transition t_i and its output place p. Transition t_i has transported base instance α in the execution which is reversed in the current execution of tr_i - the value of α is evaluated by the tr_i guard. Place p is an output place of some transition t. Molecules obtained by tr_i from its input place p_g are denoted by $(\mathcal{X}_g, \mathcal{Y}_g)$. Transition tr_i transports an idle token and $(\mathcal{X}_1, \mathcal{Y}_1)$ token which can be either an idle token or a molecule. It is an idle token if t is not the maximal transition of transitions from $dph(t_i)$ indicated by histories obtained from places h_j among those transitions which used the molecule containing α. The $(\mathcal{X}_1, \mathcal{Y}_1)$ token is equal to the molecule containing α if t is the maximal one.

$\cup$

$\{(\boldsymbol{tr_i}, \boldsymbol{p}) \mapsto (1^{\langle}(\mathcal{X}_1, \mathcal{Y}_1) + +1^{\langle}(\mathcal{X}_2, \mathcal{Y}_2))$

where

$t_i \in (T_R^{BC1} \cup T_R^{BC2}); p \in rout(t_i); \{p\} = t\bullet;$

having $(\mathcal{X}_g, \mathcal{Y}_g) = E_C(p_g, tr_i)$ and $\langle \alpha_1, \alpha_2 \rangle \in Var[G_C(tr_i)]$:

$(\mathcal{X}_1, \mathcal{Y}_1) = (\emptyset, \emptyset)$ if

$\quad t \neq max((\bigcup_{t_j \in (dph(t_i) \cup t_i)}$

$\qquad b(E_C(h_j, tr_i))|_{con(\alpha_1, \bigcup_{p_g \in rin(t_i)}(\mathcal{X}_g \cup \mathcal{Y}_g) \setminus \{\langle \alpha_1, \alpha_2 \rangle\})}));$

$\mathcal{X}_1 \cup \mathcal{Y}_1 = con(\alpha_1, \bigcup_{p_g \in rin(t_i)}(\mathcal{X}_g \cup \mathcal{Y}_g) \setminus \{\langle \alpha_1, \alpha_2 \rangle\})$ if

$\quad t = max((\bigcup_{t_j \in (dph(t_i) \cup t_i)}$

$\qquad b(E_C(h_j, tr_i))|_{con(\alpha_1, \bigcup_{p_g \in rin(t_i)}(\mathcal{X}_g \cup \mathcal{Y}_g) \setminus \{\langle \alpha_1, \alpha_2 \rangle\})}));$

$\mathcal{X}_2 \cup \mathcal{Y}_2 = (\emptyset, \emptyset)$ if

$\quad (t \neq max((\bigcup_{t_j \in (dph(t_i) \cup t_i)}$

$\qquad b(E_C(h_j, tr_i))|_{con(\alpha_2, \bigcup_{p_g \in rin(t_i)}(\mathcal{X}_g \cup \mathcal{Y}_g) \setminus \{\langle \alpha_1, \alpha_2 \rangle\})})$

$\quad \vee(\mathcal{X}_1, \mathcal{Y}_1) = (\mathcal{X}_2, \mathcal{Y}_2));$

$\mathcal{X}_2 \cup \mathcal{Y}_2 = con(\alpha_2, \bigcup_{p_g \in rin(t_i)}(\mathcal{X}_g \cup \mathcal{Y}_g) \setminus \{\langle \alpha_1, \alpha_2 \rangle\})$ if

$\quad (t = max((\bigcup_{t_j \in (dph(t_i) \cup t_i)}$

$\qquad b(E_C(h_j, tr_i))|_{con(\alpha_2, \bigcup_{p_g \in rin(t_i)}(\mathcal{X}_g \cup \mathcal{Y}_g) \setminus \{\langle \alpha_1, \alpha_2 \rangle\})})$

$\quad \wedge(\mathcal{X}_1, \mathcal{Y}_1) \neq (\mathcal{X}_2, \mathcal{Y}_2)) \}$

Description of the arc between reversing transition of BC1 or BC2 transition t_i and its output place p. Transition t_i has created a bond $\langle \alpha_1, \alpha_2 \rangle$ in the execution which is reversed in the current execution of tr_i - the value of $\langle \alpha_1, \alpha_2 \rangle$

is evaluated by the tr_i guard. Molecules obtained by tr_i from its input place p_g are denoted by $(\mathcal{X}_g, \mathcal{Y}_g)$. Place p is an output place of some transition t. Transition tr_i transports two tokens: $(\mathcal{X}_1, \mathcal{Y}_1)$ and $(\mathcal{X}_2, \mathcal{Y}_2)$ - both can be an idle ones. The $(\mathcal{X}_1, \mathcal{Y}_1)$ token is an idle token if t is not the maximal transition of transitions from $dph(t_i)$ indicated by histories obtained from places h_j among those transitions which used the molecule containing α_1 after breaking bond $\langle \alpha_1, \alpha_2 \rangle$. The $(\mathcal{X}_1, \mathcal{Y}_1)$ token is equal to the molecule containing α_1 after breaking $\langle \alpha_1, \alpha_2 \rangle$ if t is the maximal one. The same for $(\mathcal{X}_2, \mathcal{Y}_2)$ but then we consider molecule containing α_2. $(\mathcal{X}_1, \mathcal{Y}_1)$ cannot be equal to $(\mathcal{X}_2, \mathcal{Y}_2)$.

$$I_C = \{p \mapsto ConCom(M_0(p)) + +(\mathbb{K} - \#ConCom(M_0(p)))`(\emptyset, \emptyset) \mid p \in P_R\} \cup$$
$$\{h_i \mapsto \emptyset \mid t_i \in T_R\} \cup$$
$$\{h_{ij} \mapsto 0 \mid t_i, t_j \in T_R; t_i \prec t_j; t_j \in dpc(t_i)\}$$

Initial expressions of places. All places from P_R contain molecules from the initial marking of N_R and idle tokens (to fulfill $\mathbb{K}$ strong safeness), places h_i contain empty sets and places h_{ij} contain 0. For technical reasons those initial values in places are set by initialization transition t_0. That transition is a part of $dph(t)$ set for every $t \in T_R$, is executed at the initial marking and cannot be reversed. It is added to the net so that the max always exists.

References

1. CPN-Tools project website. http://cpntools.org/
2. RPNEditor: Reversing Petri Net Editor. https://www.mat.umk.pl/~folco/rpneditor
3. Barylska, K., Gogolińska, A., Mikulski, Ł., Philippou, A., Piątkowski, M., Psara, K.: Reversing computations modelled by coloured Petri nets. In: Proceedings of ATAED 2018, CEUR 2115, pp. 91–111 (2018)
4. Barylska, K., Mikulski, Ł., Piątkowski, M., Koutny, M., Erofeev, E.: Reversing transitions in bounded Petri nets. In: Proceedings of CS&P'16, CEUR 1698, pp. 74–85 (2016). CEUR-WS.org
5. Barylska, K., Koutny, M., Mikulski, Ł., Piątkowski, M.: Reversible computation vs. reversibility in Petri nets. Sci. Comput. Program. **151**, 48–60 (2018)
6. de Frutos-Escrig, D., Koutny, M., Mikulski, Ł: Investigating reversibility of steps in Petri nets. Fundam. Informaticae **183**(1–2), 67–96 (2021)
7. Jensen, K.: Coloured Petri Nets - Basic Concepts, Analysis Methods and Practical Use - Volume 1, 2nd edn. Monographs in Theoretical Computer Science. An EATCS Series. Springer, Heidelberg (1996). https://doi.org/10.1007/978-3-662-03241-1
8. Kuhn, S., Aman, B., Ciobanu, G., Philippou, A., Psara, K., Ulidowski, I.: Reversibility in chemical reactions. In: Ulidowski, I., Lanese, I., Schultz, U.P., Ferreira, C. (eds.) RC 2020. LNCS, vol. 12070, pp. 151–176. Springer, Cham (2020). https://doi.org/10.1007/978-3-030-47361-7_7
9. Melgratti, H., Mezzina, C.A., Phillips, I., Pinna, G.M., Ulidowski, I.: Reversible occurrence nets and causal reversible prime event structures. In: Lanese, I., Rawski, M. (eds.) RC 2020. LNCS, vol. 12227, pp. 35–53. Springer, Cham (2020). https://doi.org/10.1007/978-3-030-52482-1_2

10. Melgratti, H.C., Mezzina, C.A., Ulidowski, I.: Reversing place transition nets. Log. Methods Comput. Sci. **16**(4) (2020)
11. Mikulski, Ł, Lanese, I.: Reversing unbounded petri nets. In: Donatelli, S., Haar, S. (eds.) PETRI NETS 2019. LNCS, vol. 11522, pp. 213–233. Springer, Cham (2019). https://doi.org/10.1007/978-3-030-21571-2_13
12. Murata, T.: Petri nets: properties, analysis and applications. Proc. IEEE **77**(4), 541–580 (1989)
13. Philippou, A., Psara, K.: Reversible computation in nets with bonds. J. Log. Algebraic Methods Program. **124**(100718), 1–47 (2022)
14. Philippou, A., Psara, K., Siljak, H.: Controlling reversibility in reversing petri nets with application to wireless communications. In: Thomsen, M.K., Soeken, M. (eds.) RC 2019. LNCS, vol. 11497, pp. 238–245. Springer, Cham (2019). https://doi.org/10.1007/978-3-030-21500-2_15
15. Psara, K.: Reversible Computation in Petri Nets. Ph.D. thesis, Department of Computer Science, University of Cyprus (2020)

Reversibility in Erlang: Imperative Constructs

Pietro Lami[1]([⊠])(iD), Ivan Lanese[2,3]([⊠])(iD), Jean-Bernard Stefani[1]([⊠])(iD),
Claudio Sacerdoti Coen[2]([⊠])(iD), and Giovanni Fabbretti[1]([⊠])(iD)

[1] Univ. Grenoble Alpes, INRIA, CNRS, Grenoble INP, LIG, 38000 Grenoble, France
{pietro.lami,jean-bernard.stefani,giovanni.fabbretti}@inria.fr
[2] University of Bologna, 40126 Bologna, Italy
{ivan.lanese,claudio.sacerdoticoen}@unibo.it
[3] Focus Team, INRIA, Sophia-Antipolis, France

Abstract. A relevant application of reversibility is causal-consistent reversible debugging, which allows one to explore concurrent computations backward and forward to find a bug. This approach has been put into practice in CauDEr, a causal-consistent reversible debugger for the Erlang programming language. CauDEr supports the functional, concurrent and distributed fragment of Erlang. However, Erlang also includes imperative features to manage a map (shared among all the processes of a same node) associating process identifiers to names. Here we extend CauDEr and the related theory to support such imperative features. From a theoretical point of view, the added primitives create different causal structures than those derived from the concurrent Erlang fragment previously handled in CauDEr, yet we show that the main results proved for CauDEr are still valid.

Keywords: Debugging · Erlang · Reversible computing · Causality

1 Introduction

Reversible computing is a programming paradigm in which programs run both forwards (the standard computation) and backwards. Any forward computation in a reversible language can be undone with a finite number of backward steps. Reversible computing has applications in many areas, such as low-power computing [13], simulation [1], robotics [19], biological modeling [20] and others. We are particularly interested in applying reversible computing to debugging [2].

In a sequential system, undoing forward actions in reverse order of completion starting from the last one produces a backward computation. Undoing a forward action can be seen as a backward action. In a concurrent environment, one cannot

The work has been partially supported by French ANR project DCore ANR-18-CE25-0007 and by INdAM – GNCS 2020 project *Sistemi Reversibili Concorrenti: dai Modelli ai Linguaggi*. We thank the anonymous referees for their helpful comments and suggestions.

C. A. Mezzina and K. Podlaski (Eds.): RC 2022, LNCS 13354, pp. 187–203, 2022.
https://doi.org/10.1007/978-3-031-09005-9_13

easily decide which is the last action since many actions can be executed at the same time, and a total order of actions may not be available. Even if a total order exists, undoing actions in reverse order may be too restrictive since the order of execution of concurrent actions may depend on the relative speed of the processors executing them and has no impact on the final state. For instance, when looking for a bug causing a visible misbehavior in a concurrent system, independent actions may be disregarded since they cannot contain the bug.

The first definition of reversibility in a concurrent setting has been proposed by Danos and Krivine [4]: *causal-consistent reversibility*. In short, it states that any action can be undone provided that all its effects (if any) have been undone.

The idea of a causal-consistent reversible debugger was introduced in [7]. The main concept of [7] is to use causal-consistent reversibility to explore backward a concurrent execution starting from a visible misbehavior looking for the bug causing it. The CauDEr debugger [2], described in [6,16,22], applies these ideas to provide a reversible debugger for the functional, concurrent and distributed fragment of the Erlang programming language [5].

Here, we extend CauDEr and its underlying theory by adding the support for some primitives that are not considered in the previous versions. These primitives, namely register, unregister, whereis and registered, provide imperative behaviors inside the Erlang language whose core is functional. More precisely, they define a map linking process identifiers (pids) to names. They make it possible to add, delete and read elements from the map. From the technical point of view, supporting these primitives is not trivial since they introduce causal dependencies that are different from those originating from the functional and concurrent fragment of Erlang considered in [16,17,22]. In particular, read actions commute, but do not commute with add and delete actions. Such causal dependencies cannot be reliably represented in the general approach to derive reversible semantics for a given language presented in [14], because the approach in [14] considers a causal relation based on resources consumed and produced only, and does not support read operations. Similar dependencies are considered in [6], to model the set of nodes in an Erlang network, but this model does not include a delete operation, while we consider one. Similar dependencies are also used in [8] to study operations on shared tuple spaces in the framework of the coordination language Klaim, however they only access single tuples, while we also access multiple tuples or check for the absence of a given tuple. Also, their work is in the context of an abstract calculus and has never been implemented.

The paper is structured as follows. Section 2 briefly recalls the reversible semantics on which CauDEr is based [22]. Then, in Sect. 3, we extend the reversible semantics of Erlang to support imperative features. In Sect. 4 we describe our extension to CauDEr. Finally, in Sect. 5 we discuss related work and conclude the paper with hints for future work. Due to space constraints we omit some technicalities, for proofs and further details we refer the interested reader to the companion technical report [12].

2   Background

We build our technical development on the reversible semantics for Erlang in [22]. We give below a quick overview of it, while referring to [22] for further details.

$$
\begin{aligned}
program &::= mod_1 \ldots mod_n \\
mod &::= fun\_def_1 \ldots fun\_def_n \\
fun\_def &::= fun\_rule\{';' \, fun\_rule\}'.' \\
fun\_rule &::= Atom \; fun \\
fun &::= ([exprs]) \; [\textsf{when} \; expr] \rightarrow exprs \\
exprs &::= expr \; \{',' \, expr\} \\
expr &::= atomic \mid Var \mid \; '\{'[exprs]'\}' \mid \; '['[exprs|exprs]']' \mid \textsf{if} \; if\_clauses \; \textsf{end} \\
&\quad \mid \; \textsf{case} \; expr \; \textsf{of} \; cr\_clauses \; \textsf{end} \mid \textsf{receive} \; cr\_clauses \; \textsf{end} \mid expr \; ! \; expr \\
&\quad \mid \; pattern = expr \mid [Mod{:}]expr([exprs]) \mid fun\_expr \mid Opexprs \\
atomic &::= Atom \mid Char \mid Float \mid Integer \mid String \\
if\_clauses &::= expr \rightarrow exprs \; \{';' \, expr \rightarrow exprs\} \\
cr\_clause &::= pattern \; [\textsf{when} \; expr] \rightarrow exprs \; \{';' \, pattern \; [\textsf{when} \; expr] \rightarrow exprs\} \\
fun\_expr &::= \textsf{fun} \; fun \; \{';' \, fun\} \; \textsf{end} \\
patterns &::= pattern \; \{',' \, pattern\} \\
pattern &::= atomic \mid Var \mid \; '\{'[patterns]'\}' \mid \; '['[patterns|pattern]']'
\end{aligned}
$$

Fig. 1. Language syntax

The Language Syntax. Erlang is a functional, concurrent and distributed programming language based on the actor paradigm [10] (concurrency based on asynchronous *message-passing*).

The syntax of the language is shown in Fig. 1. A program is a collection of module definitions, a module is a collection of function definitions, a function is a mapping between the function name and the function expression. An expression can be a variable, an atom, a list, a tuple, a call to a function, a case expression, an if expression, or a pattern matching equation. We distinguish expressions and patterns. Here, patterns are built from atomic values, variables, tuples and lists. When we have a case *expr* of *cr_clauses* end expression we first evaluate *expr* to a value, say v, then we search for a clause that matches v and such that the guard when *expr* is satisfied. If one is found then the case construct evaluates to the clause expression. The *if* expression is very similar to the evaluation of the *case* expression just described. Pattern matching is written as *pattern = expr*. Then, $expr_1$! $expr_2$ allows a process to send a message to another one. Expression $expr_1$ must evaluate either to a pid or to an atom (identifying the receiver process) and $expr_2$ evaluates to the message payload, indicated with v. The whole function evaluates to v and, as a side-effect, the message will be sent to the target process. The complementary operation of message sending is receive *cr_clauses* end. This construct takes a message targeting the process that matches one of the clauses. If no message is found then the process suspends.

$$(Op) \quad \frac{\mathsf{eval}(op, v_1, \ldots, v_n) = v}{\theta, C[op\ (v_1, \ldots, v_n)], S \xrightarrow{\tau} \theta, C[v], S}$$

Fig. 2. A sample rule belonging to the expression level.

Erlang includes a number of built-in functions (BIFs). In [22], they only consider self, which returns the process identifier of the current process, and spawn, that creates a new process. BIFs supporting distribution are considered in [6]. For a deeper discussion we refer to [6, 22].

The Language Semantics. Here we describe the semantics of the language. We begin by providing the definitions of *process* and *system*.

Definition 1 (Process). *A process is a tuple* $\langle p, \theta, e, S \rangle$, *where* p *is the process pid,* θ *is the process environment,* e *is the expression under evaluation and* S *is a stack of process environments.*

Stack S is used to store away the process state to start a sub-computation of the expression under evaluation and then to restore it, once the sub-computation ends. We refer to [22] for a discussion on why it is needed.

Definition 2 (System). *A system is a tuple* $\Gamma; \Pi$. Γ *is the global mailbox, that is a set of messages of the form* (sender_pid, receiver_pid, payload). Π *is the pool of running processes, denoted by an expression of the form*

$$\langle p_1, \theta_1, e_1, S_1 \rangle \mid \ldots \mid \langle p_n, \theta_n, e_n, S_n \rangle$$

where "|" is an associative and commutative parallel operator.

The semantics in [22] is defined in a modular way, similarly to the one presented in [6, 16]: there is a semantics for the expression level and one for the system level. This approach simplifies the design of the reversible semantics since only the system one needs to be updated. The expression semantics is defined as a labeled transition relation, where the label describes side-effects (e.g., creation of a message) or requests of information to the system level. The semantics is a classical call-by-value semantics for a higher-order language. Figure 2 shows a sample rule of the expression level: the Op rule, used to evaluate arithmetic and relational operators. This rule uses the auxiliary function **eval** to evaluate the expression and an evaluation context C to find the redex in a larger term.

The system semantics uses the label from the expression level to execute the associated side-effect or to provide the necessary information. Below we list the labels used in the expression semantics:

- τ, denoting the evaluation of a (sequential) expression without side-effects;
- send(v_1, v_2), where v_1 and v_2 represent, respectively, the pid of the sender and the value of the message;
- rec($\kappa, \overline{cl_n}$), where $\overline{cl_n}$ denotes the n clauses of a receive expression;

$$(Send) \quad \frac{\theta, e, S \xrightarrow{\mathsf{send}(p', v)} \theta', e', S' \quad \lambda \text{ is a fresh identifier}}{\Gamma; \langle p, h, \theta, e, S \rangle \mid \Pi \to \Gamma \cup \{(p, p', \{v, \lambda\})\}; \langle p, \mathsf{send}(\theta, e, S, \{v, \lambda\}){:}h, \theta', e', S' \rangle \mid \Pi}$$

$$(\overline{Send}) \quad \Gamma \cup \{(p, p', \{v, \lambda\})\}; \langle p, \mathsf{send}(\theta, e, S, \{v, \lambda\}){:}h, \theta', e', S' \rangle \mid \Pi \leftharpoonup \Gamma; \langle p, h, \theta, e, S \rangle \mid \Pi$$

Fig. 3. A sample rule belonging to the forward semantics and its counterpart.

- spawn($\kappa, a/n, [\overline{v_n}]$), where a/n represents the name and arity of the function executed by the spawned process, while $[\overline{v_n}]$ is the list of its parameters.

Symbol κ is a placeholder for the result of the evaluation, not known at the expression level, that the system rules will replace with the correct value.

For space reasons, we do not show here the system rules, which are available in [22]. We show instead below how sample rules are extended to support reversibility.

A Reversible Semantics. Two relations describe the reversible semantics: one forward ($\to$) and one backward ($\leftharpoonup$). The former extends the system semantics using a *Landauer embedding* [13]. The latter proceeds in the opposite direction and allows us to undo an action by ensuring causal consistency, thus before undoing an action we ensure that all its consequences have been undone.

Syntactically, every process is extended with a history, denoted with h, which stores the information needed in the backward semantics to *undo* an action. In the semantic rules we highlight the history in red. The history is composed of *history items*, to distinguish the last rule executed by a process and track the related information. The history items introduced in [22] are:

$$\{\tau(\theta, e, S), \mathsf{send}(\theta, e, S, \{v, \lambda\}), \mathsf{rec}(\theta, e, S, p, \{v, \lambda\}), \mathsf{spawn}(\theta, e, S, p), \mathsf{self}(\theta, e, S)\}$$

Figure 3 shows a sample rule from the forward semantics and its counterpart from the backward semantics. W.r.t. the standard semantics, here messages also carry a unique identifier λ, without which messages with the same value could not be distinguished. This choice is discussed in [16].

In the premises of rule *Send*, we can see the expression-level semantics in action, transitioning from configuration (θ, e, S) to (θ', e', S'). The forward semantics uses the corresponding label to determine the associated side-effect: the message $(p, p', \{v, \lambda\})$ is added to the set of messages Γ. Also, the history of process p is enriched with the corresponding history item.

The reverse rule, $\overline{Send}$, can be applied only when all the consequences of the *Send*, in particular the reception of the sent message, have been undone. Such constraint is enforced by requiring the message to be in Γ. Then we can remove the message $(p, p', \{v, \lambda\})$ from Γ and restore p to the previous state.

3 Reversible Erlang with Imperative Primitives

Syntax of Imperative Primitives. In our extension, atoms and pids are central. An atom is a literal constant. Pid is an abbreviation for process identifier:

each process is identified by a pid. In Erlang, a pid can be associated to an atom. Thus, one can refer the process, e.g., when specifying the target of a message, using the associated atom instead of the pid. On the one hand, an atom is more meaningful than a pid for a human. On the other hand, this allows one to decide which process plays a given role. E.g., if a process crashes another one can be registered under the same atom so that the replacement is transparent to other processes (provided that they use the atom to interact). All pairs $\langle atom, pid \rangle$ form a map, shared among the processes of the same node (we consider here a single node, we discuss in Sect. 4 how to deal with multiple nodes).

Our extension is based on the syntax in Fig. 1, but we add the following built-in functions (BIFs):

- register/2 (where /2 denotes the arity): given an atom a and a pid p, it inserts the pair $\langle a, p \rangle$ in the map and returns the atom **true**. If either the atom a or the pid p is already registered, an exception is raised;
- unregister/1: given an atom a, it removes the (unique) pair $\langle a, p \rangle$ from the map and returns **true** if the atom a is found, raises an exception otherwise;
- whereis/1: given an atom, it returns the associated pid if it exists, the atom **undefined** otherwise;
- registered/0: returns a list (possibly empty) of all the atoms in the map.

3.1 Semantics of Imperative Features

Standard Semantics of Imperative Features. According to the official documentation [5], the BIFs above are implemented in Erlang using request and reply signals between the process and the manager of the map. To simplify the modelization, we opted to implement these BIFs as synchronous actions. This choice does not alter the possible behaviors since the behavior visible to Erlang users is determined by the order in which the request messages are processed at the manager. We begin by providing the updated definition of *system* (the definition of process is unchanged).

Definition 3 (System). *A system is a tuple* $\Gamma; \Pi; \mathsf{M}$. Γ *and* Π *are as in Definition 2.* M *is a set of registered pairs atom-pid of the form* $\{\langle a_1, p_1 \rangle; \ldots; \langle a_n, p_n \rangle\}$, *where* a_i *are atoms and* p_i *pids. Given an atom* a, M_a *is the set* $\{\langle a, p \rangle | \langle a, p \rangle \in \mathsf{M}\}$; *given a pid* p, M_p *is the set* $\{\langle a, p \rangle | \langle a, p \rangle \in \mathsf{M}\}$.

Sets M_a and M_p contain at most one element.

As in the previous section, we have a double-layered semantics: one level for expressions ($\rightarrow$) and one for systems ($\hookrightarrow$).

To simplify the presentation w.r.t. [22], we extend rule Op (Fig. 4) to deal also with built-in functions. To this end, we extend the operator **eval** to produce also the label for functions with side-effects. We define **eval** on them as:

- eval(self) = $(\kappa, \mathsf{self}(\kappa))$;
- eval(spawn, fun() $\rightarrow exprs$ end) = $(\kappa, \mathsf{spawn}(\kappa, exprs))$;

$$(Op) \quad \frac{\mathsf{eval}(op, v_1, \ldots, v_n) = (v, label)}{\theta, C[op\,(v_1, \ldots, v_n)], S \xrightarrow{\ label\ } \theta, C[v], S}$$

Fig. 4. Standard semantics: evaluation of function applications, revised.

- eval(register, $atom, pid$) = $(\kappa, \mathsf{register}(\kappa, atom, pid))$;
- eval(unregister, $atom$) = $(\kappa, \mathsf{unregister}(\kappa, atom))$;
- eval(whereis, $atom$) = $(\kappa, \mathsf{whereis}(\kappa, atom))$;
- eval(registered) = $(\kappa, \mathsf{registered}(\kappa))$.

On sequential expressions **eval** returns (v, τ), with v the result of the evaluation.

Thanks to our extension, rule Op in Fig. 4 covers all function invocations, including BIFs with side effects, while in [16,22] each such BIF requires a dedicated rule. Furthermore, new BIFs with side effects can be added without changing the expression level (function **eval** needs to be updated though).

For space reasons, the other rules for evaluating expressions are collected in the companion technical report [12].

The semantics of the system level can be found in [22], the only difference is that the system now includes the shared map M. Equivalently, the rules describing the imperative primitives can be obtained from the ones in Fig. 5, which describes the forward semantics, by dropping the red part. Rules are divided into *write rules* (above the line), which modify the map, and *read rules* (below the line), that only read it. This has an impact on their concurrent behavior, as described later on. We highlight in blue the parts related to the map.

In all the rules, the tuple representing the system includes the map M, where we store all the registered pairs atom-pid.

Rule $RegisterS$ defines the success case of the **register** BIF, which adds the tuple $\langle a, p' \rangle$ to the map. The **register** fails either when the atom a or the pid p' are already used, or when the pid p' refers to a dead process (this is checked by predicate isAlive), as described by rule $RegisterF$. Similarly, for the unregister, the success case corresponds to rule $UnregisterS$, which removes from the map the (unique) pair atom-pid for a given atom a. The failure case, when there is no pid registered under atom a, corresponds to rule $UnregisterF$. Both failure cases replace the current expression with ϵ and the current stack with $[\,]$. This denotes an uncaught exception (in this paper we do not consider exception handling). The predicate isAlive takes a pid p and the pool of running processes and controls that the process with pid p is alive ($\langle p, \theta, e, S \rangle$ with $e \neq \bot$).

Rules $SendS$ and $SendF$ define the behavior of send actions when the receiver is identified with an atom. The former is fired when the receiver is registered in the map, resulting in the addition of the message to Γ, the latter when it is not, resulting in an uncaught exception.

Rules $Whereis1$, $Whereis2$ and $Registered$ define the behavior of the respective primitives; these rules read M without modifying it. Rule $Registered$ uses the auxiliary function registered. We define it as: $\mathsf{registered}(M) = [a_1, \ldots, a_n]$ where $M = \{\langle a_1, p_1 \rangle, \ldots, \langle a_n, p_n \rangle\}$.

$(RegisterS)$ $\dfrac{\theta, e, S \xrightarrow{\text{register}(\kappa, a, p')} \theta', e', S' \quad t \text{ fresh} \quad \mathsf{M}_a = \emptyset \quad \mathsf{M}_{p'} = \emptyset \quad \text{isAlive}(p', \Pi)}{\Gamma; \langle p, h, \theta, e, S \rangle \mid \Pi; \mathsf{M} \rightarrow \Gamma; \langle p, \text{regS}(\theta, e, S, \{\langle a, p', t, \top \rangle\}){:}h, \theta', e'\{\kappa \rightarrow \text{true}\}, S' \rangle \mid \Pi; \mathsf{M} \cup \{\langle a, p', t, \top \rangle\}}$

$(UnregisterS)$ $\dfrac{\theta, e, S \xrightarrow{\text{unregister}(\kappa, a)} \theta', e', S' \quad \mathsf{M}_a = \{\langle a, p', t, \top \rangle\}}{\Gamma; \langle p, h, \theta, e, S \rangle \mid \Pi; \mathsf{M} \rightarrow \Gamma; \langle p, \text{del}(\theta, e, S, \mathsf{M}_a, \mathsf{M}^a \cup \mathsf{M}^{p'}){:}h, \theta', e'\{\kappa \rightarrow \text{true}\}, S' \rangle \mid \Pi; \mathsf{M} \setminus \mathsf{M}_a \cup \text{kill}(\mathsf{M}_a)}$

$(EndUn)$ $\dfrac{e \text{ is a value } \vee e = \epsilon \quad \mathsf{M}_p = \{\langle a, p, t, \top \rangle\}}{\Gamma; \langle p, h, \theta, e, [\,] \rangle \mid \Pi; \mathsf{M} \rightarrow \Gamma; \langle p, \text{del}(\theta, e, [\,], \mathsf{M}_p, \mathsf{M}^a \cup \mathsf{M}^p){:}h, \theta, \bot, [\,] \rangle \mid \Pi; \mathsf{M} \setminus \mathsf{M}_p \cup \text{kill}(\mathsf{M}_p)}$

$(RegisterF)$ $\dfrac{\theta, e, S \xrightarrow{\text{register}(\kappa, a, p')} \theta', e', S' \quad \mathsf{M}_a \neq \emptyset \vee \mathsf{M}_{p'} \neq \emptyset \vee \neg \text{ isAlive}(p', \Pi)}{\Gamma; \langle p, h, \theta, e, S \rangle \mid \Pi; \mathsf{M} \rightarrow \Gamma; \langle p, \text{readS}(\theta, e, S, \mathsf{M}_a \cup \mathsf{M}_{p'}){:}h, \theta, \epsilon, [\,] \rangle \mid \Pi; \mathsf{M}}$

$(UnregisterF)$ $\dfrac{\theta, e, S \xrightarrow{\text{unregister}(\kappa, a)} \theta', e', S' \quad \mathsf{M}_a = \emptyset}{\Gamma; \langle p, h, \theta, e, S \rangle \mid \Pi; \mathsf{M} \rightarrow \Gamma; \langle p, \text{readF}(\theta, e, S, a, \mathsf{M}^a){:}h, \theta, \epsilon, [\,] \rangle \mid \Pi; \mathsf{M}}$

$(SendS)$ $\dfrac{\theta, e, S \xrightarrow{\text{send}(a, v)} \theta', e', S' \quad \lambda \text{ fresh} \quad \mathsf{M}_a = \{\langle a, p', t, \top \rangle\}}{\Gamma; \langle p, h, \theta, e, S \rangle \mid \Pi; \mathsf{M} \rightarrow \Gamma \cup \{(p, p', \{v, \lambda\})\}; \langle p, \text{sendS}(\theta, e, S, \{v, \lambda\}, \mathsf{M}_a){:}h, \theta', e', S' \rangle \mid \Pi; \mathsf{M}}$

$(SendF)$ $\dfrac{\theta, e, S \xrightarrow{\text{send}(a, v)} \theta', e', S' \quad \mathsf{M}_a = \emptyset}{\Gamma; \langle p, h, \theta, e, S \rangle \mid \Pi; \mathsf{M} \rightarrow \Gamma; \langle p, \text{readF}(\theta, e, S, a, \mathsf{M}^a){:}h, \theta, \epsilon, [\,] \rangle \mid \Pi; \mathsf{M}}$

$(Whereis1)$ $\dfrac{\theta, e, S \xrightarrow{\text{whereis}(\kappa, a)} \theta', e', S' \quad \mathsf{M}_a = \{\langle a, p', t, \top \rangle\}}{\Gamma; \langle p, h, \theta, e, S \rangle \mid \Pi; \mathsf{M} \rightarrow \Gamma; \langle p, \text{readS}(\theta, e, S, \mathsf{M}_a){:}h, \theta', e'\{\kappa \rightarrow p'\}, S' \rangle \mid \Pi; \mathsf{M}}$

$(Whereis2)$ $\dfrac{\theta, e, S \xrightarrow{\text{whereis}(\kappa, a)} \theta', e', S' \quad \mathsf{M}_a = \emptyset}{\Gamma; \langle p, h, \theta, e, S \rangle \mid \Pi; \mathsf{M} \rightarrow \Gamma; \langle p, \text{readF}(\theta, e, S, a, \mathsf{M}^a){:}h, \theta', e'\{\kappa \rightarrow \text{undefined}\}, S' \rangle \mid \Pi; \mathsf{M}}$

$(Registered)$ $\dfrac{\theta, e, S \xrightarrow{\text{registered}(\kappa)} \theta', e', S' \quad \text{registered}(\mathsf{M}) = atoms}{\Gamma; \langle p, h, \theta, e, S \rangle \mid \Pi; \mathsf{M} \rightarrow \Gamma; \langle p, \text{readM}(\theta, e, S, \mathsf{M}){:}h, \theta', e'\{\kappa \rightarrow atoms\}, S' \rangle \mid \Pi; \mathsf{M}}$

(End) $\dfrac{e \text{ is a value } \vee e = \epsilon \quad \mathsf{M}_p = \emptyset}{\Gamma; \langle p, h, \theta, e, [\,] \rangle \mid \Pi; \mathsf{M} \rightarrow \Gamma; \langle p, \text{readF}(\theta, e, [\,], p, \mathsf{M}^p){:}h, \theta, \bot, [\,] \rangle \mid \Pi; \mathsf{M}}$

Fig. 5. Forward reversible semantics (standard semantics by dropping the red part). (Color figure online)

Finally, we have two rules dealing with process termination. If the pid of the process is not registered on the map, rule *End* simply changes the expression to $\bot$, denoting a terminated process. Otherwise, rule *EndUn* applies, additionally removing the pid from the map.

Reversible Semantics. The definition of the forward semantics poses a number of challenges, due to the need of balancing two conflicting requirements when defining the history information to be stored. On the one hand, we need to keep enough information to be able to define a corresponding backward semantics. This requires to understand when all the consequences of an action have been undone, and to restore the state prior to its execution. On the other hand, we need to avoid storing information allowing one to distinguish computations obtained by only swapping independent actions (this would invalidate Lemma 2, as discussed in Example 3).

We first extend the definition of system.

Definition 4 (System). *A system is a tuple* $\Gamma; \Pi; \mathsf{M}$. Γ *and* Π *are as in Definition 3. Now each element of* M *is a quadruple* $\langle a, p, t, s \rangle$ *where* a *and* p *are as in Definition 3,* t *is a unique identifier for the tuple and* s *can be either* $\top$ *or* $\bot$.

Unique identifiers t are used to distinguish identical tuples existing at different times. For example, if we have two successful pairs of register and unregister operations of the same tuple, without a unique identifier we would not know which unregister operation is connected to which register. This information is relevant since the tuple generates a causal link between a register and the corresponding unregister. This justification is similar to the one for unique identifiers λ for messages, discussed in [17].

Tuples whose last field is $\top$ match the ones in the standard semantics, we call them *alive* tuples. Those with $\bot$ are *ghost* tuples, namely alive tuples that have been removed from the map in a past forward action. We will discuss their need in Example 2.

Given an atom a, M^a is the set $\{\langle a, p, t, \bot \rangle | \langle a, p, t, \bot \rangle \in \mathsf{M}\}$; similarly, given a pid p, $\mathsf{M}^p = \{\langle a, p, t, \bot \rangle | \langle a, p, t, \bot \rangle \in \mathsf{M}\}$. Dually, from now on, sets M_a and M_p include only alive tuples. We define function kill, which takes a map and sets to $\bot$ the last field of all its tuples.

We describe below the forward and backward semantics of the imperative primitives. The semantics of other constructs is as in the original work [22], but for the introduction of the global map M.

The forward semantics is defined in Fig. 5. The following history items have been added to describe the imperative features: regS, readS, readF, sendS, readM, and del. Notably, readS is created by both rules *RegisterF* and *Whereis1* (which both read some alive tuples), readF is created by rules *UnregisterF*, *SendF*, *Whereis2* and *End* (which all require the absence of some alive tuple), del is created by both rules *UnregisterS* and *EndUn* (which both turn an alive a tuple $\langle \_, \_, \_, \top \rangle$ into a ghost $\langle \_, \_, \_, \bot \rangle$).

All the new history items, like the old ones, carry the old state θ, e, S, thus allowing the backward computation to restore it. Furthermore, they carry some additional information to enable us to understand their causal dependencies:

- regS carries the tuple inserted in the map;
- readS carries the read tuple(s);
- sendS carries the read tuple as well, but also the sent message;
- readF carries the atom or the pid which the rule tried to read and the ghost tuples for such atom or pid, if any;
- readM carries the whole map read by the rule;
- del carries the removed tuple and the ghost tuples on the same atom or pid.

Figure 6 presents the backward semantics. In previous works [6,17,22] there is one backward rule for each forward rule. Here, we were able to define one backward rule for each kind of history item, thus some backward rule covers more than one forward rule. This is possible because the history item contains enough information to correctly reverse forward rules with similar effects. E.g., both rules *RegisterF* and *Whereis1* read information from the map, and the

$$(\overline{RegisterS}) \quad \frac{\Gamma; \langle p, \mathsf{regS}(\theta, e, S, \{\langle a, p', t, \top\rangle\}):h, \theta', e', S'\rangle \mid \Pi; \mathsf{M} \cup \{\langle a, p', t, \top\rangle\} \rightharpoonup \Gamma; \langle p, h, \theta, e, S\rangle \mid \Pi; \mathsf{M}}{\text{if } \mathsf{readop}(t, \Pi) = \emptyset}$$

$$(\overline{Del}) \quad \frac{\Gamma; \langle p, \mathsf{del}(\theta, e, S, \{\langle a, p', t, \top\rangle\}, \mathsf{M}_1):h, \theta', e', S'\rangle \mid \Pi; \mathsf{M} \cup \{\langle a, p', t, \bot\rangle\}}{\rightharpoonup \Gamma; \langle p, h, \theta, e, S\rangle \mid \Pi; \mathsf{M} \cup \{\langle a, p', t, \top\rangle\}}$$
$$\text{if } \mathsf{M}_a = \emptyset \wedge \mathsf{M}_{p'} = \emptyset \wedge \mathsf{readmap}(\mathsf{M} \cup \{\langle a, p', t, \bot\rangle\}, \Pi) = \emptyset \wedge \mathsf{readfail}(t, \Pi) = \emptyset \wedge \mathsf{M}_1 = \mathsf{M}^a \cup \mathsf{M}^{p'}$$

$$(\overline{ReadS}) \quad \frac{\Gamma; \langle p, \mathsf{readS}(\theta, e, S, \mathsf{M}_1):h, \theta', e', S'\rangle \mid \Pi; \mathsf{M} \rightharpoonup \Gamma; \langle p, h, \theta, e, S\rangle \mid \Pi; \mathsf{M}}{} \quad \text{if } \mathsf{M}_1 \subseteq \mathsf{M}$$

$$(\overline{SendS}) \quad \frac{\Gamma \cup \{(p, p', \{v, \lambda\})\}; \langle p, \mathsf{sendS}(\theta, e, S, \{v, \lambda\}, \mathsf{M}_1):h, \theta', e', S'\rangle \mid \Pi; \mathsf{M} \rightharpoonup \Gamma; \langle p, h, \theta, e, S\rangle \mid \Pi; \mathsf{M}}{\text{if } \mathsf{M}_1 \subseteq \mathsf{M}}$$

$$(\overline{ReadF}) \quad \frac{\Gamma; \langle p, \mathsf{readF}(\theta, e, S, \iota, \mathsf{M}_1):h, \theta', e', S'\rangle \mid \Pi; \mathsf{M} \rightharpoonup \Gamma; \langle p, h, \theta, e, S\rangle \mid \Pi; \mathsf{M}}{} \quad \text{if } \mathsf{M}_\iota = \emptyset \wedge \mathsf{M}_1 = \mathsf{M}^\iota$$

$$(\overline{ReadM}) \quad \frac{\Gamma; \langle p, \mathsf{readM}(\theta, e, S, \mathsf{M}_1):h, \theta', e', S'\rangle \mid \Pi; \mathsf{M} \rightharpoonup \Gamma; \langle p, h, \theta, e, S\rangle \mid \Pi; \mathsf{M}}{} \quad \text{if } \mathsf{M}_1 = \mathsf{M}$$

Fig. 6. Backward reversible semantics.

history item tracks the read information. Hence, a single rule can exploit this information to check that the same read information is still available in the map.

Rule $\overline{RegisterS}$ undoes the corresponding forward action, removing the element that was added by it. To this end, rule $\overline{RegisterS}$ requires that the element added from the corresponding forward rule is still in the map (ensuring that possible deletions of the same tuple have been undone) and, as a side condition, that no process performed a read operation on a tuple with unique identifier t. This last condition is checked by the predicate $\mathsf{readop}(t, \Pi)$, which scans the histories of processes in Π looking for such reads.

Rule $\overline{Del}$ undoes either rule $UnregisterS$ or rule $EndUn$, turning a ghost tuple back into an alive one. Let us discuss its side conditions. The first two conditions require that in M there is no alive tuple on the same atom a or process p'. The third one ensures that no process performed a registered getting M, while the fourth that no process read a ghost tuple with identifier t. Finally, we require ghost tuples on both a and p' to be the same as when the corresponding forward action has been performed. The last condition ensures that rule $\overline{Del}$ will not commute with pairs of operations that add and then delete tuples on the same atom or pid, e.g., a pair register-unregister. This is needed to satisfy the properties described in Sect. 3.2, such as causal consistency.

Rule $\overline{ReadS}$ reverses rules $Whereis1$ and $RegisterF$. The only side conditions requires that the element(s) read by the forward rule must be alive. Rule $\overline{SendS}$ is analogous, but it also requires that the sent message is in Γ.

Rule $\overline{ReadF}$ undoes actions from rules $UnregisterF$, $SendF$, $Whereis2$, and End. As a side condition, we require that no alive tuple matching ι - which is either a pid or an atom - exists and that the ghost tuples related to ι are the same as when the corresponding forward action triggered.

Rule $\overline{ReadM}$ is used to undo rule $Registered$. It requires that the map M_1 stored in the history is exactly the current map M.

3.2   Properties

Here we discuss some properties of the reversible semantics introduced in the previous section. Since most of the properties are related to causality, we need to study the concurrency model of the imperative primitives. Notably, this is not specific to reversibility and the same notion can be useful in other contexts, e.g., to find races [9].

To study concurrency for the imperative primitives we define for each history item k the set of resources (atoms and pids) read or written by the corresponding transition. The idea is that two transitions (including at least a forward one) are in conflict on the map if they both access the same resource and at least one of the accesses is a write (*RegisterS, UnregisterS, EndUn*). To obtain k, we indicate with $t = (s \rightleftharpoons_{p,r,k} s')$ a (forward or backward) transition from system s to system s', where p is the pid of the process performing the action, r is the applied rule and k the item added or removed to/from the history. We call computation a sequence of consecutive transitions, and denote with ϵ the empty computation. Two transitions are co-initial if they start from the same state, co-final if they end in the same state.

Definition 5 (Resources read or written). *We define functions* read(k) *and* write(k) *as follows:*

k	read(k)	write(k)
regS(θ, e, S, $\{\langle a, p, t, \top \rangle\}$)	$\emptyset$	$\{a, p\}$
del(θ, e, S, $\{\langle a, p, t, \top \rangle\}$, M)	$\emptyset$	$\{a, p\}$
readS(θ, e, S, M)	$\{a\|M_a \neq \emptyset\} \cup \{p\|M_p \neq \emptyset\}$	$\emptyset$
sendS(θ, e, S, $\{v, \lambda\}$, $\{\langle a, p, t, \top \rangle\}$)	$\{a, p\}$	$\emptyset$
readF(θ, e, S, ι, M)	$\{\iota\}$	$\emptyset$
readM(θ, e, S, M)	$\{a\|a \text{ is an atom}\}$	$\emptyset$

Intuitively, items regS and del write on the resources a and p of the tuple added or removed. Item readS reads one or two tuples, and accesses in read modality all the involved pids and atoms. Item sendS just reads the atom and pid of the accessed tuple. Item readF accesses in read modality either an atom or a pid, as tracked in the history item. Finally, item readM exactly stores the current map, and needs to be in conflict with any transition writing on the map, even if it writes a tuple with atom and pid not previously used. Hence, we have chosen as read resources the set of all possible atoms, independently on whether they are currently used or not. We could also store all possible pids, but this will not impact the semantics, since each write access touches on an atom.

Definition 6 (Concurrent transitions). *Two co-initial transitions, $t_1 = (s \rightleftharpoons_{p_1,r_1,k_1} s_1)$ and $t_2 = (s \rightleftharpoons_{p_2,r_2,k_2} s_2)$, are in conflict if one of these conditions hold:*

- *if no transition is on the map, we refer to [17, Definition 12];*
- *if exactly one transition is on the map, they are in conflict if they are taken by the same process, namely $p_1 = p_2$, and a $\overline{SendS}$ is in conflict with a receive of the same message;*

- *if both transitions are on the map, and at least one is forward, then they are in conflict iff* $\text{read}(k_1) \cap \text{write}(k_2) \neq \emptyset$, $\text{read}(k_2) \cap \text{write}(k_1) \neq \emptyset$ *or* $\text{write}(k_1) \cap \text{write}(k_2) \neq \emptyset$;

Two co-initial transitions are concurrent if they are not in conflict.

Intuitively, concurrent transitions can be executed in any order (we will formalize this in Lemma 2). Notably, co-initial backward transitions are never in conflict.

Example 1 (Conflicting register*).* Consider a system S where two processes, say p_1 and p_2, try to register two different pids under the same atom a, and a is not already present in M (recall that an atom can be associated to one pid only). In this scenario the order in which the two actions are performed matters, because the first process to perform the action succeeds, while the second is doomed to fail. The two possibilities lead us to two states of the system, one where p_1 has succeeded and p_2 failed, say S', and the other where p_2 succeeded and p_1 failed, say S''. Clearly $S' \neq S''$, hence the two operations are in conflict. Indeed, $\text{write}(k_1) \cap \text{write}(k_2) = \{a\} \neq \emptyset$. ◊

Example 2 (Register followed by delete). Consider a system S where a process, say p_1, can do a registered operation. Another process, say p_2, performs a (successful) register followed by a delete operation (e.g., unregister) of a same tuple. In the standard semantics, executing first p_1 and then p_2 or vice versa would lead to the same state. If we were not using ghost tuples, the histories of p_1 and p_2 would be the same as well. However, we want to distinguish these two computations, since undoing the unregister would change the result of the registered, hence they cannot commute (cfr. Lemma 2). Ghost tuples are our solution to this problem. We get a similar behavior also if we consider, instead of the registered operation, any other read operation involving the added tuple. ◊

We can now discuss some relevant properties of the reversible semantics. As standard (see, e.g., [17] and the notion of consistency in [15]) we restrict to reachable systems, namely systems obtained from a single process with empty history (and empty Γ and M) via some computation. First, each transition can be undone.

Lemma 1 (Loop Lemma). *For every pair of reachable systems, s_1 and s_2, we have $s_1 \rightharpoonup s_2$ iff $s_2 \leftharpoonup s_1$.*

Let us denote with $\underline{t}$ the transitions undoing t, which exists thanks to the Loop Lemma. Next lemma shows that concurrent transitions can be executed in any order. It can be seen as a safety check on the notion of concurrency.

Lemma 2 (Square lemma). *Given two co-initial concurrent transitions $t_1 = (s \rightleftharpoons_{p_1, r_1, k_1} s_1)$ and $t_2 = (s \rightleftharpoons_{p_2, r_2, k_2} s_2)$, there exist two transitions $t_2/t_1 = (s_1 \rightleftharpoons_{p_2, r_2, k_2} s_3)$, $t_1/t_2 = (s_2 \rightleftharpoons_{p_1, r_1, k_1} s_3)$. Graphically:*

Next example shows that in order to ensure that the Square Lemma holds the semantics needs to be carefully crafted, in particular one should avoid to store information allowing to distinguish the order of execution of concurrent transitions.

Example 3 (Information carried by the register history item). If the history item of the register would contain the whole map, it would be impossible to swap the register action with an unregister action even if on a tuple with different pid and atom, because of the Square Lemma (Lemma 2). Indeed, the Square Lemma requires to reach the same state after two concurrent transitions are executed, regardless of their order. If we save the whole map in the history item of the register, we would reach two different states:

- if we execute the register operation first, the saved map would include the tuple that the unregister operation will delete;
- if we execute the unregister operation first, the map saved by the register will not contain the deleted tuple.   ◊

We now want to prove causal-consistency [4,18], which essentially states that we store the correct amount of causal and history information.

Definition 7 (Causal Equivalence). *Let $\asymp$ be the smallest equivalence on computations closed under composition and satisfying:*

1. *if $t_1 = (s \rightleftharpoons_{p_1,r_1,k_1} s_1)$ and $t_2 = (s \rightleftharpoons_{p_2,r_2,k_2} s_2)$ are concurrent and $t_3 = (s_1 \rightleftharpoons_{p_2,r_2,k_2} s_3)$, $t_4 = (s_2 \rightleftharpoons_{p_1,r_1,k_1} s_3)$ then $t_1 t_3 \asymp t_2 t_4$;*
2. *$t\underline{t} \asymp \epsilon$ and $\underline{t}t \asymp \epsilon$*

Intuitively, computations are causal equivalent if they differ only for swapping concurrent transitions and for adding do-undo or undo-redo pairs of transitions.

Definition 8 (Causal Consistency). *Two co-initial computations are co-final iff they are causal equivalent.*

Intuitively, if co-initial computations are co-final then they have the same causal information and can reverse in the same ways: we want computations to reverse in the same ways iff they are causal equivalent.

In order to prove causal consistency, we rely on the theory developed in [18]. It considers a transition system with forward and backward transitions which satisfies the Loop Lemma and has a notion of independence. The latter is concurrency in our case. The theory allows one to reduce the proof of causal consistency and of other relevant properties to the validity of five axioms: Square Property (SP), Backward Transitions are Independent (BTI), Well-Foundedness (WF), Co-initial Propagation of Independence (CPI) and Co-initial Independence Respects Event (CIRE). SP is proved in Lemma 2, BTI corresponds to the observation that two backward transitions are always concurrent (see Definition 6), and WF requires backward computations to be finite. WF holds since each backward transition consumes an history item, which are in a finite number.

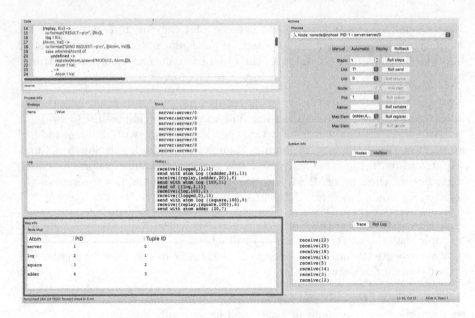

Fig. 7. A screenshot of CauDEr.

CPI and CIRE hold thanks to [18, Prop. 5.4] because the notion of concurrency is defined in terms of transition labels only. Hence, causal consistency follows from [18, Prop. 3.6]. We obtain as well a number of other properties (a list can be found in [18, Table 1]), including various forms of causal safety and causal liveness, that intuitively say that a transition can be undone iff its consequences have been undone. We refer to [18] for precise definitions and further discussion.

4   CauDEr with Imperative Primitives

We exploited the theory presented above to extend CauDEr [2,6,16,22], a Causal-consistent reversible Debugger for Erlang. CauDEr is written in Erlang and provides a graphical interface for user interaction. Previously CauDEr supported only the sequential, concurrent and distributed fragment of Erlang, and we added support for the imperative primitives. The updated code can be found at [3].

While the theory discussed so far does not consider distribution, we extended the version of CauDEr supporting distribution [6], where systems can be composed of multiple nodes. As far as the imperative primitives are concerned, the only difference is that each node has its own map, shared only among its processes.

Figure 7 shows a snapshot of the new version of CauDEr. The interface is organized as follows. On the left, from top to bottom, we can see (i) the program under debugging, (ii) the state, history and log (log is not discussed in this paper) of the selected process, (iii) the map of the node of the current process (the main novelty in the interface due to our extension, highlighted with a red square). On the top-right we can find execution controls (they are divided in multiple tabs, here we see the tab about rollback, described below), and on the bottom-right information on the system structure and on the execution.

CauDEr works as follows: the user selects the Erlang source file, then CauDEr loads the program and shows the source code to the user. Then, the user can choose the function that will act as an entry point, specify its arguments, and select the identifier of the node where the first process should run. The user can perform single steps on some process (both forward and backward), n steps in the chosen direction in automatic (a scheduler decides which process will execute each step), or use the rollback operator.

The rollback operator allows one to undo a selected action (e.g., the send of a given message) far in the past, including all and only its consequences. This is convenient to look for a bug causing a visible misbehavior, as described below. The semantics of the rollback operator roughly explores the graph of consequences of the target action, and undoes them in a causal-consistent order using the backward semantics. A formalization of the rollback operator can be found in the companion technical report [12].

Case Study. We consider as a case study a simple server dispatching requests to various mathematical services, and logging the results of the evaluation on a logger. Services can be stateful, and are spawned only when there is a first request for them. Our example includes two stateless services, computing the square and the logarithm, respectively, and a stateful service adding all the numbers it receives. The logger keeps track of the values it receives, and answers each request with the sequential number of the element in the log. For space reasons we omit the full code of our case study, which anyway can be found either in the companion technical report [12] or in the repository [3].

In our sample scenario, we invoke the program with the list of requests [{square, 10}, {adder, 20}, {log, 100}, {adder, 30}, {adder, 100}].

The two first requests are successfully answered, while the request to compute the logarithm of 100 is not. By checking the history of the server (this is exactly the one shown in Fig. 7, relevant items are grayed, most recent items are on top) we notice that the request has been sent by the server as message 11. By using CauDEr rollback facilities to undo the send of message 11 (including all and only its consequences), one notice that the send has been performed at line 24 (also visible in the screenshot, upon rollback the line becomes highlighted), which is used for already spawned services. This is wrong since this is the first request for a logarithm. One can now require to rollback the register of atom log (used as target of the send). We can now see that the system logger has been registered under this atom in the main function:

register (log,spawn(?MODULE, logger,[0,[]])),

This is wrong. The bug is that the same atom has been used both for the system logger and for logarithm service.

Finding such a bug without the support of reversibility, and rollback in particular, would not be easy. Also, rollback allows us to go directly to points of interest (e.g., where atom log has been registered), even if we do not know which process performed the action. Hence, debugging via rollback scales better than standard techniques to larger programs, where finding the bug without reversibility would be even more difficult.

5   Conclusion, Related and Future Work

We have extended CauDEr and the underlying reversible semantics of Erlang to support imperative primitives used to associate names to pids. This required to distinguish write accesses from read accesses to the map, since the latter commute while the former do not. Also, the interplay between delete and read operations required us to keep track of removed tuples. Notably, a similar approach needs to be used to define the reversible semantics of imperative languages, such as C or Java.

While we discussed most related work, in particular work on reversibility in Erlang, in the Introduction, we mention here some related approaches. Indeed, reversibility of imperative languages with concurrency has been considered, e.g., in [11]. There however actions are undone (mostly) in reverse order of completion, hence their approach does not fit causal-consistent reversibility. Generation of reversible code is also studied in the area of parallel simulation, see, e.g., [21], but there reversed code is sequential, and concurrency is added on top of it by the simulation algorithm. Also, this thread of research lacks theoretical results.

The current approach, as well as the theory in [18] on which we rely to prove properties, defines independence as a binary relation on transitions. We plan to extend this approach in future work by defining independence as a binary relation on sequences of transitions, since we found cases where single transitions do not commute, while sequences can.

For instance, a registered() does not commute with either register(a, _) or unregister(a), but it can commute with their composition since the set of registered tuples is the same before and after. Notably, covering this case would require to extend the theory in [18] as well.

References

1. Carothers, C.D., Perumalla, K.S., Fujimoto, R.: Efficient optimistic parallel simulations using reverse computation. TOMACS 9(3), 224–253 (1999)
2. CauDEr repository (2022). https://github.com/mistupv/cauder
3. CauDEr with imperative primitives repository (2022). https://github.com/PietroLami/cauder
4. Danos, V., Krivine, J.: Reversible communicating systems. In: Gardner, P., Yoshida, N. (eds.) CONCUR 2004. LNCS, vol. 3170, pp. 292–307. Springer, Heidelberg (2004). https://doi.org/10.1007/978-3-540-28644-8_19
5. Erlang/OTP 24.1.5. https://www.erlang.org/doc/index.html
6. Fabbretti, G., Lanese, I., Stefani, J.-B.: Causal-consistent debugging of distributed erlang programs. In: Yamashita, S., Yokoyama, T. (eds.) RC 2021. LNCS, vol. 12805, pp. 79–95. Springer, Cham (2021). https://doi.org/10.1007/978-3-030-79837-6_5

7. Giachino, E., Lanese, I., Mezzina, C.A.: Causal-consistent reversible debugging. In: Gnesi, S., Rensink, A. (eds.) FASE 2014. LNCS, vol. 8411, pp. 370–384. Springer, Heidelberg (2014). https://doi.org/10.1007/978-3-642-54804-8_26
8. Giachino, E., Lanese, I., Mezzina, C.A., Tiezzi, F.: Causal-consistent rollback in a tuple-based language. J. Log. Algebraic Methods Program. **88**, 99–120 (2017)
9. González-Abril, J.J., Vidal, G.: A lightweight approach to computing message races with an application to causal-consistent reversible debugging. CoRR (2021)
10. Hewitt, C., Bishop, P.B., Steiger, R.: A universal modular ACTOR formalism for artificial intelligence. In: IJCAI, pp. 235–245. William Kaufmann (1973)
11. Hoey, J., Ulidowski, I.: Reversible imperative parallel programs and debugging. In: Thomsen, M.K., Soeken, M. (eds.) RC 2019. LNCS, vol. 11497, pp. 108–127. Springer, Cham (2019). https://doi.org/10.1007/978-3-030-21500-2_7
12. Lami, P., Lanese, I., Stefani, J., Sacerdoti Coen, C., Fabbretti, G.: Improving CauDEr with imperative features - Technical report (2022). https://hal.archives-ouvertes.fr/hal-03655372
13. Landauer, R.: Irreversibility and heat generation in the computing process. IBM J. Res. Dev. **5**(3), 183–191 (1961)
14. Lanese, I., Medic, D.: A general approach to derive uncontrolled reversible semantics. In: CONCUR, vol. 171. LIPIcs, pp. 33:1–33:24. Schloss Dagstuhl - Leibniz-Zentrum für Informatik (2020)
15. Lanese, I., Mezzina, C.A., Stefani, J.: Reversibility in the higher-order π-calculus. Theor. Comput. Sci. **625**, 25–84 (2016)
16. Lanese, I., Nishida, N., Palacios, A., Vidal, G.: CauDEr: a causal-consistent reversible debugger for Erlang. In: Gallagher, J.P., Sulzmann, M. (eds.) FLOPS 2018. LNCS, vol. 10818, pp. 247–263. Springer, Cham (2018). https://doi.org/10.1007/978-3-319-90686-7_16
17. Lanese, I., Nishida, N., Palacios, A., Vidal, G.: A theory of reversibility for Erlang. J. Log. Algebraic Methods Program. **100**, 71–97 (2018)
18. Lanese, I., Phillips, I., Ulidowski, I.: An axiomatic approach to reversible computation. In: FoSSaCS 2020. LNCS, vol. 12077, pp. 442–461. Springer, Cham (2020). https://doi.org/10.1007/978-3-030-45231-5_23
19. Laursen, J.S., Schultz, U.P., Ellekilde, L.: Automatic error recovery in robot assembly operations using reverse execution. In: IROS, pp. 1785–1792. IEEE (2015)
20. Phillips, I., Ulidowski, I., Yuen, S.: A reversible process calculus and the modelling of the ERK signalling pathway. In: Glück, R., Yokoyama, T. (eds.) RC 2012. LNCS, vol. 7581, pp. 218–232. Springer, Heidelberg (2013). https://doi.org/10.1007/978-3-642-36315-3_18
21. Schordan, M., Oppelstrup, T., Jefferson, D.R., Barnes, P.D., Jr.: Generation of reversible C++ code for optimistic parallel discrete event simulation. New Gener. Comput. **36**(3), 257–280 (2018)
22. González-Abril, J.J., Vidal, G.: Causal-consistent reversible debugging: improving CauDEr. In: Morales, J.F., Orchard, D. (eds.) PADL 2021. LNCS, vol. 12548, pp. 145–160. Springer, Cham (2021). https://doi.org/10.1007/978-3-030-67438-0_9

A Reversible Debugger for Imperative Parallel Programs with Contracts

Takashi Ikeda and Shoji Yuen[(✉)]

Graduate School of Informatics, Nagoya University, Furo-cho, Chikusa-ku, Nagoya,
Aichi 4648601, Japan
{tikeda,yuen}@sqlab.jp

Abstract. We present a reversible debugger for imperative parallel programs with block structures. A program runs in the runtime of abstract machines executed concurrently, where each abstract machine has the instruction set both for forward executions and backward executions. In order to efficiently localize a defect, we annotate a program by contracts with `expects` and `ensures` as C++ contracts. When a condition at `ensures` is violated, there exists some defect. Then, the reversible runtime traces back to the last ensure annotation and check the configuration to find out the source of the problem. By repeating this process, it is possible to localize the defect efficiently, preserving the environment of that particular execution. For controlling executions of parallel blocks, annotations are with the condition expressions of blocks running in parallel and those for variables. We illustrate the debugging process by presenting a prototype implementation by Python.

Keywords: Concurrency · Reversible debugging · Contract
annotations

1 Introduction

Reversing concurrent programs is a novel way to analyze the behaviour. We focus on debugging imperative parallel programs with the nested block structure. Debugging concurrent programs is not straightforward since blocks executed in parallel vary for every execution. Uncertain synchronization mismatches between concurrent processes may cause an unexpected action. The problem may not always appear as in sequential programs. Making a runtime reversible [4–6] eases debugging concurrent programs [3] in that the runtime suspends the program at a breakpoint and traces backwards until the cause of the fault is found. For this purpose, debugging requires a *backward* breakpoint. For specifying these dual breakpoints, we incorporate *contract annotations* for reversible debugging, intending contract annotations identify the fragment to be executed forwards and backwards for debugging. We extend contract annotations to assert conditions for the running status of parallel blocks in the environment[1].

---

[1] An implementation of the reversible debugger in this paper is at: https://github. com/syuen1/RevDebugger/.

C. A. Mezzina and K. Podlaski (Eds.): RC 2022, LNCS 13354, pp. 204–212, 2022.
https://doi.org/10.1007/978-3-031-09005-9_14

2   Reversible Runtime for Parallel Programs

P ::= **begin** bn BB **end** | **par** an $P(\| P)^+$ **rap** | S
BB ::= DV DP DF $P(;P)^+$ RV
S ::= **skip** | X = E | **if** C **then** P **else** P **fi** |
        while C **do** P **od** | **call** cn $a(X?)$
DV ::= (**var** $X;$)*
DP ::= (**proc** pn $a(X?)$ **is** P **end**)*
DF ::= (**func** fn $b(X?)$ **is** P **return**)*
RV ::= (**remove** $X;$)*
E ::= X | n | (E) | E op E|{cn $b(X?)$}
C ::= **true** | B | C && C | **not** C | (C)
B ::= E == E | E > E
(X: Variable,n: Integer,a: Procedure name,b: Function name, op: {+,-,×})

Following [4], we define the programming language as below[2].

The reversible runtime proposed by the authors [5,6] executes a program by the abstract machines with byte-code instructions for forward and backward. In the forward execution of a program, the history of variable updates and branching flows are kept in two system stacks, called V-stack and L-stack, respectively. The runtime forks abstract machines for a **par** block, and the forked abstract machines execute its sub-blocks concurrently. The sub-blocks are merged at the end of the parallel block. The blocks are forked at the merge point and merged at the fork point at the backward execution. Variable updates and branching flows are extracted by popping up from the V-stack and the L-stack, respectively, enabling to trace back the forward execution.

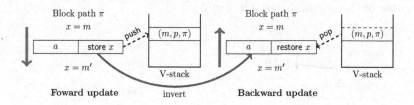

Fig. 1. Reversible update

Figure 1 shows the basic mechanism to reverse the variable value update. All variables are treated as global variables with *block path*. The block path is the sequence of block labels an, bn, cn, pn and fn specifying the context of the block which the variable belong to. When the abstract machine process labelled by p executes `store` for x, the previous value of x with the process id p and the context path π is stored in the global stack called 'V-stack', and then x is

---

[2] Here we use the extended BNF where A^* and A^+ is the repetition of A more than 0-times and once respectively, and $A?$ is either A or ε.

updated. At the backward execution, `store` is converted as `restore`. `restore` pops up the value to x with the block path π from the V-stack matching the process id p. The L-stack is used in reversing the joining control flows in an abstract machine.

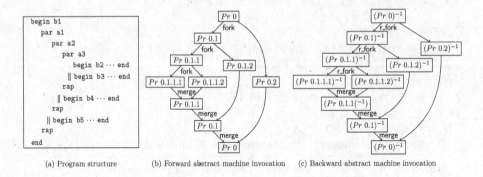

(a) Program structure   (b) Forward abstract machine invocation   (c) Backward abstract machine invocation

Fig. 2. Parallel blocks and abstract machine invocation

A `par` block is translated as shown in Fig. 3. `fork` n invokes new n abstract machines, $M_1, \ldots, M_n$, are invoked. Each abstract machine executes a block in the `par` block. The `par` block terminates when all of its sub-blocks terminates. `merge` terminates the abstract machines invoked by the corresponding `fork`. A block invoked by `fork` is identified by the sequence of numbers. The initial block has id 0. The i-th block in `par` invoked by the block of π is $\pi.i$. A `par` block may have a nested structure. For example, the block invoked by the i-th block in the j-th block is identified by $0.j.i$. Figure 2(b) shows forks and merges in the execution of the program shown in Fig. 2 (a).

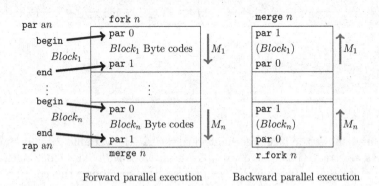

Forward parallel execution   Backward parallel execution

Fig. 3. Reversible parallel blocks

To execute a `par` block backwards, `merge` is replaced by `r_fork` and `fork` is replaced by `merge`. `r_fork` differs from `fork` in that `r_fork` pops local variable values from V-stack. The abstract machines are invoked in the way of replaced by r_fork and reverse the arrows as show in Fig. 2 (c) where $(Pr\ \pi)^{-1}$ is the reverse of $Pr\ \pi$. Each par block is reversed, and new abstract machines are invoked to execute the sub-blocks concurrently. Since each entry of the V-stack stores the process id, restore is executed to roll back the forward execution. Details of instructions and the runtime are presented in [5,6].

3   Reversible Debugging with Contract Annotations

We incorporate *contract annotations* in the reversible debugging. Contract annotations assert preconditions and postconditions of methods and functions.

An ensures annotation checks a property as a forward breakpoint and suspends the execution when the property is violated. The corresponding expects annotation checks the condition to reach the ensures annotation as a backward breakpoint. Checking the property of expects at the forward execution is useful to filter the execution to identify the problem.

```
1   begin b1
2     var seats; var agent1; var agent2;
3     proc p1 airline() is
4       par a1
5         begin b2
6           while (agent1==1) do
7             if (seats > 0) then
8               seats = seats - 1
9             else
10               agent1 = 0
11             fi
12           od
13         end
14      || begin b3
15           while (agent2==1) do
16             if (seats > 0) then
17               seats = seats - 1
18             else
19               agent2 = 0
20             fi
21           od
22         end
23       rap
24     end
25     seats = 3; agent1 = 1; agent2 = 1;
26     call c1 airline();
27     remove agent2; remove agent1; remove seats;
28   end
```

Fig. 4. Airline example [3]

Contract annotations are commonly used in object-oriented programming languages such as Java and C++ to specify the properties the methods should satisfy. In concurrent object-oriented programming language SCOOP [10], expects annotations are extended for synchronizing methods by waiting until the property holds. We adopt this mechanism in reversible debugging. ensures works as a forward breakpoint, and expects notation works as a backward breakpoint filtering the forward execution that reaches the corresponding ensures.

A pair of contract annotations is inserted before and after blocks or statements in the form following [11]:

[[expects dn *LP C PR*]]   [[ensures dn *LP C PR*]]

where dn is a *label* paring corresponding expects and ensures, *LP* is a *location path* referring to a parallel block specified relatively by the path. A condition of variables C and a built-in predicate PR are checked in the environment of the specified parallel block. The built-in predicates TERMINATED hold if the parallel block reaches the merging point. LIVING is holds otherwise. * holds always.

The location path specifies a parallel block by the relative position. When a par block is executed, the runtime forks abstract machines (AMs) as shown in Fig. 2. A contract annotation in a block of an abstract machine with id π can refer to other blocks by tracing the invocation path.

SELF :   a block in own AM   PARENT : a block in the parent AM
CHILD :   a block in the first child AM   FOLLOW : a block in the next sibling AM
PRECEND : a block in the previous sibling AM

For example, the block in AM with id of 0.1.1.1 refers to the block in the block of 0.1.2 by PARENT.FOLLOW. The annotation checks if the AM is terminated or not with the state of variables.

Reversible Debugging Steps: The reversible debugging proceeds as follows:

Step 1. The initial pair of contracts are placed.
Step 2. When the ensures condition is violated, roll back to the corresponding expects annotation.
Step 3. Update the contract annotations to narrow down the fragment.
Step 4. Run forward to trace the previous execution.
Step 5. Go back to step 2 until identifying the problem.

We apply our debugging to the airline example [3] shown in Fig. 4, assuming seats ended with -1. Contract annotations are added as follows. Figure 5 shows where the contracts are attached as break points in the execution flow of the example, where an initial call starts with the call of procedure of airline and two parallel blocks are invoked. In a backward execution, the flow goes backward by inverting arrows in the flow along with the V-stack and L-stack to preserve the order of the forward exection.

① [[expects d1 SELF true *]] and [[ensures d1 SELF seats > -1 *]] before and after line 26: call c1 airline();.

② Stop when seats is -1 where seats>-1 is violated. roll back to before line 26 with seats=3, agent1=agent2=1.

③ Update annotations: [[expects d2 SELF true *]] before line 6 and [[ensure d2 seats > -1]] after line 13, and [[expects d3 SELF true *]] before line 15 and [[ensures d3 SELF seats>-1 *]] after line 24. These contracts gnerate break points as shown ③ in Fig. 5.

④ Trace forward the previous execution and stop at one of ensures.

⑤ Let ensures d2 violated the condition with seats=-1. And roll back until expects d2 for the first time. At this point, agent1=0 and seats=-1. Go backward again.

⑥ Stopping at expects d2, agent1=1 and seats=1 since agent2 is rolled back. (Otherwise, the problem does not happen.)

⑦ Update annotations: [[expects d4 SELF true *]] before line 7 and [[ensures d4 SELF seats>-1 *]] after 8.

⑧ Trace forward the previous execution and the program stop at ensures labelled by either d4 or stop at ensure d3.

⑨ In the former case, roll back till expects d4 or expects d3. Then, it is found that both blocks are trying to check seats > 0 simultaneously. Inserting another pair of contract for b3 as d5 will find the similar problem.

By the debugging scenario above, checking seats>0 is not done properly by the blocks in par a1. One way to correct the program is to incorporate a mutual exclusion, such as Dekker's algorithm.

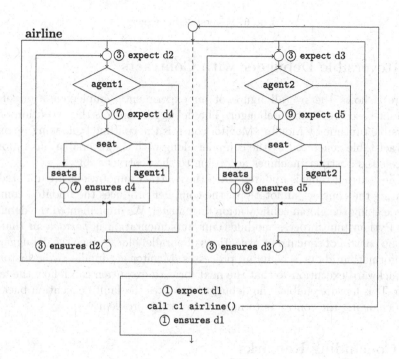

Fig. 5. Contract annotations as breakpoints for debugging

Another way for correction is to run forward by changing the built-in predicate condition. In the above debugging scenario, at ⑦, [[expects d4 FOLLOW true TERMINATED]] before line 7. Then, ensures is never violated. In this case, if the process waits for the other agent to terminate when seats = 1, seats does not become negative. This correction suggests introducing a priority at the last ticket so that one agent waits for the other agent to complete selling it.

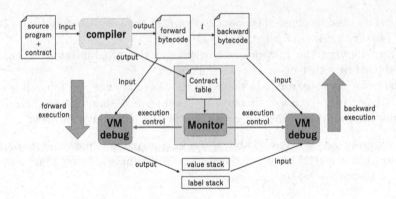

Fig. 6. Reversible debugger

4 Reversible Debugger with Contracts

Figure 6 shows the overall figure of an experimental implementation of the contract-based reversible debugger. The debugger controls the execution of the reversible runtime by Monitor. Monitor controls the runtime by looking up at the contract table generated by the compiler along with the reversible code. Monitor controls the abstract machines according to the contract table.

The contract table is updated when the contract annotations are updated. At updating the contract annotations, the compiler produces the updated contract table keeping the global configuration unchanged. We implemented the debugger with Python multiprocess module. Our implementation is *portable* in that, we have no control of concurrent executions of parallel blocks since the debugger has no information about scheduling processes. Monitor accumulates the history of the backward execution so that the next forward execution can follow the faulty trace. This feature enables the debugger executes the faulty execution back and forth changing the contracts to narrow down the problem.

5 Concluding Remarks

We presented the reversible debugging for imperative parallel programming with contracts. Contract annotations define the pairs of breakpoints in forward and backward executions. `ensures` annotations assert the conditions for forward breakpoints, and `expects` annotations work as the backward breakpoints. A backward breakpoint checks the condition at the backward execution and at the forward execution to suspend the execution to filter the execution. Our reversible debugging eases locating the cause of the problem concerning synchronization between parallel blocks. We presented a prototype of the reversible debugger using contract annotations as breakpoint specifications.

From the viewpoint of debugging, our method needs to be strengthened for practical use. In particular, a location path in a contract specifies a single parallel block. This works for a simple case but is insufficient since it is uncertain where the problem exists. A location path is better to specify the set of parallel blocks running. However, this mechanism requires more formal investigation for runtime as shown in [9] for debugging.

The reversible debugging methods for concurrent programs have been proposed [7,8], where the annotations of execution history dynamically added to the programs are used for debugging. [2] proposes the reversible debugging of communicating programming language μOz. [12] tracks message passings in reverse graphically. Contracts in concurrent programs may be seen as monitoring communication patters specified by sessions [1]. Our debugging framework much simpler than sessions and our contracts focus on particular pairs with causality. Incorporating more sophisticated specifications such as sessions is future work. Since our reversible runtime uses the history information accumulated on the execution stacks, our debugger checks the property by contract annotations from the program. Updating contract annotations to locate the problem is not straightforward, but we believe it improves the efficiency of finding the problem in reversing executions.

Acknowledgement. The authors thank Dr. Irek Ulidwoski and Dr. James Hoey for their valuable discussion and suggestions while Dr. Ulidowski's visit for JSPS Fellowship S21051. This work was supported b0y JSPS KAKENHI Grant Numbers JP17H01722 and JP21H03415.

References

1. Burlò, C.B., Francalanza, A., Scalas, A.: On the monitorability of session types, in theory and practice. In: Proceedings of ECOOP 2021. LIPIcs, vol. 194, pp. 20:1–20:30 (2021)
2. Giachino, E., Lanese, I., Mezzina, C.A.: Causal-consistent reversible debugging. In: Gnesi, S., Rensink, A. (eds.) FASE 2014. LNCS, vol. 8411, pp. 370–384. Springer, Heidelberg (2014). https://doi.org/10.1007/978-3-642-54804-8_26
3. Hoey, J., Lanese, I., Nishida, N., Ulidowski, I., Vidal, G.: A case study for reversible computing: reversible debugging of concurrent programs. In: Ulidowski, I., Lanese, I., Schultz, U.P., Ferreira, C. (eds.) RC 2020. LNCS, vol. 12070, pp. 108–127. Springer, Cham (2020). https://doi.org/10.1007/978-3-030-47361-7_5
4. Hoey, J., Ulidowski, I., Yuen, S.: Reversing parallel programs with blocks and procedures. In: Proceedings of EXPRESS/SOS 2018. EPTCS, vol. 276, pp. 69–86 (2018)
5. Ikeda, T., Yuen, S.: A reversible runtime environment for parallel programs. In: Lanese, I., Rawski, M. (eds.) RC 2020. LNCS, vol. 12227, pp. 272–279. Springer, Cham (2020). https://doi.org/10.1007/978-3-030-52482-1_18
6. Ikeda, T., Yuen, S.: A reversible runtime for parallel programs with recursive blocks. IPSJ Trans. Program. (PRO) **14**(5), 34–48 (2021). (in Japanese)
7. Lanese, I., Nishida, N., Palacios, A., Vidal, G.: CauDEr: a causal-consistent reversible debugger for Erlang. In: Gallagher, J.P., Sulzmann, M. (eds.) FLOPS 2018. LNCS, vol. 10818, pp. 247–263. Springer, Cham (2018). https://doi.org/10.1007/978-3-319-90686-7_16

8. Lanese, I., Palacios, A., Vidal, G.: Causal-consistent replay debugging for message passing programs. In: Pérez, J.A., Yoshida, N. (eds.) FORTE 2019. LNCS, vol. 11535, pp. 167–184. Springer, Cham (2019). https://doi.org/10.1007/978-3-030-21759-4_10

9. Lienhardt, M., Lanese, I., Mezzina, C.A., Stefani, J.-B.: A reversible abstract machine and its space overhead. In: Giese, H., Rosu, G. (eds.) FMOODS/FORTE-2012. LNCS, vol. 7273, pp. 1–17. Springer, Heidelberg (2012). https://doi.org/10.1007/978-3-642-30793-5_1

10. Morandi, B., Bauer, S.S., Meyer, B.: SCOOP – a contract-based concurrent object-oriented programming model. In: Müller, P. (ed.) LASER 2007-2008. LNCS, vol. 6029, pp. 41–90. Springer, Heidelberg (2010). https://doi.org/10.1007/978-3-642-13010-6_3

11. Reis, G.D., Garcia, J.D., Lakos, J., Meredith, A., Myers, N., Stroustrup, B.: Support for contract based programming in C++ (2018). http://www.open-std.org/jtc1/sc22/wg21/docs/papers/2018/p0542r3.html

12. Shibanai, K., Watanabe, T.: Actoverse: a reversible debugger for actors. In: Proceedings of AGERE 2017, pp. 50–57. ACM (2017)

Towards Causal-Consistent Reversibility of Imperative Concurrent Programs

James Hoey[✉] and Irek Ulidowski

School of Computing and Mathematical Sciences, University of Leicester, Leicester,
UK
{jbh13,iu3}@leicester.ac.uk

Abstract. We describe an ongoing work of defining and implementing a
form of reversibility of concurrent programs where causally independent
steps can be undone out of backtracking order. We introduce a notion
of causal independence between steps of reverse execution and adjust
the previously developed method for backtracking reversibility to move
towards obtaining causal-consistent reversibility.

Keywords: Reversible computation · Causal-consistent reversibility ·
Backtracking reversibility

1 Introduction

Reversible execution of concurrent imperative programs is important for many
applications, including debugging [5,9,10] and Parallel Discrete Event Simulation [15,16]. Faithfully reversing to all intermediate states can help locate a software defect, and undo invalid optimistic simulation. Work including RCC [13]
and reversible flowcharts [17] describe reversal of sequential programs. These
"backtrack" by undoing execution steps in exactly the inverted forward order.

Research into reversibility of message-passing systems introduced causal-
consistent reversibility [4,14], where steps of an execution can be reversed out
of backtracking order. Any step (or action) can be undone provided all of its
consequences have previously been reversed. This relaxation offers several benefits. One application-specific benefit, namely causal-consistent reversible debugging [6,8], is described by Lanese et al. through Cauder, a causal-consistent
reversible debugger for Erlang [10,11]. Other approaches of reverse debugging
are summarised by Engblom [5]. The cause of a concurrent program bug may
be in a less dominant thread. Backtracking requires reversal of all steps, including this more dominant, but irrelevant, thread. Provided causality is maintained
across threads, time and resources could be saved by reversing only the thread
of interest (including those necessary from other threads). Lanese, Phillips and
Ulidowski [12] describe further properties for reversing that preserves causes,
namely Causal Safety and Causal Liveness.

© The Author(s), under exclusive license to Springer Nature Switzerland AG 2022
C. A. Mezzina and K. Podlaski (Eds.): RC 2022, LNCS 13354, pp. 213–223, 2022.
https://doi.org/10.1007/978-3-031-09005-9_15

P ::= ε | S | P; P | {P} par {P}

S ::= skip | X = E | if B then P else Q end | while B do P end | begin BB end

BB ::= DV; P; RV   DV ::= ε | var X = E; DV   RV ::= ε | remove X = E; RV

E ::= X | n | (E) | E Op E   B ::= T | F | ¬B | (B) | E == E | E > E | B ∧ B

Fig. 1. Syntax of a concurrent programming language.

2   Backtracking Reversibility

The concurrent imperative programming language we use to discuss causal-consistent reversibility is shown in Fig. 1. Supported constructs are assignments (both destructive (such as X=3) and constructive (such as X=X+1)), conditionals, while loops, blocks, local variables and a parallel composition operator. Operational semantics defining forward (and reverse) execution are given in [7]. This approach has been proved to be correct [7] and applied to debugging [9].

The reversal of a program execution by reversing statements in exactly the inverted forward order is named backtracking [1]. Our previous work [7,9] has proposed backtracking reversibility of executions of programs written in the syntax from Fig. 1[1]. We do this by recording (otherwise unrecoverable) information lost during forward execution, and introducing identifiers to capture the concurrent interleaving order (determined by the parallel composition operator par). Information lost during forward execution is saved to an auxiliary store δ, and includes values overwritten during an assignment and control flow information (result of condition evaluation for branching and looping). As each statement executes, the next available identifier (the next natural number in ascending order) is assigned to it. In the following examples, identifiers assigned to statements are displayed within the program syntax.

When reversing an execution, identifiers are used in descending order to determine the correct reverse interleaving order (backtracking). Information saved onto δ is then used to undo the effects of each statement. All use of δ and identifiers is defined in the operational semantics as in [7]. Transitions that use an identifier, namely assignments, opening (evaluating) a conditional statement or a condition of a while loop, closing of conditionals and loops, local variable declarations and removals, are called *identifier transitions*. All other transitions (those have no affect on the program state), such as removing a sequentially composed skip statement or opening or closing a completed block statement, are called *skip transitions*. Such skip transitions (or steps) can therefore already be reversed out of backtracking order.

---

[1] Additionally, previous work included the reversal of potentially recursive procedures. We omit procedures here and defer reversing them to future work.

2.1   Proposed Relaxations of Backtracking

In preparation for the following relaxation of backtracking reversibility, we first describe a number of changes required to our current approach. The auxiliary store δ previously contained a minimal amount of stacks to store control flow information (such as the result of evaluating a conditional statement). A single stack was used to store information for all conditional statements. This works for backtracking reversibility, as the final conditional statement will be reversed first. This is no longer sufficient for reversing out of backtracking order, as a stack element below the head may need to be accessed first. We therefore introduce separate arrays for each conditional statement here for the first time. In a similar manner, we also introduce separate arrays for each while loop and each (global or local) version of a variable.

In our previous work without causal-consistent reversibility, identifiers were used in descending order (implemented as a counter) to enforce backtracking reversibility. This is no longer sufficient for causal-consistent reversal, where identifiers could be used in any order. Hence, we move away from implementing this as a counter, and instead maintain an array of used identifiers. Elements can then be removed (when used during a step of the reverse execution) in any order. Identifiers are no longer required to be used in descending order.

3   Towards Causal-Consistent Reversibility

Having set out the necessary background, we now define and illustrate how to reverse concurrent programs in a causally-consistent manner. Before we continue, we note that the syntax shown in Fig. 1 defines traditional and irreversible programs (and is a subset of languages used in our previous work). For ease of reading, we omit parts of the syntax that are not critical for this work. This includes the unique names given to constructs (such as Wn for while loops) and statement paths Pa (used for evaluation). In the following examples, we introduce a notation for displaying statement identifiers within the syntax. Further details of this notation can be found in [7].

To consider causality we introduce a new notion of *execution sequences*. An execution sequence consists of identifier or skip transitions between programs. Each program is named P_i, where i is the highest identifier used so far. This identifier appears in program code as a element of an array, for example [i] or [i,j]. A transition from P_i that results from executing a non-skip statement produces the program P_{i+1}. A skip transition from P_i produces the program P_i^a, where a is a fresh number that uniquely identifies the execution of this skip. An identifier transition is labelled with the statement (including its identifier) that caused it, and a skip transition is labelled with the word "skip" and an appropriate a in round brackets.

Example 1. Consider an execution of the following program containing a parallel statement followed by a destructive assignment. Let X, Y and Z initially equal 0, where the conditional branch executes first (since the par operator allows execution interleaving). Though multiple execution orders exist, the precise order of statement execution used here is indicated by the identifiers.

$$\{\text{while } (\text{X} < 2) \text{ do} \qquad\qquad \{\text{if } (\text{Y} < 1) \text{ then}$$

$$\text{X} = \text{X} + 1 \ [4,7]; \qquad\qquad\qquad \text{Y} = \text{Y} + 2 \ [2]$$

$$\text{Y} = \text{Y} + \text{X} \ [5,9] \qquad \text{par} \qquad \text{else } \text{Z} = 3 \ []$$

$$\text{end } [3,6,10]\} \qquad\qquad \text{end } [1,8]\}; \qquad\qquad \text{X} = 4 \ [11]$$

Complete execution of this program produces the following execution sequence:

$$P_0 \xrightarrow{\text{if}..[1]} P_1 \xrightarrow{\text{Y=Y+2[2]}} P_2 \xrightarrow{\text{while}..[3]} P_3 \xrightarrow{\text{X=X+1[4]}} P_4 \xrightarrow{\text{skip(14)}} P_4^{14} \xrightarrow{\text{Y=Y+X[5]}} P_5 \xrightarrow{\text{skip(15)}} P_5^{15}$$

$$\xrightarrow{\text{while}..[6]} P_6 \xrightarrow{\text{X=X+1[7]}} P_7 \xrightarrow{\text{skip(16)}} P_7^{16} \xrightarrow{\text{ifend[8]}} P_8 \xrightarrow{\text{Y=Y+X[9]}} P_9 \xrightarrow{\text{skip(17)}} P_9^{17}$$

$$\xrightarrow{\text{whilend[10]}} P_{10} \xrightarrow{\text{skip(18)}} P_{10}^{18} \xrightarrow{\text{skip(19)}} P_{10}^{19} \xrightarrow{\text{X=4[11]}} P_{11} \ (= \text{skip})$$

The skip transition skip(14) (among others) labels a transition that removes a sequentially composed skip statement, while skip(18) labels a skip transition closing parallel composition. The program state at P_5 is that X=1, Y=3, Z=0. The final program state is such that X=4, Y=5 and Z=0.   □

To reverse the execution of the above program, we first generate the inverted program. Reverse execution of the inverted program produces a corresponding execution sequence. The transitions are between inverted programs named IP_i, where i is the highest previously used identifier at that point (due next for reversal via backtracking). Inverted programs use the same syntax as forward programs, with expressions and conditions still presented. Such expressions and conditions are included to help with our application to debugging, in which seeing such constructs is crucial. However, they are *not re-evaluated* during reversal, with old values and evaluation results retrieved from the auxiliary store δ.

Example 2. Consider the inverted version of the program (augmented with arrays of identifiers representing a specific forward execution order) from Example 1. Note that the constructive assignments that were increments are inverted as decrements, hence, unlike destructive assignments, do not rely on saved values. The expressions X < 2 and Y < 1, and the statements X = 4 and Z = 3, are each not re-evaluated during reverse execution.

$$\text{X} = 4 \ [11]; \ \{\text{while } (\text{X} < 2) \text{ do} \qquad\qquad \{\text{if } (\text{Y} < 1) \text{ then}$$

$$\text{Y} = \text{Y} - \text{X} \ [5,9]; \qquad\qquad\qquad \text{Y} = \text{Y} - 2 \ [2]$$

$$\text{X} = \text{X} - 1 \ [4,7] \quad \text{par} \qquad \text{else } \text{Z} = 3 \ []$$

$$\text{end } [3,6,10]\} \qquad\qquad \text{end } [1,8]\}$$

If the order of executing statements is from the highest identifier to the lowest, then we obtain the following *backtracing reversal execution sequence*:

$$IP_{11} \overset{X=4[11]}{\rightsquigarrow} IP_{10} \overset{skip(19)}{\rightsquigarrow} IP_{10}^{19} \overset{while..[10]}{\rightsquigarrow} IP_9 \overset{Y=Y-X[9]}{\rightsquigarrow} IP_8 \overset{skip(18)}{\rightsquigarrow} IP_8^{18}$$

$$\overset{if..[8]}{\rightsquigarrow} IP_7 \overset{X=X-1[7]}{\rightsquigarrow} IP_6 \overset{skip(17)}{\rightsquigarrow} IP_6^{17} \overset{while..[6]}{\rightsquigarrow} IP_5 \overset{Y=Y-X[5]}{\rightsquigarrow} IP_4$$

$$\overset{skip(16)}{\rightsquigarrow} IP_4^{16} \overset{X=X-1[4]}{\rightsquigarrow} IP_3 \overset{skip(15)}{\rightsquigarrow} IP_3^{15} \overset{whilend[3]}{\rightsquigarrow} IP_2 \overset{Y=Y-2[2]}{\rightsquigarrow} IP_1$$

$$\overset{ifend[1]}{\rightsquigarrow} IP_0 \overset{skip(14)}{\rightsquigarrow} IP_0^{14}$$

The transition $\overset{X=4[11]}{\rightsquigarrow}$ reverses an assignment to X by retrieving the previous value (2) from δ. The transitions $\overset{while..[10]}{\rightsquigarrow}$ and $\overset{if..[8]}{\rightsquigarrow}$ open a while loop and a conditional statement respectively (retrieving appropriate boolean values from δ), while $\overset{whilend[3]}{\rightsquigarrow}$ and $\overset{ifend[1]}{\rightsquigarrow}$ replace the completed constructs with skip. This execution begins in the state X=4, Y=5 and Z=0 (the final state of forward execution), and produces a final state of X=0, Y=0 and Z=0 (as required). As in Example 1, the program state at IP_5 is the same as in P_5, namely X=1, Y=3, Z=0.

An example of a reversal of a different forward execution of the program from Example 1 is shown in Appendix A.   □

A backtracking execution sequence corresponds tightly to the matching forward execution sequence. Identifier transitions each have an inverse equivalent. The majority of skip transitions also have such a match, though this is not as tight. Since skip steps do not change the program state, this causes no issues.

Following the backtracking execution sequence will correctly restore the program state to as it was prior to the forward execution, as proved to be correct in [7]. We note here that we propose changes to δ in this work not present in [7], however these changes are only to the structure of the auxiliary store and therefore are still consistent with our original proof. Causal-consistent reversibility allows us to reverse via a different execution sequence while maintaining correctness. As stated in [4,12], two execution traces are causally-equivalent if the only difference between them is the order of independent steps. This requires the notion of *independence* between statements.

3.1   Data Race and Causal Independence

Independence of statements has been widely studied in the context of parallelisation of sequential programs, instruction scheduling in compilers and in Data Flow Machines [2,3]. In its simplest form, it means that the effect of X=X+1;Y=2 on the program state is the same as that of Y=2;X=X+1 or X=X+1 par Y=2 because X=X+1 and Y=3 update memory independently, so the order in which they are executed or reversed is irrelevant. In this work-in-progress paper, we are interested in independence of statements when executing individual versions of inverted programs (as in Example 2). When reversing in our setting, since no evaluation of conditions of loops or conditionals takes place (control flow information is instead read from δ [7]), and since statements that produce skip transitions do not update memory, there will only be causal independence between some assignment statements.

In general, two assignments are dependent if there is a data race between them, where the order of execution directly impacts the final program state. Appendix B contains a detailed discussion of the independence of assignments to local and global variables. We denote statements by S_1 and S_2, though also use $S(n)$ and $S(m)$ to represent the statement that uses the given identifier n respectively m.

Definition 1. *There is a data race between S_1 and S_2 (S_1 and S_2 race) if*

- *S_1 and S_2 are destructive assignments to the same (version of a) variable.*
- *S_1 is a constructive assignment to a variable used within the expression of the assignment S_2, or S_2 is a constructive assignment to a variable used within the expression of the assignment S_1.*

Example 3. Consider execution of an inverted program below, where initially X = 3 and Y = 15. The forward execution began with X = Y = 0. The assignments to Y race according to Definition 1.

$$\{X = 3 \ [3]; \ Y = Y + 8 \ [2]\} \ \textbf{par} \ \{Y = 7 \ [1]\}$$

With the sequential ordering of statements on each side of the parallel maintained, the first reversal step must be the statement with identifier 3 or 1. It is not possible for any other statement to execute at this point. Each of the possible first steps can be retrieved simply by analysing the program syntax. These assignments do not race as they are to different variables, so we might be tempted to reverse first Y=7[1]. After this, we have that X = 3 and Y = 0 because initially going forwards Y=7 overwrote the value 0. Backtracking order is followed for the remaining assignments (with identifiers 3 and 2), producing the final state with X = 0 (as required) and Y = −8 (incorrectly). This error is a result of allowing racing statements with identifiers 2 and 1 to be reversed out of order. Hence, when deciding if to reverse Y=7[1] before X=3[3], we also need consider if reversing Y=7[1] before Y=Y+8[2] is safe. This motivates causal independence.   □

Before we define causal independence, we introduce a helpful notation. When reversing an arbitrary program IP_8, the next statement to undo under backtracking has the identifier 8. To undo an independent statement with the identifier say 4, we need a notation for the resulting program. We introduce $IP_i^{\{a,b\}}$, where i is as before, a identifies a skip step, and b is now a fresh number indicating a program produced by causal-consistent reversibility. We use $*$ to represent an arbitrary value. Our resulting program would now be uniquely labelled $IP_8^{\{*,4\}}$.

For a statement $S(m)$ to be reversed before $S(n)$ (due next in backtracking order), with $n > m$, we must determine whether $S(m)$ races with $S(n)$ and with any intermediate statements $S(i)$.

Definition 2. *(Causal Independence) Assume* S(n) *and* S(m) *are non skip statements with identifiers* n *and* m *respectively such that* n > m. *Assume*

$$IP_n \overset{S(n)}{\rightsquigarrow} IP_{n-1} \ldots \overset{S(i)}{\rightsquigarrow} \ldots IP_m \overset{S(m)}{\rightsquigarrow} IP_{m-1} \quad and \quad IP_n \overset{S(m)}{\rightsquigarrow} IP_n^{\{*,m\}}$$

and let S(i) *be either a statement with identifier* i *such that* $n \geq i > m$, *or* S(i) *labels a skip transition for some appropriate* i *such that* $n > i > m$. *We say that* S(n) *and* S(m) *transitions from* IP_n *are causally independent if* S(m) *is not in a data race with any* S(i).

Example 4. Recall the program and its backtracking execution in Example 2. Let the backtracking reversal execute as previously described up until the use of the identifier 5 via the statement Y=Y-X [5]:

$$IP_{11} \overset{X=4[11]}{\rightsquigarrow} IP_{10} \overset{skip(19)}{\rightsquigarrow} IP_{10}^{19} \overset{while..[10]}{\rightsquigarrow} IP_9 \overset{Y=Y-X[9]}{\rightsquigarrow} IP_8 \overset{skip(18)}{\rightsquigarrow} IP_8^{18}$$

$$\overset{if..[8]}{\rightsquigarrow} IP_7 \overset{X=X-1[7]}{\rightsquigarrow} IP_6 \overset{skip(17)}{\rightsquigarrow} IP_6^{17} \overset{while..[6]}{\rightsquigarrow} IP_5$$

At this point, the next available step of reversal is either the assignment within the loop body (Y=Y-X [5]) or the assignment within the conditional (Y=Y-2 [2]). By Definition 2, these two statements race as both are assignments to the same variable. So, backtracking order must be followed reversing them. After reversing Y=Y-X [5], the choice is now between the skip(16) followed by X=X-1[4] transitions and the assignment within the conditional (Y=Y-2[2]). By Definition 2, we can see that Y=Y-2 [2] does not race with skip(16) nor on X=X-1[4]. This means we can reverse it out of backtracking order and therefore produce an alternative execution sequence:

$$IP_5 \overset{Y=Y-X[5]}{\rightsquigarrow} IP_4 \overset{skip(16)}{\rightsquigarrow} IP_4^{16} \overset{Y=Y-2[2]}{\rightsquigarrow} IP_4^{*,2} \overset{X=X-1[4]}{\rightsquigarrow} IP_3 \overset{skip(15)}{\rightsquigarrow} IP_3^{15}$$

$$\overset{whilend[3]}{\rightsquigarrow} IP_1 \overset{ifend[1]}{\rightsquigarrow} IP_0 \overset{skip(14)}{\rightsquigarrow} IP_0^{14}$$

We note that the skip transition $\overset{skip(15)}{\rightsquigarrow}$ would be performed before the assignment reversed early under uniform execution. This alternative execution sequence begins in the state X=1, Y=3 and Z=0 (as required), and produces a final state of X=0, Y=0 and Z=0 (meaning the reversal is indeed correct).   □

4   Conclusion and Future Work

We have presented our initial work aimed at causal-consistent reversibility of imperative concurrent programs. We have described key notions with examples, including causal independence between transitions. Future work will extend our approach with recursive procedure calls, provide a proof of correctness.

Though not presented here, our simulator, Ripple [7], is currently being extended with causal-consistent reversibility. Future development will complete this implementation and explore the link to debugging.

A   Causally Independent Interleavings

The backtracking reversal execution sequence from Example 2 is shown in Fig. 2 as the path from IP_{11} via IP_8^{18} and IP_7, then all the way down to IP_2 before finishing at IP_0^{14}. The alternative reversal shown in Example 4 is the path described above but with the detour from IP_4^{16} to IP_1. As seen from the rest of the diagram, any full path is a valid execution that can be gotten from the main execution by changing order of causally independent transitions.

There are many possible executions of the forward program from Example 1. For each such execution, there is a particular inverted program which will have a backtracking execution sequence. Moreover, there will be potentially many other execution sequences originating from that backtracking sequence that preserve causal independence. This is illustrated in the next example.

Example 5. Consider a different execution of the program from Example 1, where one full iteration of the while loop is executed first. Then we perform the entire conditional statement (executing the false branch), and follow it by doing the second loop iteration, producing the following execution sequence.

$$P_0 \xrightarrow{\text{while..}[1]} P_1 \xrightarrow{X=X+1[2]} P_2 \xrightarrow{\text{skip}(14)} P_2^{14} \xrightarrow{Y=Y+X[3]} P_3 \xrightarrow{\text{skip}(15)} P_3^{15} \xrightarrow{\text{while..}[4]} P_4 \xrightarrow{\text{if..}[5]} P_5$$

$$\xrightarrow{Z=3[6]} P_6 \xrightarrow{\text{ifend}[7]} P_7 \xrightarrow{X=X+1[8]} P_8 \xrightarrow{\text{skip}(16)} P_8^{16} \xrightarrow{Y=Y+X[9]} P_9 \xrightarrow{\text{skip}(17)} P_9^{17}$$

$$\xrightarrow{\text{whilend}[10]} P_{10} \xrightarrow{\text{skip}(18)} P_{10}^{18} \xrightarrow{\text{skip}(19)} P_{10}^{19} \xrightarrow{X=4[11]} P_{11}\ (=\text{skip})$$

Under backtracking reversal, the second while loop iteration must be reversed first. This would produce the following execution sequence.

$$IP_{11} \xrightsquigarrow{X=4[11]} IP_{10} \xrightsquigarrow{\text{skip}(19)} IP_{10}^{19} \xrightsquigarrow{\text{while..}[10]} IP_9 \xrightsquigarrow{Y=Y-X[9]} IP_8 \xrightsquigarrow{\text{skip}(18)} IP_8^{18}$$

$$\xrightsquigarrow{X=X-1[8]} IP_7 \xrightsquigarrow{\text{skip}(17)} IP_7^{17} \xrightsquigarrow{\text{if..}[7]} IP_6 \xrightsquigarrow{Z=3[6]} IP_5 \xrightsquigarrow{\text{ifend}[5]} IP_4$$

$$\xrightsquigarrow{\text{while..}[4]} IP_3 \xrightsquigarrow{Y=Y-X[3]} IP_2 \xrightsquigarrow{\text{skip}(16)} IP_2^{16} \xrightsquigarrow{X=X-1[2]} IP_1 \xrightsquigarrow{\text{skip}(15)} IP_1^{15}$$

$$\xrightsquigarrow{\text{whilend}[1]} IP_0 \xrightsquigarrow{\text{skip}(14)} IP_0^{14}$$

By Definition 2, we have that the opening/closing of a conditional statement is independent of any statements of the loop (no re-evaluation of the expression). The false branch statement Z=3 is independent of any statements of the loop. The entire conditional statement can be reversed prior to any reversal of the loop. This causally consistent reversal produces the following execution sequence.

$$IP_{11} \xrightsquigarrow{X=4[11]} IP_{10} \xrightsquigarrow{\text{skip}(19)} IP_{10}^{19} \xrightsquigarrow{\text{if..}[7]} IP_{10}^{*,7} \xrightsquigarrow{Z=3[6]} IP_{10}^{*,6} \xrightsquigarrow{\text{ifend}[5]} IP_{10}^{*,5}$$

$$\xrightsquigarrow{\text{while..}[10]} IP_9 \xrightsquigarrow{Y=Y-X[9]} IP_8 \xrightsquigarrow{\text{skip}(18)} IP_8^{18} \xrightsquigarrow{X=X-1[8]} IP_7 \xrightsquigarrow{\text{skip}(17)} IP_7^{17}$$

$$\xrightsquigarrow{\text{while..}[4]} IP_3 \xrightsquigarrow{Y=Y-X[3]} IP_2 \xrightsquigarrow{\text{skip}(16)} IP_2^{16} \xrightsquigarrow{X=X-1[2]} IP_1 \xrightsquigarrow{\text{skip}(15)} IP_1^{15}$$

$$\xrightsquigarrow{\text{whilend}[1]} IP_0 \xrightsquigarrow{\text{skip}(14)} IP_0^{14}$$

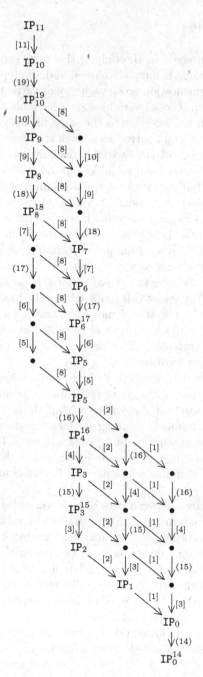

Fig. 2. All possible executions of the inverted program from Example 2 preserving causal independence. To improve presentation of transition labels we have only retained bracketed identifiers or skip numbers omitting the names of statements. For example instead of X=4[11] we write [11] as the label of the first transition, and we write (19) instead of skip(19) in the second transition.

B   Local Variables

The programming language used throughout this work supports global and local variables. A global variable is uniquely named and assumed to exist prior to the execution. At an implementation level, each global variable is associated with a unique memory location. Global variables are accessible from any point within the program, with each use referring to the same memory location.

The syntax shown in Fig. 1 introduces block statements of the form DV; P; RV, where DV is a sequence of local variable declaration statements, P is a program and RV is a sequence of local variable removal statements. A local variable declaration statement (only possible at the beginning of a block) creates a new variable local to the block statement. A unique memory location is associated with this local variable, keeping the value it holds separate to that of the global version. This local variable is only accessible from within the same block statement. If a local variable is named uniquely (including to global variables), then this is treated exactly the same as a global variable. Should a local variable share its name with a global variable, the global variable is no longer accessible within this block statement. Any use of this name within the block statement will refer to the local version (and not the memory location associated with the global version). At the end of a block, each local variable must then be removed via a local variable removal statement. This deletes the final value this variable held and releases the memory location.

Let us first consider whether local variable declaration statements can race. Within a single block, our syntax does not support parallel statements within DV. Therefore two declaration statements within the same block cannot race. Two blocks can be in parallel, meaning declaration statements from different blocks can be executed in parallel. Since each will use a fresh memory location and therefore refer to a different variable (or version if the same name is used), these also cannot race. Similar reasoning can be given for removal statements but is omitted here.

We now consider races between uses of local variables. A parallel statement within a block may contain uses of the same local variable in parallel. Such statements will race according to Definition 1. Two block statements can be in parallel, each of which may declare a local variable with the same name. Any two statements such that each is from a different side of this parallel statement cannot race as this name will refer to a different version of this variable (a different memory location). Two uses of the same variable name on a single side of the parallel will race as explained above.

We conclude that local variable declaration and removal statements cannot race, and are therefore not included in our definition of a data race (Definition 1).

References

1. Bergstra, J.A., Ponse, A., van Wamel, J.J.: Process algebra with backtracking. In: de Bakker, J.W., de Roever, W.-P., Rozenberg, G. (eds.) REX 1993. LNCS, vol. 803, pp. 46–91. Springer, Heidelberg (1994). https://doi.org/10.1007/3-540-58043-3_17

2. Bernstein, D., Rodeh, M.: Global instruction scheduling for superscalar machines. In: SIGPLAN 1991 Conference on Programming Language Design and Implementation, Proceedings of the ACM, pp. 241–255 (1991)

3. Cooper, K.D., Torczon, L.: Instruction scheduling. In: Engineering a Compiler, 2nd edn., pp. 639–677. Morgan Kaufmann (2012)

4. Danos, V., Krivine, J.: Reversible communicating systems. In: Gardner, P., Yoshida, N. (eds.) CONCUR 2004. LNCS, vol. 3170, pp. 292–307. Springer, Heidelberg (2004). https://doi.org/10.1007/978-3-540-28644-8_19

5. Engblom, J.: A review of reverse debugging. In: Proceedings of the 2012 System, Software, SoC and Silicon Debug Conference (2012)

6. Giachino, E., Lanese, I., Mezzina, C.A.: Causal-consistent reversible debugging. In: Proceedings of FASE 2014 (2014). https://doi.org/10.1007/978-3-642-54804-8_26

7. Hoey, J.: Reversing an Imperative Concurrent Programming Language. Ph.D. thesis, University of Leicester (2019)

8. Hoey, J., Lanese, I., Nishida, N., Ulidowski, I., Vidal, G.: A case study for reversible computing: reversible debugging of concurrent programs. In: Ulidowski, I., Lanese, I., Schultz, U.P., Ferreira, C. (eds.) RC 2020. LNCS, vol. 12070, pp. 108–127. Springer, Cham (2020). https://doi.org/10.1007/978-3-030-47361-7_5

9. Hoey, J., Ulidowski, I.: Reversible imperative parallel programs and debugging. In: Thomsen, M.K., Soeken, M. (eds.) RC 2019. LNCS, vol. 11497, pp. 108–127. Springer, Cham (2019). https://doi.org/10.1007/978-3-030-21500-2_7

10. Lanese, I., Nishida, N., Palacios, A., Vidal, G.: CauDEr: a causal-consistent reversible debugger for Erlang. In: Gallagher, J.P., Sulzmann, M. (eds.) FLOPS 2018. LNCS, vol. 10818, pp. 247–263. Springer, Cham (2018). https://doi.org/10.1007/978-3-319-90686-7_16

11. Lanese, I., Palacios, A., Vidal, G.: Causal-consistent replay reversible semantics for message passing concurrent programs. Fundamenta Informaticae **178**(3), 229–266 (2021)

12. Lanese, I., Phillips, I., Ulidowski, I.: An axiomatic approach to reversible computation. In: FoSSaCS 2020. LNCS, vol. 12077, pp. 442–461. Springer, Cham (2020). https://doi.org/10.1007/978-3-030-45231-5_23

13. Perumalla, K.: Introduction to Reversible Computing. CRC Press (2014)

14. Phillips, I., Ulidowski, I.: Reversing algebraic process calculi. J. Log. Algebraic Program. **73**, 70–96 (2007)

15. Schordan, M., Oppelstrup, T., Jefferson, D.R., Barnes, P.D.: Generation of reversible C++ code for optimistic parallel discrete event simulation. New Generation Comput. **36**(3), 257–280 (2018)

16. Vulov, G., Hou, C., Vuduc, R.W., Fujimoto, R., Quinlan, D.J., Jefferson, D.R.: The backstroke framework for source level reverse computation applied to parallel discrete event simulation. In: WSC 2011 (2011)

17. Yokoyama, T., Axelsen, H.B., Glück, R.: Fundamentals of reversible flowchart languages. Theore. Comput. Sci. **611**, 87–115 (2016)

Optimizing Reversible Programs

Niklas Deworetzki[1], Martin Kutrib[2], Uwe Meyer[1(✉)],
and Pia-Doreen Ritzke[1]

[1] Technische Hochschule Mittelhessen, Wiesenstr. 14, 35390 Giessen, Germany
{uwe.meyer,niklas.deworetzki,pia-doreen.ritzke}@mni.thm.de
[2] Institut für Informatik, Universität Giessen, Arndtstr. 2, 35392 Giessen, Germany
kutrib@informatik.uni-giessen.de

Abstract. Reversible programming languages have been a focus of research for more than the last decade mostly due to the work of Glück, Yokoyama, Mogensen, and many others. In this paper we report about our recent activities to optimize reversible code with respect to execution time. Based on our *rc3*-compiler which compiles Janus to reversible static-single-assignment form RSSA, we had explored and implemented optimization algorithms for local common-subexpression elimination, constant propagation, and folding and have presented those at SOAP 2021. This paper focuses on new achievements for procedure inlining as well as elimination of dead code. Our compiler is—to our knowledge—the first optimizing compiler for reversible languages. Whereas these optimizations are well established for "traditional" languages, programs that can be executed forwards and backwards require different and novel approaches.

Keywords: Reverse computing · Reversible programming languages · Janus · Reversible static-single-assignment · Optimization

1 Introduction

Reverse computing, although the initial ideas can be traced back to the 1960s [11], has been a major research area over the last decade. With the growing importance of sustainability and reduced energy consumption, reverse computing promises contributions by avoiding the waste of energy through deletion of information [6].

More than twenty years after the first creation of a reversible language called Janus [12], the papers of the Copenhagen group [18] brought new life into the area of reversible languages by formally defining and extending Janus. Interpretation and partial evaluation [13] as well as self-interpretation [20] were studied and in [3], Axelsen published his results on compilation of Janus. In [19] a reversible flowchart language is described as a foundation for imperative languages and their r-Turing-completeness is proved, i.e. its ability to compute exactly all injective computable functions.

C. A. Mezzina and K. Podlaski (Eds.): RC 2022, LNCS 13354, pp. 224–238, 2022.
https://doi.org/10.1007/978-3-031-09005-9_16

Whilst it was now possible to execute programs forwards and backwards, there seem to be no previous results about optimization of reversible programs. Optimization in this regard refers to improving the execution time of programs or their memory consumption [15]. In this paper, we will mainly focus on execution time.

It is well known from the discipline of compiler construction that optimization can most effectively be performed on some intermediate representation of the source rather than the source code itself or its abstract syntax tree. Such intermediate representations include three-address-code [1] and static-single-assignment [16].

In 2015, Mogensen published his work on RSSA, which is a special form of static-single-assignment that can be executed forwards and backwards [14]. Our *rc3*-compiler (*reversible computing compiler collection*) [17] is able to compile Janus to RSSA (and three-address-code) [10].

In [4] we have reported on our first successes in implementing local common-subexpression elimination as well as constant propagation and folding. In this paper we are going to describe two further optimization techniques, namely procedure inlining and dead-code elimination, and will present the results of the application of these optimizations on some typical Janus programs that have been compiled to RSSA.

2   The Compiler *rc3*

This section briefly explains the structure and implementation of our compiler's front-end and back-ends (see Fig. 1). Our approach to implement the compiler in Java largely resembles the approach for a classical multi-pass compiler [2]. The back-ends are pluggable, such that adding new back-ends is easy.

The front-end consists of a dedicated scanner and a parser, which are generated using the scanner generator *JFlex* [9] and the parser generator *CUP* [7] respectively. The scanner performs the lexical analysis, converting the input characters into a sequence of tokens. These tokens are then passed to the parser, which performs the syntactic analysis and constructs an abstract syntax tree. After the construction of an abstract syntax tree, it is passed to the semantic analysis.

With the implementation of the semantic analysis, the particularities arising from the properties of a reversible language become clear: As in a conventional language, Janus defines rules for the visibility of identifiers and restrictions on types of variables and expressions. In addition to classical analysis passes, that insert declarations into a symbol table and check the visibility and types of used variables and expressions, another pass has to be defined, the aim of which is to check the reversibility of individual instructions. Most importantly, assignments need to be reversible. For instance, assigning a constant value to a variable is not reversible, as the previous value of the variable would be required in order to be able to assign it to the variable in backwards execution. An exception are `local` and `delocal` statements which initialize respectively delete a variable. These are mutually inverse and thus need to occur in pairs.

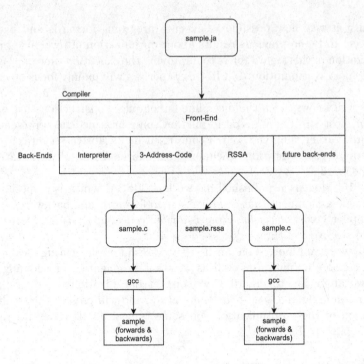

Fig. 1. Overview of our compiler.

To circumvent this problem with assignment, Janus only allows +=, -=, and ^= (the latter representing an XOR operation). The operations += and -= are mutually inverse, ^= is inverse to itself. In addition, control constructs such as conditional or loop require assertions at the end, such that the assertion becomes the condition during backwards execution and vice versa. Procedure calls in Janus are call-by-reference and use the keyword `call`; during backwards execution, the procedure body will simply be executed backwards; the inverse of a `call` is `uncall`. Please note that variable-aliasing would prevent reversibility and is thus forbidden.

RSSA is, as mentioned before, a reversible form of SSA, i.e., each variable can only be assigned once and different "versions" of a variable need to be used when a variable has got multiple assignments. In "conventional" SSA, Φ-functions are used to merge two versions into a new one, for example after a conditional statement where one version of each variable exists for each of the two branches.

Mogensen observed that this technique, although well known, is not applicable in RSSA, as the merge operation is not reversible since it turns two pieces of information into one. Thus, RSSA uses entry- and exit points: In the simplest form, `l(x1, ..., xn) <-` is an unconditional entry point and represents just a label. `l1(x1, ..., xn)l2 <- c`, where c is a condition, is a conditional entry point with the following semantics: If entered through a jump to `l1`, c is evaluated and is verified to be true, or a runtime-error will be generated; if entered though a jump to 12, c is verified to be false, or a runtime error is created. Exit points are either `-> l(x1, ..., xn)` (unconditional) or `c -> l1(x1, ..., xn)l2` (conditional), where `c` is evaluated and a jump to `l1` is performed if true, or to `l2` otherwise. The parameters `x1, ..., xn` are passed from exit- to entry-point by value. In backwards execution, jumps are performed from entry- to exit-point accordingly.

In RSSA, the semantics of procedure calls is call-by-value-result (see the second but last line on the right in the example depicted in Fig. 2), which is equivalent to call-by-reference when aliasing is forbidden.

In Janus, as well as in RSSA, all variables need to be deleted properly to avoid memory garbage, as it would prevent reversibility. In Janus, local variables can be created with a `local` declaration and need to be explicitly destroyed using a `delocal` statement. A `local`-statement is of the form `local t x=e`, where t is a type, x is a variable and e is an expression; a `delocal`-statement is of the same form. In forwards execution, a runtime occurs, when the evaluation of e in the `delocal`-statement yields a value different to the current value of x. In backwards execution, this applies to the `local`-statement accordingly.

Such a `delocal`-statement is translated to an assignment with a constant value on the left-hand side (!) – see line 11 in the example in Fig. 4 – and is called *finalizer*. If this constant value is not equal to the value of the expression on the right-hand side, a runtime error will be generated.

The RSSA semantics ensure proper destruction of the first variable on the right-hand-side of assignment, as well as variables passed as parameters in exit points.

An example of a Janus program together with its RSSA translation is shown in Fig. 2.

procedure inc(int n, int res)	begin inc(n_0, res_0)
res += n	res_1 := res_0 + (n_0 ^ 0)
res += 1	res_2 := res_1 + (1 ^ 0)
	end inc(n_0, res_2)
procedure main()	
int i	begin main(i_0, x_0)
int x	i_1 := i_0 + (10 ^ 0)
i += 10	(i_2,x_1) := call inc(i_1,x_0)
call inc(i, x)	end main(i_2, x_1)

Fig. 2. Example for translation of a procedure call.

3   Optimizations

Optimization in our compiler is performed on the RSSA-code. Prior to all optimizations, the RSSA-Code is split into building blocks, such that all statements in the building blocks are executed in the same order from the first to the last statement. A building block consists of the largest possible set of instructions such that the above requirement is fulfilled. In RSSA, building blocks can be identified easily as each entry-point is the start of a new block, and each exit-point is the end of the current block. The **begin**-statement of a procedure is a start of a block, too. Thus, in the example of Fig. 4, there are four building blocks: Lines 1–3, 4–6, 7–8, 9–12. The building blocks form a set of vertices in a graph, where the (directed) edges are determined through the jumps from an exit-point to the corresponding entry-point. This graph is usually called *program graph*.

3.1   Procedure Inlining

Procedure inlining is independent of the direction of execution and can thus be implemented in a straightforward manner by substituting the procedure call with the procedure body. Of course, it needs to be ensured that variables are renamed and care needs to be taken that recursion does not lead to infinite inlining or huge programs. **uncall** statements are inlined by replacing them with the inverse of the procedure body, i.e., the statements are inserted in reverse order and inverted according to their semantics. Our strategy is to first inline procedures smaller than a given size (configurable via the command-line), followed by procedures which are called only once (leading to the fact that these procedures can be eliminated completely). In addition, it is possible to specify allow-lists and block-lists of procedures to be always inlined or never.

3.2   Local Common-Subexpression Elimination

We have developed and implemented a new algorithm that uses a directed-acyclic multigraph to represent the different dependencies between common-subexpressions local to a block but also their sequence and relations between the creation of a variable and its destruction. This approach is different to conventional local common-subexpression elimination where a simple graph is sufficient (see for example [1]). Since common-subexpressions do occur frequently, this optimization typically leads to considerable performance improvements.

We have described our algorithm in detail in [4].

3.3   Constant Propagation and Folding

Constant propagation identifies occurrences of variables with a constant value. Constant folding is a technique to evaluate expressions at compile-time when the operands are known to have constant values [15].

It turns out that constant propagation for reversible programs can be performed twice, i.e., forwards and backwards: Not only definitions such as (in Janus) `local int i=0` but also their inverse `delocal int i=10` can be taken into account since the semantics enforce that the value of i in this case needs to be 10 when reaching the `delocal`-statement. These are translated to RSSA initializers and finalizers, and the same rule applies.

Our compiler will invert the current building block and perform constant propagation and folding again by replacing constants and computing the values of expressions in case all their operands are constant. The idea for this approach was suggested by Mogensen in [14]. As far we know, our compiler is the first implementation.

Again, more details are provided in [4]. Especially when used together with inlining, constant propagation is a very powerful optimization technique as shown in Fig. 3, which shows a simple Janus program with two procedures on the left, and the optimized RSSA code on the right. As one can see, both procedure calls have been inlined completely. In addition, constant propagation recognizes the fact that x is a constant and thus can be removed from the list of parameters passed to the procedure. Thus, the whole program is reduced to only three lines of code.

```
procedure i1(int n, int r)
   n -= 1
   call i2(n, r)

procedure i2(int n, int r)
   r += n*n                          begin main(y_0)
                                        in9_in3_r_1 := y_0 + (9 * 9)
procedure main()                     end main(in9_in3_r_1)
   int y
   local int x = 10
   call i1(x,y)
   delocal int x=9
```

Fig. 3. Example for inlining and constant propagation.

3.4   Dead-Code Elimination

As the name of this optimization already suggests, the aim is to remove code that does not change the behavior of the program, such as code that will never be executed or only changes the state of variables that will not be used thereafter.

To our knowledge, this is the first description of such an optimization for reversible programs.

Prior to describing the algorithm, a few definitions need to be given.

Definition 1. *"A definition is an assignment of some value to a variable."* [15, p. 218].

Definition 2. *"A variable is considered dead if it is not used on any path in the program graph from the position of its definition in the code to the exit point. An instruction is dead if it computes only values that are not used on any executable path from this instruction to the exit point."* [15, p. 592].

"Use" in this regard refers to an occurrence of the variable where the current value of the variable is required. A formal definition for RSSA is given in Table 1.

Rarely do programmers include dead instructions in their code – the typical use case for dead-code elimination is after the application of other optimization techniques, such as constant propagation and common-subexpression elimination. It is thus worthwhile implementing dead-code elimination.

We are going to look at intra-procedural analysis only as opposed to inter-procedural analysis. I.e., the analysis required for dead-code elimination examines each procedure individually, and it is assumed that through procedure calls and uncalls all variables in the argument lists are used and defined.

Accordingly, all output parameters of a procedure (when analysing the procedure for forwards execution) and all input parameters (in case of backwards execution) must be considered to be used. Thus, it is possible to focus the analysis on local variables only, as shown in the example of Fig. 4.

		1	begin $f(x_0, y_0)$
		2	$z_0 := 0 \char`^ (0 \char`^ 0)$
1	procedure $f(\text{int } x, \text{ int } y)$	3	$x_0 == 0 \,-> \, Lf_5(y_0, z_0, x_0)Lf_6$
2	local int $z = 0$	4	$Lf_5(y_1, z_1, x_1) <-$
3		5	$y_4 := y_1 + (1 \char`^ 0)$
4	if x=0	6	$-> \, Lf_7(z_1, y_4, x_1)$
5	y+=1	7	$Lf_6(y_2, z_2, x_2) <-$
6	fi x=0	8	$-> \, Lf_8(z_2, y_2, x_2)$
7		9	$Lf_7(z_7, y_8, x_7)Lf_8 <- x_7 == 0$
8	z+=x+y	10	$z_8 := z_7 + (x_7 + y_8)$
9	delocal int $z = x + y$	11	$0 := z_8 \char`^ (0 \char`^ 0)$
		12	end $f(x_7, y_8)$

Fig. 4. Example for dead-code elimination.

Let us informally perform the analysis for the Janus program:

Firstly, a local variable z is declared and defined. Because of the += operator, line 8 in the Janus program is a use of and at the same time another definition of z. Lastly, in line 9 the variable z is destroyed. Thus, z does not contribute to the computation of the final values of x and y (it only contributes to itself) and thus, lines 2, 8, and 9 can be eliminated. Obviously – and this was already mentioned in [14] – a local variable can only exist between its local and delocal instructions.

Observation 1. A local variable, i.e., a variable that is not a formal parameter of the procedure (in Janus), respectively a formal parameter of a **begin** or **end**-instruction in RSSA , can only exist between its local and delocal instructions (in Janus), respectively its initialization and its finalization in RSSA.

Since a local variable always needs to be destroyed via a `delocal`-statement in Janus, respectively a finalizer statement in RSSA, the final value of this variable needs to be available in these statements. This leads us to the second observation:

Observation 2. It is not possible to remove a definition of a variable only. Thus, the variable needs to be completely removed by eliminating all its occurrences or not at all.

Please note that this is different to conventional dead-code elimination, where, for example, in a C-fragment such as `int x; x=0; x=1;` the definition `x=0` could be eliminated.

It is well-known that liveness in conventional programming is a backwards data-flow problem that is solved by iterating through the program bottom-to-top. When looking at the RSSA program, we come to the same conclusion as above when tracing the different versions of z: z_8 is finalized in line 11, in line 9 it is created using z_7 which in turn is a parameter of the conditional entry point $Lf_7(\ldots)Lf_8$. Hence, we need to look at the two building blocks that end with exit points to Lf_7 resp. Lf_8. In these, no version of z is used, hence the parameters of the respective entry points Lf_5 and Lf_6 are not required, neither is z_0 in the exit point in line 3. Finally, we conclude that this variable is dead and all occurrences of versions of z can be eliminated.

Before analysing backwards execution, we need to provide some basic concepts:

The well-known data-flow algorithm for liveness analysis for "forwards-only" programs [15], firstly computes the sets of variables defined prior to being used (if at all) in a block b ($DEF(b)$) and the set of variables used prior to being defined (if at all) ($USE(b)$). $DEF(b)$ and $USE(b)$ are then used to compute the set of live variables $IN(b)$ at the beginning of the block, starting with the last block, i.e., the block containing the `end`-Statement. The IN-set is propagated upwards to the predecessors of b. For each predecessor b', the set $OUT(b')$ is the union of all successors of b'. These computations form a system of equations that can be solved iteratively as a fixpoint always exists. Please note that loops in the program will lead to the fact that we may need to compute IN and OUT multiple times for a given block. Kildall's worklist algorithm [8] is a well-established solution for data-flow problems.

Observation 3. Since RSSA is a reversible static-single-assignment form, there can't be any uses prior to a definition in a block. Consequently, USE (as defined above) would always be empty and DEF would always contain all variables. It is thus sufficient for RSSA to define USE as the set of all variables used after its definition and focus on this set only.

Due to the semantics of procedure calls (in the case of intra-procedural analysis), we conclude that variables which are parameters of the `end`-statement are live after the statement since they will be passed back to the caller. Due to the symmetry of forwards and backwards execution, the converse is also true: All variables that are parameters of the **begin**-statement are live at the start of the **begin**-statement.

There are cases, where a variable is live at some point when looking only at forwards execution, but is considered dead at the same point looking at backwards execution. As an example, we use the code shown in Fig. 4 (on the left-hand side) and show the reverse RSSA code on the right-hand side.

```
1   begin  f(x0, y0)                    1   begin  f(x7, y8)
2     z0 := 0 ^ (0 ^ 0)                 2     z8 := 0 ^ (x7 + y8)
3     x0 == 0 -> Lf5(y0, z0, x0)Lf6     3     z7 := z8 - (x7 + y8)
4                                        4     x7 == 0 -> Lf7(z7, y8, x7)Lf8
5   Lf5(y1, z1, x1) <-                   5
6     y4 := y1 + (1 ^ 0)                 6   Lf7(z1, y4, x1) <-
7     -> Lf7(z1, y4, x1)                 7     y1 := y4 - (1 ^ 0)
8                                        8     -> Lf5(y1, z1, x1)
9   Lf6(y2, z2, x2) <-                   9
10    -> Lf8(z2, y2, x2)                 10  Lf8(z2, y2, x2) <-
11                                       11    -> Lf6(y2, z2, x2)
12  Lf7(z7, y8, x7)Lf8 <- x7 == 0       12
13    z8 := z7 + (x7 + y8)               13  Lf5(y0, z0, x0)Lf6 <- x0 == 0
14    0 := z8 ^ (0 ^ 0)                  14    0 := z0 ^ (0 ^ 0)
15  end  f(x7, y8)                       15  end  f(x0, y0)
```

Fig. 5. Example for differences in forwards and backwards execution.

In forwards execution, z is only used after the **if**-statement, whereas it is used before when the procedure is executed backwards. Since procedure f consists of four building blocks, forwards analysis would report z to be used in different building blocks than in backwards analysis. Thus, the sole information which variables are live, is not sufficient. In traditional liveness-analysis, the set of variables that are live at the beginning of a block is computed by taking the set of live variables at the end of the block, subtracting the set of variables defined in the block prior to being used in the block, and joining the result with the set of variables used in the block prior to being defined in the block.

For reversible programs, our approach is to utilize only USE-sets and not remove the variables that are defined in the block (DEF), since in backwards execution the inverse would happen.

By utilizing USE only, we collect all used variables from the **end**-statement up to the **begin**-statement. I.e., we will finally end up not only with the parameters of the **end**-statement, as pointed out already, but with all used variables.

In the example of Fig. 4, our algorithm will identify all versions of x and y as begin used in procedure p. In the Janus program, z is not required, and thus, the different versions of z are neither required in the RSSA program.

As RSSA contains statement types that are quite different from conventional procedural programming languages, the definitions of USE for all kinds of RSSA-instructions are different, too, as can be seen in Table 1. Should an operand of an instruction be a constant, it is ignored. Hence, in Table 1 a, b, c, r, x, y, z refer to variables only.

Table 1. USE for RSSA statements.

Statement	USE
$L(a_1, \ldots, a_n) \leftarrow$	$\emptyset$
$L_1(a_1, \ldots, a_n) L_2 \leftarrow c == d$	$\{c, d\}$
$begin\ f(a_1, \ldots, a_n)$	$\emptyset$
$\rightarrow L(a_1, \ldots, a_n)$	$\emptyset$
$c == d \rightarrow L1(a_1, \ldots, a_n) L2$	$\{c, d\}$
$end\ f(a_1, \ldots, a_n)$	$\emptyset$
$x := y + (r * t)$	$\begin{cases} \{r, t, y\}, & \text{if } x \in OUT \\ \emptyset, & \text{otherwise} \end{cases}$
$a, b := x, y$	$\begin{cases} \{x, y\}, & \text{if } a \in OUT \vee b \in OUT \\ \emptyset, & \text{otherwise} \end{cases}$
$M[x] + = y * z$	$\{x, y, z\}$
$M[x] < - > M[y]$	$\{x, y\}$
$x := M[y] := z$	$\{y, z\}$
$(r_1, \ldots, r_i) := call\ f(a_1, \ldots, a_j)$	$\{a_1, \ldots, a_j\}$
$(r_1, \ldots, r_i) := uncall\ f(a_1, \ldots, a_j)$	$\{a_1, \ldots, a_j\}$

Since we have already identified that DEF-sets are not meaningful in case of reversible programs, we have chosen to simplify the computation of IN and OUT by utilizing USE only. Note, USE depends on OUT because we will just propagate USE in each block from bottom to top. For dead-code elimination analysis, we need to work backwards and start at the last block, which we will call b_{end}, – as we did already in our informal analysis. All variables that are parameters of the **end**-instruction will be passed back to the caller and are thus live.

Combining all previous observations leads to the algorithm for determining used variables as shown in Algorithm 1.

As we pointed out above, the analysis might yield different results when the program is executed backwards. In a reversible program, however, both execution directions are relevant. Consequently, we must assume that a variable contained in either of the result sets is used by the program. We execute the algorithm twice on any procedure p, once on the forward version of a procedure and once on its inverse. The union of both sets is constructed as a single result. We call this set $USED(p)$.

As the set of variables in a procedure is finite, and $IN(b)$ can only grow, the algorithm will terminate with a fix point for $In(b_{begin})$. The algorithm is also correct, i.e., a variable that is used in the procedure will finally always be contained in $USED(p)$, which is ensured by the conservative definition of USE for each instruction and the fact that the algorithm joins these to compute $IN(b)$. Branches are merged together by joining the sets of the successors (line 12).

Algorithm 1 Used variables Algorithm.

1: **procedure** USEDVARS(p)   ▷ Used variables of procedure p
2:     $Pending := \{b : b$ is a block$\}$
3:     **for all** block b **do**
4:         $IN(b) := \emptyset$
5:     **end for**
6:     **while** $Pending \neq \emptyset$ **do**
7:         Choose block b from $Pending$ and remove b from $Pending$
8:         $TEMP(b) := \emptyset$
9:         **if** $b = b_{end}$ **then**
10:            Set $OUT(b_{end})$ to the set of all variables in the parameter list
11:        **else**
12:            $OUT(b) := \bigcup_{b\prime \in Succ(b)} IN(b\prime)$
13:        ▷ $Succ(b)$ denotes the set of all successors of block b in the program graph.
14:        **end if**
15:        **for all** Statement s in b in reverse order **do**
16:            $TEMP(b) := TEMP(b) \cup USE(s)$
17:        **end for**
18:        **if** $IN(b) \neq TEMP(b)$ **then**
19:            $IN(b) := TEMP(b)$
20:            $Pending := Pending \cup Pred(b)$
21:        ▷ $Pred(b)$ denotes the set of all predecessors of block b in the program graph.
22:        **end if**
23:     **end while**
24:     **return** $In(b_{begin})$
25:                    ▷ b_{begin} denotes the block containing the **begin**-statement
26: **end procedure**

Loops lead to a next iteration and thus a potentially larger $IN(b)$ set. Induction over all instructions and blocks will provide a formal proof.

In order to eliminate dead code, we finally iterate through all blocks of the procedure, to eliminate all statements where a variable v occurs that is not contained in $USED(p)$. Please note that it is not possible that other variables occuring in the same statement depend on v, since the analysis would otherwise have indicated that v is used. Likewise, we eliminate v from all parameter lists of entry points, as well as the corresponding parameters in the respective exit points.

The final resulting code of the application of the algorithm to the program in Fig. 5 is shown in Fig. 6.

```
1    begin  f(x₀,  y₀)
2        x₀ == 0 -> Lf₅(y₀,  x₀)Lf₆
3        Lf₅(y₁,  x₁) <-
4            y₄ := y₁ + (1 ^ 0)
5            -> Lf₇(y₄,  x₁)
6        Lf₆(y₂,  x₂) <-
7            -> Lf₈(y₂,  x₂)
8        Lf₇(y₈,  x₇)Lf₈ <- x₇ == 0
9    end  f(x₇,  y₈)
```

Fig. 6. Example after dead-code elimination.

4   Example

In order to demonstrate our results, we are going to reuse the example from
S. Muchnick's book [15] in Fig. 7 with the Janus code on the left and the RSSA
code on the right.

```
                                    1    begin  m(n₀)
1    procedure  m(int  n)           2        i₀ := 0 ^ (1 ^ 0)
2        local int  i=1             3        j₀ := 0 ^ (2 ^ 0)
3        local int  j=2             4        k₀ := 0 ^ (3 ^ 0)
4        local int  k=3             5        l₀ := 0 ^ (5 ^ 0)
5        local int  l=5             6        -> Lm₁(i₀, l₀, j₀, n₀, k₀)
6                                   7        Lm₁(i₁, l₁, j₁, n₁, k₁)Lm₃ <- i₁ == 1
7        from i=1 do                8            i₂ := i₁ + (j₁ ^ 0)
8            i += j                 9            l₂ := l₁ + (j₁ + 1)
9            l += j + 1            10            j₂ := j₁ + (2 ^ 0)
10            j += 2               11            j₂ <= n₁ -> Lm₄(k₁, j₂, l₂, i₂, n₁)Lm₂
11        loop                     12        Lm₂(k₂, j₃, l₃, i₃, n₂) <-
12            k -= j               13            k₃ := k₂ - (j₃ ^ 0)
13        until (j <= n)           14            -> Lm₃(i₃, l₃, j₃, n₂, k₃)
14                                 15        Lm₄(k₄, j₄, l₄, i₄, n₃) <-
15        delocal int  l=8         16            0 := l₄ ^ (8 ^ 0)
16        delocal int  k=3         17            0 := k₄ ^ (3 ^ 0)
17        delocal int  j=4         18            0 := j₄ ^ (4 ^ 0)
18        delocal int  i=3         19            0 := i₄ ^ (3 ^ 0)
                                   20    end  m(n₃)
```

Fig. 7. Example from Advanced Compiler Design and Implementation.

The compiler will compute the $USED$-set for m as $\{ i_4, j_2, i_2, i_3, j_1, i_0, j_4, j_3, i_1, n_2, n_1, j_0, n_3, n_0 \}$.

Thus, variables k and l with their instances k_0, k_1, k_2, k_3, k_4 and l_0, l_1, l_2, l_3, l_4 are not used and will be eliminated from the program, resulting in the code in Fig. 8.

Calling the unoptimized procedure 10 000 times leads to the execution of 230 003 RSSA instructions in 348 ms in our Java-based virtual machine (also available at [17]), whereas the optimized procedure requires only 180 003 instructions which are executed in 227 ms, which is a 34% improvement for this (artificial) example. Using our new stack-based virtual machine [5], we are able to call

```
1    begin m(n₀)
2        i₀ := 0 ^ (1 ^ 0)
3        j₀ := 0 ^ (2 ^ 0)
4        -> Lm₁(i₀, j₀, n₀)
5    Lm₁(i₁, j₁, n₁)Lm₃ <- i₁ == 1
6            i₂ := i₁ + (j₁ ^ 0)
7            j₂ := j₁ + (2 ^ 0)
8            j₂ <= n₁ -> Lm₄(j₂, i₂, n₁)Lm₂
9    Lm₂(j₃, i₃, n₂) <-
10            -> Lm₃(i₃, j₃, n₂)
11    Lm₄(j₄, i₄, n₃) <-
12            0 := j₄ ^ (4 ^ 0)
13            0 := i₄ ^ (3 ^ 0)
14    end m(n₃)
```

Fig. 8. Optimized example from Advanced Compiler Design and Implementation.

the procedure 10 000 000 times in 7 089 ms, respectively 5 073 ms for the optimized version, which is a speed-up of 28%. In reality, improvements from dead code elimination alone will be lower for real-world examples (as is also the case for traditional languages), and depend heavily on the programming style of the developer.

For the Janus self-interpreter [20] executing the Fibonacci example 10 times, the number of RSSA instructions executed in the virtual machine could be reduced by constant propagation, common sub-expression elimination, procedure inlining as well as dead code elimination from 199 000 instructions to 178 000 instructions, which is a 11% improvement. The execution time was reduced from 633 ms to 547 ms, which is a 14% improvement.

A further example is a program that calls and uncalls a procedure for matrix inversion 10 000 times. The Janus program contains 182 lines, the unoptimized RSSA code 465 lines, and the optimized version 918 lines (due to inlining). Using the Java-based virtual machine, the unoptimized program executes 35,4 million instructions within 12 787 ms; the optimized version executes only 20,8 million instructions (41% less) and requires 9 515 ms, which is a speedup of 25.5%.

It is worthwhile noticing that, although only reversible updates are allowed in Janus and RSSA—which leads to fewer optimization opportunities, as explained above—, we also eliminate the cleanup (finalization) of unused variables, leading to further savings in execution time.

5   Conclusions and Outlook

We have briefly shown optimization algorithms for procedure inlining, common-subexpression elimination, and constant propagation and folding, as well as in detail for dead-code elimination. As far as we know, these are the first algorithms for optimization of reversible programs.

Mogensen [14] provides some suggestions on potential optimizations, further work or implementations of these are currently not known to us. Our *rc3* compiler is to our knowledge the first optimizing compiler for reversible languages. It is publicly available for download from our university's GIT repository (see [17]).

The inherent requirements of reversible computing require extensions of "traditional" algorithms to be able to apply them to reversible languages: Traditional data-flow analysis determines IN and OUT sets either in a forwards manner, i.e. stepping from one basic block to its successors, or vice versa. But, in a reversible world, "forwards" and "backwards" in terms of direction of execution are not distinguishable, making the application of these well-known algorithms by Kildall [8] and others quite difficult.

Further optimizations we are currently exploring are the extension of the above from the local scope, i.e., within a building block, to a global one, i.e., across all blocks of a procedure, as well as loop optimizations such as loop-unrolling or loop-invariant code motion. Using loop-unrolling, loop variables will be replaced by constant values leading to further opportunities for constant-propagation and folding.

With regards to applicability to other programming language paradigms, we conclude that these do require a translation to intermediate code, too. To our mind, RSSA is independent from high-level languages and could thus be used for example for other reversible imperative languages including object-oriented languages as well. Obviously (as is also the case for conventional languages), polymorphism in object-oriented languages can lead to the fact, that it is unknown at compile-time which method will be called. As is the case for conventional object-oriented languages, the correct method to be invoked can only be determined at runtime via the dispatch table of the current object. RSSA does not provide such a means for dynamic binding, and inlining is only possible if the compiler knows which method will be called, whereas the other shown optimisations within a procedure can be applied. Of course, each reversible intermediate language will require a corresponding definition of USE for each kind of statement.

Functional languages typically require different optimization techniques such as strictness analysis or tail recursion elimination, i.e. the transformation of recursion into simple loops. The latter seems to be very difficult for reversible imperative languages due to the requirement for loops to be reversible.

Acknowledgements. We would like to thank the reviewers who had provided valuable feedback and suggestions for improvement.

References

1. Aho, A., Sethi, R., Ullman, J.: Compilers: Principles, Techniques and Tools. Addison-Wesley, Boston (1986)
2. Appel, A.W.: Modern Compiler Implementation in Java. Cambridge University Press, Cambridge (1998)
3. Axelsen, H.B.: Clean translation of an imperative reversible programming language. In: Knoop, J. (ed.) CC 2011. LNCS, vol. 6601, pp. 144–163. Springer, Heidelberg (2011). https://doi.org/10.1007/978-3-642-19861-8_9

4. Deworetzki, N., Meyer, U.: Program analysis for reversible languages. In: Proceedings of the 10th ACM SIGPLAN International Workshop on the State of the Art in Program Analysis, SOAP 2021, pp. 13–18. Association for Computing Machinery, New York (2021). https://doi.org/10.1145/3460946.3464314

5. Deworetzki, N., Meyer, U.: Designing a reversible stack machine. In: Mezzina, C.A., Podlaski, K. (Eds.): RC 2022, LNCS 13354, pp. 65–72. Springer, Cham (2022, to appear)

6. Frank, M.P.: The future of computing depends on making it reversible. IEEE Spectrum, September 2017

7. Hudson, S.E., Flannery, F., Ananian, S.C., Wang, D., Petter, M.: Cup user's manual, June 2014. http://www2.in.tum.de/projects/cup/docs.php

8. Kildall, G.A.: A unified approach to global program optimization. In: Fischer, P.C., Ullman, J.D. (eds.) POPL, pp. 194–206. ACM Press (1973). http://dblp.uni-trier.de/db/conf/popl/popl73.html

9. Klein, G., Rowe, S., Décamps, R.: Jflex user's manual, version 1.8.2 edn., February 2020. https://www.jflex.de/manual.html

10. Kutrib, M., Meyer, U., Deworetzki, N., Schuster, M.: Compiling Janus to RSSA. In: Yamashita, S., Yokoyama, T. (eds.) RC 2021. LNCS, vol. 12805, pp. 64–78. Springer, Cham (2021). https://doi.org/10.1007/978-3-030-79837-6_4

11. Landauer, R.: Irreversibility and heat generation in the computing process. IBM J. Res. Dev. 5(3), 183–191 (1961)

12. Lutz, C.: Janus - A Time-Reversible Language (1986). http://tetsuo.jp/ref/janus.pdf. Letter to R. Landauer

13. Mogensen, T.Æ.: Partial evaluation of the reversible language Janus. In: Khoo, S.C., Siek, J.G. (eds.) PEPM, pp. 23–32. ACM (2011). http://dblp.uni-trier.de/db/conf/pepm/pepm2011.html

14. Mogensen, T.Æ.: RSSA: a reversible SSA form. In: Mazzara, M., Voronkov, A. (eds.) PSI 2015. LNCS, vol. 9609, pp. 203–217. Springer, Cham (2016). https://doi.org/10.1007/978-3-319-41579-6_16 http://dblp.unitrier.de/db/conf/ershov/ershov2015.html

15. Muchnick, S.S.: Advanced Compiler Design and Implementation. Morgan Kaufmann (1997)

16. Rosen, B.K., Wegman, M.N., Zadeck, F.K.: Global value numbers and redundant computations. In: Ferrante, J., Mager, P. (eds.) POPL, pp. 12–27. ACM Press (1988). http://dblp.uni-trier.de/db/conf/popl/popl88.html

17. Technische Hochschule Mittelhessen: Reversible computing compiler collection (rc3), February 2022. https://git.thm.de/thm-rc3/release

18. Yokoyama, T., Axelsen, H.B., Glück, R.: Principles of a reversible programming language. In: Ramírez, A., Bilardi, G., Gschwind, M. (eds.) Conference Computing Frontiers, pp. 43–54. ACM (2008). http://dblp.uni-trier.de/db/conf/cf/cf2008.html

19. Yokoyama, T., Axelsen, H.B., Glück, R.: Fundamentals of reversible flowchart languages. Theor. Comput. Sci. 611, 87–115 (2016). http://dblp.uni-trier.de/db/journals/tcs/tcs611.html

20. Yokoyama, T., Glück, R.: A reversible programming language and its invertible self-interpreter. In: Ramalingam, G., Visser, E. (eds.) PEPM, pp. 144–153. ACM (2007). http://dblp.uni-trier.de/db/conf/pepm/pepm2007.html

Author Index

Printed in the United States
by Baker & Taylor Publisher Services